中国社会科学院语言研究所 主办
中国语言学会语音学分会 会刊
PHONETIC ASSOCIATION OF CHINA

中国语音学报

第17辑

CHINESE JOURNAL OF PHONETICS

中国社会科学出版社

图书在版编目（CIP）数据

中国语音学报. 第17辑／中国社会科学院语言研究所主办. —北京：中国社会科学出版社，2022.6

ISBN 978 - 7 - 5227 - 0989 - 5

Ⅰ.①中… Ⅱ.①中… Ⅲ.①汉语—语音学—文集 Ⅳ.①H11 - 53

中国版本图书馆 CIP 数据核字(2022)第 205537 号

出 版 人 赵剑英
责任编辑 张 林
特约编辑 张 虎
责任校对 韩海超
责任印制 戴 宽

出 版 中国社会科学出版社
社 址 北京鼓楼西大街甲 158 号
邮 编 100720
网 址 http://www.csspw.cn
发 行 部 010 - 84083685
门 市 部 010 - 84029450
经 销 新华书店及其他书店

印 刷 北京君升印刷有限公司
装 订 廊坊市广阳区广增装订厂
版 次 2022 年 6 月第 1 版
印 次 2022 年 6 月第 1 次印刷

开 本 787×1092 1/16
印 张 12.75
插 页 2
字 数 337 千字
定 价 76.00 元

目　录

韵律作为互动的资源：以话语延伸和会话重叠为例*

乐 耀 乔雪玮 郑上鑫

摘 要 在自然会话中，韵律作为一种重要资源参与互动的组织过程。本文首先介绍了会话语音学研究范式的两大理论背景，即弗斯的语言学思想和会话分析学派的方法；其次，以话语延伸和会话重叠为例，整理和回顾了这两种互动现象中语音韵律相关的重要研究成果。文章最后强调会话中的语音韵律研究需要紧密联系社会行为，并具体阐释了自然会话语音分析的七条研究原则。
关键词 韵律，会话语音学，话语延伸，会话重叠

Prosody as an Interactional Resource: Increment and Overlap

YUE Yao QIAO Xuewei ZHENG Shangxin

Abstract Prosody is an integral component of language use; it is constantly deployed in organizing social interactions and constructing social actions, together with grammar, body movements, hand gestures and other modalities. This article sets out a review of the theories, methodologies, and major findings of the study of phonology-for-conversation. It firstly introduces the two theoretical foundations for this research paradigm, then looks at the studies of phonetics and prosody in two particular interactional phenomena—increment and overlap. The article is concluded with an elucidation of the seven principles for noticing and analysing phonetic and prosodic patterns in conversation, underscoring the use of naturally occurring data, participants' perspective, and the omnirelevance of sequential positions and social actions.
Keywords Prosody, Phonology-for-conversation, Increment, Overlap

1. 互动韵律研究的背景

将语音韵律①作为互动交际的重要资源来研究，较早来自于英国约克大学的语音学家（York phoneticians），尤其是 John Local、John Kelly 和 Bill Wells② ［17，36，37，40］。他们以会话分析理论和方法为基础，系统地研究真实言谈交际中语音韵律资源的互动意义，由此开创了会话语音学（phonology-for-conversation）的研究范式。该研究范式深受英国语言学家弗斯（John Rupert Firth）和社会学领域会话分析学派（Conversation Analysis）的影响，下面分别介绍相关的理论背景。

1.1 弗斯的语言学思想

英国语言学家、现代语言学伦敦学派的创始人弗斯的核心语言学思想是：语言研究的目标不是语言系统本身，而是应该将语言的使用作为“社会过程”的一部分来观察。他认为意义不仅与一个特定情景和声音环境相连，而且深深地根植于人们赖以生存的社会活动过程之中［70］。

---

* 文章由三位作者分工合作完成。文中若有任何错误由第一作者负责。

① 一般认为韵律是超音段或非音段的，语音是音段的。但一方面，二者并非截然二分；另一方面，会话分析和互动语言学研究领域的语音学家发现，在真实的言语交际中，参与者组织和构建社会互动时，常常是同时以韵律和语音作为资源（如［38］）。所以，本文多数时候使用“语音韵律”并称。

② Bill Wells 和 William H. G. Wells 为同一位学者，见［37］。

弗斯有关语境、功能和言语交际之间关系的立场涉及三方面［12，13］：第一，语言被认为是一种社会工具，它是社会行为的载体。在说话时，交际双方都是社会成员，有社会角色和身份，有社会交际的目标和任务，有情感和认知立场，所有这些都可以随着即时交际而改变。第二，语境化（contextualization）的意义是语言学的中心问题。对我们来说，语境包括对话的序列和相互作用的语境，以及语言和社会互动场景。第三，语言被视为一套交互系统，语言分析在其领域（如语音、词汇、句法和形态学等）内或跨领域分析，这体现了语言使用的多系统性（polysystematicity）。

就韵律研究而言，弗斯将韵律限制在单个说话人的话语中。而专门从事会话语音韵律研究的英国约克学派认为，韵律研究可以延伸到会话双方的话轮之间。比如，在会话的特定话轮或序列位置上，一个说话人的语音模式（sound pattern）设计与另一个说话人的会话具有意义的关联。会话语音韵律研究与弗斯所关注的一致性在于：意义主要是社会性的，因为它是由社会中的人们共享的，并被社会互动环境语境化。而在语言会话的多系统性中，韵律研究也应该从交际双方的互动视角来看它对构建会话意义的贡献。

1.2 会话分析学派方法

在方法论上，会话互动的语音韵律研究深受会话分析学派（以下简称 CA）的启发。而 CA 植根于对话互动的实证研究传统，这源自哈罗德·加芬克尔（Harold Garfinkel）［18，19］创立的“常人方法论”（ethnomethodology）的社会学理论［21］。这种方法的主要分析假设是，社会互动是由互动者自己不断构建和理解的，而不是预先给定的，对其解释离不开社会背景。也就是说，社会互动及其社会秩序是不断浮现的（emergent）；参与者在社会互动中对意义的理解，很大程度上依赖于所有符号线索的语境敏感性，或者用常人方法论的术语来说，即索引性（indexicality）。

在常人方法论的社会学理论的影响下，CA 认为社会互动是有序的、成系统的，语言是用于互动的资源，在特定的会话环境中，交际者用它来实现适当的社会行为。因此，会话分析不应该从社会互动中分离出来，互动是有结构组织的，这种组织的痕迹可以在互动本身中找到。同时，会话分析也不应该置于互动上，而应从会话参与者的视角选择进行分析的范畴、单位来解释。因此，CA 特别强调实证研究，它的一系列假设是在细致分析音频或视频记录的、真实发生的言谈会话基础上产生的。会话分析学家是要试图将每一次社会言谈互动展现为互动参与者共同合作的活动。

那么，回到会话互动的语音韵律研究领域，我们也可以认为，语音韵律的使用模式在互动中也是有序的，是会话参与者完成社会行为所依赖的必要资源，也是构建和识解互动意义的重要手段。一些语音韵律的参数和特征可以被作为交际者的工具，用于社会互动中会话序列的组织和管理。它们可以作为符号系统的一部分，与句法、词汇、身姿和其他语境化线索一起，被用来分析和解释话轮构建、话轮转换、序列组织等互动机制。

在对日常会话序列组织和互动功能进行分析时，有必要对语音韵律细节进行考察。因此，我们应该平等对待所有语音资源，不应给予一种语音参数比另一种语音参数更优先的分析特权，不应有预设的语音分析范畴。我们应该对所描述的、以言谈参与者取向（participant orientation）观察到的语音特征提供严谨的分析证据。当要发展一种语音解释理论时，应该将其与言谈互动中基于行为的序列分析相关联。

总之，在做互动中的语音韵律研究时，要将自然发生的语料分析放在首位。任何其他形式的语料数据（如问卷调查、访谈、实验产出或焦点小组访问①）都对日常互动序列分析帮助不大，因为它们不

① 焦点小组访谈是社会科学研究中常用的质性研究方法。一般由一个经过研究训练的调查者主持，采用预先设定部分访谈问题的方式与一组被调查者交谈。

能揭示会话互动结构的特点。在分析自然语料的时候，要将其视为上下文的一个组成部分。并且，任何会话都是在实时行进的互动中浮现的，因此要将分析的范畴植根于自然会话本身，通过言谈参与者的取向来论证分析范畴的有效性。

下面分别以日常互动中的话语延伸(increment)① 和会话重叠（overlap）为例，择要介绍这两类互动现象在会话语音韵律研究中的一些重要成果，从而勾勒出互动语音韵律研究的理念、方法和原则。当然，会话语音韵律研究所关涉的互动现象不只本文所讨论的这两类，还有很多是有关话轮的投射（projection)、话轮的转换、会话序列的行进、修补（repair）现象、特定社会行为的构建等方面的语音韵律研究［5，6，7，9，43，44，52，57，59，60，65］。

2. 话语延伸现象的语音韵律研究

话语延伸是指在言语互动中，一个话轮构建单位（turn-constructional unit，TCU）完结之后，说话人会延续该话轮，常会临时添加一些话语。而这些话语通常与前一个 TCU［也被称为宿主（host)］在句法、韵律、语义、行为上存在或多或少的联系，以此区别于新的、独立 TCU。如 Ford 等［15］(24 页）中的例子所示②：

1 Abbie：［Ah：
2 Terry：［We <u>had</u> him，(.) this <u>sum</u>-
3 mer，(1.5) for <u>f：i：ve</u>
4 <u>weeks.</u> (0.8) **when we were**
5 **out at the campground**?
6 Rachel：Oh really.

第 4 行的 TCU 到达了可能完结处(possible completion point）后，听话人没有接话。在 0.8 秒的沉默（silence）后，Terry 在第 4、5 行继续产出了与宿主 TCU 在句法、语义、行为、韵律上均有连续性的话语，提供了第二个话轮转换相关位置(transition-relevance place，TRP)［15］。

因此，这种现象可以看作是话轮（句子）在口语交际中被或紧或松地扩展和延伸了，体现了 TCU 的可扩展性［46］。随着跨语言的对比研究增多，更多类型的话语延伸现象被纳入研究视野［72］。于是，语音韵律作为重要资源在话语延伸中的互动意义被逐渐认识到，并且进一步揭示了互动会话中韵律和句法等其他资源的相互协作和制约关系。下文以研究的对象语言为线索，评介话语延伸韵律研究方面一些的重要成果，其中也分析关注了汉语话语延伸的韵律研究的现状。

2.1 英语的相关研究

Schegloff［51］从语法的连续性上来界定增量的不独立性，尚未考虑韵律上的因素③。Ford 等［15］的研究除了涉及句法、语用和语义因素，还注意到了两种不同的增量在韵律上也表现出差异。其中扩展的第一个重读音节和前一个 TCU 最后一个重读音节的音高相同或更低，而自由成分则有音高重置（pitch reset）的特点④。这种韵律特征的差异进一步说明扩展类的依附性更强，而自由成分类则是介于依附与独立之间的中间状态。虽然两类增量都出现

① 本文中的“话语延伸”属于话轮延续（turn continuation）这一大类，囊括了各类 TCU 延续（TCU continuation）和自由成分（free constituent)，但不包括完全独立的新 TCU。Schegloff［51，53］提出的增量(increment）是话语延伸的一个次类。在许多文献中也常常使用“increment”来泛指话语延伸各类相关现象，是较宽泛的理解，故本文英文标题和摘要也沿用该术语翻译。

② Ford 等［15］原文中的转写符号说明如下：“［”表示重叠开启处，“(.)”表示小于0.2秒的停顿，“(1.5)”为停顿的时长，“：”表示声音延长（sound stretch)，下划线表示重音，“，.?”分别表示延续、下降和上升语调。下文例子中出现的相同符号同理。

③ 例如在 Schegloff［51］（90 页）中的例子，时间状语从句“When I get home”出现在“I' ll give you call tomorrow”这一完整的 TCU（句法、语用、韵律均完结）后，二者在句法上衔接在一起可以构成完整的句法结构。

④ 该文中的“扩展”等同于 Schegloff［51，53］和下文 Walker［62，63］所指的“增量”，但将自由成分也囊括入“增量”中。自由成分通常为非附属的名词短语（unattached NPs)，如“She had it yesterday. **Ten pounds.**”［15］(27 页)。

在听话人接管话轮出现问题的情况下，但扩展类是对前一TCU的行为延续，提供了TRP。而自由成分则是一个新的行为，大多实施评价并表达立场态度。文章还发现有的扩展类也会像自由成分一样表达立场，这种功能的不对应现象主要是由于韵律上的音高重置所导致的。因此，这种现象在一定程度上表明了韵律可以压过句法，对交际互动中的行为影响较大。

以上有关话语延伸韵律特点的研究主要是基于听觉感知的。Walker［62］结合了听觉和声学的分析方法，较为系统地研究了英语自然会话中增量的语音韵律特征，主要从音高（pitch）、音强（loudness）、语速（rate of articulation）和特定的发音特征（articulatory characteristics）等参数进行了实证分析。在音高表现上，大多数增量的最后一个音步（foot）的音高曲拱（pitch contour）、音域（pitch range）都和宿主TCU的近似。同样，音强的最高峰值（peak intensity）和语速也大体相同，还可能会和宿主TCU一样表现出嘎裂声（creaky voice）和呼吸（breath）等其他发音特征。文章通过语音分析进一步证明了韵律也是一种重要的互动资源，强调增量对宿主TCU的延续性。对于增量在互动中的功能而言，间隔后（post-gap）的增量出现在听话人缺乏回应的情况下，可以消解宿主TCU中潜在的歧义，避免听话人理解困难；他人话语后（post-other-speaker-talk）的增量在听话人已经接话之后增补信息；毗邻（next-beat）增量出现在宿主TCU刚刚完结后，立刻对可能造成理解困难和立场分歧的话语进行处理。

在此基础上，Walker［63］详细分析了话轮在开端、完结和延续这三个敏感位置的语音特征。其中，话轮的延续有三种不同的韵律模式，与两个TCU突然连接（abrupt-join）相比（下文3.1将有介绍），枢纽（pivot）① 和增量则较为特殊。与枢纽不同，增量开启之前呈现的是韵律完结的特征，而音高、音强、语速和其他语音特征都表现出与之前话语的连续性，这说明增量的性质是隶属于宿主TCU的单位。该文通过将增量和另外两种话轮延续的韵律模式进行对比，揭示了相同序列位置不同延续类型的韵律差异。

总之，话语延伸的研究虽然最初只关注了语法在互动中的作用，但Ford等［15］和Walker［62，63］逐渐认识到了韵律资源在互动会话中的重要作用，全面地总结了不同类型话语延伸的韵律特征和互动功能。但是，以上研究都是以英语为对象语言，基于英语研究的发现有待于更多其他语言类似现象的验证。只有这样才可以发现互动交际中与话语延伸相关的语音韵律模式使用的个性和共性。

2.2 跨语言视角研究

Vorreiter［61］基于跨语言（英语、日语和德语）的对比分析，对话轮延续进行了更加系统的分类。在这个分类体系中，整个话轮延续根据句法、语义、语用和韵律四个因素逐层划分②。作者特别将TCU延续从韵律上分为附加（add-on）和非附加（non-add-on）两大类。附加类主要指延续的成分与宿主TCU之间有韵律断裂（prosodic break），在听感上是明显添加上去的。相反，非附加则与宿主TCU形成一个韵律曲拱。该文没有严格地界定韵律断裂的标准，但展示了几个比较典型的特征。例如，停顿、音高曲拱和节奏模式（rhythmic pattern）的断裂都是比较常见的韵律断裂表现。附加类和非附加类对听话人而言有明显的感知差异。因此，附加类在间隔后或他人话语后通常实施修补，而非附加类则更常表达情感［20］。

Couper-Kuhlen和Ono［8］基于Vorreiter［61］的分类体系对英语、德语和日语进行了更详细的对比分析。文章认为韵律上为非附加类型的TCU延续在句法和语义上表现为错位（out of place）或右偏置

① 枢纽是指说话人通过语音手段在TCU句法、语用完结后继续说话，使其成为前后都能融入的语法成分。枢纽是前一TCU的末端，同时也是后一TCU的开端。

② 在该体系中话轮延续分为TCU延续和新TCU，自由成分则介于二者之间。

(right dislocation)①，与宿主TCU之间没有韵律断裂，形成了一个韵律融合的整体。这种非附加的韵律表现在三种语言中出现的频率差异较大：英语中很少出现②，而日语和德语中则较频繁出现。这一韵律倾向性差异主要是因为不同语言的语序差异：英语是左向中心语（left headed）；而日语和德语则是右向中心语（right headed）。语序的差异导致TCU延续类型的倾向性不同，也伴随着韵律特征的差异。另外，文章还注意到在英语中较丰富的黏着(glue-on)③类延伸成分前面必须有韵律断裂，否则就不存在TCU延续了。

在韩语这样的音节节拍型（syllable-timed）语言中，TCU延续和宿主TCU在语音连贯性（phonetic coherence）上有不同表现。Kim［30］发现韩语的TCU延续的音节节拍与宿主TCU相同。延伸成分重复了宿主TCU的韵律结构，通过平行的韵律结构特征展示出二者的延续性关联。如果TCU延续和宿主TCU最末成分的音节数量不对应时，韩语会表现出加快语速或添加停顿等特征，以此来实现与宿主TCU的韵律平行。这种韵律特征可被视作再次完结手段（re-completer），促进听话人接管话轮做出回应。

2.3 汉语的相关研究

Luke和Zhang［41］强调韵律在识别汉语TCU扩展中具有重要作用。文章从句法、韵律、语义/语用和信息焦点四个参数区分了TCU扩展和新TCU。作者强调句法连续性只是TCU扩展的必要不充分条件，韵律因素也需要考虑。句法和韵律虽然常常是协调一致的，但有时会有相互矛盾的复杂表现。具有句法连续性的话轮延续也可能是韵律上独立的单位，其性质就是独立的TCU，而非TCU扩展。如下例［41］（627页）中：

1 Ming：尤其到（0.3）最市中心的地
2 　　　方，那真是密度绝对是北京赶
3 　　　不上的.（0.4）↑**广州也赶不上.**

第1—3行是一个话题和说明结构的TCU。在TRP和0.4秒的停顿后，第3行新添加的小句是同一话题的第二个说明，通过副词“也”构成平行结构。但第3行的完整语调④和承载的信息焦点使其成为独立的TCU［41］。

TCU扩展在韵律上要表现出连续性或依附性，具体包括音高和音强与宿主TCU相同或更低，语速也常常加快，即非完整语调（non-full intonation）或从属语调(subordinate intonation)。文章发现在区分TCU扩展和新TCU的四个参数中，韵律上的从属语调更具有区别作用。在语义/语用上，TCU扩展总是回溯性的（retrospective），具有对宿主TCU进行修补或增添信息等互动功能。

Zhang［68］和Zhang等［69］两篇文章都关注了话轮延续和宿主TCU之间衔接的韵律表现以及互动功能。Zhang［68］发现在缺少听话人接话的情况下，说话人的话轮延续成分之前可能出现一个间隔。另一种情况下，说话人在TCU可能完结处之前快速冲破（rush-through)⑤边界立刻开启下一话语内容，或者将下一话语内容的开端与前一TCU紧密相扣（latching)。快速冲破和紧密相扣这两种韵律表现都是维持话轮的手段，其功能在于抢先（pre-emptive）进行话轮延续。但文章认为二者存在差异，快速冲破只能发生在同一说话人的话轮内，而紧密相扣则既可能出现在同一说话人的话轮内，也可以出现在两个不同说话人的话轮间。此外，紧密相扣的

① 错位即插入（insertable）类型，如“Silly thing **that**”；右偏置即替换（replacement）类型，如“Cyd rang this evening **Cyd Arnold**”［8］（518页）。

② Geluykens［20］的英语口语语料中123个右偏置只有17个是韵律上非附加类的。

③ 这里的黏着等同于Schegloff［51］的“增量”和Ford等［15］的“扩展”。

④ 该文［41］中标注“↑”表示音高重置。

⑤ “快速冲破”是除‘突然连接’以外，另一个在TRP处使用韵律资源进行多单位话轮（multi-unit turn）组织的惯例（practice）［48，49，51］。Schegloff［49］（77—78页）如此形容该惯例：“当前说话人接近TCU的可能完结处时，加快语速，使语调曲拱（intonation contour）和语调短语越过完结点持续行进至一个新序列（或另一个TCU），直至放慢语速或进行吸气……”

话轮延续成分之前的TCU一般表现为韵律完结语调特征，只是缺乏TCU间自然的沉默（natural beat of silence），而快速冲破的话轮延续成分之前的TCU在韵律上并未完结①，并且最后一个音节常常被压缩，前后两部分没有可识别的韵律断裂。虽然存在以上差异，但文章认为紧密相扣是更大的一个上位概念，可以包括快速冲破，二者都用于模糊话轮转换相关位置，抢先进行话轮延续以此调整立场、避免可能遇到的问题和提供更多信息②。

基于以上的探讨，Zhang等［69］进一步从音高变化、音强和元音音长等方面分析了汉语普通话中快速冲破和紧密相扣的具体差异。快速冲破的前一个TCU最末音节被压缩、音长缩短，音高范围也相应被缩短。快速冲破前后的两个音节流畅地融合在一起，没有清晰明显的交界处。这一韵律表现比较明显地预示了说话人在当前TCU完结后会产生话轮延续，确保了维持话轮的权利。与此不同，紧密相扣的前一TCU最末音节没有被压缩和加速，反而可能被延长，其音高变化不如典型的韵律边界调那么明显。与快速冲破相比，紧密相扣不明显预示话轮延续。该文还发现汉语中有些现象是介于二者之间的韵律表现，前一TCU的最末音节时长没有被压缩，但是音高也几乎没有变化。这很可能是说话人准备产出话轮延续的一种表现。可见，对于汉语这种有声调的语言而言，音高在话轮维持中的重要性还有待进一步研究。

Lim［34］赞同Luke和Zhang［41］对汉语TCU延续的界定和分类，认为韵律上的从属语调是判断汉语TCU延续最主要的标准。汉语TCU延续在会话互动中具有调整立场、阐明或消除歧义、重构序列行为、确保或寻求听话人的接收等功能。这些互动动能的实现可以依赖句法和韵律这两种互补的资源。一方面，话轮延续如果是句法不连续的类型，则往往通过从属语调、紧密相扣或快速冲破等韵律手段来弥补，加强其会话连续性。另一方面，话轮间隔后和他人话语后的话轮延续是韵律上断裂的，则可以通过黏着的句法手段来加强其连续性③。因此，韵律和句法都是话轮延续这一交际互动过程中重要的资源，二者相互协作和制约，共同构建TCU延续这一互动行为。

2.4 小结

话语延伸中的语音韵律作为重要的资源，与句法等其他资源共同构建互动行为。在不同的语言中，各类型话语延伸的使用频率差异较大，往往也伴随着韵律上的明显差异。对于汉语而言，韵律特征是识别和判断TCU延续的重要因素，从属语调、快速冲破和紧密相扣等韵律特征都证明汉语话语延伸与宿主TCU的韵律依赖度较高。在一定程度上，汉语TCU延续的韵律依赖度和强化立场态度的人际功能成正比，但与信息功能、会话结构功能成反比［71］。但是，汉语作为一种有声调的语言，自然口语中语调和声调的复杂关系会给界定话语延伸造成困难，这是今后需要进一步解决的课题。

3. 会话重叠现象的语音韵律研究

话轮转换系统是社会互动的基础设施之一，其基本原则是“一时一人”（one-speaker-at-a-time）［46］。虽然“一时无人”（no-speaker-at-a-time；即发生沉默）［22，46］和“一时多人”（more-than-one-speaker-at-a-time；即发生重叠）的情况本身并不罕见，但自然会话中并非所有的沉默或重叠都是对话轮转换规则的违反；同时，多数沉默和重叠是有序的、成系统的，亦可反证会话参与者对遵守话轮转换规则的取向。其中，本节将关注的重叠现象尤为如此［26，54］。

---

① 因此，快速冲破的话轮延续前一个TCU只是从句法和语用两个参数上判断为到达了可能完结处。

② 该文认为快速冲破和紧密相扣在互动功能上没有明显差异，但紧密相扣的话轮延续可能更容易发生重叠。

③ 文章统计表明70%韵律不连续的话轮延续都是句法关系衔接较紧密的黏着类型，话轮延续和宿主TCU之间构成连动、动宾、动补、偏正等句法结构关系。

在会话分析领域，Jefferson［26，27，28，29］和 Schegloff［54，55］可以说是关于会话重叠的奠基性研究。二人均将重叠视为是一个由参与者共同协商、逐步塑造的过程，因此分别探讨了重叠的不同阶段及其内在有序性［29，54］，并展现了重叠与话轮转换系统之间的相关性［27］（特别是［54］）。下文将按照重叠不同发展阶段的顺序，在已有研究的基础上，分别考察和总结语音韵律作为互动资源在重叠各阶段中的使用惯例与相关的互动意义。

3.1 预开启

投射和投射性（projectability）是会话分析中的核心概念，同时也是互动言谈的实现基础［1，11］。说话人可以通过各种资源（语法、韵律、体势等）在实时互动中投射出尚未说出的话语，甚至于是整个 TCU/话轮所承载的社会行为；同样，受话人在逐步理解当前行进的话轮（turn-in-progress）时，也可以根据各种资源或大或小的投射性预测出当前说话人随后的话语与行为。重叠现象也不例外。所以，与重叠相关的第一阶段并非是重叠的开启（onset），而是预开启（pre-onset），即当前尚未处于重叠的说话人有可能观察到其他尚处沉默的受话人即将发话的预开启（pre-beginning）① 行为（比如吸气、头或眼神的转向等，详见［51］），随即通过某些特定惯例在重叠的预开启阶段提前遏止对方即将开启的话语。

Schegloff［54］提到在重叠预开启阶段，当前说话人用于提前阻断重叠开启（即阻断某位/些受话人即将开启的话语）的语音惯例有：（1）提高音强（volume）或音高；（2）加快语速。不论是音强或音高的增强还是语速的加快，都可以理解为是当前占据话轮空间（turn space）的说话人在面对其他参与者可能发话并造成重叠时所使用的互动惯例；当前说话人通过动用韵律资源（这里涉及音强、音高以及语速），提前巩固自己对于话轮空间的控制，并向可能的发话人发出信号，阻断其即将开启的话语。②

除了即将发话的预开启行为，重叠预开启处所出现的韵律变化还与一个重要的 TCU/话轮位置有关，那就是话轮转换相关位置（TRP）。话轮转换规则决定了潜在的下一说话人在 TRP 处发话的合法性或常规性，不管是通过他选（other-select）还是自选（self-select）［46］。因而当前说话人如果计划——特别是在当前 TCU 临近结束时临时计划——继续开启下一 TCU，即形成一个多单位话轮的话，就必须要面临潜在的下一说话人进行合法话轮转接并与之造成重叠的风险。Local 和 Walker［38］发现，当前说话人在当前 TCU 接近 TRP③ 时，可能会使用“突然连接”的手段继续开启新的 TCU、完成新的社会行为，其语音特征主要有：（1）前一 TCU 末尾音节的音高和音强上升，持续到后一 TCU 首个重读音节；（2）前一 TCU 末尾音节的语速加快，但突然连接后语速明显减慢；（3）前一 TCU 末尾音节从不出现声门闭合（glottal closure）或其他截断（cut-off）特征。

3.2 开启

下一阶段是重叠的开启。对于重叠开启，需要考虑的问题是：第二说话人（即重叠前未占据话轮空间的说话人，与第一说话人相对，参看注②是否有可能意识到在此处发话会造成重叠？如果有，其仍要发话的原因是什么？如果没有，是什么造成了这种情况？如果是两人同时发话（即不存在第一/第二说话人之分），那其在此处发话的原因又是什么？Jefferson［26］部

① 此处的“预开启”是话轮组织的一个阶段［51］，注意与重叠的“预开启”阶段区分。

② 另外一类 Schegloff［54］没有谈到，但我们在语料中却时常会观察到的现象是：重叠中的第一说话人（即重叠前占据话轮空间的说话人）虽然通过某些预开启行为察觉到了潜在的下一说话人可能要发话，但没有以任何手段阻断其即将开启的话语，而是提前放弃当前行进的话轮，常表现为语音的截断，将话轮空间顺势让给下一说话人，最终并未与之形成重叠。

③ 具体而言，是指当前 TCU 句法和语用的可能完结处的前一音节。

分回答了上述问题。她认为会话中大部分重叠开启都是成系统的，总共可以归为三类：（1）转换型开启（transitional onsets）；（2）识别型开启（recognitional onsets）；（3）前进型开启（progressional onsets）。其中，转换型开启和前进型开启尤其涉及第二说话人对于第一说话人当前话语韵律特征的关注，是韵律在重叠中作为互动资源的另一表现。

3.2.1 转换型开启

在转换型开启中，第二说话人发话时关注的是当前话轮的可能完结处，其发话实质上可视为是合法的话轮转换。但是，并非每次合法的话轮转换都是无缝对接的（clean transition），下一说话人早一些或晚一些都有可能造成重叠①，尽管这些重叠大多是很短暂的，甚至（对于参与者和分析者来说）是不起眼的。

过往对于参与者如何投射和预测 TRP 这一问题已有过许多讨论（如［14，16］；相关综述见［73］），其中发现 TRP（或所谓 TCU 的可能完结处）不仅表现在句法和语用的完结，还反映在韵律的完结。说话人和受话人为此所动用的韵律资源，并不是单一的［比如只依赖于语调曲拱的（末尾）走势］，而是多样的、组合使用的。已有研究所发现的能够指示“转换就绪”（transition readiness）的韵律资源包括：（1）音高重音（pitch accent）［52，66］；（2）不同类型的沉默［36］；（3）音高、音强、音长、语速等的组合［37，66，67］；（4）节奏和语速［2，4］；（5）特殊音质（non-modal voice quality）（如嘎裂声、气声、耳语声、假声等［42，45］）。

参与者可以通过上述韵律资源在当前 TCU 的实时构建中投射和预测 TRP，而这反映在重叠的转换型开启。例如，当第二说话人通过第一说话人当前正在构建的 TCU 的韵律信息判断出其何时到达 TRP 时，他就可以距该 TRP 稍早一些发话。此时虽然会造成重叠，但这样的重叠往往是微小的、短暂的——可能只是当前 TCU 最后一个音素或音节［26］。因而，距当前 TCU 的可能完结处稍早一些的转换型开启仍然是合法的，或者至少是可预测的。另外，Jefferson［26，28］发现，会话中常见的话轮转换非但不是无缝转接或稍早转接，反倒是稍晚转接，即在当前话轮结束后、下一说话人发话前会出现一段自然沉默，称之为“无标记的下一位置”（unmarked next position）。当下一说话人稍晚发话，而当前说话人却在当前 TCU 可能完结处后继续产出话语时，就会发生重叠；这类重叠开启从话轮转换系统来看同样是合法的，虽然表面上看会被误认为是第二说话人在企图打断第一说话人。针对这类重叠开启，Couper-Kuhlen［4］从韵律角度给出了解释，认为在英语或其他重音节拍型（stress-timed）语言中，沉默的“无标记”与言语节奏（speech rhythm）密切相关，只有符合相邻言语节奏而产生的沉默才不会被受话人注意到并认为是需要解释的。

3.2.2 前进型开启

在互动言谈中，参与者始终关注并偏好互动进程保持连续性或前进性（progressivity）；这种前进性既包括微观的 TCU/话轮中话语（或其他模态）的连续向前产出，也包括宏观的行为序列之间的连贯进展［47，58］。因而，当重叠中的第二说话人被视为由于当前的话轮在行进中出了问题而发话，就称之为前进型开启。当前话轮在行进上出现了问题可以直接表现为语法的不连贯，比如某些语言成分的重复（如“**我我**今天好多了”）；但更常见的是表现为语音/韵律的不连贯，而这就涉及互动言谈中的修补组织（organisation of repair），特别是其中的修补开启标记（repair initiator，下称修补标记）［56］。

---

① 还有一种可能是，第二说话人的发话位置相对于当前行进中的话轮的可能完结处不早也不晚，但第一说话人（即当前说话人）同时继续产出话语，这时也会发生重叠。Jefferson［26］称这样的重叠为“副产品”（byproduct），与“取得的重叠”（achieved overlap）相对。前者是两个参与者不同行为的附带结果，后者则是第二说话人能够预测到在下一位置发话可能会造成重叠，却依然选择在此处发话，因而随后的重叠应视为是其“取得”的。

韵律实现的修补标记一般被视为会话中的障碍（hitch）和扰乱（perturbation），包括语音的截断（一般表现为声门闭合[23，24，31]）和延长、节奏的断裂和音高或音强的急剧提升[10]，以及各种形式的填声停顿（pause filler）[①] 和未填充的停顿（unfilled pause）[36]。这些所谓韵律形式的障碍或者扰乱，既可以被说话人用来投射当前话轮的组织遇到了问题（有时也可以投射问题的类型），同样也可以被受话人用来监测（monitor）当前行进的话轮，判断其在前进性上受到了阻碍或破坏，从而在下一位置（非TRP）开启话轮，以帮助恢复互动的前进性。如果此时第一说话人也选择继续产出话语，就会与第二说话人的话语形成重叠，使之成为前进型开启。这些在前进性上表现出困难和阻碍、虽然并非位于TRP但仍然经常发生话轮转换（即前进型开启）的地方，也是话轮转换的机会空间（opportunity space）中除TRP外的另一重要位置[32，33]。值得注意的是，在某些前进型开启中，第二说话人恰恰利用了这些韵律资源和转换位置，表面看是为了促进前进性，但实际上却关注和实现着其他互动功能[74]。

3.3 重叠期间：开启后与预解决

上一节总结了韵律在重叠开启阶段——特别是在转换型开启和前进型开启中——是如何作为互动资源被参与者关注和使用。即将讨论的下一阶段是重叠期间（within-overlap）。该阶段所涵盖的位置较广，从重叠开启后一直到重叠解决前都可以视为重叠期间，只要当前话轮空间仍然被两人或多人占据。由于持续较长的重叠在互动言谈中并不常见[②]，所以下面我们将重点关注重叠期间首尾两个关键位置：开启后（post-onset）与预解决（pre-resolution）。

在开启后这一位置，重叠双方所面对的互动任务可分为两方面。一方面，任意一方在认识到重叠开启之后，可以选择放弃当前行进的话轮，从话轮空间的竞争中退出，使下一时刻的会话重新恢复一时一人的常态；而放弃当前话语，通常表现为语音上的截断。另一方面，任意一方也可以选择继续组织当前行进的话轮，持续竞争话轮空间。当然，做此选择的说话人可以正常地产出话语，使其看起来好像并未认识到自己身处重叠[③]；但时常发生的是，重叠一方或多方通过韵律的调整为其在重叠期间的竞争加码。与预开启处类似，Schegloff[54]观察到重叠一方可能在重叠开启后以放慢语速或提高音强的方式对当前所发生的重叠做出反应。但注意，同样涉及语速这一韵律参数，说话人在预开启处表现的是加快语速，而在开启后则是放慢语速。同一互动资源的实际使用在不同互动位置上的变化正是互动言谈“对位置敏感的语法”（positionally sensitive grammar）的体现[51，75]。

而所谓重叠的预解决，并不是分析者能够看到的所有重叠临近结束的位置都是“预解决”；重叠预解决的识别及其中韵律的变化实际上与TRP相关。当重叠一方的话语接近可能完结处时，另一方就可能在此时延长某个/某些音以“吸收”（absorb）[④] 对方即将到达TRP的话语，从而将自己尚未完结的话语保留至重叠解决后，并在重叠的竞争中获得优势。在重叠预解决处的语音延长也被称为“预解决延长”（pre-resolution stretch）[54]。

3.4 解决后与重叠话语的恢复

经过短暂或持久的重叠后，重叠获得解决，会话重新回到正常秩序。本小节将聚焦重叠解决后（post-resolution）以及双方在重叠结束后试图恢复（retrieve）因重叠而受到破坏的话语时，是如何运用韵律资源达到该互动目的的。

---

① 有一些停顿填充成分（如英语的uh和um）在言谈互动中可能已经具有词汇的性质[3，25]。

② 这类重叠也被称为“持久延展重叠”（extended overlap），详见Schegloff[54]及其个案分析。

③ Jefferson[29]称之为“无标竞争”（unmarked competition），另可参看Schegloff[54]。

④ 关于重叠的吸收及对方的回应策略，参看Schegloff[49]。

重叠解决后这一位置紧邻重叠结束处。重叠双方有可能在意识到重叠发生后，同时或接近同时放弃自己的当前话语，将话轮空间分别让给对方，此时带来的结果可能是节奏上的断裂，也就是沉默。或者，其中一方放弃当前话语或达到完结点，此时另一方便失去了通过韵律升级（upgrade）或其他手段竞争话轮空间的理由，但其往往只有在重叠结束后稍晚一些（具体而言是第二个节拍［54］）才能认识到会话已经恢复至一时一人的状态，因此我们经常可以发现结束后的一方可能会将重叠期间的韵律（如音强增大、语音延长）带到重叠解决后这一位置，随后伴随着一时一人的恢复，其韵律表现也回到了常规的无标记状态。

重叠作为非常规的话轮转换，会对其后话轮和序列的发展产生影响。先前重叠的双方在重叠结束后所面临的一个重要问题便是：如果重叠对话语在听、说、理解任一方面产生了破坏，那么对重叠话语的恢复和修补就是紧邻重叠结束后①的相关行为。重叠结束后的恢复与修补相同，可以分为自我恢复（self-retrieval）与他人恢复（other-retrieval）［29］。自我恢复可以通过有标记的重启（restart）先前话语和无标记的接续先前话语完成。这里值得从韵律方面考虑的问题是：参与者“重启”和“接续”时的语音韵律特征是否存在差异？如果存在差异，那又是否与实时互动相关，或者说是否真正得到了参与者的关注？“重启”和“接续”的语音韵律特征与语法是否对应？对应或不对应是否也反映了不同的行为［35］？与之相对，他人恢复的手段包括有标记的请求对方重复相关话语（repeat request）和无标记的对对方重叠中的话语表示确认（acknowledgement）或将其部分或全部重复并嵌入至自己随后的话语中（embedded repeat）［29］。这些手段同样涉及韵律作为互动资源的运用，比如进行他人恢复的说话人在嵌入重复时，不同的语音韵律表现可以使得相同的形态句法成分实施不同的社会行为，或表现不同的认识地位、立场态度等。

3.5 小结

本节按照重叠发展的顺序，即重叠的预开启、开启（转换型与前进型）、重叠期间（开启后与预解决）、解决后与重叠话语的恢复，讨论并总结了说话人在不同阶段运用韵律资源参与互动的惯例及互动意义。目前以汉语会话作为语料，使用会话分析的方法研究韵律作为互动资源参与重叠构建和发展的成果甚少。通过综述上述研究，至少能够得到两点研究启示：（1）关注不同互动位置对于韵律作为互动资源在使用时的限制与塑造；（2）韵律/语音特征的描写本身可以不断细化，但只有那些被参与者关注或使用的，才是真正参与互动组织、具有互动价值的资源。

4. 余论和总结

4.1 余论

我们通常把言语交际理解为意义从言者的思想传递转移到听者的思想之中，而语言是这一转移最重要的载体。但是，互动语言学家认为意义的传达是由交际参与者在话轮交替的互动模式中共同协商完成。语音韵律资源是会话交际最重要的资源之一，交际中语音的设计在一定程度上是它所处会话序列的产物，同时它也受所传达的社会行为的制约。

若从言谈参与者的视角看，交际双方是通过听觉分析（auditory analysis）和感知来看语音线索在互动交际中的作用，所以在做会话语音韵律分析时，需要通过反复比较声音记录中可听辨识别的语音范畴来做互动功能的理解。若从分析研究者的视角看，会话参与者取向的听觉分析可通过声学分析（acoustic analysis）手段来验证，因此听觉分析和声学分析相结合的方法在该领域研究中越来越普遍［64］。但是，依靠耳朵的听觉分析依旧是根本，比

① 如果对重叠话语的恢复和修补延后至非紧邻重叠结束后的位置进行，那么其相关性就会大大减弱，同时还要与其他序列所蕴含的行为竞争或协调，致使其恢复效果相应降低（比较 Schegloff［50］）。

如会话分析学派的创始人之一盖尔·杰斐逊（Gail Jefferson）为记录真实的自然会话而设计的精细转写系统，就反映了社会学家认识到语音细节潜在的社会互动相关性。

4.2 总结

英国约克学派语音学家John Local和Gareth Walker［39］提出了自然会话语音分析领域有关研究方法的七条“律令”（imperatives）。在此，以我们对这七条研究原则的理解和解读作为本文的总结。

（1）**只使用互动言谈（talk-in-interaction）的语料**。因为互动言谈语料能从会话序列结构展现参与者取向的研究视角，它反映了数据的有效性和自然性。正如Schegloff［51］所言:“在日常会话和其他形式的言谈互动中，会话中的话轮序列是重要而贴近的互动组织结构的‘生态龛’（the key proximate organizational niche），它是语言使用和适应的环境。”这里的“生态龛”是借用生态学术语（也叫“生态位”ecological niche），是指一个物种所处的环境以及其本身生活习性的总称。而语言的生态龛是社会互动交际，这是它的使用环境，其具体的使用模式就是一轮一轮的言谈互动序列。因此，来自实验环境产出的或来自内省的数据并不能准确地反映对话互动参与者的实际行为。

（2）**语音分析和互动分析是并行（parallel）的，而不是有先后之分的**。言语交际是口耳相传的，研究者在对言语做交际功能的解释时不能回避听得见的语音线索。也就是说，在分析处理来自交际对话的语料时，一些语音细节和特定的互动功能是密不可分的，两者分析缺一不可。因此，从这个角度来看，我们在对自然会话做互动分析的时候，应该同时做语音分析，两者是并行的，而不应把语音分析当作是额外的、可选的内容。

（3）**对提出的任何分析范畴和主张都要从参与者取向来论证**。当分析者想要论证某些语音特征是构成一个特定话轮或序列的重要因素时，就需要证明会话参与者自己也将其视为重要因素对待。不能仅依靠分析者的直觉或者心理猜测，应该依赖参与者取向的论证原则。这样才能够确保所描述的各种语言资源（包括语音韵律资源）的使用惯例对参与者自身具有某种现实意义，并且这是参与者语言能力的一部分。

（4）**确保个案分析解释和个案集合的分析解释一样具有说服力**。任何单一的交际事件都是参与者在进行互动时，综合使用一系列交际惯例（各种模态资源）的结果。但是，互动现象的个案研究不是孤例研究。要通过仔细考察相似的、复现（recurring）的个案总和（the aggregate）来概括互动现象的语言手段或语音韵律模式，这样才能发现互动结构和语言资源之间的关系。

（5）**在反复听语音材料的过程中仔细检查每一个言谈片段**。在分析真实的言谈材料时，所有层面（语音韵律、句法语义、互动行为、其他模态等）的讨论都应该认真细致地参考音频/视频所记录的语料，依靠上述原则方法和研究范式来查验所研究分析的言语片段。这种检查不是孤立地从会话序列中抽离出来做去语境化的分析，而应不断地联系前后话轮来展示参与者取向的交际场景。

（6）**将所有层级的所有细节都视为与言谈参与者潜在相关**。这一点是很困难的，作为分析者我们总是有预设地将一些分析范畴作为假定的分析对象。但是，从会话参与者的视角来看，从一开始，我们就不知道哪些细节可能与言谈双方有关，哪些细节在当下可能具有特定的交际功能。这一要求不仅适用于语音细节，也适用于整个言谈组织的语言和非语言模态资源。

（7）**要注意所考察的对象在互动序列和结构中的位置**。会话语音韵律研究的主要内容之一是要弄清语音参数群和语音模型的互动功能。涉及的重要方法是作比较，要为实例建立可靠的可比性。这需要观察特定的语音范畴在话轮中和序列间的位置分布。不同的序列位置——横向看话轮内、纵向看话轮构成的序列——对语音参数群构建的使用模式要求不一样，不同的语音模式在不同的序列位置上所具有的互动功能也不同。所以，这体现了语法（此处的“语法”是包括语音韵律使用规律的“大语法”）对序列位置的敏感性。

5. 致谢

本文得到2020年国家社科基金一般项目“汉语口语修补现象的语法研究”（20BYY175）的资助。感谢匿名审稿专家的意见。论文写成后，张惟老师通读全文并给予了宝贵的意见，在此表达诚挚的谢意。

参考文献

[1] Auer, P. 2005. Projection in interaction and projection in grammar. *Text* 25(1), 7 – 36.

[2] Auer, P., Couper-Kuhlen, E., Müller, F. 1999. *Language in Time: The Rhythm and Tempo of Spoken Interaction*. New York: Oxford University Press.

[3] Clark, H. H., Fox Tree, J. E. 2002. Using *uh* and *um* in spontaneous speaking. *Cognition* 84, 73 – 111.

[4] Couper-Kuhlen, E. 1993. *English Speech Rhythm: Form and Function in Everyday Verbal Interaction*. Amsterdam/Philadelphia: John Benjamins.

[5] Couper-Kuhlen, E. 2009. Prosody. In: D' hondt, S., Östman, J. – O., Verschueren, J. (eds), *The Pragmatics of Interaction*. Amsterdam / Philadelphia: John Benjamins, 174 – 189.

[6] Couper-Kuhlen, E. 2011. Pragmatics and prosody: Prosody as social action. In: Bublitz, W., Norrick, N. (eds), *Foundations of Pragmatics*. Berlin: Mouton de Gruyter, 491 – 510.

[7] Couper-Kuhlen, E., Ford, C. E. (eds), 2004. *Sound Patterns in Interaction*. Amsterdam/Philadelphia: John Benjamins.

[8] Couper-Kuhlen, E., Ono, T. 2007. ' Incrementing' in conversation. A comparison of practices in English, German and Japanese. *Pragmatics* 17 (4), 513 – 552.

[9] Couper-Kuhlen, E., Selting, M. (eds), 1996. *Prosody in Conversation: Interactional Studies*. Cambridge: Cambridge University Press.

[10] Cutler, A. 1983. Speakers' conceptions of the function of prosody. In: Cutler, A., Ladd, D. R. (eds), *Prosody: Models and Measurements*. Berlin: Springer-Verlag, 79 – 91.

[11] Deppermann, A., Mondada, L., Doehler, S. P. 2021. Early responses: An introduction. *Discourse Processes* 58 (4), 293 – 307.

[12] Firth, J. R. 1968 [1957]. A synopsis of linguistic theory (1930 – 1955). Reprinted in: Frank R. P. (ed), *Selected Papers of J. R. Firth (1952 – 1959)*. Bloomington: Indiana University Press, 168 – 205.

[13] Firth, J. R. 1957 [1935]. The technique of semantics. Reprinted in: Firth, J. R. *Papers in Linguistics (1934 – 1951)*. London: Oxford University Press, 7 – 33.

[14] Ford, C. E. 2004. Contingency and units in interaction. *Discourse Studies* 6(1), 27 – 52.

[15] Ford, C. E., Fox, B. A., Thompson, S. A. 2002. Constituency and the grammar of turn increments. In: Ford, C. E., Fox, B. A., Thompson, S. A. (eds), *The Language of Turn and Sequence*. New York: Oxford University Press, 14 – 38.

[16] Ford, C. E., Thompson, S. A. 1996. Interactional units in conversation: Syntactic, intonational, and pragmatic resources of the management of turns. In: Ochs, E., Schegloff, E. A., Thompson, S. A. (eds), *Interaction and Grammar*. Cambridge: Cambridge University Press, 134 – 184.

[17] French, P., Local, J. 1983. Turn-competitive incomings. *Journal of Pragmatics* 7(1), 17 – 38.

[18] Garfinkel, H. 1963. A conception of, and experiments with, “trust” as a condition of stable concerted actions. In: Harvey, O. J. (ed), *Motivation and Social Interaction*. New York: Ronald Press, 187 – 238.

[19] Garfinkel, H. 1967. *Studies in Ethnomethodology*. Englewood Cliffs, New Jersey: Prentice-Hall.

[20] Geluykens, R. 1994. *The Pragmatics of Discourse Anaphora in English: Evidence from Conversational Repair*. Berlin/New York: Mouton de Gruyter.

[21] Heritage, J. 1984. *Garfinkel and Ethnomethodology*. Cambridge: Polity Press.

[22] Hoey, E. M. 2020. *When Conversation Lapses: The Public Accountability of Silent Copresence*. New York: Oxford University Press.

[23] Jasperson, R. M. 1998. *Repair after cut-off: Explorations in the grammar of focused repair of the turn-constructional unit-so-far* [doctoral dissertation]. University of Colorado at Boulder.

[24] Jasperson, R. M. 2002. Some linguistic aspects of closure cut-off. In: Ford, C. E., Fox, B. A.,

Thompson S. A. (eds), *The Language of Turn and Sequence*. New York: Oxford University Press, 257 – 286.

[25] Jefferson, G. 1974. Error correction as an interactional resource. *Language in Society* 3 (2), 181 – 199.

[26] Jefferson, G. 1983a. Two explorations of the organization of overlapping talk in conversation, 1: Notes on some orderlinesses of overlap onset. *Tilburg papers in language and literature* 28.

[27] Jefferson, G. 1983b. Two explorations of the organization of overlapping talk in conversation, 2: On a failed hypothesis: ' Conjunctionals' as overlap-vulnerable. *Tilburg papers in language and literature* 28.

[28] Jefferson, G. 1986. Notes on ' latency' in overlap onset. *Human Studies* 9, 154 – 183.

[29] Jefferson, G. 2004. A sketch of some orderly aspects of overlap in natural conversation. In: Lerner, G. H. (ed), *Conversation Analysis: Studies from the First Generation*. Amsterdam/Philadelphia: John Benjamins Publishing Company, 43 – 59.

[30] Kim, K. 2007. Sequential organization of post-predicate elements in Korean conversation: Pursuing uptake and modulating action. *Pragmatics* 17(4), 573 – 603.

[31] Laakso, M., Sorjonen, M. – L. 2010. Cut-off or particle — devices for initiating self-repair in conversation. *Journal of Pragmatics* 42(4), 1151 – 1172.

[32] Lerner, G. H. 1987. *Collaborative turn sequences: Sentence construction and social action* [doctoral dissertation]. University of California, Irvine.

[33] Lerner, G. H. 1996. On the ' semi-permeable' character of grammatical units in conversation: Conditional entry into the turn space of another speaker. In: Ochs, E., Schegloff, E. A., Thompson S. A. (eds), *Interaction and Grammar*. Cambridge: Cambridge University Press, 238 – 276.

[34] Lim, N. – E. 2014. *Retroactive operations: on ' increments' in Mandarin Chinese conversations* [doctoral dissertation]. University of California, Los Angeles.

[35] Local, J. 1992. Continuing and restarting. In: Auer, P., Di Luzio, A. (eds), *The Contextualization of Language*. Amsterdam/Philadelphia: John Benjamins, 273 – 296.

[36] Local, J., Kelly, J. 1986. Projection and ' silences': Notes on phonetic and conversational structure. *Human Studies* 9, 185 – 204.

[37] Local, J., Kelly, J., Wells, W. H. G. 1986. Towards a phonology of conversation: Turn-taking in Tyneside English. *Journal of Linguistics* 22 (2), 411 – 437.

[38] Local, J., Walker, G. 2004. Abrupt-joins as a resource for the production of multi-unit, multi-action units. *Journal of Pragmatics* 36, 1375 – 1403.

[39] Local, J., Walker, G. 2005. Methodological imperatives for investigating the phonetic organization and phonological structures of spontaneous speech. *Phonetica* 62(2 – 4), 120 – 130.

[40] Local, J., Wells, W. H. G., Sebba, M. 1985. Phonology for conversation: Phonetic aspects of turn delimitation in London Jamaican. *Journal of Pragmatics* 9(2 – 3), 309 – 330.

[41] Luke, K. K., Zhang, W. 2007. Retrospective turn continuations in Mandarin Chinese conversation. *Pragmatics* 17(4), 605 – 635.

[42] Ogden, R. 2004. Non-modal voice quality and turn-taking in Finnish. In: Couper-Kuhlen, E., Ford, C. E. (eds), *Sound Patterns in Interaction*. Amsterdam/Philadelphia: John Benjamins, 29 – 62.

[43] Ogden, R. 2012. Prosodies in conversation. In: Niebuhr, O. (ed), *Understanding Prosody: The Role of Context, Function and Communication*. Berlin/Boston: Walter de Gruyter, 201 – 217.

[44] Ogden, R. 2022. The phonetics of talk in interaction. In: Knight, R. – A., Setter, J. (eds), *The Cambridge Handbook of Phonetics*. Cambridge: Cambridge University Press, 657 – 681.

[45] Ogden, R., Routarinne, S. 2005. The communicative functions of final rises in Finnish intonation. *Phonetica* 62, 160 – 175.

[46] Sacks, H., Schegloff, E. A., Jefferson, G. 1974. A simplest systematics for the organization of turn-taking for conversation. *Language* 50 (4), 696 – 735.

[47] Schegloff, E. A. 1979. The relevance of repair to syntax-for-conversation. In: Givón, T. (ed), *Syntax and Semantics 12: Discourse and Syntax*. New York: Academic Press, 261 – 286.

[48] Schegloff, E. A. 1982. Discourse as an interactional achievement: Some uses of ' uh huh' and other things that come between sentences. In: Tannen, D. (ed), *Analyzing Discourse: Text and Talk*. Washington: Georgetown University Press, 71 – 93.

[49] Schegloff, E. A. 1987. Recycled turn beginnings: A precise repair mechanism in conversation's turn-taking organization. In: Button, G., Lee,

J. R. E. (eds), *Talk and Social Organization*. Clevedon: Multilingual Matters, 70 – 85.

[50] Schegloff, E. A. 1992. Repair after next turn: The last structurally provided defense of intersubjectivity in conversation. *American Journal of Sociology* 97 (5), 1295 – 1345.

[51] Schegloff, E. A. 1996. Turn organization: one intersection of grammar and interaction. In: Ochs, E. Schegloff, E. A., Thompson, S. A. (eds), *Interaction and Grammar*. Cambridge: Cambridge University Press, 52 – 133.

[52] Schegloff, E. A. 1998. Reflections on studying prosody in talk-in-interaction. *Language and Speech* 41 (3 – 4), 235 – 263.

[53] Schegloff, E. A. 2000a, September. On turn's possible completion, more or less: Increments and trail-offs [paper presentation]. The Euro-Conferences on Interactional Linguistics, Spa, Belgium.

[54] Schegloff, E. A. 2000b. Overlapping talk and the organization of turn-taking for conversation. *Language in Society* 29(1), 1 – 63.

[55] Schegloff, E. A. 2001. Accounts of conduct in interaction: Interruption, overlap, and turn-taking. In: Turner, J. H. (ed), *Handbook of Sociological Theory*. New York: Kluwer Academic / Plenum Publishers, 287 – 321.

[56] Schegloff, E. A., Jefferson, G., Sacks, H. 1977. The preference for self-correction in the organization of repair in conversation. *Language* 53 (2), 361 – 382.

[57] Selting, M. 2010. Prosody in interaction: State of the art. In: Barth-Weingarten, D., Reber, E., Selting, M. (eds), *Prosody in Interaction*. Amsterdam/Philadelphia: John Benjamins, 3 – 40.

[58] Stivers, T., Robinson, J. D. 2006. A preference for progressivity in interaction. *Language in Society* 35 (3), 367 – 392.

[59] Szczepek Reed, B. 2007. *Prosodic Orientation in English Conversation*. London: Palgrave Macmillan.

[60] Szczepek Reed, B. 2013. Conversation analysis and prosody. In Chapelle, C. A. (ed), *The Encyclopedia of Applied Linguistics*. Oxford: Wiley-Blackwell, 1082 – 1086.

[61] Vorreiter, S. 2003. Turn continuations: Towards a cross-linguistic classification. *Interaction and Linguistic Structures* (39), 1 – 25.

[62] Walker, G. 2004a. On some interactional and phonetic properties of increments to turns in talk-in-interaction. In: Couper-Kuhlen, E., Ford, C. E. (eds), *Sound Patterns in Interaction: Cross-linguistic Studies from Conversation*. Amsterdam/Philadelphia: John Benjamins, 147 – 169.

[63] Walker, G. 2004b. *The phonetic design of turn endings, beginnings, and continuations in conversation* [doctoral dissertation]. University of York.

[64] Walker, G. 2013. Phonetics and prosody in conversation. In: Sidnell, J., Stivers, T. (eds), *The Handbook of Conversation Analysis*. Oxford: Wiley-Blackwell, 455 – 475.

[65] Walker, T. 2014. Form ≠ function: The independence of prosody and action. *Research on Language and Social Interaction* 47(1), 1 – 16.

[66] Wells, B., Macfarlane, S. 1998. Prosody as an interactional resource: Turn-projection and overlap. *Language and Speech* 41 (3 – 4), 265 – 294.

[67] Wells, B., Peppé, S. 1996. Ending up in Ulster: Prosody and turn-taking in English dialects. In: Couper-Kuhlen, E., Selting, M. (eds), *Prosody in Conversation*. Cambridge: Cambridge University Press, 101 – 130.

[68] Zhang, W. 2012. Latching/Rush-through as a turn-holding device and its functions in retrospectively oriented pre-emptive turn continuation: Findings from Mandarin conversation. *Discourse Processes* 49(3 – 4), 163 – 191.

[69] Zhang, W., Li, B., Chan, A. 2012. Preliminary observations of phonetic characteristics cuing turn continuation in spoken Mandarin. In: *Proceedings of Meetings on Acoustics 163 ASA* (Vol. 15), Acoustical Society of America.

[70] 冯志伟（2013）《现代语言学流派》（增订本）。北京：商务印书馆。

[71] 刘奕（2014）《汉语会话增量研究：语言结构与功能》。上海外国语大学博士学位论文。

[72] 乔雪玮、乐耀（2021）（将刊）话语延伸及相关现象的研究述评及思考。《语言教学与研究》。

[73] 乐耀（2017）互动语言学研究的重要课题——会话交际的基本单位。《当代语言学》第2期，246—271页。

[74] 郑上鑫、乐耀（2021，4月17—18日）《修补与重叠的相关性：以汉语会话的修补中重叠为例》。第四届互动语言学与汉语研究国际学术讨论会，线上。

[75] 郑上鑫、乔雪玮、乐耀（2002）（将刊）论对位置敏感的嵌入修补。《语言教学与研

究》第6期。

乐　耀　厦门大学人文学院中文系教授、博导，博士研究生学历。主要研究方向为理论语言学、话语功能语法、会话分析和互动语言学。
Email：yueyao82@163.com
乔雪玮　厦门大学人文学院中文系博士研究生。主要研究领域为话语功能语言学。
Email：qiaoxuewei@stu.xmu.edu.cn
郑上鑫　厦门大学人文学院中文系硕士研究生。研究兴趣为会话分析和互动语言学。
Email：marat1988@stu.xmu.edu.cn

COMPARISON OF THE ACOUSTIC FEATURES OF PROSODIC BOUNDARIES IN CHINESE FORMAL AND INFORMAL SPEECH

BU Xiaoke, FENG Hui, ANG Qiuxiang, CHEN Jiangchao

Abstract According to Register Grammar, prosody, as an aspect of grammar, is one way to realize different registers. This study explored the differences in the acoustic features of prosodic boundaries between Chinese formal and informal speech. Results suggested that: (1) Pauses occurred more frequently and lasted longer at prosodic boundaries in formal speech, best reflected at the Prosodic Clitic level and at the Prosodic Phrase level respectively. In formal speech, pauses at Prosodic Phrase boundaries lasted significantly longer than those at Prosodic Clitic boundaries, while this difference was not significant in informal speech. The distribution of pause duration displayed greater dispersion as the prosodic level increased. (2) In informal register, Prosodic Phrase boundaries performed higher degrees of pre-lengthening than Prosodic Clitic boundaries, while this difference was not significant in formal speech. Prosodic Clitic boundaries in formal and informal speech displayed pre-lengthening and post-lengthening, respectively. (3) Pre-strengthening in the intensity of prosodic words at prosodic boundaries existed at all three levels in both registers, but it was probably a weak cue to discriminate the two registers. (4) Only slight pitch reset was found at Prosodic Clitic boundaries in formal speech and at Prosodic Phrase boundaries in informal speech.

Keywords Register, Prosodic boundaries, Acoustic features, Pre-lengthening, Pitch reset

1. INTRODUCTION

Register is a language mechanism used to determine or adjust the social relationships and distances between the speaker and the hearer in communication [6]. Differences of language in different politeness degrees, attitudes and occasions have been extensively studied from the aspects of sound [9,26], lexicon [16,24] and grammar [7,20]. Feng [7] proposed Chinese Register Grammar (CRG), providing theoretical evidence for an interface between register and grammar. Based on the theory of CRG, a number of Chinese researchers reported lexical, morphological and syntactic differences between different registers of Mandarin Chinese [7,13,24]. Regarding the prosodic aspect, Feng and Hu [5] discovered that Chinese formal speech featured more pauses or breaks, longer syllable duration and larger pitch range. It is noted that the interaction of register with prosody remains an under-examined field, especially with prosodic boundaries, which were found crucial in speech engineering [9,21,30].

Prosodic boundaries refer to the boundaries between prosodic units [3]. The proposed model of Prosodic Hierarchy holds that an utterance can be divided into a hierarchy of prosodic units shared by all human languages, including Syllable, Foot, Prosodic Word, Prosodic/Phonological Phrase, Intonational Phrase, and Utterance [14]. In Mandarin Chinese, Wang [22] and Feng [8] suggested that between Prosodic Phrase and Prosodic Word there is also a level for Prosodic Clitic, which is usually made up of a prosodic word and a clitic attached to it.

Previous research agreed that the acoustic features of prosodic boundaries mainly include silent pauses, pre-boundary lengthening, and syllable pitch reset in the vicinity of boundaries [21]. Pitch reset is essentially the reset of the downward slope of the pitch, which manifests as the upward movement of the syllable bass point after the prosodic boundary [3]. The acoustic features of prosodic boundaries differ among different prosodic levels. Ladd [12], Wightman et al. [25] and Kim et al. [10] found longer silent pauses and more significant pre-boundary lengthening and pitch reset as the level of prosodic boundaries increases.

With regard to prosodic boundaries in Chinese speech, one focus lies in speech engineering. The acoustic characteristics of prosodic boundaries, e. g. co-articulation at the Prosodic Word boundaries, proved critical in speech communication, syntactic disambiguation, rhythm adjustment and the improvement of the naturalness and intelligibility of speech synthesis [9,29,30].

In addition, studies focusing on prosodic boundaries in Chinese of particular registers have also been conducted. For example, based on large corpus with both slow and fast speech rates, Wang et al. [21] investigated the acoustic correlates to prosodic hierarchical boundaries in Chinese. Chen and Duan [4] compared the prosodic features of storytelling discourses and news broadcasts, and found that the prosody of flowing sentences in storytelling discourses is reflected in the various combinations of rhythmic units at different prosodic levels.

To sum up, language differences in different registers have been extensively investigated from various aspects in previous studies, of which some have reported lexical and grammatical differences in different registers of Mandarin Chinese. According to Chinese Register Grammar [7], prosodic differences are expected to be found across different registers. Nevertheless, few prosodic cues for distinguishing the formal and informal registers have been reported, let alone studies focusing on the features of prosodic boundaries in different registers. However, Hu et al. [9], Wang et al. [21] and Zheng [30] suggested that research on prosodic boundaries is important for both speech recognition and synthesis.

Thus, the focus of the present study is the acoustic features of prosodic boundaries (at the levels of Prosodic Word, Prosodic Clitic and Prosodic Phrase) in Chinese speech of different formality. Specifically, this paper aims to address two questions: (1) Will boundary pauses behave differently in Chinese formal and informal speech? (2) Is there any difference in the acoustic features of prosodic words in the vicinity of prosodic boundaries between Chinese formal and informal speech? It may be noted that we chose to examine the features of pre- and post-boundary prosodic words rather than the more extensively examined units, syllables. Although previous studies mainly focused on syllables at boundaries, some of them pointed out that prosodic words as a whole show certain prosodic patterns [4, 19,23,27]. According to Cao [2], prosodic words are the most basic and important prosodic units in the Chinese prosodic hierarchy. Therefore, we focus on the features of prosodic words as a whole.

The remainder of this paper is organized as follows. Section 2 describes the experimental design and data collection. Section 3 discusses the findings on boundary pauses and on pre- and post-boundary prosodic words at the three prosodic levels. Section 4 is the conclusion.

2. EXPERIMENT

To examine the afore-mentioned research questions, we utilized the materials in Feng and Hu's [5] experiment. This section first gives a brief introduction to the subjects, materials and procedures, and then specifies how the data needed were collected and processed.

2.1 Subjects, materials and procedures

The 20 subjects were from Feng and Hu's [5] study, including ten Chinese announcers and ten Beijing Mandarin speakers (gender balanced in each group). Materials are available in the appendix in Feng and Hu [5].

The settings of the materials are listed in Table 1. Our current study made use of the first six pairs of Feng and Hu's [5] stimuli. Each pair consisted of a formal sentence and its informal counterpart, which were consistent in tonal combinations and syntactic structures but different in the degree of formality.

Table 1 Register details of stimuli [5]

	Formal	Informal
Relation	Announcer and audience	Family members
Attitude	Neutral	Intimate
Occasion	Broadcast	Talking with family members
Content	Politics	Daily life

Utterances were recorded with Praat [1] in a quiet (environment noise level < 30 dB) small (10 – 15 m^2) room; all recordings were directly recorded as 16 bit mono wav files at a 44 kHz sampling rate. All sentences were presented with corresponding instructions for each setting. A total of 120 recordings were chosen from Feng and Hu [5] for this study.

In this study, the independent variables were register (formality) and prosodic levels (Prosodic Word level, Prosodic Clitic level or Prosodic Phrase level); the dependent variables were a series of acoustic parameters measured, including the frequency and duration of pauses, and the duration, intensity and minimal pitch of prosodic words in the vicinity of prosodic boundaries.

2.2 Data collection

2.2.1 Annotation

All the files were first segmented with Forced Aligner [28], and then syllable boundaries were manually adjusted according to the features of boundary vowels and consonants [11]. Based on the annotation in Feng and Hu [5], a break index tier was added with Praat.

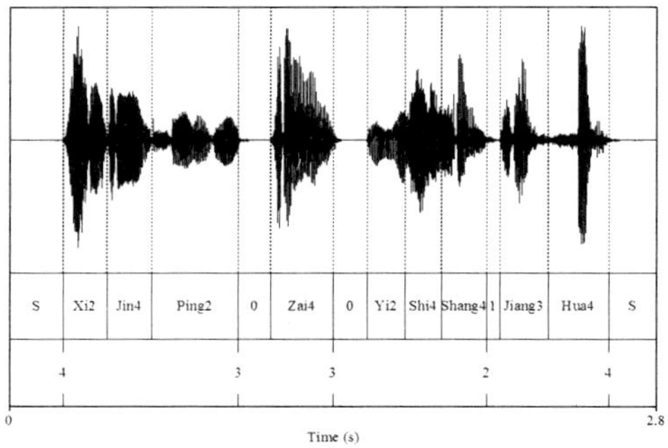

Figure 1 An example of annotation for the target sentences

Thus, the resulting annotation contained two tiers: the Pinyin tier and the Break Index tier, as shown in Figure 1. In the Pinyin tier, syllable boundaries were determined; each word was represented by Pinyin, followed by its tone (0, 1, 2, 3 or 4, representing the neutral tone, first tone, second tone, third tone and fourth tone in Standard Chinese, respectively). Silent pauses within sentences were marked with "0" and filled pauses "1". According to the standards used in the Annotated Speech Corpus of Chinese Discourse (ASCCD) [15], the key to determining the break index after a prosodic unit is to see how closely the unit is perceived to conjoin with the following unit. In the Break Index tier, "1", "2", "3" and "4" represented the boundaries of prosodic words (PW), prosodic clitics

(PC), prosodic phrases (PP) and intonational phrases (IP), respectively.

2.2.2 Data extraction

VoiceSauce [17] was used to extract the duration, pitch and intensity of the recordings. A Praat script was utilized to extract the annotation data, including the break index information. The duration, mean intensity and pitch (maximal and minimal) of prosodic words at each boundary were calculated with Microsoft Excel. Altogether, there are 389 PW/PC/PP boundaries in 120 utterances. Detailed statistics are listed in Table 2.

Table 2 Numbers of prosodic boundaries by registers and prosodic levels

	PW	PC	PP	Total
Formal	95	39	65	199
Informal	106	40	44	190

2.2.3 Data processing

All the duration, intensity and pitch values of pre- and post-boundary prosodic words extracted were standardized into logarithmic z-scores (lz-scores for short) for each speaker to minimize the effect of individual differences [31] with the formula below:

$$lz = 10 + 5 \times \frac{\log_{10}x - \frac{1}{n}\sum_{i=1}^{n}\log_{10}x_i}{\sqrt{\frac{1}{n-1}\sum_{i=1}^{n}\left(\log_{10}x_i - \frac{1}{n}\sum_{i=1}^{n}\log_{10}x_i\right)^2}} \tag{1}$$

where x is the value to be normalized; lz is the standardized value; n is the sample size for each speaker.

3. RESULTS AND DISCUSSION

The acoustic data of the pauses and of the prosodic words at prosodic boundaries in formal and informal speech are presented and discussed as follows.

3.1 Pauses at prosodic boundaries of the three levels

Boundary pauses were analyzed from the aspects of frequency and duration. The former measures how likely pauses are to occur at boundaries of a certain level; the latter implies the duration of pauses at the three levels of boundaries where there exists a pause.

3.1.1 Frequency of pauses

The frequency of PW/PC/PP pauses is the ratio of PW/PC/PP boundaries with pauses to all PW/PC/PP boundaries. Figure 2 displays the frequencies of silent, filled and total pauses at boundaries of the three levels in the two registers.

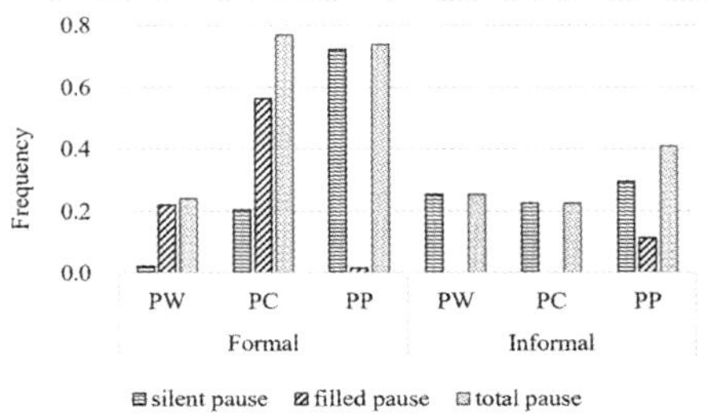

Figure 2 Frequency of pauses at prosodic boundaries in formal and informal speech

According to the frequency of total pauses, the three levels rank as PC > PP > PW in formal register; and for informal register, the order is PP > PW > PC. Particularly, it is remarkable that PC boundaries display a significant difference between the two registers: the occurence of pauses at PC boundaries in formal speech is much higher than that in informal speech (a frequency of 0.77 in formal speech versus 0.22 in informal speech). This suggests that the difference in the frequency of pauses between two registers is best reflected at PC boundaries.

Considering each prosodic level individually, it can be found that at PW boundaries, there is no significant difference in the frequency of total pauses between formal and informal speech; while at PC and PP boundaries, pauses are much more likely to occur in formal speech than in informal speech. This can be explained by the fact that in Chinese formal speech, speakers use more pauses to make clearer utterances, while in informal speech they speak more casually and pause less. And the pause frequencies that are similarly low at PW boundaries in both registers are probably due to the consistent close juncture between prosodic words—the smaller prosodic units, regardless of the degree of formality.

As to the distribution of pause types, in formal register, pauses are less likely to be filled ones at major boundaries, with about 91% of pauses being filled ones at PW boundaries, 73% at PC boundaries and only 2% at PP boundaries, while in informal register, filled pauses only occur at PP boundaries, with a proportion of 27%.

3. 1. 2 Duration of pauses

Figure 3 shows the mean duration of boundary pauses. Both registers display increasing pause duration as the prosodic level goes higher, which coincides with the findings of Wang et al. [21]. In formal register, pauses at PP boundaries (median = 105 ms) are significantly longer than those at PC boundaries (median = 56 ms) (Mann-Whitney U = 1161, $n_1 = 47$, $n_2 = 30$, $p < .001$ two-tailed); while in informal register, the difference in the duration of the pauses at PP (median = 36 ms) and PC boundaries (median = 45 ms) is not significant (Mann-Whitney $U = 63$, $n_1 = 18$, $n_2 = 9$, $p = .375$ two-tailed).

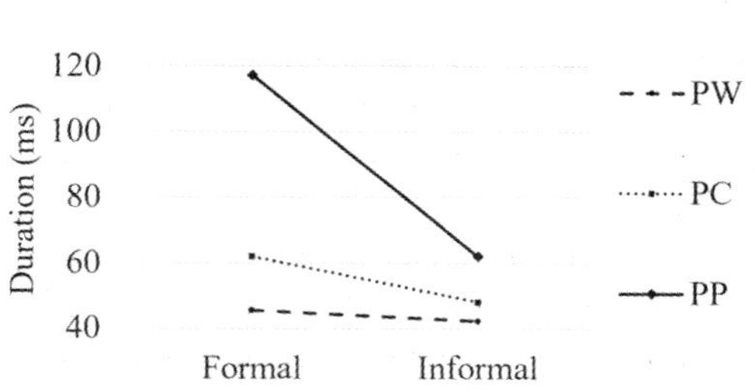

Figure 3 Mean duration of pauses at prosodic boundaries in formal and informal speech

At all the three levels, formal speech shows longer pauses than informal speech, with different degrees, though. This is shown in Table 3: as the prosodic level rises from PW to PP, the p-value of the Mann-Whitney U test decreases, indicating increasingly significant difference between the pause duration of the two registers.

Table 3 Results of Mann-Whitney U tests of pause durations

Level	Median (ms)		U	n_1	n_2	p
	Formal	Informal				
PW	44	45	696	23	27	.460
PC	56	45	180	39	9	.140
PP	105	36	349	47	18	< .001

Such different degrees can also be observed in Figure 4, which shows the distribution of pause duration at prosodic boundaries of the three levels in the two registers. PW boundaries display a similar distribution of pause duration in these two registers, so do the PC boundaries. Thus, in Figure 3, these two levels show no significant difference in pause duration between two registers. For PP boundaries, however, the distributions of two registers differ significantly. The duration of formal pauses mainly ranges from 40 – 220 ms; and that of informal pauses, 10 – 100 ms. This can explain their mean difference illustrated in Figure 3. In addition, at the PP level, the duration distribution of formal pauses (SD = 79. 68 ms) shows greater dispersion compared with informal pauses (SD = 56. 66 ms).

Across the three levels, it can be observed that PC pauses have the most centralized distribution, then come the PW pauses; and PP pauses show the greatest dispersion. Wang et al. [21] found increasing dispersion as the prosodic level increases from PP (Prosodic Phrase) to IP (Intonational Phrase). If we consider prosodic clitics as a subcategory of prosodic words (as the ASCCD

[15] prescribes), it is plausible to make such a generalization that the distribution of pause duration displays greater dispersion as the prosodic level increases.

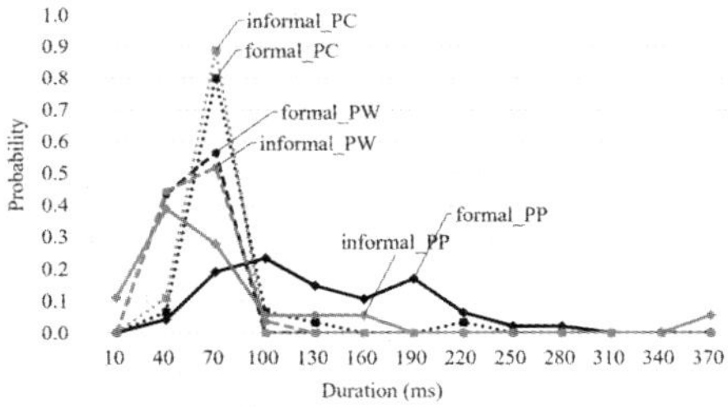

Figure 4 Distribution of pause duration at prosodic boundaries in formal and informal speech

3.2 Acoustic features of prosodic words before and after prosodic boundaries

As for the prosodic words in the vicinity of prosodic boundaries, acoustic variables measured include duration, intensity and the lowest pitch. These variables were examined to observe whether there are acoustic phenomena like pre-boundary lengthening, pre-boundary strengthening and pitch resetting.

3.2.1 Duration

Pre-boundary lengthening is one acoustic feature at prosodic boundaries [3]. Figure 5 shows the mean duration of prosodic words before and after different prosodic boundaries and the corresponding differences between formal and informal speech.

At the PW level, the duration of post-boundary prosodic words is 11.80% and 28.32% longer than that of pre-boundary ones in formal and informal register respectively, indicating post-lengthening in both registers. Segmental lengthening not only occurs at pre-boundary but also at post-boundary, as was discovered by Zu and Chen [32], whose results suggested a tendency for minor prosodic boundaries to display post-lengthening, as opposed to major prosodic boundaries. Given an average pre-lengthening of −10.56%, 14.20% and 16.49% in formal register, and that of −22.07%, 9.62% and 14.28% in informal register at PW, PC and PP boundaries respectively, it may thus be assumed that the lower the level of the prosodic boundary is, the slighter the degree of pre-lengthening is, to the extent that post-lengthening may occur.

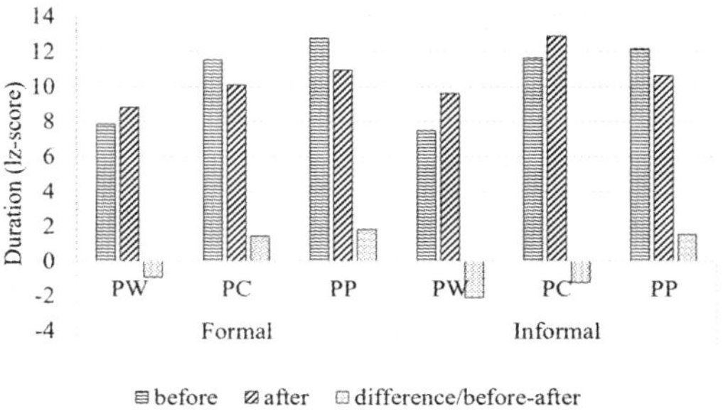

Figure 5 Mean duration of prosodic words before and after prosodic boundaries in formal and informal speech

A Kruskal-Wallis test indicates no significant differences ($\chi^2 = 4.48$, $df = 2$, $p = .107$) among the amount of pre-lengthening at the three prosodic levels in formal register; whereas in informal speech, significant differences ($\chi^2 = 12.03$, $df = 2$, $p = .002$) were found in pre-lengthening among the three prosodic levels. A *post hoc* Dunn's test on the pre-lengthening of the three levels in informal register suggests significant differences between the PP level and the PW level ($p = .002$), and between the PP level and the PC level ($p = .029$). Therefore, the afore-mentioned assumption that the degree of pre-lengthening correlates positively to the level of prosodic boundaries holds good only for the informal register.

As is shown in Figure 5, at all the three levels, formal speech shows greater degree of pre-lengthening than informal speech. But Mann-Whitney U tests on formal/informal samples at the three levels indicate significant difference merely at the PC level (Mann-Whitney $U = 1055$, $n_1 = 39$, $n_2 = 40$, $p = .007$ two-tailed), rendering Prosodic Clitic a level discriminating the two registers—at PC boundaries, formal speech tends to display pre-lengthening; while informal speech has a tendency to lengthen the post-boundary prosodic words.

3.2.2 Intensity

The intensity feature at prosodic boundaries in different speech styles tends to be different, as Chen and Duan [3] discovered. Figure 6 shows the mean intensity of prosodic words before and after prosodic boundaries and the corresponding differences.

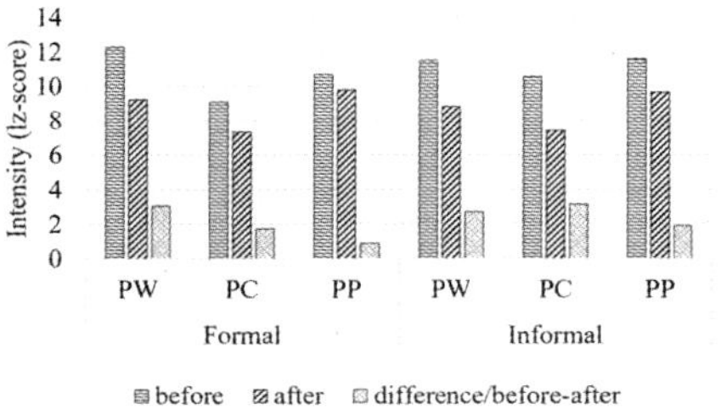

Figure 6 Mean intensity of prosodic words before and after prosodic boundaries in formal and informal speech

It appears that in both registers, pre-boundary intensity is higher than post-boundary intensity (called "pre-strengthening" hereafter) at all the three levels. At all the three levels, formal register and informal register display no significant difference in pre-strengthening (Mann-Whitney $p = .442$, $.280$ and $.265$ for the PW level, PC level and PP level, respectively).

The intensity variation presented in our study is consistent with Streeter [18], which suggested that intensity variation is a weak cue for phrase boundary. The intensity feature of prosodic words at the vicinity of prosodic boundaries may not be an effective prosodic factor for differentiating Chinese formal speech from informal speech.

3.2.3 Pitch

Wang et al. [21] examined the degree of pitch reset at prosodic boundaries "by analyzing the lowest pitch of the prosodic syllables before and after the boundaries." For PW boundaries, the increase in the lowest pitch indicates discontinuity of the bass contour; for PC and PP boundaries, such increase indicates pitch reset [21]. Here the minimal pitch of prosodic words before and after boundaries is analyzed. Figure 7 illustrates the maximal and minimal pitch of pre-boundary prosodic words and post-boundary ones at the three levels.

Specifically, at the PW level, in both registers, the minimal pitch is even lower after boundaries, indicating no discontinuity of the bottom line. At the PC level, the minimal pitch in informal speech continues to decrease, showing no pitch reset; while in formal speech it slightly climbs up, indicating a small degree of reset.

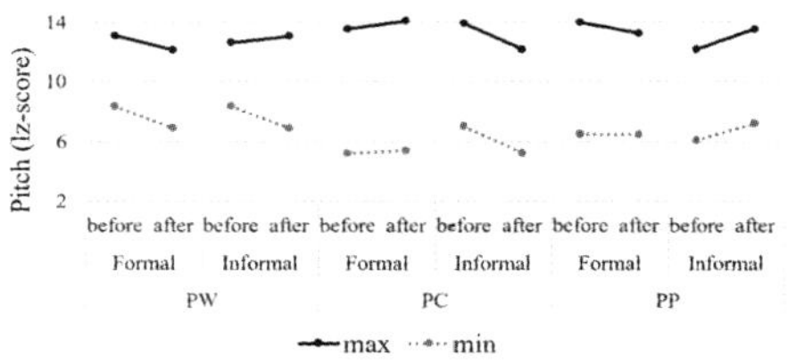

Figure 7 Maximal and minimal pitch of prosodic words before and after prosodic boundaries in formal and informal speech

Two notions are interesting here. First, compared with informal speech, formal speech tends to "tense" at the tail, reversing the general declining pitch contour. Second, taking into consideration the pause difference in PC boundaries between the two registers in Section 3.1, it is plausible that in informal speech, there is not enough time for pitch resetting in the vicinity of PC boundaries where pauses are less and shorter. As an example, Figure 8 shows a pair of formal and informal utterances with this feature.

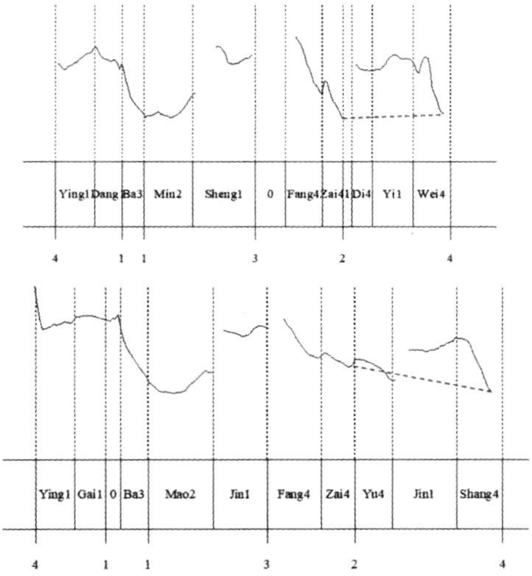

Figure 8 An example of the pitch contours at prosodic clitic boundaries in formal (top) and informal (bottom) speech

As shown in Figure 8, in the formal utterance, the lowest pitch of the prosodic word *dìyīwèi* (第一位, the first place) is slightly higher than that of its pre-boundary counterpart *fàngzài* (放在, put something on a certain place). In the informal utterance, however, the bass point of the post-boundary *yùjīnshàng* (浴巾上, on the bath towel) is obviously lower than that of the pre-boundary *fàngzài*. The formal utterance displays a minor pitch reset after the PC boundary; and the pitch of the informal utterance still keeps declining.

At the PP level, the minimal pitch in formal speech levels out and informal speech shows reset. Therefore, pitch reset was found at PC boundaries in formal speech and at PP boundaries in informal speech. But Wilcoxon signed-rank tests on the corresponding paired bass samples suggested that both were not significant (p = .317 and .339 for PC boundaries in formal register and for PP boundaries in informal register, respectively).

4. CONCLUSIONS

This study focused on the differences between Chinese formal and informal speech in the acoustic features of prosodic boundaries. Boundaries at the Prosodic Word level, Prosodic Clitic level and Prosodic Phrase level were examined in detail regarding the frequency and duration of pauses, and the duration, intensity and bass points of pre- and post- boundary prosodic words. The findings are as follows.

With regard to boundary pauses, pauses generally occurred more frequently and lasted longer at prosodic boundaries in formal speech, which was probably due to the need for clearer utterances in formal speech. Pauses in formal speech outnumbered those in informal speech, especially at the PC and PP boundaries. As to the differences in pause duration between the two registers, first, pauses at PP boundaries lasted significantly longer than those at PC boundaries in formal speech, while this difference was not significant in informal speech. Second, the higher the prosodic level was, the more significant was the difference in pause duration between formal and informal register. Third, as the prosodic level increased, the distribution of pause duration probably displayed greater dispersion.

As to the duration of pre- and post-boundary prosodic words, first, in informal register, PP boundaries performed more significant pre-lengthening than PC boundaries; while this difference was not significant in formal speech. Second, the most considerable difference between the two registersd lied in the PC level, where formal speech displayed pre-lengthening, while informal speech displayed post-lengthening.

At all the three levels, pre-boundary intensity was observed higher than post-boundary intensity in both registers. Pre-strengthening of prosodic words at prosodic boundaries was regarded as a weak cue to discriminate the two registers, as all the three levels demonstrated no significant difference in prestrengthening between formal and informal register.

Concerning the pitch contour at prosodic boundaries, in both registers, prosodic word boundaries showed no discontinuity of the bass point. Pitch reset was observed but tested not significant at PC boundaries in formal speech and at PP boundaries in informal speech.

The findings in the present study suggest observable differences in the acoustic features of prosodic boundaries between Chinese formal and informal speech. For future studies, we will sort out prosodic words/clitics/phrases to find more about the differences between the two registers, for example, prosodic words of different tonal combinations; clitics in different kinds of phrases such as *zài* (在, at) in the verbal phrase *fàngzài* (放在, to put something on a certain place) and in the prepositional phrase *zài yíshì shàng* (在仪式上, at the ceremony).

5. ACKNOWLEDGEMENTS

The research is supported by Social Science Foundation of Tianjin, China (TJWW19-009 and TJWW17-010).

REFERENCES

[1] Boersma, P., Weenink, D. (1992 - 2022): Praat: doing phonetics by computer [Computer Program]. Versin 6. 1. 16, retrieved 2020 from https://www.praat.org.

[2] Cao, J. 2011. Prosodic structure and speech sound variation. *Journal of School of Chinese Language and Culture Nanjing Normal University* 3, 12 - 22. [In Chinese]

[3] Chen, M. 2013. The characteristics of oral Chinese prosodic boundaries of American English speaking CSL learners. *Chinese Teaching in the World* 27 (1), 95 - 104. [In Chinese]

[4] Chen, Y., Duan, R. 2020. The prosodic expression of flowing sentences in storytelling. *Cotemporary Rhetoric* (1), 74 - 87. [In Chinese]

[5] Feng, H., Hu, D. 2020. Prosodic features in Chinese formal and informal speech. *Studies in Prosodic Grammar* (2), 103 - 124. [In Chinese]

[6] Feng, S. 2010. On mechanisms of register system and its grammatical property. *Studies of the Chinese Language* (5), 400 - 412 + 479. [In Chinese]

[7] Feng, S. 2012. The grammar of yuti: Exploring languages with ' the rules of form-function correspondence'. *Contemporary Rhetoric* (6), 3 - 12. [In Chinese]

[8] Feng, S. 2013. *Prosodic Syntax in Chinese* (enlarged). Beijing: The Commercial Press. [In Chinese]

[9] Hu, W., Xu, B., Huang, T. 2002. An experimental study on prosodic boundary in Chinese Mandarin. *Journal of Chinese Information Processing* 1, 43 - 48. [In Chinese]

[10] Kim, H., Yoon, T., Cole, J., Hasegawa-Johnson, M. 2006. Acoustic differentiation of L- and L-L% in switchboard and radio news speech. *Proceedings of Speech Prosody*, Dresden.

[11] Kong, J. 2015. *Basic Course of Experimental Phonetics*. Beijing: Peking University Press. [In Chinese]

[12] Ladd, D. R. 1988. Declination ' reset' and the hierarchical organization of utterances. *The Journal of the Acoustical Society of America* 1, 530 - 544.

[13] Luo, J. 2017. On the syntactic and register difference between monosyllabic and disyllabic verbs carrying objects. *Language Teaching and Linguistic Studies* 1, 14 - 24. [In Chinese]

[14] Nespor, M., Vogel, I. 2007. *Prosodic Phonology: With a New Foreword*. Berlin: Mouton de Gruyter.

[15] Phonetics Lab, Institute of Linguistics, Chinese Academy of Social Sciences. 2008. ASCCD-Annotated speech corpus of Chinese discourse. [In Chinese]

[16] Romaine, S. 2009. Handbook of multilingualism and multilingual communication. *Language* 85 (2), 457 - 458.

[17] Shue, Y. - L. 2010. *The Voice Source in Speech Production: Data, Analysis and Models*. PhD dissertation, UCLA.

[18] Streeter, L. A. 1978. Acoustic determinations of phrase boundary perception. *The Journal of the Acoustical Society of America* 64, 1582 - 1592.

[19] Sun, Y., Shi, F. 2012. Durational performance of focus sentences in Standard Chinese. *Chinese Journal of Phonetics* 3, 70 – 76. [In Chinese]
[20] Tao, H. 1999. The grammatical significance of register classification. *Contemporary Linguistics* 3, 15 – 24 + 61. [In Chinese]
[21] Wang, B., Yang, Y., Lü, S. 2004. Acoustic analysis on prosodic hierarchical boundaries of Chinese. *Acta Acustica* 1, 29 – 36. [In Chinese]
[22] Wang, H. 2008. *Non-Linear Phonology of Chinese*. Beijing: Peking University Press. [In Chinese]
[23] Wang, L., Shi, X. 2016. A sample analysis of the lengthening ratio of declarative sentence in Guangzhou Mandarin. *Chinese Journal of Phonetics* 7, 107 – 117. [In Chinese]
[24] Wang, Y. 2016. *A Study on the Pan-Temporal Spatialization of Written Formal Grammar in Chinese*. Beijing: China Social Sciences Press. [In Chinese]
[25] Wightman, C. W., Shattuck-Hufnagel, S., Ostendorf, M., Price, P. J. 1992. Segmental durations in the vicinity of prosodic phrase boundaries. *The Journal of the Acoustical Society of America* 91 (3), 1707 – 1717.
[26] Winter, B., Grawunder, S. 2012. The phonetic profile of Korean formal and informal speech registers. *Journal of Phonetics* 40 (6), 808 – 815.
[27] Yin, Z. 2019. Speaking rate in Chinese reading discourse based on prosodic hierarchy model. *Chinese Journal of Phonetics* 12, 63 – 74. [In Chinese]
[28] Yuan, J., Liberman, M. 2008. Speaker identification on the SCOTUS corpus. *Proceedings of Acoustics* '08 Paris, 5687 – 5690.
[29] Zhang, J., Zhu, W., Garding, E. 2002. Temporal structures of spoken Chinese Mandarin. *Acta Acustica* 27(5), 389 – 392. [In Chinese]
[30] Zheng, Y. 2008. Coarticulation at the boundary of prosodic words—Consideration on the naturalness of synthesized speech. *Journal of Tsinghua University (Science and Technology)* 48 (S1), 645 – 651. [In Chinese]
[31] Zhu, X. 2004. F0 normalization: How to deal with between-speaker tonal variations? *Linguistic Sciences* 2, 3 – 19. [In Chinese]
[32] Zu, Y., Chen, X. 1999. Segmental durations and lengthened syllables. *Proceedings of the 14th International Congress of Phonetic Sciences*, San Francisco, 277 – 280.

BU Xiaoke BA. She is a graduate of Tianjin University. Her research interests include phonology and syntax.
Email: charon09502@ 163. com

FENG Hui PhD. She is an associate professor of Tianjin University. Her research interests include speech perception and production, and sociolinguistics. She is the corresponding author of this paper.
Email: fenghui@ tju. edu. cn

ANG Qiuxiang BA. She is a graduate of Tianjin University. Her research interest is speech perception.
Email: 15288020162@ 163. com

CHEN Jiangchao BA. She is a graduate of Tianjin University. Her research interest is speech prosody.
Email: shaynachan@ 163. com

粤方言区英语学习者焦点重音产出与感知研究

曹　冲　李爱军

摘　要　本文在自主音段节律理论的框架下，以40名粤方言区英语学习者为研究对象，通过行为产出和感知实验考察粤方言区英语学习者一般疑问句焦点重音的习得情况。研究发现：（1）学习者采用上升和下降两类边界调实现疑问语气，并且升调边界调和降调边界调的使用频次非常接近；（2）当学习者采用升调边界调结尾时，如学习者明确句中焦点的位置，焦点词实现的音高模式主要是 L^* 和 L^*+H，相反则是 L^* 和 H^*。但是，当学习者采用降调边界调结尾时，焦点词实现的音高模式主要是 H^* 和 L+H^*，与学习者是否明确焦点位置无关；（3）学习者感知句中焦点重音的正确率在72%左右，不同类型音高重音的感知结果没有显著差异。

关键词　粤方言，焦点重音，产出，感知

A Study of Cantonese EFL Learners on Producing and Perceiving Nuclear Accent in English

CAO Chong　LI Aijun

Abstract Based on Auto-segmental Metrical Theory, the study investigated the processing of nuclear accent in yes-no questions from the perspectives of realization and perception by 40 Cantonese EFL learners of English. Results showed that: (1) learners applied both the rising and falling boundary tones to realize the interrogative intonation, and the frequency of occurrence of each boundary tone was nearly matched; (2) when learners adopted the rising boundary tone, the nuclear accent was mainly marked by L^* and L^*+H pitch accent if learners were clear of the location of nuclear accent, but L^* and H^* pitch accent if learners were less clear of the location of nuclear accent. However, when learners adopted the falling boundary tone, the nuclear accent was mainly marked by H^* and L+H^* pitch accent, independent of the awareness of the location of nuclear accent; (3) The perception accuracy of the nuclear accent was about 72%, and there was no significant differences in the perception accuracy of different types of pitch accents.

Keywords Cantonese, Nuclear accent, Production, Perception

1. 引言

英语是一种重音节拍语（stress-timed language），重音是英语最显著的韵律特征之一［25］。英语中的重音可以分为词重音和句重音，词重音的位置不固定，属于自由重音（free stress），句重音作用于话语层面，通常是话语焦点在语音上的表现形式之一。

焦点是话语的语义中心，是说话者期望强调和突出的核心内容［8］。在语篇理解过程中，焦点通常与信息结构有关，一个句子按照信息结构可以划分为焦点/背景、新信息/旧信息等，一般来说，焦点对应新信息，背景对应旧信息［3，5，21，23］。焦点可以通过句法、语义和语音等手段来突显［22，24］。已有研究显示，焦点与重音密切相关，英语突显焦点的语音手段主要是焦点重音，语流中成为焦点的词或成分会以音高重音的形式表现出来［4］。

汉语是一种音节节拍语（syllable-timed language），具有音节相对等时性。

同时汉语又是一种声调语言，包括十大方言，分别是官话、晋、徽、吴、赣、闽、客家、湘、粤和平话方言，这些方言在调类和调型上相互间存在差异。对声调语言来说，语调的实现会受到字调的影响。已有学者采用实验语音学手段对中国不同方言区英语学习者焦点重音的产出进行了详细的声学分析。例如，尽管学习者和英语本族语者都采用抬高基频调域的策略来实现焦点重音，但由于受到方言字调的影响，学习者在实现基频最高点、基频升降幅度、焦点后压缩（Post focus compression，简称 PFC）等方面都表现出不同于英语本族语者的特点；其次，学习者每个词甚至每个音节的发音都清晰、饱满，抹掉了重读音节的突显性，表现出强弱对比不明显的特点［7，11，16］。

除了声学分析，也有学者依据自主音段节律理论（Auto-segmental Metrical Theory，简称 AM 理论）对英语学习者焦点重音产出的语调模式进行了考察。AM 理论采用高目标值和低目标值标注英语语调变化，包括5个音高重音，分别是 H*、L*、L*+H、L+H* 和!H+H*［10］。从焦点重音实现的音高模式来看，英语本族语者往往采用 H* 和 L+H* 表达陈述句中的焦点重音，采用 L*+H 或 L* 表达是非问句中的焦点重音，焦点重音实现的音高模式与焦点所处的位置无关。而对英语学习者来说，如果焦点位于句中，则采用 H* 表达陈述句和是非问句中的焦点重音。如果焦点位于句末，则采用 H* 表达陈述句中的焦点重音，采用 L*+H 或 H* 表达是非问句中的焦点重音，并且有且仅当焦点重音位于句末最后一个音节时，英语学习者才会使用 L*+H 类音高重音，随着焦点成分内音节数量的增加，学习者使用 H* 音高重音的倾向越明显。可以看出，英语学习者在表达不同句型中的焦点重音时主要依赖 H* 音高重音［6，9，11，13］。

与产出相比，感知研究成果相对没有那么丰富。已有研究发现英语学习者可以准确感知陈述句中的焦点重音，但是对一般疑问句焦点重音的感知则存在困难，主要表现在学习者不能准确感知 L* 类音高重音，倾向将疑问句句末音节感知为重读音节。同时，学习者对焦点重音的感知受到句子形式—意义匹配与否的影响。如果让学习者和英语本族语者依据音高重音对不同语调类型的句子进行分类，学习者主要根据句子中音高重音的个数，而英语本族语者主要根据音高重音的位置。也就是说，在焦点重音的感知上，学习者关注的是焦点重音在语音实现上基频曲线的变化，而英语本族语者更关注焦点重音表达的意义［19］。

粤方言虽然在节奏归类上也属于音节节拍语，但在韵律结构和类型上与英语、汉语其他方言（如官话、吴方言等）存在较大的差异。在焦点重音的语音实现上，英语依赖的主要声学线索是基频，其次是时长，而粤方言主要依靠时长［17］；其次，英语焦点的实现既有焦点处的基频扩张，也有焦点后的基频压缩（焦点前的基频基本保持不变）［15］。英语是典型的存在焦点后压缩（PFC）现象的语言，而粤方言是不存在 PFC 现象的语言，焦点对焦点后成分的基频不存在压缩［17］。因此，粤方言和英语在韵律形式上的差异可能会对粤方言区英语学习者焦点重音的习得造成一定影响。已有考察粤方言区英语学习者重音习得的研究多集中在产出，感知研究相对欠缺。产出研究发现粤方言区英语学习者词重音的产出较英语本族语者相比，具有音高更高、时长更短、音强更低等特点［18］，句重音的产出具有调型使用单一［2］、重读音节与非重读音节时长差异不明显［12］等特点。

已有考察粤方言区英语学习者焦点重音习得的研究关注的是焦点重音实现的声学表现，因而更注重声学分析。而焦点重音实现的音高模式及知觉表现却少有研究涉及。本研究以自主音段节律理论为理论依据，通过行为产出与感知实验，考察粤方言区英语学习者焦点重音产出的音高模式与感知特点。

2. 产出实验

产出包括两个实验：实验 1“看图说话”和实验 2“看文本朗读”，两者的区别在于产出过程中是否明确告诉被试句中的重读词。“看图说话”考察的是学习者在口语表达过程中是否具有重音意识，即是否会重读句子的焦点，因此该环节并未明确告知被试句中哪个词需要重读。“看文本朗读”，朗读文本上有明确的重音标记，考察的是学习者在具有重音意识的情况下，会采用哪种重读模式实现句中的焦点重音。

2.1 方法

2.1.1 被试

40 位粤方言区的英语学习者参加了此次实验，粤方言是他们的第一语言。他们都是广州高校的在校大学生，包括大一、大二英语专业的大学生和通过大学英语六级的非英语专业的大学生。所有被试均是右利手，没有听说读写障碍。实验结束后获得一定报酬。

2.1.2 实验 1：看图说话

采用两台电脑分别向被试和实验者呈现幻灯片，幻灯片上呈现若干幅图片，被试幻灯片上的图片整齐有序地摆放，如图 1 所示，上下图片为一组，共 6 组，图 1 中的数字表示组别顺序，从左上至右下分别是第 1 组至第 6 组。实验者幻灯片上的图片与被试幻灯片上的图片一样，但摆放却是杂乱无章的，如图 2 所示。

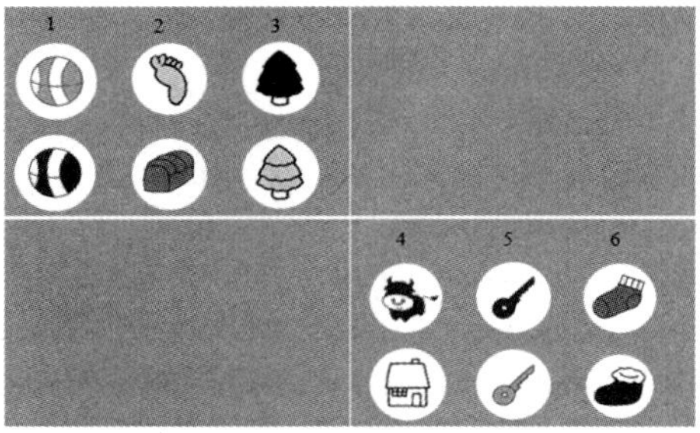

图 1 被试幻灯片上的图片示例

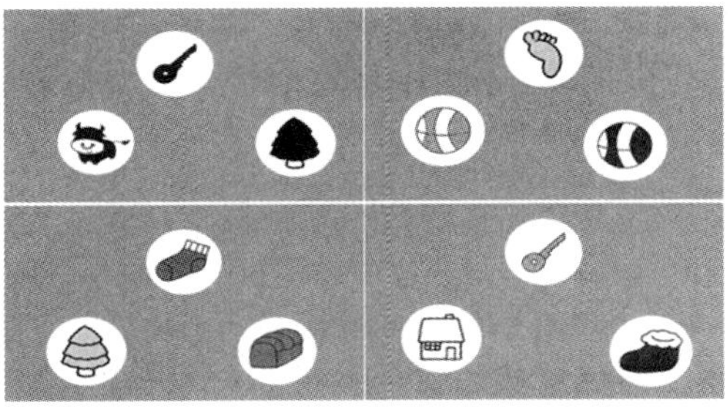

图 2 主试幻灯片上的图片示例

实验要求被试根据幻灯片上图片呈现的相对位置，用规定的负载句形式“Could you put the 颜色词 1 + 名词 1 over the 颜色词 2 + 名词 2?”向主试描述每组图片的颜色和形状，并指导实验员将实验者幻灯片上的图片摆放至被试电脑屏幕上幻灯片显示的两幅图片的相对位置。

被试幻灯片上图片的摆放包含三种情况：第一，上下图片形状相同、颜色不同；第二，上下图片颜色相同、形状不同；第三，上下图片颜色、形状各不相同。根据本文的研究目的，第一种语境下被试产出的句子是本实验考察的目标句，其余是填充句。以图 1 为例，被试一共产出 6 个句子，其中 3 个是目标句，分别是：

（1）Could you put the green ball over the brown ball? 对应第 1 组图片；

（2）Could you put the black tree over the pink tree? 对应第 2 组图片；

（3）Could you put the brown key over the green key? 对应第 5 组图片。

从目标句的形式来看，颜色词是目标句的对比焦点所在，其中第二个颜色词承担全句的核心重音，也是产出实验 1 考察的目标词。

图片所对应的英语单词提前发放给被试以让被试熟悉。每位被试需完成 20 张幻灯片的描述任务，一共产出 104 个句子，其中目标句和填充句各 52 句。该环节一共采集到 4160 个句子，其中目标句2080句（52个目标句 × 40位被试 = 2080）。实验大致持续35分钟。

2.1.3 实验2：看文本朗读

文本包含30个句子，均选自实验1“看图说话”环节中的104个实验句，其中10句选自52个目标句，20句选自52个填充句。句中的重读词汇用大写和加粗的方式加以突显，如：

“Could you put the green ball over the BROWN ball ?”

句中的对比焦点BROWN为句重音。

被试在完成“看图说话”任务后再进行“看文本朗读”实验。该环节一共采集到1200个句子，其中目标句400句（10个目标句 × 40位被试 = 400）。实验大致持续10分钟。

2.1.4 语音标注与处理

采用Praat软件对采集到的目标句进行标注，标注内容包括音段、句重音位置、音高重音类型以及边界调等。标注工作由三位标注人分别独立完成，之后三位标注人对不一致的数据进行讨论并确定最终标注结果。韵律标注采用ToBI标注体系，ToBI标注的理论基础是Pierrehumbert提出的AM理论［9］。

根据标注结果提取句中每个单词浊音段的基频（每个浊音段11个点）和时长。采用z-score方法对所有提取到的原始基频值进行归一化处理，以消除个人音域差异，转换公式为：

$$z = (x - M) / SD \qquad (1)$$

z表示归一后的基频值，x表示原始基频值，M和SD分别表示每位被试的基频均值和标准差。

2.1.5 录音

产出实验在安静的录音室完成。使用Thinkpad电脑和Lexicon外置声卡，录音采用中国社会科学院熊子瑜编写的“xPerception”（“看图说话”实验）和“xRecorder”（“看文本朗读”实验）软件。采样率22050Hz，量化精度16 bit，单声道，所有录音保存为“.wav”格式，方便后续分析。

2.2 结果

2.2.1 实验1：看图说话

本文主要关注目标词的重读模式，但是在标注过程中我们发现被试采用了两种边界调来实现疑问语气：升调边界调和降调边界调，为了避免边界调的音高表现影响目标词重读模式的分析，我们依据边界调类型和目标词的音高重音类型对目标句进行了分类处理。

首先，按照边界调的标注结果将2080个目标句分成两类：采用升调表示疑问语气的句子（边界调的标注结果为L-H%和H-H%）和采用降调表示疑问语气的句子（边界调的标注结果为H-L%和L-L%）。经统计，共有1070个句子实现为升调疑问句，占比51.4%，1010个句子实现为降调疑问句，占比48.6%。

其次，按照目标词实现的音高重音类型，对第一步分出的两类句子进行再次分类，分类结果见表1。

表1 看图说话实验中目标词实现的音高重音类型及占比（个数和百分比）

音高重音	升调疑问句	降调疑问句
H*	241（22.5%）	896（88.7%）
L+H*	3（0.3%）	114（11.3%）
L*+H	12（1.1%）	0
L*	814（76%）	0
总计	1070（100%）	1010（100%）

表1结果显示，如果学习者采用升调边界调（边界调标注结果是L-H%和H-H%）实现疑问语气，目标词实现的音高重音类型包括H*、L+H*、L*+H和L*四类，其中，L+H*和L*+H的使用比例非常小，目标词实现的音高重音类型主要是L*，其次是H*，句子的基频曲线如图2（a－b）所示。如果学习者采用降调边界调（边界调标注结果是H-L%和L-L%）结尾，目标词实现的音高重音类型主要是H*，其次是L+H*，句子的基频曲线如图3（a－b）所示。图2、图3的纵坐标表示

归一后的基频值（z-score 值），下文同（图 4 和图 5），矩形框所示的位置是目标词在句中所处的位置。图 2 至图 5 中每个单词的纵坐标值分别是同类句子里相同位置上所有单词基频归一后的平均值。从左至右每个单词分别表示：

“Could | you | put | the | 颜色词 1 | 名词 | over | the | 颜色词 2 | 名词?”

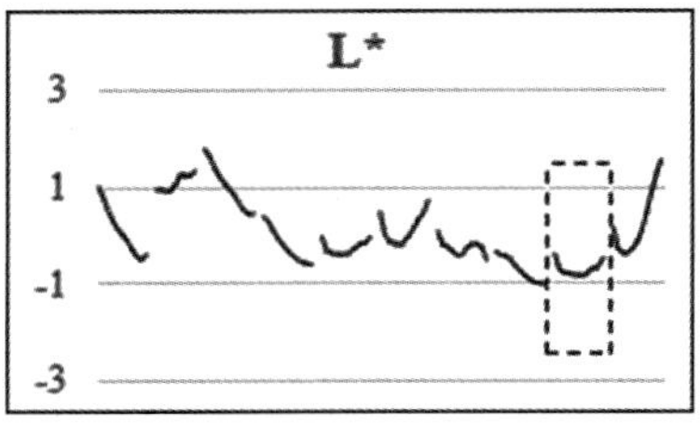

图 2a　目标词音高重音实现为 L* 和边界调为升调

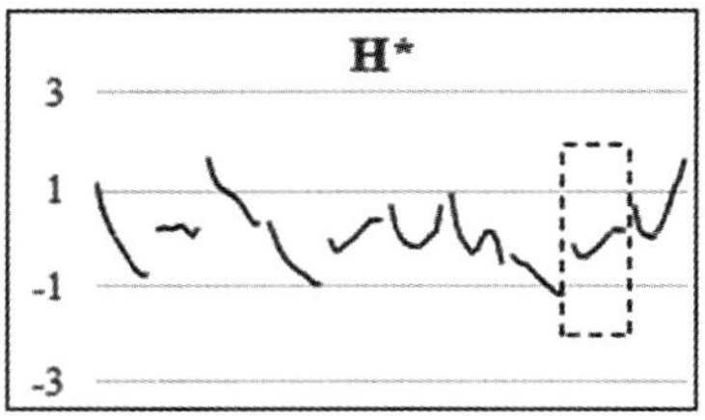

图 2b　目标词音高重音实现为 H* 和边界调为升调

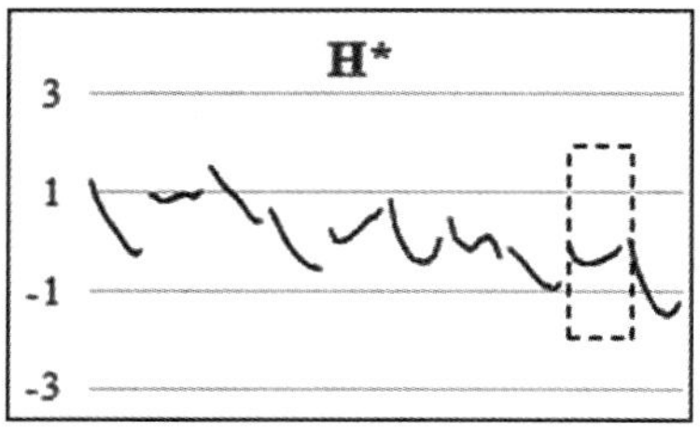

图 3a　目标词音高重音实现为 H* 和边界调为降调

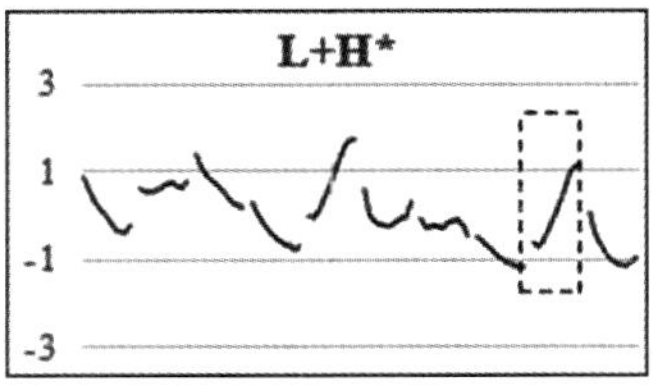

图 3b　目标词音高重音实现为 L+H* 和边界调为降调

学习者在“看图说话”环节一共采用了六种重读模式来产出是非问句中的焦点重音，在升调边界调句子中，学习者采用了 H*、L+H*、L*+H 和 L* 实现目标词重读，以 L* 音高重音为主。在降调边界调句子中，学习者采用了 H* 和 L+H* 实现目标词重读，其中以 H* 音高重音为主。

2.2.2　实验 2：看文本朗读

数据分析方式与实验 1 一致。

首先，根据边界调的标注结果将 400 个句子分成两类：采用升调表示疑问语气的句子和采用降调表示疑问语气的句子。经统计，共有 197 个句子实现为升调疑问句，占比 49.25%，203 个句子实现为降调疑问句，占比 50.75%。

其次，按照目标词所实现的音高重音类型对这两类句子进行进一步的分类，分类结果如表 2 所示。

表 2　看文本朗读实验中目标词实现的音高重音类型及占比（个数和百分比）

音高重音	升调疑问句	降调疑问句
H*	17（8.8%）	129（63.55%）
L+H*	19（9.8%）	58（28.57%）
L* +H	20（10.4%）	7（3.45%）
L*	141（73%）	9（4.43%）
总计	197（100%）	203（100%）

表 2 结果显示，无论被试采用何种边界调实现疑问语气，目标词实现的音高重音类型都包括 H*、L+H*、L*+H 和 L* 四类。如果被试采用升调边界调结尾，目标

词最常实现的音高重音类型是 L^*，其次是 L^*+H，句子基频曲线如图4（a－b）所示。如果被试采用降调边界调结尾，目标词最常实现的音高重音类型是 H^*，其次是 L+H^*，句子基频曲线如图5（a－b）所示。

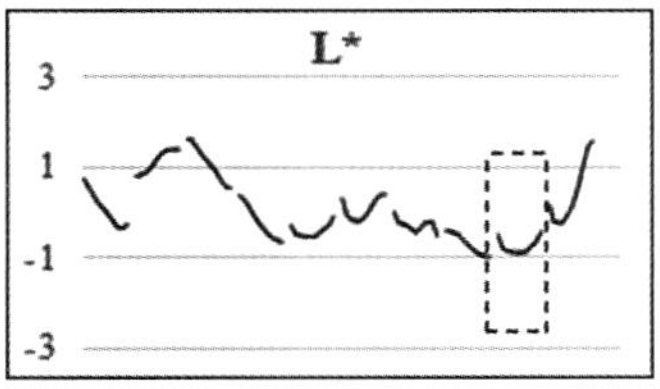

图4a 目标词音高重音实现为 L^* 和边界调为升调

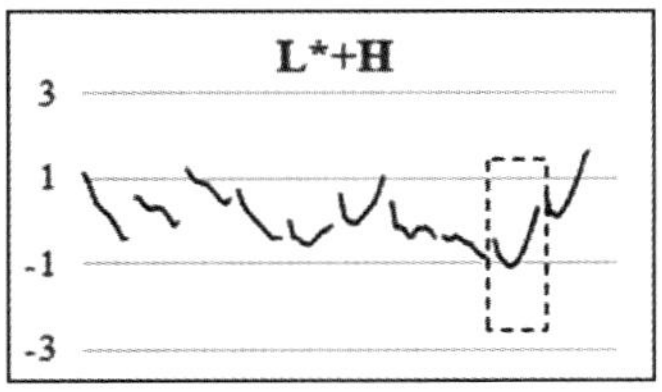

图4b 目标词音高重音实现为 L^*+H 和边界调为升调

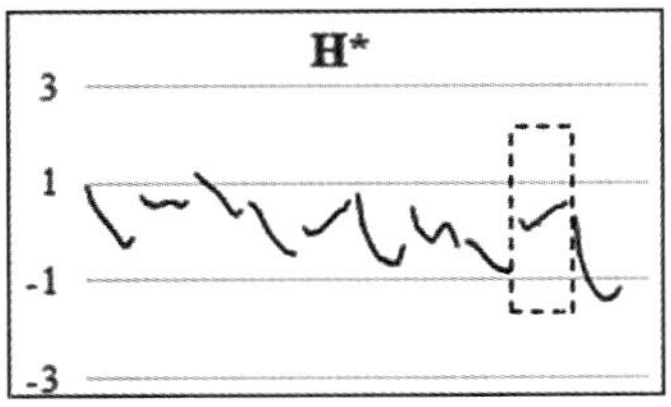

图5a 目标词音高重音实现为 H^* 和边界调为降调

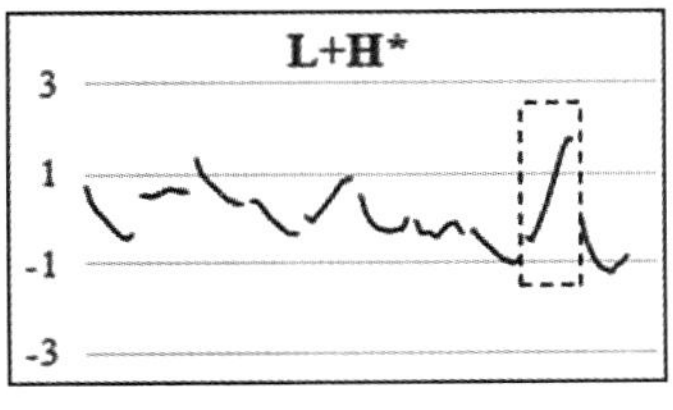

图5b 目标词音高重音实现为 L+H^* 和边界调为降调

学习者在“看文本朗读”环节一共采用了八种语调模式来产出是非问句中的焦点重音，升调边界调句子中目标词重读的音高重音类型与“看图说话”环节基本一致，包括 H^*、L+H^*、L^*+H 和 L^* 四类，其中以 L^* 为主。降调边界调句子中目标词重读的音高重音类型除了 H^* 和 L+H^* 外，还包括 L^*+H 和 L^*，其中仍以 H^* 为主。

3. 感知实验

3.1 方法

3.1.1 被试

与实验1被试一致。

3.1.2 声学刺激

言语声学刺激包括30个一般疑问句，句中的核心重音由窄焦点承担。窄焦点由两类音高重音实现，分别是 L^*+H 和 H^*。为了避免实验的单调性，实验还设置了宽焦句。L^*+H、H^* 类音高重音句子及宽焦句各10句。

本实验目标句由一名英语本族语者录制完成，要求发音人在朗读一个引导句后，以自然的方式说出目标句，例如：

窄焦点实现的音高重音类型为 L^*+H：

引导句：What did Tina play in a class at school?

目标句：Did Tina play the DRUM in a class at school?

图6为所示目标句的基频曲线。

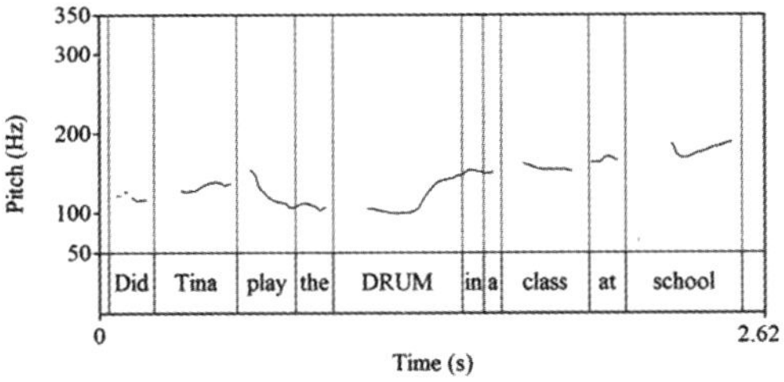

图6 焦点重音实现为 L^*+H 的基频曲线示例

H^* 是中国英语学习者常出现的偏误重读模式，为了让录音人说出此类句子，录制过程中不仅向录音人播放中国英语学习者产出的偏误语音，同时向录音人展示句子的基频曲线。

窄焦点实现的音高重音类型是 H*：

引导句：What does Susan teach in the university?

目标句：Does Susan teach PHYSICS in the university?

图7为所示目标句的基频曲线。

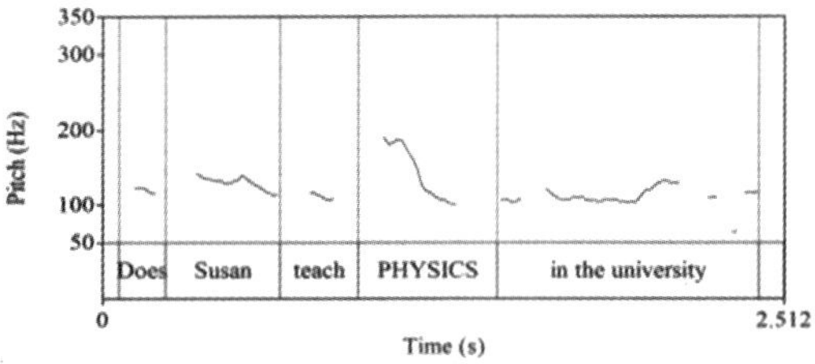

图7 焦点重音实现为 H* 的基频曲线示例

3.1.3 流程

感知实验在一间安静的实验室进行。提前录制的句子通过耳机播放给被试，同时句子文本呈现在电脑屏幕上，如图8所示。听辨过程中被试可以单选也可以多选，如果被试认为听到的句子中只有一个重读单词，则单选；如果被试认为句子中有多个重读单词，则多选；如果被试认为听到的句子中没有重读的单词，则选择句末的标点符号，这样设计的目的是避免句子在未完全播放完毕的情况下被试已经快速地做出选择。当被试确定自己的选择后，点击界面中的“确定”按钮即播放下一个句子。30个句子随机播放。整个过程大概持续10分钟。

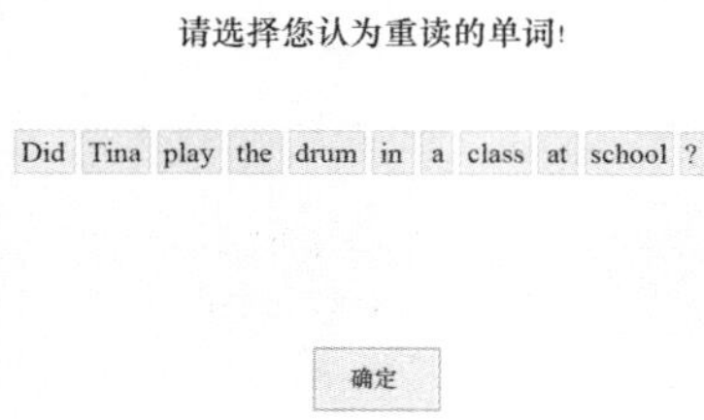

图8 感知实验程序界面

3.2 结果

由于我们关注的只是英语学习者对听辨句子中预设的焦点重音（核心重音）的感知情况，因此，无论被试的感知结果是单选还是多选，只要被试在听辨过程中选择了句子中的窄焦点词为句中的重读词，就计1分，相反则计0分。每个被试同类句子最高得分10分，最后对所有被试同类句子的分数进行累积，所有被试同类句子最高得分400分。最后结果如图9所示。

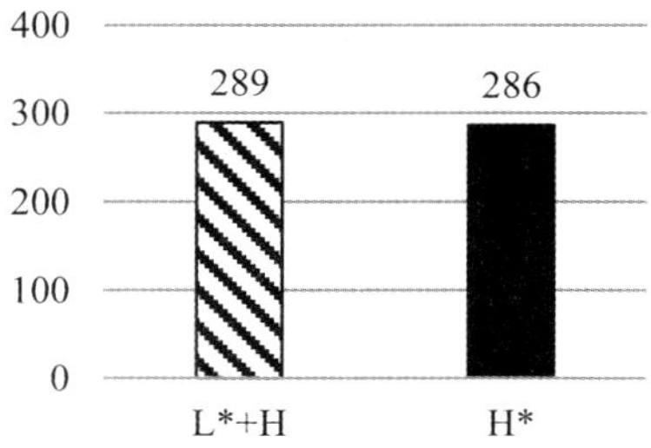

图9 L*+H 和 H* 类音高重音感知得分

从图9可以看出，学习者对 L*+H 和 H* 音高重音的感知得分非常接近，L*+H 音高重音的感知得分是289分，感知正确率是72.2%，H* 音高重音的感知得分是286分，感知正确率是71.5%。配对样本 t 检验结果显示被试对两类音高重音的感知结果没有显著差异（$t=0.147$，$df=39$，$p=0.884$）。

4. 讨论与结论

（1）本文通过行为产出和感知实验考察了粤方言区英语学习者一般疑问句焦点重音的习得表现。产出结果显示，英语学习者一般疑问句焦点重音的语调产出模式与英语本族语者存在两点不同。首先，英语本族语者往往使用升调边界调实现疑问语气[1]，而英语学习者同时使用升调边界调和降调边界调，且两类边界调使用的频次非常接近。“看图说话”实验升调边界调句子占目标句总数的51.4%，降调边界调句子占目标句总数的48.6%。“看文本朗读”实验升调边界调句子占目标句总数的49.25%，降调边界调句子占目标句总数的50.75%。其次，英语本族语者往往使用低平调（L^*）或者低升调（L^*+H）实现一般疑问句中的焦点重音［6］，而英语学习者焦点重音实现的音高方式与边界调有关。当边界调实现为降调时，无论是“看图说话”还是“看文本朗读”，焦点最常实现的音高重音类型是H^*，其次是$L+H^*$；当边界调实现为升调时，“看图说话”环节，焦点实现的音高重音类型主要是L^*，其次是H^*；“看文本朗读”环节，焦点实现的音高重音类型主要是L^*，其次是L^*+H。总体来看，英语学习者一般疑问句焦点重音的产出主要表现为两类优势语调，分别是“焦点重音实现为低平调L^*，边界调实现为升调边界调”（$L^*+L-H\%$）和“焦点重音实现为高平调H^*，边界调实现为降调边界调”（$H^*+H-L\%$）。

（2）本文的产出研究结果与以往以普通话或其他方言为母语背景的英语学习者为研究对象的研究有相似也有不同。相似的是实验结果都显示中国英语学习者习惯采用H^*音高重音实现不同句型的音高重音，不同的是，以往的研究仅发现学习者在产出L^*音高重音时存在困难，本文在此基础上进一步发现学习者在产出是非问句中的焦点重音时，目标词实现的音高重音类型与边界调实现的类型有关。当是非问句实现为下降的边界调时，目标词的重读模式以H^*音高重音为主，但当是非问句实现为上升的边界调时，目标词的重读模式以L^*音高重音为主，不存在产出困难。需要注意的是，本文设定的目标词在句中所处的位置接近句末，不排除L^*音高重音的实现与句末实现的上升边界调（$L-H\%$）有关。

（3）当学习者使用升调边界调实现句子的疑问语气时，不论是“看图说话”环节还是“看文本朗读”环节，学习者都主要采取L^*音高重音实现目标词的重读。当学习者采用降调边界调形式产出是非问句时，无论学习者是否明确句中的重读信息，学习者主要采用H^*音高重音。两种产出语境下焦点重音实现的语音突显程度有所差异，“看文本朗读”语境下（被试具有明确的重音意识），重读的语音突显程度明显强于“看图说话”，体现在H^*类音高重音的基频均值更高、音高重置幅度以及升降幅度更大，L^*音高重音的基频均值更低、基频最低点更低。“看图说话”环节中音高重音的基频表现或许与粤方言实现焦点重音的语音手段有关。粤方言主要依靠时长，重读对音高的影响不大，所以“看图说话”环节音高重音在基频上的表现并不突显。

（4）结合英语学习者焦点重音的感知表现来看，尽管学习者对低升调L^*+H和高调H^*音高重音的感知没有显著差异，但这两类音高重音在产出中出现的语境截然不同。高调H^*主要使用在边界调类型实现为$H-L\%$和$L-L\%$的一般疑问句中，低升调L^*+H主要使用在边界调类型实现为$H-H\%$和$L-H\%$的一般疑问句中。并且当学习者具有明确的重音意识时（看文本朗读语境），焦点重音的语音实现程度也更强（如基频均值更高、升降幅度更大），重读模式的韵律实现也越靠近英语本族语者。

（5）已有研究表明话语中的焦点重音具有层级性，核心重音是必需的，不可或缺的，但是一个句子除了核心重音之外，还可以包含核心前重音或核心后重音［20］。从本研究设计的目标句来看，颜色词承担句子中的对比焦点所在，其中第二个颜色词（目标词）承担全句的核心重音。本研究的英语学习者在产出目标句时往往将一个句子实现为2—3个韵律短语，以“Could you put the green ball over the brown ball?”目标句为例，学习者在“over the”前往往有一个较大的停顿，整句实现为“could you put the green ball”和“over the brown ball”2个韵律短语，但是有的学习者也会在单词“you”后有一个停顿，整句实现为“Could you / put the green ball / over the brown ball?”3个韵律短语。由于我们主要关注目标词在音高维度上的韵律实现，因而只分析了目标词所在的韵律短语，在该短语内目标词往往承担了短语内的重音，而其他韵律短语内重音的实现方式并未深入分析。另外，文中对目标词语音实现程度的论述只是基于定性的描写分析，缺少具体的定量的语音声学参数（基频均值、最大值、最小值、升降幅度，时长，能量等）的支持，这些留待今后做更加深入细致的研究。

5. 致谢

本研究得到国家社科基金重大课题“中国方言区英语学习者语音习得机制的跨学科研究”（15ZDB103）、中国社会科学院博士后创新项目“中国学习者的英语节奏学习和加工”(ZBH20191006）和“中国博士后科学基金会第13批特别资助”（2020T130718）的经费支持。

参考文献

[1] Bolinger, D. 1978. *Intonation Across Languages*. Stanford: Stanford University Press.

[2] Chu, S. 2002. The prosodic transcription of a corpus of Hong Kong English: collection criteria, transcription system and preliminary findings. *Proceedings of the Third Sigdial Workshop on Discourse and Dialogue* 2: 11 – 14.

[3] Cutler, A. 1976. Phoneme-monitoring reaction time as a function of preceding intonation contour. *Perception & Psychophysics* 20(1): 55 – 60.

[4] Gussenhoven, C. 1983. Focus, mode and the nucleus. *Journal of Linguistics* 19: 377 – 417.

[5] Halliday, M. A. K. 2004. *An Introduction to Functional Grammar*. Edward Arnold Press.

[6] Ji, X., Wang, X., Li, A. 2009. Intonation patterns of yes-no questions for Chinese EFL learners. *Proceedings of International Symposium on Chinese Spoken Language Processing*, 88 – 93.

[7] Jia, Y., Li, A. 2013. Phonetic realization of accent from Chinese English learners in various dialectal regions. *Proceedings of International Symposium on Chinese Spoken Language Processing*, 296 – 300.

[8] Ladd, D. R. 1978. Stylized intonation. *Language* 54(3): 517 – 540.

[9] Lian, X. R., Duan, W. J., Jia, Y., Anne, R. 2013. Phonetic realization of narrow focus by Beijing EFL learners in English yes-no sentences. *Proceedings of O – COCOSDA*, 1 – 5.

[10] Pierrehumbert, J. B. 1980. *The Phonology and Phonetics of English Intonation*. MA: MIT.

[11] Qian, D., Jia, Y., Li, A., Xu, L. 2014. An experimental comparative study on prosodic features between Ningbo EFL learners and American Native speakers-in the case of production of yes-no questions. *Proceedings of International Symposium on Chinese Spoken Language Processing*, 236 – 240.

[12] Setter, M. 2003. A comparison of speech rhythm in British and Hong Kong English. *Proceedings of the 15th International Congress of Phonetic Sciences*, 467 – 470.

[13] Wang, H. Y., Jia, Y., Li, A., Tang, Y. 2014. Intonation patterns of yes-no questions with narrow focusing of Chinese northern EFL learners. *Proceedings of International Symposium on Chinese Spoken Language Processing*, 212 – 217.

[14] Watson, D. G, Tanenhaus, M. K., Gunlogson, C. A. 2008. Interpreting pitch accents in online comprehension: H* vs. L + H*. *Cognitive Science* 32(7): 1232 – 1244.

[15] Xu, Y., Xu, C. 2005. Phonetic realization of focus in English declarative intonation. *Journal of Phonetics* 33(2): 159 – 197.

[16] 段文君、贾媛、冉启斌：《山东方言焦点语音实现的共性和差异性特征—以济南、聊城、淄博方言为例》，《清华大学学报（自然科学版）》2013年第8期，第835—838页。

[17] 葛淳宇：《汉语语调的跨方言研究》，博士学位论文，中国社会科学院大学，2020年。

[18] 郭兴荣、陈晓湘：《北京话和粤语背景学习者英语词重音产出研究》，《外语教学与研究》2017年第2期，第188—201页。

[19] 纪晓丽、张辉、李爱军、龚箭：《不同水平学习者对英语语调感知的实证研究》，《外语教学与研究》2018年第3期，第393—406页。

[20] 李爱军、袁一：《普通话多焦点的语音实现》，《中国语音学报》2019年第11辑，第1—26页。

[21] 李晓庆、杨玉芳：《不一致性重读对口语语篇加工中信息激活水平的影响》，《心理学报》2005年第3期，第285—290页。

[22] 刘丹青、徐烈炯：《焦点与背景、话题及汉语“连”字句》，《中国语文》1998年第4期，第243—252页。

[23] 王丹、杨玉芳：《论元结构的焦点和重音关

系对话语理解的影响》，《心理科学》2010年第3期，第526—529页。
[24] 徐烈炯、潘海华：《焦点结构和意义的研究》，外语教学与研究出版社2005年版。
[25] 许希明、沈家煊：《英汉语重音的音系差异》，《外语教学与研究》2016年第5期，第643—656页。

曹　冲　中国社会科学院语言研究所，博士后。主要研究领域为言语韵律、语音习得。
Email：caochong2013@126.com

李爱军　中国社会科学院语言研究所，语料库暨计算语言学研究中心，博士，研究员。主要研究领域为言语韵律、L1 & L2 语音习得、情感语音。
Email：liaj@cass.org.cn

普通话无标［ma］字句韵律研究

王炤宇　曹梦雪

摘　要　“吗”是普通话中常见的疑问语气词，在言语活动中有时会与另外一个非疑问语气词“嘛”产生混淆。通过对已有研究进行梳理可以发现，“吗”“嘛”混淆反映了语气信息的不确定。语音形式、语言使用都会影响语气信息的表达和理解，但具体的影响的方式尚不明晰。因此，本研究首先通过产出实验考察了无标陈述句、无标疑问句、“吗”字句和“嘛”字句的声学表现。结果表明：（1）“吗”字句和“嘛”字句都更接近疑问语调；（2）句调中语气词的目标音高是［ma］字句最主要的语气声学相关量；（3）语气词“吗”倾向于实现较高的目标音高，“嘛”倾向于实现较低的目标音高。进一步，通过听感实验考察了［ma］的目标音高对［ma］字句语气信息理解的作用。结果表明：（1）句调中语气词的目标音高也是［ma］字句的语气听感线索；（2）“吗”和“嘛”的目标音高听感空间存在交叉；（3）“吗”的目标音高听感空间范围大于“嘛”。综合两个实验可以发现：（1）发音人可以在［ma］字句中通过调整语气词的目标音高传递不同语气；（2）听音人也可以根据语气词的目标音高理解语气信息，但在目标音高“不够低”的情况下，听音人会倾向于将句子理解为疑问句。
关键词　［ma］字句，句末语气词，韵律

Prosody of Unmarked [ma] Sentences in Mandarin Chinese

WANG Zhaoyu　CAO Mengxue

Abstract “吗” [ma] is a common interrogative modal particle in Mandarin Chinese, but it is sometimes confused with the non-interrogative “嘛” [ma] in our speech. Previous research attributed the confusion to the vagueness of the moods. Our study first investigated acoustic characteristics of the unmarked readings of declarative sentences and interrogative sentences with “吗” and “嘛” endings respectively. The results showed: (1) Both “吗” sentences and “嘛” sentences are closer to interrogative intonation; (2) The acoustic correlates of the mood information in [ma] sentences is the target pitch of [ma]; (3) “吗” tends to achieve a higher target pitch, while “嘛” a lower target pitch. Further, in the identification and discrimination experiments we investigated the effect of the target pitch of [ma] on sentence mood information understanding. The results showed: (1) The auditory clue in the [ma] sentences is also the target pitch of [ma]; (2) There exists overlap between the auditory space of “吗” and “嘛”; (3) The auditory space of “吗” is larger than “嘛”. Combining these results, we find that: (1) Speakers can convey different mood information by adjusting the target pitches of the modal particles; (2) Listener can also understand the mood information according to the target pitches of the modal particles, but when the target pitch is “not low enough”, listeners tend to interpret the sentence as interrogative.
Keywords [ma] Sentences, Modal particles, Prosody

1. 引言

现代汉语普通话拥有丰富的语气词，语气词在句子里的语气作用和语音表现也是学界关注的话题之一。“语气”是一个很大的范畴，包括陈述、疑问、祈使、感叹这四种狭义的“语气”［14］。“吗”是普通话中常见的疑问语气词，在言语活动中有时会与另外一个非疑问语气词“嘛”产生混淆［5，10，15］。这种混淆反映了语气信息表达和理解的不确定。因为语气词不能独立成句，所以研究“吗”和“嘛”需要以句子为依托。包含句末语气词“吗”或“嘛”的句子可以称为［ma］字句，按照其传递的语气分为“吗”字疑问句、

“嘛”字祈使句和“嘛”字陈述句。

语音形式会影响语气信息的表达和理解。已有研究认为，“吗”字句通过疑问语调和语气词“吗”共同传递疑问信息。具体来说，典型的“吗”字句使用疑问语调，与没有语气词、只依靠疑问语调传递疑问信息的是非问句（即“无标是非问句”）语调基本相同，只是音高范围小于语调是非问句，原因在于语气词“吗”也承担了部分疑问信息［3，17，22］。

还有学者认为，语气词“吗”可以独立传递疑问信息。“吗”字句使用陈述语调依然可以通过语气词“吗”表达疑问语气［9，13，18］，不论前一音节调形如何，“吗”音节末尾音高都倾向于达到同一水平［7，21］。

也有学者不认为语气词“吗”可以独立表达疑问信息，指出“吗”音高表现包含高平、速升、缓降等特点，这些都是疑问语调作用的结果，不是语气词自身的音高特征［20］。

已有研究对“嘛”字句的语音表现讨论较少。在祈使句研究方面，有学者提出祈使句通常使用降调［8］，一般的祈使句和陈述句的语调特征一致［6］。“嘛”字祈使句句调是否也具有上述特点，还需要进一步考察。

在“嘛”字陈述句研究方面，熊子瑜、林茂灿［20］通过实验发现，“嘛”字句末尾音高表现包括低平、缓升、速降等特点，并认为这些特点是陈述语调作用的结果，不是语气词自身的属性。

已有研究通过对［ma］字句的语音表现进行声学分析，对语气词的语气功能产生了不同的认识。因此本研究将从“吗”“嘛”混淆现象入手，综合采用声学分析和听感实验，明确语气词的韵律特征和语气作用，深入了解“吗”“嘛”因语音形式引起的语气功能混淆。

2.［ma］字句的语气声学相关量

2.1 实验方案

2.1.1 语料和发音人

实验句需要排除语气副词、否定副词等干扰因素，在自然焦点无标陈述句的基础上添加语气词［ma］。因为语气词没有固定的调形，很容易受到前一音节的顺同化作用影响，所以实验设计了四个不同声调的变量来控制前一音节声调对语气词的影响。由于“嘛”字陈述句和“嘛”字祈使句典型的句法表现存在很大差异，所以我们通过两组实验句，分别比较“嘛”字祈使句与“吗”字疑问句（表1）、“嘛”字陈述句与“吗”字疑问句（表2）。其中无标陈述句、无标疑问句每句均由两个韵律词构成，“你吃”组包括目标韵律词1“你吃”和目标韵律词2“山X”，“他是”组包括目标韵律词1“他是”和目标韵律词2“朱X”；“吗”字句和“嘛”字句除了目标韵律词1、目标韵律词2，还包含语气词“吗”或“嘛”。［ma］前一音节均没有鼻音韵尾，以便较为清晰地切分出语气词［20］。

发音人为六名北京师范大学文学院汉语言文字学专业的研究生，其中男女各三人，平均年龄为22.67±1.21岁，均来自官话区，普通话水平较高，可以准确理解并产出无标陈述句、无标疑问句和不同语气［ma］字句。

录音在语音实验室完成，使用praat［2］软件，采用单声道录制，采样率为44100Hz。录音时，首先请一位发音人进入实验室，用纸质材料把需要录制的实验句呈现给该发音人，请他用3到5分钟，在实验负责人的协助下，通过练习朗读熟悉实验材料，以确保正式实验中语气的准确性。随后进入试录环节，请发音人自然朗读无标陈述句，熟悉录音环境，掌握录音流程。在适应录音环节之后，开始正式录制，请发音人自然朗读全部实验句，一遍结束之后，稍事休息，开始第二遍录制。六位发音人两遍产出实验句共计384句。

本研究在正式实验之前进行了预实验，目的在于评估发音人表达情感的能力和准确性。在预实验阶段，由主试和另一位现代汉语方向的硕士研究生一起对产出结果进行了语气听辨，确定与预设一致，所有发音人均满足情感录音的需求。

表 1 “你吃”组祈使—疑问实验句

	无标陈述句	无标疑问句	“吗”字疑问句	“嘛”字祈使句
阴平句	你吃山楂。	你吃山楂?	你吃山楂吗?	你吃山楂嘛。
阳平句	你吃山竹。	你吃山竹?	你吃山竹吗?	你吃山竹嘛。
上声句	你吃山枣。	你吃山枣?	你吃山枣吗?	你吃山枣嘛。
去声句	你吃山菜。	你吃山菜?	你吃山菜吗?	你吃山菜嘛。

表 2 “他是”组陈述—疑问实验句

	无标陈述句	无标疑问句	“吗”字疑问句	“嘛”字祈使句
阴平句	他是朱基。	他是朱基?	他是朱基吗?	他是朱基嘛。
阳平句	他是朱迪。	他是朱迪?	他是朱迪吗?	他是朱迪嘛。
上声句	他是朱喜。	他是朱喜?	他是朱喜吗?	他是朱喜嘛。
去声句	他是朱弟。	他是朱弟?	他是朱弟吗?	他是朱弟嘛。

2.1.2 数据测量与处理

研究通过语调格局［19］，确定词调域位置。在此基础上依据每一个音高数据点百分值描绘发音人语调格局中的音高曲线，用以直观反映［ma］字句的音高变化。

录音完成后，对所得结果进行归一化处理，过滤个人特征。词调域归一化首先以四个声调句为一组，计算出每位发音人产出的四个句子中各个词调域上线极大值和下线极小值；然后分别计算发音人各个词调域上线极大值和下线极小值的平均值，得到［ma］字句和无标句句调中各个词调域的范围。音高曲线归一化用通过语调格局计算出来的各个音节 11 个数据点的百分比绘制每位发音人的音高曲线，再将发音人的数据进行平均，得到［ma］字句和无标句句调的音高曲线。

产出结果中部分音节存在嘎裂现象。根据已有研究［23］，嘎裂作为“极低”的表现，其语调格局百分值低于 0，具体数值无法测算。本研究将出现嘎裂的数据点的数值统一记做 0.00，这部分数据对应的数据点归一后的平均值实际上要低于所得结果。

2.2 实验结果

2.2.1 陈述语调与疑问语调的比较

图 1 展示了无标陈述句和无标疑问句各个词调域在语调格局中的位置。其中每张图的柱形从左到右依次表示目标韵律词 1 和目标韵律词 2。可以发现无标疑问句目标韵律词 1、目标韵律词 2 调域都高于无标陈述句。

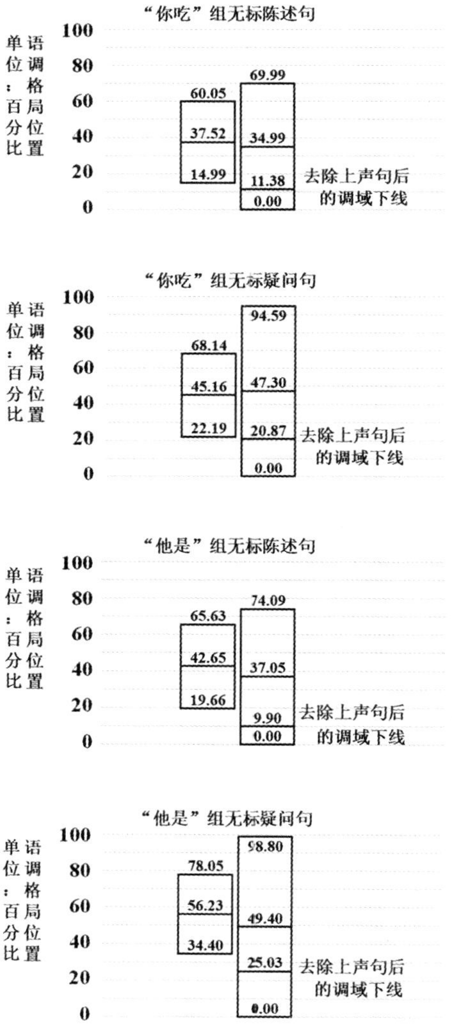

图 1 无标句词调域

图 2 是无标陈述句和无标疑问句语调格局中的音高曲线，无标疑问句音高高于无标陈述句，且目标韵律词 2 的调域差异大于目标韵律词 1 调域。

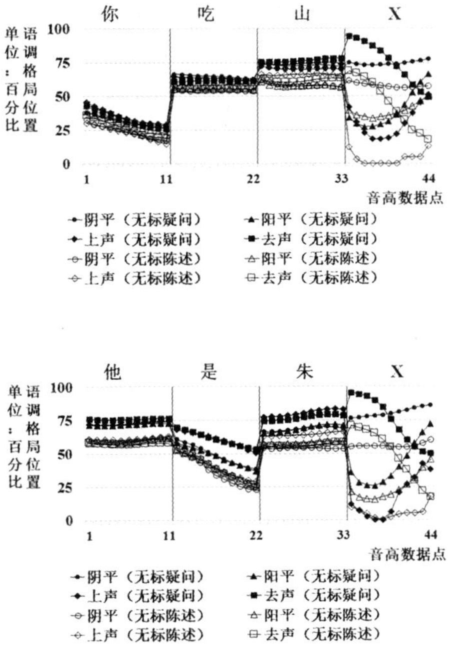

图 2　无标句音高曲线

综上所述，无标疑问句目标韵律词 1、目标韵律词 2 的调域在语调格局中的位置都高于无标陈述句，其中目标韵律词 2 的调域差异较大，与石锋［19］、Yuan［1］等学者结论一致。

2.2.2　［ma］字句句调与功能语调的比较

图 3 展示了［ma］字句语调格局中的词调域位置。其中每张图的柱形从左到右依次表示目标韵律词 1、目标韵律词 2 和语气词。对比图 3 和图 1 可看出，“吗”字句目标韵律词 1 调域上线、下线高于无标陈述句；与无标疑问句差异不大。目标韵律词 2 调域上线高于无标陈述句，略低于无标疑问句；下线高于无标陈述句，与无标疑问句差异不大。“嘛”字祈使句、陈述句目标韵律词 1 调域上下线和目标韵律词 2 调域上线也与无标疑问句差异不大，目标韵律词 2 调域下线介于无标陈述句和无标疑问句之间。

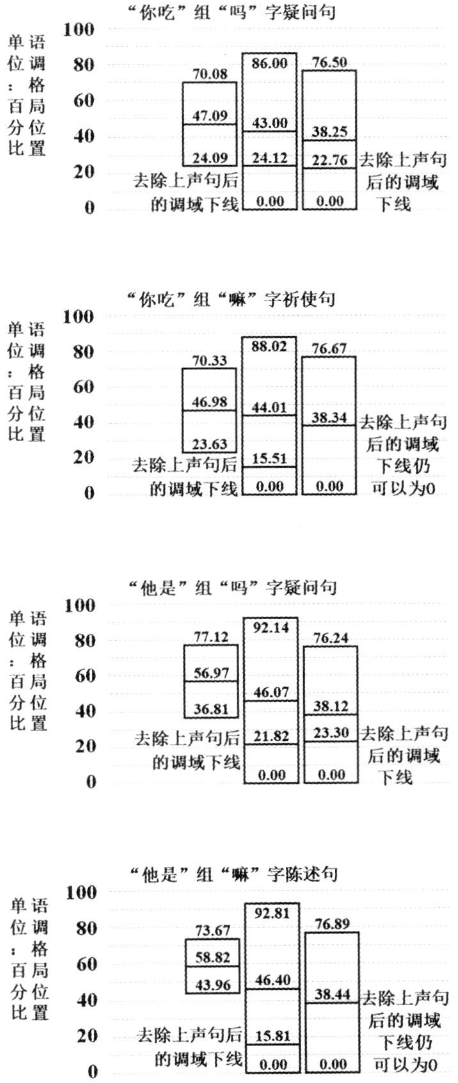

图 3　［ma］字句词调域

图 4 展示了“吗”字句语调格局中的音高曲线。可以看出在目标韵律词 1、目标韵律词 2 调域中，“吗”字句除去声句目标韵律词 2 第二音节较低外，其余均高于无标陈述句，与无标疑问句基本没有差异。

图 5 表示的是“嘛”字祈使句和“嘛”字陈述句的音高曲线。无论是祈使句还是

陈述句,“嘛”字句在目标韵律词1、目标韵律词2调域,除上声、去声句目标韵律词2第二音节较低外,其余均高于无标陈述句,与无标疑问句基本没有差异。

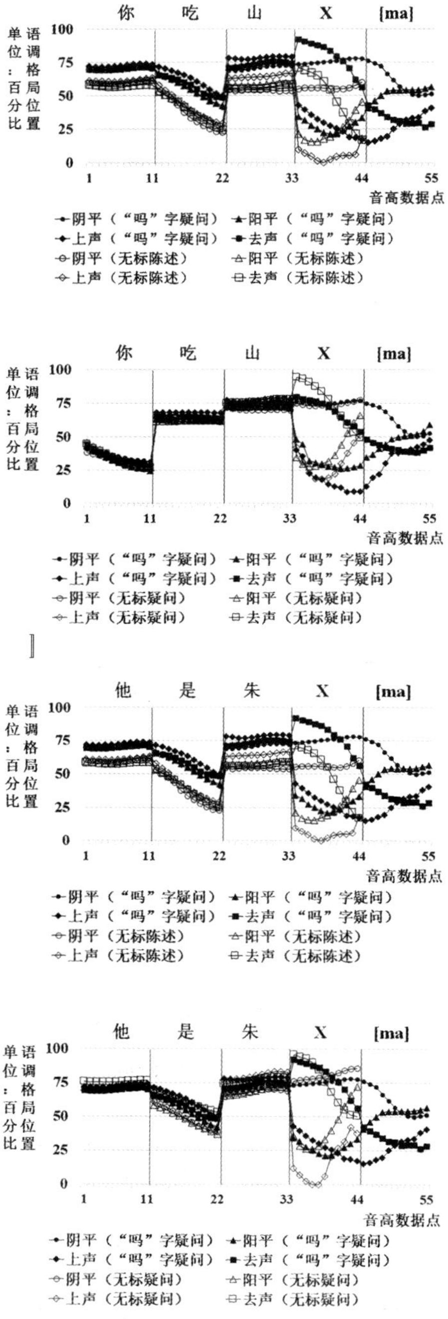

图4 “吗”字句音高曲线

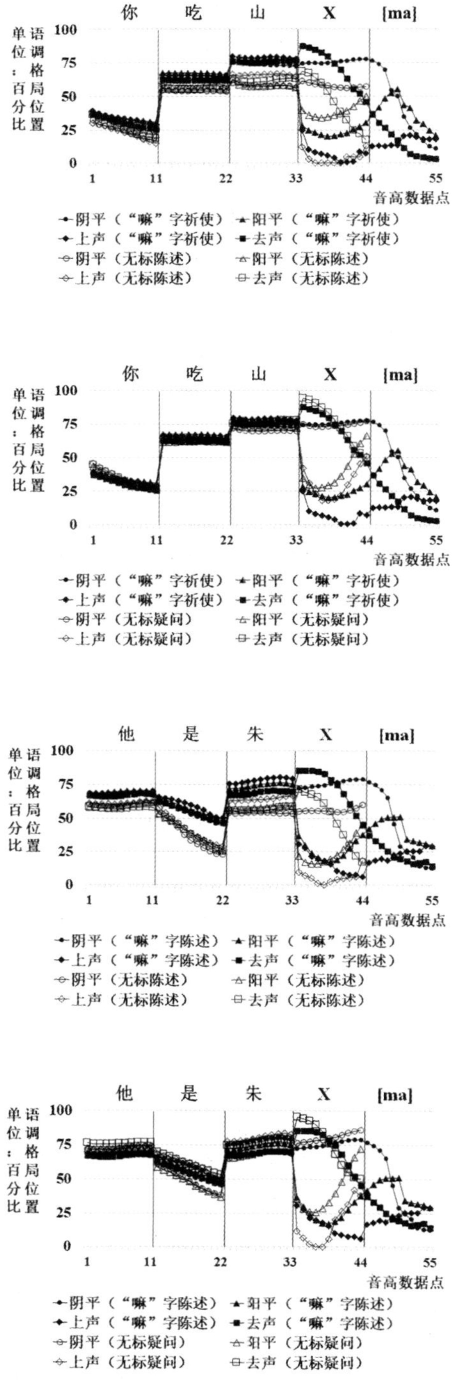

图5 “嘛”字句音高曲线

综上所述，无论是“吗”字疑问句，还是“嘛”字祈使句、“嘛”字陈述句，在目标韵律词1、目标韵律词2的音高表现都更接近疑问语调，这反映了两点问题。

第一，因为“吗”字句和“嘛”字句的音高表现都很接近疑问语调，所以二者可能很难通过目标韵律词1、目标韵律词2调域的音高表现传递语气。这个问题还需要通过2.2.3不同语气［ma］字句句调的比较，做进一步的分析。

第二，“嘛”字句的句调“接近”疑问语调，并不是因为“嘛”字句传递疑问信息，而是因为“嘛”字句句调自身的音高表现与疑问语调的表现产生重合。这一发现提醒我们进一步思考“吗”字疑问句的句调表现是否仅仅是疑问语调的结果。

2.2.3　不同语气［ma］字句句调的比较

观察图3，分别对比“吗”字疑问句与“嘛”字祈使句、“嘛”字陈述句的词调域位置，发现目标韵律词1上下线、目标韵律词2上线和语气词上线基本一致。差异主要表现在目标韵律词2和语气词下线上，“吗”字句目标韵律词2和语气词下线均高于“嘛”字句。

图6分别对比了“吗”字疑问句与“嘛”字祈使句、“嘛”字陈述句的音高曲线。可以发现“吗”字句与“嘛”字句在目标韵律词1、目标韵律词2差异不大，在语气词部分灰色表示的“嘛”字祈使句的音高曲线低于黑色表示的“吗”字疑问句。在“你吃”组中，“吗”的最后一个音高数据点（即目标音高，下称“目标音高”）高于40%，“嘛”的目标音高低于20%。在“他是”组中，“吗”“嘛”目标音高以30%为界，前者高于30%，后者低于30%。

综上所述，“吗”字句和“嘛”字句在目标韵律词1调域基本一致，在目标韵律词2、语气词调域存在一定差异。语气词“吗”倾向于实现较高的目标音高，而“嘛”则倾向于实现较低的目标音高。

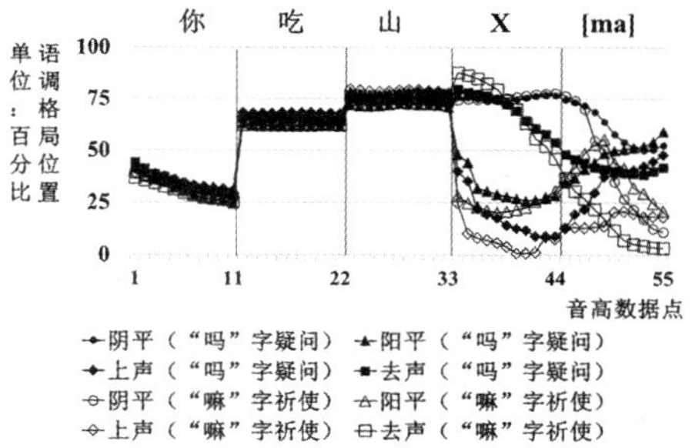

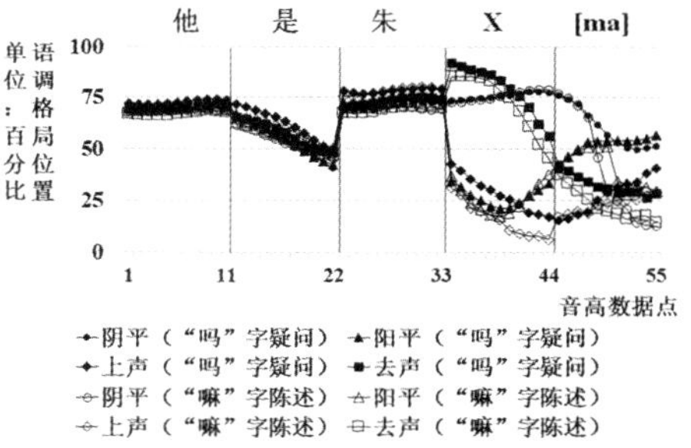

图6　［ma］字句音高曲线

2.3　结果讨论

以往研究多用调型来区别不同语气的语气词［ma］，指出“吗”多为升调，而“嘛”多为降调［7，11，21］。但是本研究赞同熊子瑜、林茂灿［20］的观点，认为调型描述的是语气词实现目标音高的音程，目标音高才是区分不同语气的根本。“吗”“嘛”的差异能否说明语气词［ma］的目标音高是［ma］字句语气表达的主要声学相关量，我们接下来将会进一步作出说明。

语气词是一个轻声音节，它的目标音高和调形在句子中都会受到前一音节声调的影响。语气词［ma］的音高曲线大多前半部分变化显著，后半部分趋于平缓。对照频谱和音高曲线（图7）可以发现，［ma］前半部分衔接前一音节，与鼻音段［m］基本对应，后半部分与元音段［a］基本对应。因此，我们称前半部分鼻音段［m］为过渡段，称后半部分元音段［a］为稳定段。前一音节的声调对语气词

［ma］在句调中的调形和目标音高都会产生影响。如图 6 所示，在不同声调的前接音节音高同化作用下，同一语气词的调形和目标音高具体数值不尽相同，但是疑问语气词“吗”的目标音高区间依然高于祈使语气词、陈述语气词“嘛”，说明语气词［ma］的调形对其语气功能实现的影响不大，［ma］字句的语气声学相关量应该是语气词的目标音高。

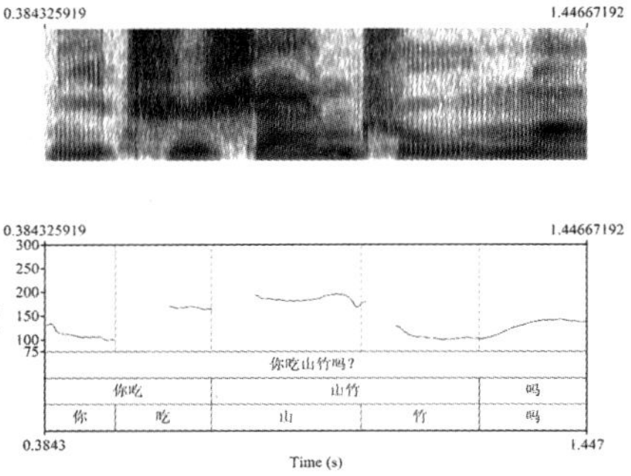

图 7　阳平“吗”字句频谱和基频曲线

目标韵律词 2 调域下线的差异是语气词音高逆同化作用的结果，不是功能语调调节的结果。图 6 中阳平组、上声组和去声组“吗”字句目标韵律词 2 第二音节音高曲线均高于“嘛”字句。如果是功能语调带来的差异，那么作为基式的阴平句也应该有相同的表现。但是如图 6 所示，在阴平组“吗”字句和“嘛”字句中，这个音节的音高曲线基本完全一致，说明这个差异是作为变式的阳平音节、上声音节和去声音节受到了语气词［ma］音高逆同化的影响，不是功能语调叠加的结果。这也说明语气词［ma］的目标音高是［ma］字句主要的声学相关量。

综上所述，可以说明句调中语气词的目标音高是［ma］字句最主要的语气声学相关量。疑问语气词“吗”可以和祈使语气词“嘛”、陈述语气词“嘛”分别构成连续统，根据目标音高差异形成各自的音高区间。

3. ［ma］字句的语气听感线索

3.1　实验方案

3.1.1　刺激音录制与合成

本实验朗读材料与产出实验相同。发音人为一名 23 岁女性研究生，来自中原官话区，普通话水平较高。录音在语音实验室完成，使用 praat［2］软件，采用单声道录制，采样率为 44100Hz。

在计算得到发音人语调格局后，与产出实验结果进行对照，确定结果符合参照依据，进一步在“你吃山 X 吗?”“他是朱 X 吗?”两组 8 句“吗”字句录音基础上，通过修改语气词［ma］的目标音高合成刺激音连续统。由产出实验结果可知，元音［a］部分较为稳定，所以把元音［a］作为听感目标对象。

根据产出实验结果可知，疑问语气词“吗”可以通过目标音高与祈使、陈述语气词“嘛”相区别，“吗”的目标音高较高，“嘛”的目标音高较低。因此，可以通过听音人对由“吗”到“嘛”的刺激音连续统语气作出的判断，找到“吗”“嘛”的听感边界。

“吗”字疑问句和“嘛”字祈使句连续统合成操作如下。通过测量发音人产出结果，找到阴平句、阳平句、上声句和去声句中［a］的起点在发音人语调格局的位置分别位于 61.72%、55.82%、31.39% 和 35.94% 处。四个句子［ma］的目标音高均在语调格局中以 10% 为步幅从 100% 降至 0%。由此得到 4 个刺激音连续统，每个连续统包括 11 个刺激音。

用同样的方法合成“吗”字疑问句和“嘛”字陈述句连续统。测量找到阴平句、阳平句、上声句和去声句中［a］的起点在发音人语调格局中分别处于 75.07%、55.67%、19.89% 和 29.23% 的位置。［ma］的目标音高也均在语调格局中以 10% 为步幅从 100% 降至 0%。由此得到 4 个刺激音连续统，每个连续统也包含 11 个刺激音。

3.1.2　实验流程

听音人为中国大陆地区非汉语言专

业普通话使用者，共14人，其中男性6人，女性8人，平均年龄27.93±9.30岁，均为右利手，且无视听障碍。实验时间在25分钟左右，难度较大，考虑到听音人的状态，刺激音只播放一遍。刺激音的播放和行为数据的采集通过praat［2］完成。

辨认实验的具体环节包括：听音人阅读实验说明，点击开始→播放刺激音并显示选项画面→听音人按键选择→进入下一环节。刺激音以乱序播放，每次播放一句话，每句话播放一遍，听音人必须在两个选项中选择一个。对于“你吃”句，两个选项分别为“问你吃不吃”和“让你吃”，实际对应“疑问”和“祈使”两个语气判断；对于“他是”句，两个选项分别为“问你他是谁”和“告诉你他是谁”，对应的是“疑问”和“陈述”两个语气判断。更便于非汉语言专业的听音人理解实验要求，完成实验任务。

区分实验的具体环节包括：听音人阅读实验说明，点击开始→播放实验句并显示选项画面→听音人按键选择，如“一致”“不一致”→进入下一环节。刺激音按照音高升序播放，每次播放一对刺激音，每对刺激音中两句话间隔2秒，语气词目标音高在语调格局中相差20%，例如第1对刺激音是以0%和20%为目标音高的［ma］字句。听音人必须判断两句话的语气意义是否一致。再通过计算所有听音人的平均值，得到［ma］字句语气区分结果，此时每两个音高数据点之间的区分率应该在0%到100%之间，区分率0%意味着所有听音人都认为该对音高所表达的语气意义一致，100%则意味着所有听音人对该对句子都作出语气“不一致”的判断。

3.1.3　参数提取

辨认率：计算14位听音人某一句话辨认结果的平均值，即为该刺激音目标韵律词2目标音高的语气辨认率。

边界位置：疑问语气和祈使语气辨认曲线、疑问语气和陈述语气辨认曲线各自的交点在语调格局中对应的位置。

边界宽度：语气辨认率为75%和25%时在语调格局中对应的位置的差值［15］。

区分率：计算14位听音人某一对刺激音区分结果的平均值，作为两个刺激语调格局中间位置的语气区分率。

峰值位置：最大区分率在语调格局中对应的位置。

峰界对应：区分曲线峰值位置与辨认曲线边界位置的对应情况。

3.2　实验结果

3.2.1　“吗”“嘛”目标音高的听感分界

图8两条方点折线表示的是“吗”与“嘛”（祈使）的语气辨认率，圆点折线表示的是二者的区分率。“吗”“嘛”边界位置位于20%到30%之间。但交点前后曲线变化不够陡峭，边界宽度较大。区分曲线峰值位置出现在40%处，说明［ma］最后一个音高数据点落在30%和50%时的听感区分程度最大，峰值位置与辨认曲线边界位置相比右移，峰界不对应，且峰值不高。由此可见，句调中疑问语气词“吗”和祈使语气词“嘛”目标音高听感空间存在一定的交叉。

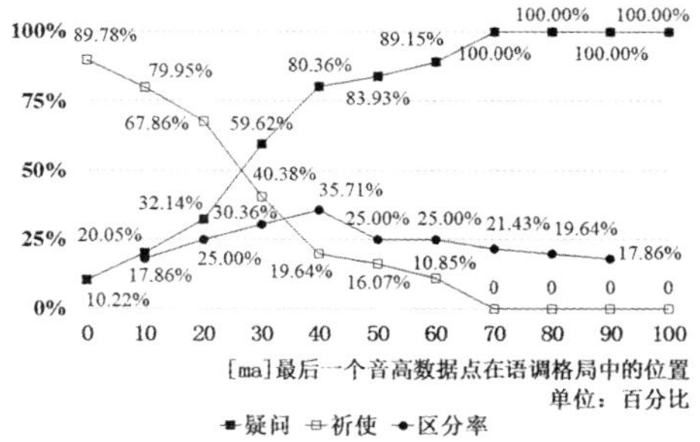

图8　“吗”“嘛”（祈使）的听辨结果

图9两条方点折线表示的是“吗”与“嘛”（陈述）的语气辨认率，圆点折线表示的是二者的区分率。“吗”“嘛”边界位置在0%到10%之间，但前后曲线变化缓慢，边界宽度较大。区分曲线峰值位置出现在20%处，说明［ma］最后一个音高数据点落在10%和30%时的听感区分程度最大，但峰值不高，且与辨认曲线

边界相比峰值位置右移，峰界不对应。表明疑问语气词“吗”和陈述语气词“嘛”目标音高听感空间分界不够清晰，存在一定的交叉。

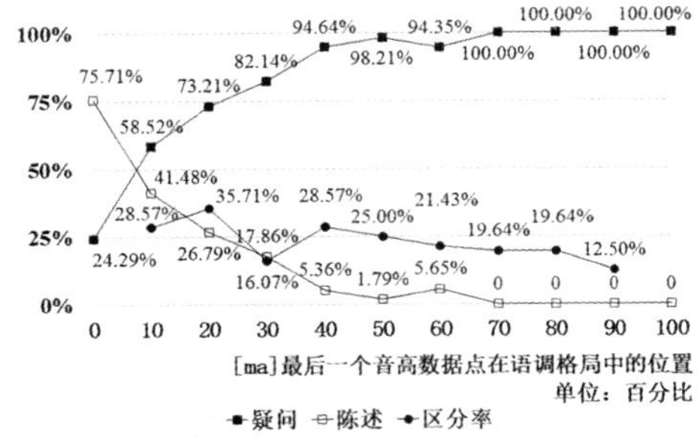

图9　“吗”“嘛”（陈述）的听辨结果

3.2.2　［ma］的目标音高听感空间

以往研究中缺少有关语气词［ma］目标音高区间的讨论，但是Yuan［1］的研究为这个问题的解释提供了参考。Yuan［1］考察了无标陈述句和无标疑问句的听感情况，发现陈述语调是无标记的，疑问语调是有标记的，在没有足够的信息表明句子传递的是疑问语气时，听音人倾向于把句子识别为陈述语气。这里的“无标记”和“有标记”反映的是使用频率，杜建鑫［3］通过语料库研究发现，与“嘛”相比，“吗”的使用频率更高，说明语言使用者对语气词［ma］表疑问的情况更熟悉。受此启发，我们可以在“吗”“嘛”之间把疑问语气词“吗”看作无标记的。在［ma］的目标音高不够低时，没有足够的信息表明［ma］传递的是祈使或陈述语气，听音人会倾向于理解为疑问语气，因此连续统上疑问语气的听感空间大于祈使语气和陈述语气。

“不够低”的说法说明了我们不能明确指出目标音高在什么位置算“低”，反映了语气词［ma］目标音高听感空间边界不清晰的情况。本研究探索的正是语气与语气词［ma］目标音高的对应关系，即意义与形式之间具有规约性的对应关系。这种在语言使用过程中形成的规约性关系说明［ma］的目标音高和语气信息的认识会受到语言使用的影响。

3.3　结果讨论

以往研究讨论过［ma］的声韵部分是否具有语气功能。从语音产出的角度来看，杨纯莉［20］、胡灏［6］通过对自然产出的“吗”字句进行声学分析发现，语气词没有固定的调型，句末处句调的走势与前一音节调形基本一致，由此认为功能语调在语气信息传递方面的作用不大，主要是语气词在表达疑问。但因为两位学者已经提出语气词是轻声音节，本身不具有固定调值，所以他们实际上认为疑问信息是由语气词的声韵部分而非声调来传递的，这一观点有其局限性。本研究通过产出实验发现，在目标音高较低的时候［ma］可以用来传递祈使或陈述语气，说明［ma］的声韵结构并非只能表达疑问语气。

从听感角度来看，江海燕［8］通过在无标陈述句句末添加疑问语气词“吗”的方式，发现听音人无一例外认为句子传递的是疑问语气。这是因为拼接上去的［ma］是从“吗”字句中剪切的，目标音高“不够低”，听音人只能把［ma］理解为疑问语气词。因为“吗”的目标音高听感空间大于“嘛”，所以在没有语境的情况下，当［ma］的目标音高“不够低”时，听音人会依据语气词［ma］的声韵，把句子理解为疑问句。由此可以推断，语气词［ma］的声韵本身能够提示语气信息，但是具体的语气类型还需要通过目标音高实现。

［ma］字句的语气听感线索与声学相关量相同，都是［ma］的目标音高。目标音高空间的建构需要同时考虑发音人角度的目标音高区间和听音人角度的目标音高听感空间。“吗”的目标音高听感空间位置较高、范围较大，“嘛”的位置较低、范围较小，与产出实验语气声学相关量的结论基本一致。

但在［ma］目标音高边界方面，两个实验结果存在较大差异。“吗”“嘛”目标音高听感空间之间存在交叉，边界不清晰。而“吗”“嘛”的声学区间交叉情况不显著。造成二者存在差异的可能原因是，在没有语境的情况下，发音人倾向于产出语音形式典型的［ma］来传递相应的语气。也正因为如此，为了区别更容易混淆的“嘛”字祈使句和“吗”字句，产出结果中祈使语气词“嘛”的上线反而低于陈述语气词“嘛”。

综上所述，语气词［ma］的目标音高既是［ma］字句的语气声学相关量，也是其语气听感线索。在目标音高连续统上，“吗”的位置较高，范围较大；“嘛”位置较低，范围较小。

4. 结论

本研究从“吗”“嘛”混淆现象出发，通过产出实验和听感实验，明确了［ma］字句的语气声学相关量和语气听感线索都是其语气词的目标音高。

疑问语气词“吗”和祈使语气词、陈述语气词“嘛”的目标音高存在较大差异。发音人可以通过实现较高的目标音高传递疑问语气，通过产出较低的目标音高表达祈使语气或陈述语气。听音人也可以根据语气词的目标音高判断［ma］字句传递的语气信息，但在目标音高“不够低”的情况下，听音人会倾向于将句子理解为疑问句。

5. 致谢

本文研究得到了国家社会科学基金青年项目“‘方言—普通话’双语环境下的婴幼儿声调习得机制研究”（18CYY021）和中宣部文化名家暨“四个一批”人才自主选题项目“语调类型学研究”的经费支持。

参考文献

［1］Yuan，J. 2011. Perception of intonation in Mandarin Chinese. *Journal of the Acoustical Society of America* 6，4063－4069.

［2］Boersma，P. 2001. Praat，a system for doing phonetics by computer. *Glot International* 5：9－10，341－345.

［3］陈茸、石媛媛（2009）普通话疑问句语调的声学实验分析。《牡丹江教育学院学报》第4期，29—31页。

［4］杜建鑫（2011）语气词“嘛”“吗”混用问题研究。《理论界》第4期，176—179页。

［5］傅由（1997）小议语气助词“嘛”。《中国人民大学学报》第6期，95—98页。

［6］贺阳、劲松（1992）北京话语调的实验探索。《语言教学与研究》第2期，71—96页。

［7］胡灏（2017）《汉语自然话语疑问句语调的音高模式研究》。暨南大学硕士学位论文。

［8］黄伯荣（1984）《陈述句、疑问句、祈使句、感叹句》。上海：上海教育出版社。

［9］江海燕（2005）疑问语气意义的两种表达途径。《南开语言学刊》第2期，45—52页。

［10］江海燕（2010）《汉语语调问题的实验研究》。北京：首都师范大学出版社。

［11］李明（1996）语气助词的音高分析。《世界汉语教学》第4期，45—55页。

［12］李智（2010）《现代汉语口语疑问句语调升降规律及其成因研究》。暨南大学硕士学位论文。

［13］刘月华（1988）语调是非问句。《语言教学与研究》第2期，25—34页。

［14］吕叔湘（1979）《汉语语法分析问题》。北京：商务印书馆。

［15］强星娜（2006）《现代汉语语气词ma（吗、嘛）》。上海师范大学硕士学位论文。

［16］荣蓉（2013）《汉语普通话声调的听感格局》。南开大学博士学位论文。

［17］阮吕娜（2004）《汉语疑问句语调研究》。北京语言大学硕士学位论文。

［18］沈炯（1992）汉语语调模型刍议。《语文研究》第4期，16—24页。

［19］石锋（2013）《语调格局：实验语言学的奠基石》。北京：商务印书馆。

［20］熊子瑜、林茂灿（2003）语气词“ma0”的疑问用法和非疑问用法。载《第七届全国人机语音通讯学术会议（NCMMSC7）论文集》，243—246页。

［21］杨纯莉（2016）疑问句句末语气助词“吗”的音高和语调关系研究。载《第六届东亚汉语教学研究生论坛暨第九届北京地区对外汉语教学研究生学术论坛论文集》，13页。

［22］阎锦婷、高晓天（2017）普通话语调问句和“吗”字问句的不同韵律分布模式。《南开语言学刊》第2期，72—80页。

［23］朱晓农（2010）《语音学》。北京：商务印书馆。

王炤宇 武汉大学文学院，博士研究生。主要研究领域为汉语语音学、韵律学、社会语言学、语用学。
Email：miranda2121@163.com

曹梦雪 北京师范大学文学院，副教授。主要研究领域为语音学、儿童语言习得、语言习得计算模型、汉语方言学。
Email：mengxue.cao@bnu.edu.cn

互动视角下陈述疑问句的韵律特征初探

张欣阳　陈玉东

摘　要　本文以《圆桌派》第一季约600分钟的自然口语会话语料为研究依据，从中选取陈述句、疑问句和陈述疑问句，采用实验语音学的方法，针对陈述疑问句的韵律特征进行分析。研究发现：与陈述句和疑问句相比，（1）陈述疑问句整体音长较长，调尾音长有显著的延宕，这可以表现出说话人对问题有一定了解但又不十分确定的部分［K+］的认识地位；（2）陈述疑问句的音强整体较弱，并且在句末音节明显减弱；（3）陈述疑问句的音高在调核后与陈述句类似，但在调核前明显较高，这可能与其序列结构有关。总的来说，与陈述句和疑问句相比，陈述疑问句的音节较长、较弱，特别是调尾音节的持续延宕与句末音节骤然变弱的相互配合，构成其较明显的韵律特征。

关键词　陈述疑问句，韵律，互动

A Preliminary Study on the Prosodic Features of Declarative Questions from the Perspective of Interaction

ZHANG Xinyang　CHEN Yudong

Abstract This paper analyzes the prosodic features of declarative questions. The experimental data include declarative sentences, interrogative sentences and declarative questions selected from 600 minute conversations produced in the first season of a reality TV show called: "Yuan Zhuo Pai". The findings are as follows: Compared with declarative sentences and interrogative sentences, (1) The duration of declarative questions is long with a distinct delay at the tail, which can show epistemic stance of partially [K+] (having more or less clear expectations about what the answer will be). (2) The intensity of declarative questions is weak as a whole, while syllables at the end of the sentence are significantly weakened. (3) The pitch of declarative questions after nucleus is similar to that of declarative sentences, and then a sequential organization may contribute to a significantly higher pitch before nucleus. Generally speaking, compared with declarative sentences and interrogative sentences, declarative questions are featured by longer and weaker syllables as well as the coordination between continuous delay of tail and sudden weakening at the end of the sentence.

Keywords Declarative questions, Prosody, Interaction

1. 引言

1.1　陈述疑问句的定义

提问（Question）是一种社会行为，通过这种行为，提问者要求被提问者提供关于提问者认为被提问者了解得更多的信息。在自然口语会话中，听话人可以通过疑问形态或语调来识别对方是否在提问，但是Couper-Kuhlen和Selting［2］指出，即使在完全可以将语句标记为疑问句的语言中，说话者也可以产生所谓的“陈述疑问句”（declarative question），即构建为要求听话人确认的陈述句的话轮。在汉语学界，赵元任［20］曾提及一种不同于一般是非问句语调特点的求证问句（要求证实的问话）。他指出，这种问句的语调整句都低，常常是粗糙的，句末常有语气助词“啊”。贺阳、劲松［12］观察到，这种求证问句的句末也可以不带语气助词“啊”。

杭宝桐［11］认为，英语的陈述疑问句是一种和陈述句结构相同的疑问句，只是书面语要在陈述句句末加上问号，口语要在句末用升调。但是，句末用升调这样的描述是早期学者对英语陈述疑问句的认识。

Couper-Kuhlen［1］发现，在英国一档电台电话答疑节目的电话语料库中，带有句末降调的是非问句几乎与句末升调的是非问句一样多，而且大多数陈述性疑问句实际上都是句末降调。由此可见，学界对英语陈述疑问句语调的认识有了改变，陈述疑问句不再是“升调”。

根据以上研究，本文把汉语陈述疑问句定义为，词汇和句法形态上无疑问标记，句末调听起来无明显上敛、功能上是请求确认的、实施的是提问行为的句子。

1.2 韵律特征

赵元任［21］提出，要把汉语的“字调”和“句调”区分开，“因为这每字固有的腔调和说话读书时抑扬的句调不是一件事情，也不是言语学上一类的现象”。“字调”即“声调”，“句调”即一句话的“语调”。关于声调和语调的关系，赵元任立足于汉语的声调语言特征，提出了三种说法——“代数和”“橡皮带”“波浪说”。由此可见，声调和语调虽然时常相互影响，但它们仍然是相对独立的。

在《语音学和音系学词典》［14］中，语调（intonation）的定义为：“为了传达意义而在通常长于一个单词的一串话语中，对音高，还可能加上响度、音速、停顿等韵律要素的运用。语调可以用于各种目的：标示语法边界（短语、小句），提示句子类型（如陈述句、疑问句），传达说话人的态度（惊异、反讥、愤怒等）。”

可以看出，与声调区分语义的作用相比，语调的作用在于区分语句不同的功能或目的，包括句法上的功能和说话人的情感态度等。陈述疑问句是一种比较特殊的句子类型，说话人使用陈述疑问句通常是对有所了解但又不十分确定的问题进行提问，而这正是通过语调来实现的。葛淳宇、李爱军［10］指出，“语调一般指与音高有关的语音表现”，而本文是在接近自然口语的对话中分析陈述疑问句，除了音高之外，还讨论陈述疑问句的音长、音强特征。

Palmer［6］引入了 Klinghardt、Klemm 德语著作的术语，将英语语调按照线性顺序切分为调核（nucleus）——核心调开始处最突显的音节、调头（head）——调核前的延伸部分（the pre-nucleus stretch）、调尾（tail）——调核后的延伸部分（the stretch following the nucleus），为语调构造分析理论奠定了基础。

赵元任［21］在 Palmer 的基础上，将汉语语调划分为调头（head）和调干（body）两大部分，调头包括调冠（anacrusis）、主调头（main head），调干包括调核（nucleus）、调尾（tail）。

沈炯［16］继承并发展了赵元任的思想，提出了“双线模型”，认为“汉语语调是高音线和低音线两方面调节配合起来的结果”。沈炯［17］指出，汉语音高系统包括有声性和区别性，“有声性是语言外壳的有声实质，区别性是语言成分的本质属性”，声调的区别性在于调类，语调的区别性在于类型，“为语句添加功能意义或口气色彩”。沈炯［15］还发展了汉语语调构造理论，把语调分为调冠（prehead）、调头（head）、调核（nucleus）、调尾（tail）四个部分。他认为，“高音线和低音线的语调调节要通过语调构造来说明……从调冠到调尾是分段处理的，每一段的变化都包含语调信息”，并且，在调冠到调尾的每一段中，“调核和调尾是主要部分，有时调冠也起重要作用”，这些变化是区别语调类型的主要手段。

Pierrehumbert［8］将自主音段音系学与节律音系学结合起来，开创了自主音段—节律理论（Autosegmental-Metrical Theory，简称 AM 理论）。Ladd［7］正式提出“语调音系学”（Intonational Phonology）这一概念，并对 AM 理论的原则、方法及理论系统化。AM 理论认为，重音和边界调是语调的核心要素，其中重音用于突显重要信息，而边界调则可以实现调群切分，并表达语气与语篇功能，二者相互组合，构成完整的语调曲拱。林茂灿［13］汲取了 AM 理论的边界调（boundary tone）提法，主张句末语调观，并通过汉语陈述句和疑问句的感知和声学实验得出结论，“疑问语气和陈述语气由短语的边界音节携带”“疑问边界调的时长比其陈述的长”。

总的来说，沈炯的语调构造理论关注语调的各个部分，是一种整句语调观，而AM理论观测语调的重点是重音和边界调。本研究以语调构造理论为基本框架，使用“双线模型”全面关注汉语陈述疑问句调冠、调头、调核和调尾的总体变化。同时，还特别关注处在调尾部分的句末非轻声音节的局部变化特征，也就相当于句末边界调特征，这样更便于观察句末调的细微变化。

2. 实验设计

2.1 语料来源

本研究的语料来源为文化类综艺节目《圆桌派》第一季的20期，约600分钟。共涉及13位发音人，包括6位女性发音人和7位男性发音人。这种对话节目的语料比较接近自然口语。本文从中共选取了47个陈述疑问句、46个陈述句和26个疑问句。语料中带疑问标记的疑问句使用频率较高，同时考虑到疑问句的判定，本文的疑问句均选择带“吗”字的疑问句。陈述疑问句均选择没有语气词的陈述疑问句。

本文对陈述疑问句的判定是在言语互动的视角下进行的：在对话序列中，（1）说话人的语句在句法上是陈述句，句末调没有显著的上敛，功能上是请求确认的、能够实施提问行为的句子；（2）在后续的话轮中，听话人的回答是确认或不确认的。如果听话人仅仅是“哦”“知道了”这类回应，则表明听话人没有把前一话轮识别为问句，那么说话人的语句就不是陈述疑问句。例如，下面序列中“唯一的解放”和“心灵的解放”是本文探讨的陈述疑问句，但是像“心灵的解放”这种存在语音交叠的语句，由于提取准确声学特征比较困难，暂不在本研究的考察范围内。

1 B 那个是一个（0.5）他：要努力地把自己往下拉，就是别人觉得那叫无限止的堕落，但是对他来讲那是唯一的出路

2 A 唯一的解放

3 B 唯一的解放

4 A 心灵的解［放

5 B ［对 =

6 B = 要不断地把自己往下，那：那个往下是很有勇气的，那是要冒险的

本例的转写标记包括：圆括号内为停顿时长，中括号表示言谈重叠，等号表示急接，冒号表示音节延长。

2.2 数据获取

使用Praat对句子中符合条件的音节进行逐一切分和标注，同时根据主观听感标注句子重音，标记为3。

以沈炯的语调构造理论为基础，标记调冠为P、调头为H、调核为N、调尾为T。重音词中非调核音节标记为W。

除此之外，标记句子类型层、话语层、说话人层，如图1所示。

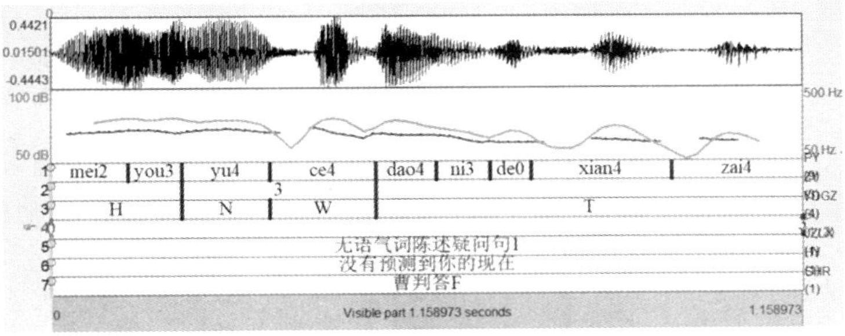

图1 Praat标注示例图

用中国传媒大学自编的Alldata数据提取软件将20期节目中音节的音长、音强和手工修正后的音高数据提取到Excel表格中。

2.3 数据处理方法

将所需数据提取至Excel表格中后，对数据进行处理。其中，句末音节选取的是处在调尾部分的句末的两个非轻声音节，音强提取的是各音节的平均音强，音高的提取则以沈炯的双线模型为基础提取音高特征点。沈炯［16］提出："语调研究中，最好把声调调域分成两个音区，即高音区和低音区。用这两个音区来说明的声调特征就是高音特征和低音特征。它们的实际音高用高音点和低音点的实测数据来表示。就声调和轻声的核心段来看，阴平、阳平和去声三种声调，以及上声后边的轻声，都有高音特征，上声以及非上声后边的轻声都有低音特征。因此它们内部都包含音高的对偶变化……轻声跟前边的声调总是组成音高对偶变化。很明显，声调音域的变化可以从这些对偶关系里反映出来。"因此，在本文的实验中，根据声调提取有声带振动的韵母的音高，阴平提取音高最大值为高音点，上声提取音高最小值为低音点，阳平和去声分别提取最大值和最小值为高音点和低音点；阴平、阳平和去声后的轻声提取最小值为低音点，上声后的轻声提取最大值为高音点。轻声后的轻声音节数量不多，在数据处理过程中删除。

然后，对音高特征点的数据进行半音化处理，以消除性别之间的差异，转换公式为：

$$st = 12 \times \lg(f/f_{ref})/\lg 2 \quad (1)$$

其中，f是提取的音高频率，f_{ref}是参考频率。男声的参考频率是50Hz，女声的参考频率是90Hz。

最后，为了尽量消除个体间的随机差异，再以说话人为单位分别对时长（只包括音节，不包括无声段）、音高、音强进行归一化处理。归一化公式为：

$$Z = 10 + 5 \times (X - \overline{X})/S \quad (2)$$

其中，X是需要归一化的数值，$\overline{X}$是平均值，S是标准差。得到的Z值是以10为均值，以5为标准差的正态分布的标准分值。

所有相关数据整理完成后用SPSS对音长、音强、音高的高音点和低音点进行独立样本t检验，三种句子类型的音节数量分布如表1所示。其中，音长和音强的样本量相同，列于表1各句子类型中三组数据的第1列，音高的高音点（三组数据第2列）和低音点（三组数据第3列）两组样本分别列出。

表1 音节数量表

	陈述疑问句	陈述句	疑问句
调冠	31/23/27	63/43/48	19/10/16
调头	132/88/110	232/166/182	65/42/52
调核	55/51/36	59/50/47	31/19/26
调尾	190/137/150	222/148/171	124/81/94
句末	67/50/53	67/38/49	39/27/30

3. 实验结果及讨论

对比陈述疑问句、疑问句、陈述句的数据，对音长、音强、音高的高音点和低音点分别进行整体、语调构造、句末音节的独立样本t检验，结果如下。

3.1 音长

音长的独立样本t检验结果显示，陈述疑问句的音长整体特征与疑问句、陈述句都存在显著差异（陈述疑问句与疑问句：$t(702)=3.870$，$p=0.000$；陈述疑问句与陈述句：$t(1034)=2.802$，$p=0.005$），陈述疑问句的音长平均值比疑问句长1.52，比陈述句长0.94。在语调构造方面，陈述疑问句与疑问句、陈述句在调尾上都存在显著差异（疑问句：$t(312)=3.273$，$p=0.001$；陈述句：$t(410)=2.264$，$p=0.024$），陈述疑问句的调尾音长均值比疑问句长1.79，比陈述句长1.15。我们称之为"延宕"。

除此之外，陈述疑问句与疑问句在调

冠上存在显著差异（t（48）=2.415，p=0.020）。在句末音节方面，陈述疑问句与疑问句存在显著差异（t（104）=2.945，p=0.004），与陈述句不存在显著差异（t（132）=1.044，p=0.298）。

将陈述疑问句与陈述句、疑问句的音长平均值进行对比，如图2所示，可以发现，除了调冠之外，陈述疑问句的调头、调核、调尾、句末音节的音长都是三者中最长的；疑问句是三者中整体音长最短的。

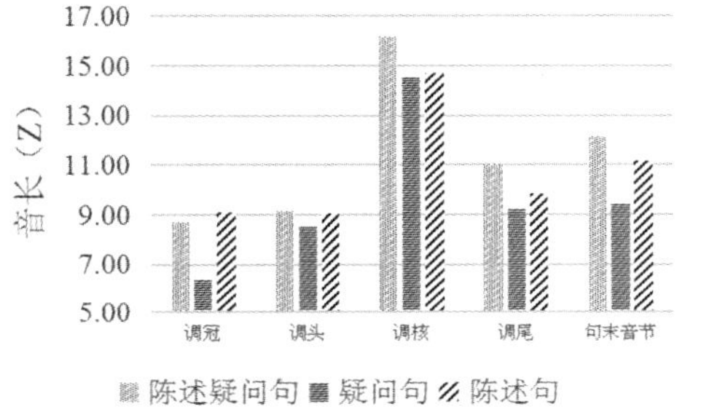

图2　音长平均值图

沈炯［17］指出，“疑问句末了的音节有加长的倾向，除了语调的调核、调尾和少数强语势音节外，其他音节的时长减小”。林茂灿［13］也指出，“疑问的边界调时长比其陈述的长”。本文中疑问句的句末音节没有呈现出音长加长的倾向，甚至是三种句子类型中最短的，这与本文选取的疑问句类型有关。沈炯和林茂灿先生探讨的是无疑问标记的疑问句，而本文涉及的疑问句都是“吗”字问。从柴丹丹［9］的实验数据中也可以看出，“吗”字问在音长方面的表现与无疑问标记疑问句不同，其末字（“吗”的前一音节）时长比陈述句和无疑问标记疑问句都短，全句时长也比陈述句短。这是因为疑问标记“吗”本身就可以表示提问，因此不一定需要语调来表达疑问语气，较短的音长反而有助于提问者表达疑问。

分别对三种句子类型内部相邻环节的音长进行独立样本t检验，其中呈现出的明显变化主要是由重音引起的（三种句子类型的调核与调头、调尾的音长相比都明显更长），本文对此不再做详细说明。值得注意的是，陈述疑问句调尾音长的延宕一直持续到句末音节，调尾与句末音节的音长没有显著差异（t（255）=－1.469，p=0.143），而陈述句的句末音节与调尾的音长相比有明显的延长（t（287）=－1.983，p=0.048），但仍然没有陈述疑问句长。也就是说，陈述疑问句音长的延宕是从调尾开始一直持续到句末音节的，而陈述句只在句末音节有些延长。

Heritage［4，5］指出，在提问行为中，提问者将自己定位为未知（［K－］）方，将被提问者定位为更了解（［K+］）方。值得注意的是，［K+］和［K－］都可以是完全的或者部分的，当提问者对答案多多少少有一些清楚的期待时，就是部分［K+］。［K+］的程度越高，即说话人对信息的知晓度越高，说话人对所说内容的确定性就越强。陈述疑问句是说话人以陈述句的形式向听话人求证的，用来提问已知但不十分确定的信息，此时说话人将自己定位在部分［K+］的认识地位。

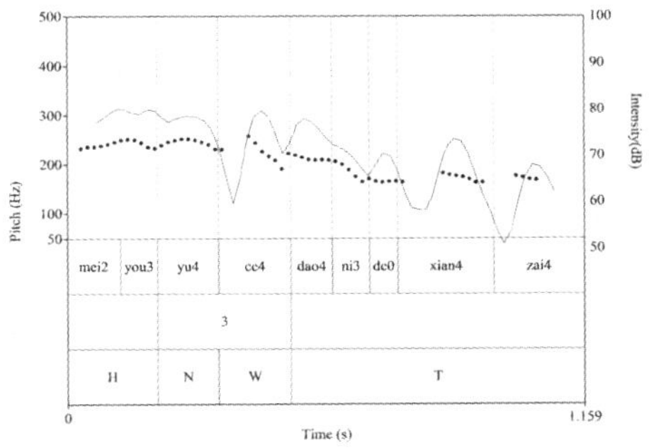

图3　“没有预测到你的现在?”韵律图

陈述疑问句调尾的音长较长，与陈述句和疑问句都有明显差异，并且这种延宕一直持续到句末音节。陈述句的调尾音长是标记话轮结束的特征之一，以陈述句为参照，陈述疑问句调尾音长的额外的延宕是其最突出的特征。这种延宕可以表现出说话人对所说内容的不确定和犹豫不决，也就是部分［K+］的认识地位，期待听话人的进一步确认，从而被听话人识别为一种提问行为。

例如：曹判答（女）：“没有预测到你的现在?”

如图3所示，图中虚线为例句的音高变化虚线，实线为例句的音强变化曲线。本句调尾的句末音节“现在”的音长明显较长。

3.2 音强

音强的独立样本t检验结果显示，陈述疑问句的音强整体特征与疑问句存在显著差异（t（702）=−3.937，p=0.000），平均值比疑问句低1.56，与陈述句的音强没有显著差异（t（1034）=−0.778,p=0.437）。在语调构造和句末音节方面，陈述疑问句与疑问句的调头、调尾和句末音节存在显著差异（调头：t（195）=−2.258，p=0.025；调尾：t（312）=−4.182，p=0.000；句末音节：t（104）=−2.785，p=0.006），陈述疑问句的音强平均值分别比疑问句低1.28、2.75、3.66。

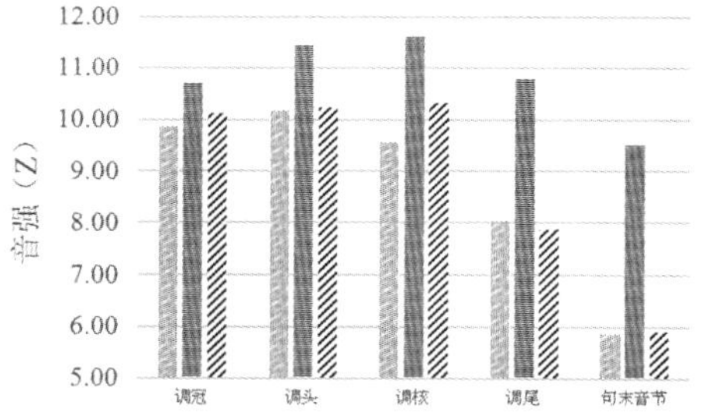

图4　音强平均值图

将陈述疑问句与陈述句、疑问句的音强平均值进行对比，如图4所示，可以发现：陈述疑问句的音强是三者中最弱的；疑问句在语调构造各个位置的音强都要强于陈述句，是三者中音强最强的。分别对三种句子类型内部相邻环节的音强进行独立样本t检验，结果显示，陈述疑问句只有调尾与句末音节的音强存在显著差异（t（255）=2.465，p=0.014）；陈述句的调尾与其前后环节都存在显著差异（调核与调尾：t（279）=3.101，p=0.002；调尾与句末音节：t（287）=2.508，p=0.013）；疑问句各相邻环节的音强都没有显著差异。也就是说，陈述疑问句的音强与陈述句相似，整体比疑问句弱得多，并且在句末音节明显减弱，但陈述句的音强在调核后便逐级减弱，而疑问句的音强整体变化不大。

这种现象也与说话人的认识地位有关。在本文的三种句子类型中，疑问句是说话人处于完全［K−］的认识地位时使用的，是针对整个命题的提问，说话人对所说内容的不确定性最强、最明显，说话人采用一种直截了当的提问方式，使得音强相对增强，以期望听话人能够直接提供可信的答案，因此疑问句的音强最强、最稳定。陈述句是说话人处于完全［K+］的认识地位时使用的，说话人对所说内容的确定性比较强，不需要听话人确认，伴随着总体音高下倾的趋势（见3.3节），音强在调核后逐级下降，直到句末音节降到最弱。而陈述疑问句是说话人处于部分［K+］的认识地位时使用的，音强整体上稍弱于陈述句，但陈述疑问句的音强只在句末音节才明显减弱。如图3所示，图中实线为例句的音强变化曲线。本句调核“预”的音强均值为77.73dB，调尾的非轻声音节“到”为76.19dB，句末音节“在”为62.67dB，比“到”弱了很多。

从图3中可以看出，陈述疑问句句末音节音强的减弱与调尾音节音长的持续延宕相互配合，构成了陈述疑问句较为明显的韵律特征。

3.3 音高

音高的高音点和低音点的独立样本t检验结果显示，陈述疑问句与疑问句音高高音点、低音点的整体特征都存在显著差异（高音点：t（473）=4.691，p=0.000；低音点：t（556）=2.534，p=0.012），陈述疑问句的平均值分别比疑问句高1.77、1.09，与陈述句都不存在显著差异。在语调构造方面，陈述疑问句与疑问句和陈述句的调头高音点都存在显著差异（疑问句：t（128）=4.498，p=0.000；陈述句：t（252）=2.839，p=0.005）。陈述疑问句的调尾高音点与疑问句存在显著差异（t（216）=2.023，p=0.044）。

对比陈述疑问句与陈述句、疑问句的高音点和低音点的均值，如图5所示，可以发现，陈述疑问句的高音点和低音点整体略高，尤其是调核前音节，高音点在句末音节下降到最低，低音点在句末音节下降到疑问句与陈述句之间。

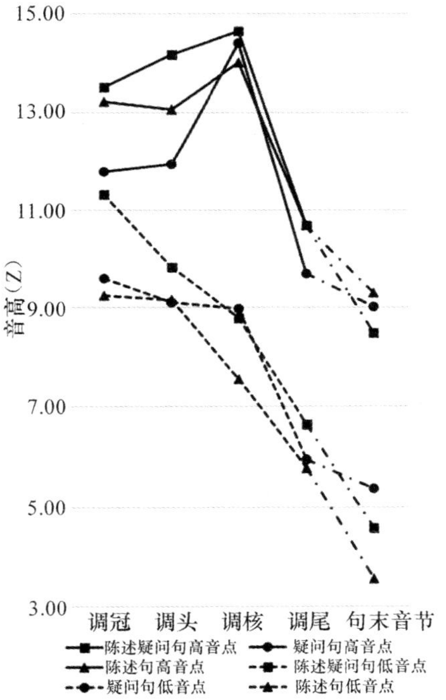

图5　音高平均值图

陈述疑问句调核前音节的音高较高可能与其序列结构有关。谢心阳［19］指出，“陈述式问句很多是基于背景知识和互动语境所提出的要求确认的行为，因而很可能出现在对方叙述过程中，从而构成一种插入式问句”。在本文的语料中，陈述疑问句出现的语境通常是说话人A正在听B讲述一段经历或故事，说话人A对此加以求证，求证的话轮位于一个会话序列的中间位置，仅仅是一个插入扩展序列，说话人A在这个序列提问，往往需要打断B的讲述，将B的话语权争夺过来，构成一种插入式问句。如2.1节例句“唯一的解放”。French和Local［3］发现，与同一说话人在其他地方开始话轮转换时的标准相比，竞争性话语的音高水平显示出明显的增加。因此，位于插入扩展序列的陈述疑问句需要争夺话语权，其调冠、调头音节的音高相对较高。

分别对三种句子类型内部相邻环节的音高进行独立样本t检验并结合前文，我们发现，在低音线上，三种句子类型都呈下倾趋势，但在具体环节上有一些不同。陈述疑问句与陈述句相比总体略高，在调冠位置高得更多一些（t（73）=1.945，p=0.056）；陈述疑问句与疑问句相比，差异主要在调尾与句末音节之间的变化，疑问句句末音节明显上敛，即向上拉平，调尾与句末音节的低音点没有显著差异（t（122）=0.599，p=0.550），而陈述疑问句和陈述句在继续显著下降，调尾和句末音节的低音点之间存在显著差异（陈述疑问句：t（201）=2.560，p=0.011；陈述句：t（218）=2.312，p=0.022）。沈炯［15］指出，“句末一个音节的低音线极易受口气语调调节的影响”。沈炯［16］指出，“陈述语调的低音线起伏比较大，句末部分特别低。这是低音线的下延形式。疑问语调的低音线起伏比较小，句末虽然也很低，但是比陈述句相应部分要高得多……这是低音线的上敛形式”。本研究的实验结果与沈炯先生的结论基本一致，疑问句句末音节的低音线明显上敛；陈述疑问句与陈述句类似，句末音节的低音线明显下延。

在高音线上，三种句子类型调核到调尾之间的语势都有明显的下降（独立样本t检验的p值均小于0.01），相比而言，陈述句下降得最少，疑问句下降得最多。但是调尾和句末音节相比，疑问句明显改变了直线下降的趋势，伴随着低音线的上敛出现了一定的抬升，调尾和句末音节之间没有显著差异（t（106）=0.933，p=

0.353)。而陈述疑问句和陈述句则比较相似,都是继续显著下降,调尾和句末音节之间存在显著差异(陈述疑问句:t(185)= 3.423,p = 0.001;陈述句:t(184)=2.074,p=0.040)。沈炯[16]指出,“陈述语调在调核后有一个全句性的比较大的落差,……这是高音线的骤落形式。疑问语调……这个落差大体上要比陈述语调的小,这是高音线的渐落形式”。王韫佳[18]指出,“带疑问语气词的疑问句和陈述句的差别基本上与无标记的疑问句和陈述句的差别相同”。也就是说,在沈炯和王韫佳的实验语料中,有无疑问标记的疑问句句末都是上敛的,只是上敛程度有所不同。在本研究的实验结果中,三种句子类型的高音线在调核和调尾之间总体都出现了骤降,只是在疑问句调尾的最后音节呈现出了明显的拉平。

总的来说,陈述疑问句的音高在调核前较高,与调核没有明显差异,这可能与陈述疑问句的序列结构有关,但在调核后持续显著下降。如图3所示,该句调核和调头音节的音高差异不大,但调核后音节的音高在持续下降。

另外,从图5中还可以看出,陈述疑问句的调域基本处于陈述句和疑问句之间;三种句子类型在调核位置的调域都比较宽,陈述疑问句的调域在调尾的收窄最多;在句末音节,陈述疑问句的调域有一定程度的加宽。结合前文的分析可知,调尾调域的收窄主要是由高音线的骤落造成的,句末音节调域的加宽主要是由低音线的下延造成的。

4. 结论

根据本文对《圆桌派》第一季接近自然口语会话语料进行的初步分析,针对陈述疑问句的韵律特征可以得出如下结论:

(1)陈述疑问句整体的音长较长,调头后音节都是音长最长的,尤其是调尾音节。这与说话人的认识地位有关,调尾音节的延宕可以表现出说话人对所说内容的不确定和犹豫不决,也就是部分[K+]的认识地位,期待听话人的进一步确认,从而被听话人识别为一种提问行为。

(2)陈述疑问句的音强整体比疑问句弱,与陈述句的音强差异不明显。疑问句的音强整体较强,变化不大;陈述句的音强在调核后便逐级减弱;而陈述疑问句的音强在句末音节才明显减弱。

(3)陈述疑问句的音高整体比疑问句高,与陈述句的音高较为类似,只是在调核前较高,这可能与其多位于插入扩展的序列结构有关。高音线在调核后持续骤落,低音线在调核后持续下延。调域基本处于陈述句和疑问句之间。

总的来看,与陈述句和疑问句相比,陈述疑问句音长较长,调尾音长有显著的延宕;音强较弱,并且在句末音节明显减弱。整体音高较高,但是在调核后持续显著下降。调域基本处于陈述句与疑问句之间。陈述疑问句调尾音节音长的持续延宕与句末音节音强的骤然变弱相互配合,构成其较为明显的韵律特征。

由于现有语料数量有限,本文结论还将通过扩大语料规模或设计实验来进一步验证。

5. 致谢

本文研究得到了国家社科基金重大项目“汉语自然口语对话的互动语言学研究”(20&ZD295)的经费支持。

参考文献

[1] Couper-Kuhlen, E. 2012. Some truths and untruths about final intonation in conversational questions. Jan P. (eds), *Questions: Formal, Functional and Interactional Perspectives*. Cambridge: Cambridge University Press.

[2] Couper-Kuhlen, E., Selting, M. 2018. *Interactional Linguistics: An Introduction to Language in Social Interaction*. Cambridge: Cambridge University Press.

[3] French, P., Local, J. 1983. Turn-competitive incomings. *Journal of Pragmatics* 7, 17-38.

[4] Heritage, J. 2012. Epistemics in action: Action formation and territories of knowledge. *Research*

on Language and Social Interaction 45, 1 – 29.
[5] Heritage, J. 2012. The epistemic engine: Sequence organization and territoriesof knowledge. *Research on Language and Social Interaction* 45, 30 – 52.
[6] Palmer, H. 1922. *English Intonation with Systematic Exercises*. Cambridge: Cambridge University Press.
[7] Ladd, D. R. 1996. *Intonational Phonology*. Cambridge: Cambridge University Press.
[8] Pierrehumbert, J. B. 1980. *The Phonology and Phonetics of English Intonation*. Ph. D, MIT.
[9] 柴丹丹（2017）普通话不同语用功能疑问句的语调研究。南京师范大学，硕士论文。
[10] 葛淳宇、李爱军（2018）语调类型学研究综述。《中国语音学报》第 10 辑，57—71 页。
[11] 杭宝桐（1979）关于英语陈述疑问句。《外语教学与研究》第 2 期，79—80 页。
[12] 贺阳、劲松（1992）北京话语调的实验探索。《语言教学与研究》第 2 期，71—96 页。
[13] 林茂灿（2006）疑问和陈述语气与边界调。《中国语文》第 4 期，364—376 页。
[14] R. L. 特拉斯克（2000）《语音学和音系学词典》。北京：语文出版社。
[15] 沈炯（1994）汉语语调构造和语调类型。《方言》第 3 期，221—228 页。
[16] 沈炯（1992）汉语语调模型刍议。《语文研究》第 4 期，16—24 页。
[17] 沈炯（1995）汉语音高系统的有声性和区别性。《语言文字应用》第 2 期，13—18 页。
[18] 王韫佳（2008）试论普通话疑问语气的声学关联物。载《语言学论丛》第 37 辑，北京：商务印书馆，183—205 页。
[19] 谢心阳（2021）多模态资源与汉语口语中陈述式问句的解读。《当代修辞学》第 3 期，84—95 页。
[20] 赵元任（1979）《汉语口语语法》。北京：商务印书馆。
[21] 赵元任（2002）《赵元任语言学论文集》。北京：商务印书馆。

张欣阳 中国传媒大学，硕士在读。主要研究领域为语言学及应用语言学专业，对外汉语教学方向。
Email：zhangxinyang2021@126. com

陈玉东 中国传媒大学人文学院教授。主要研究领域包括实验语音学、发声学、语言学。
Email：edwardcyd@163. com

基于系统声学实验的赣语遂川话声调研究

曾　玲　余俊毅　刘新中

摘　要　本文运用熊子瑜博士开发的汉语方言字音实验分析工具，对赣语遂川话声调的共时面貌和古今对应规律进行了系统考察，以赣语吉茶片为参照，探讨遂川话声调演变的个性和共性。研究发现，遂川话的上声分阴阳，去声不分阴阳，且保留入声调，与吉茶片大多数方言点存在差异。从具体的分化路径上看，古浊上归去声和阳上而非阴平；古清去不归阳平，并依声母送气与否分为两个调类，送气归入声，不送气归去声；古入声按清浊二分，清入为入声，全浊入归去声，次浊部分随清入，部分随浊入，与赣方言次浊入的分化大规律一致。
关键词　赣语，遂川话，声调古今对应，汉语方言字音系统

Tone Features of the Suichuan Gan Dialect Based on Acoustic Data

ZENG Ling　YU Junyi　LIU Xinzhong

Abstract This paper aims to describe the tonal evolution of the Suichuan dialect and to make a detailed comparison with other Gan dialects with the help of the research tool developed by Dr. XIONG Ziyu. We found that the *Shang* tone in this dialect split into the *Yin* and *Yang* categories, but the *Qu* tone did not split. The *Ru* tone still remains in the dialect, different from most other dialects in the Jicha dialect group. Specifically, the *Shang* tone with voiced initials merged with the *Qu* tone and the *Yangshang* tone rather than the *Yinping* tone. The *Qu* tone with voiceless initials did not merge with the *Yangping* tone; rather it split into two categories—the *Ru* tone with the aspirated initial and the *Qu* tone with the unaspirated initial. The *Ru* tone spilt into two categories, following the voicing of the initials: The *Ru* tone with the voiceless initials remained the *Ru* tone, but it merged with the *Qu* tone when the initials are voiced. When the initials are sonorants, the syllables merged with the *Ru* tone with voiceless and voiced initials respectively. The similar pattern is attested in other Gan dialects.
Keywords Gan dialect, Suichuan dialect, Tonal evolution, Chinese Dialect Phonetic System

1. 引言

在传统的方言调查中，方言学家依靠听辨典型例字记录某方言点的声韵调系统。对有经验的调查者来说，这是一种快速且有效的调查方法，但如果每位调查者听辨音的标准不一致，在调值的记录上往往就有很多的分歧。此外，调查者也不可能详尽展示字表中所有例字语音的声学数据。随着计算机技术的发展，运用实验手段来调查方言已成为常态，以数据为支撑的汉语方言调查受到越来越多研究者的重视。一大批以 Praat［1］为代表的语音分析软件，在汉语方言学界得到了广泛应用。一些以研究汉语方言为目的的研究工具，也为汉语方言研究者提供了极大的便利。本文就是利用熊子瑜博士研发的汉语方言字音系统实验研究工具［16］，对遂川话声调的进行系统考察的一个尝试。

从地理位置上看，遂川县隶属江西省吉安市，位于江西省西南边境，吉安市西南部。在《中国语言地图集》（第 2 版）［20］中，遂川话属于赣语吉茶片，多位学者曾对其声调系统进行调查，但在调类分布及调值上略有差异。前人及笔者的调

查描写如表 1 所示。

表 1 已有的遂川话声调系统描写记录

	平声		上声		去声		入声	调类数
	阴平	阳平	阴上	阳上	阴去	阳去	入声	
颜森［18］	53	22	31		24	213	5	6
陈昌仪［4］	53	22	31		213	34	5	6
刘纶鑫［8］	42	22	21	24	213	55	/	6
辛世彪［14］	53	22	31	24	213		5	6
方志编委会［6］	53	33	33	35	55	213	/	6
昌梅香［2］	53	33	31	35	324		5	6
笔者①	53	33	31	35	304②		5	6

表 1 所列举的对遂川话调类调值的描写，各研究有不同程度的差异，主要分歧在古上声和去声的分化和演变。但这些研究采用的都是传统的听音记音调查法，具有一定的主观性，需要通过实验数据进一步系统考察。本文借助汉语方言字音系统实验研究工具，以《方言调查字表》［5］中所有有效音节与遂川话音节全表③的语音数据为基础，对赣语遂川话调类的共时分布和历时演变进行考察。分析过程大都由程序集中实现，在系统声学数据的支撑下，完成对遂川话声调的共时全貌和古今演变规律的考察，最终用可视化的图表形式呈现研究结果，并以此为依据观察遂川话声调的有关特点。

2. 实验设计

2.1 实验材料与发音人

本次实验的字表主要根据《方言调查字表》［5］和遂川话音节全表编制。去除同音的成分，这两个调查表在音类和音节分布上保持一致，能够涵盖音节层面的所有语音信息。

此次调查共采集了老中青男女共六人的录音数据，六位发音人都是土生土长的江西遂川人，青年发音人虽在外地求学，但口音未受影响；中年和老年发音人未离开过遂川，发音地道、稳定。本文的声学数据主要来自一位中年女性（48 岁）和一位青年女性发音人（25 岁）。其余人的数据作为参考，所反映的规律与两位主要发音人一致。两位主要发音人同时掌握遂川话和普通话，日常交流使用遂川话，口齿清晰，语言表达流利，能够代表遂川话的语音面貌。为证明声调演变规律的准确性，两位发音人采用不同的录音字表，验证在以字表为实验变量的情况下两位发音人的数据所体现的规律是否一致。其中，青年发音人的录音材料来自《方言调查字表》［5］，有效的录音材料共计 3455 个；中年发音人的录音材料来自遂川话音节全表，有效的录音材料共计 1045 个。两个字表所用到的例字数量分别如表 2 和表 3 所示。

表 2 《方言调查字表》各古调类例字数量及占比

	古平	古上	古去	古入	合计	百分比
全清	538	306	356	207	1407	41%
次清	166	95	118	77	456	13%
全浊	377	145	213	113	848	25%
次浊	292	155	185	112	744	21%
合计	1373	701	872	509	3455	100%
百分比	40%	20%	25%	15%	100%	

① 基于笔者 2019 年对遂川话的调查，发音人为吕园生，男，61 岁。

② 去声音节在听感上有明显的断裂，具有不连续特征，语图上表现为基频的中断，因此将去声确定为中折调，用［30 4］表示。

③ 表格由笔者归纳整理，笔者为母语者。

表3 遂川话音节全表古调类例字数量及占比

	古平	古上	古去	古入	合计	百分比
全清	148	122	109	51	430	36%
次清	75	48	58	21	202	17%
全浊	125	49	75	39	288	25%
次浊	96	66	65	35	262	22%
合计	444	285	307	146	1182	100%
百分比	38%	24%	26%	12%	100%	

上述两份字表虽然音节数量有差异，但是，与中古各个调类的比例对应基本一致，可以反映共时声调与古今声调的演变大势。

2.2 实验工具

本文主要使用熊子瑜博士研发的汉语方言字音系统实验研究工具①（2018年版）[16]，对遂川话声调的古今演变及共时分布进行研究。该套研究工具共有“字音录制”“字音标注”“声学数据分析”“字音数据提取”“字音数据展示”和“字表数据展示”六个流程。需要依据脚本要求整理筛选好字表，然后按照顺序依次运行脚本，完成对录音数据的采集、标注、分析和提取等一系列操作，最终结果以分类数据和图表的形式呈现。

2.3 实验方法

实验主要的操作流程如下：

（1）从《方言调查字表》[5]中筛选整理录音字表，剔除一些在遂川话中不常使用的汉字，以保证录音条目的代表性和有效性；

（2）使用xRecorder程序在一间安静的房间中进行录音，尽量减少噪音对采集声学数据的影响；

（3）使用脚本自动生成并检校TextGrid和PitchTier数据，对全部录音材料进行音段切分和标注，对断点、跳点以及非正常截断的音高数据进行校正；

（4）添加声、韵、调、IPA等关联信息到字表数据文件；

（5）根据声调音高数据文件按古调类和古声母清浊提取音高数据并进行均值分析，制作出“古调+古声清浊”分类的音高调型图；

（6）依据古调类来源与今读的共时分布情况输出该方言点古今字音对应关系数据，主要有“古—今”和“今—古”两条路径。

（7）依据古调类的今读类型和今调类的古音来源分析计算古调类的分化系数和合并系数，同时为了进一步了解古调类的分化情况，还将各个古调类的合并系数两两比较，较为全面地展现遂川话古调类的今读分合情况。

汉语方言声调的演变主要根据古声母的清浊所决定的古声调类型作为观察线索。对赣语而言，声调演变还涉及共时层面声母送气与否等再分调的问题。本文以赣语遂川话全部共时音节声学的实验数据为出发点，以汉字的古声调类型为分类的主要依据，同时兼顾声母送气与否等因素，分析各类例字的实际音高情况，在此基础上考察、分析古声调在遂川话中的分化与合并情况。

3. 系统实验所反映的遂川话声调的共时面貌和古今对应关系

3.1 古声调均值音高调型图

我们将两个字表的语音信息作系统处理，在使用者标注并校检完相应的声学数据后根据相关指令自行对提取出的音高数据进行均值分析，并作出“古调+古声清浊”分类的音高调型图。图1—图8是该脚本根据两套不同的字表制作生成的遂川话各古调类的音高调型图。

① 该套工具可在公众号“语音学堂”获取。

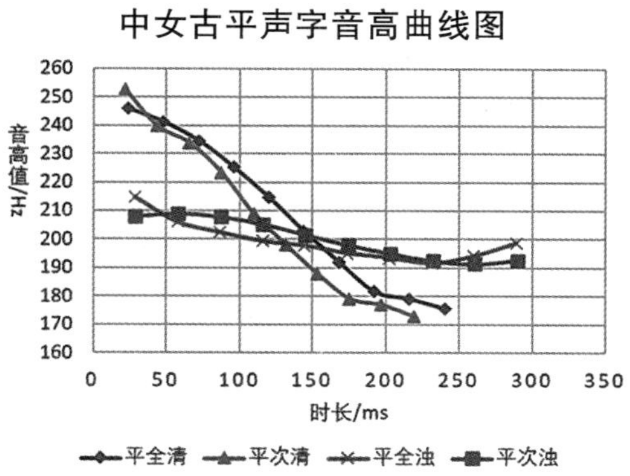

图1　中年古平声音高曲线图

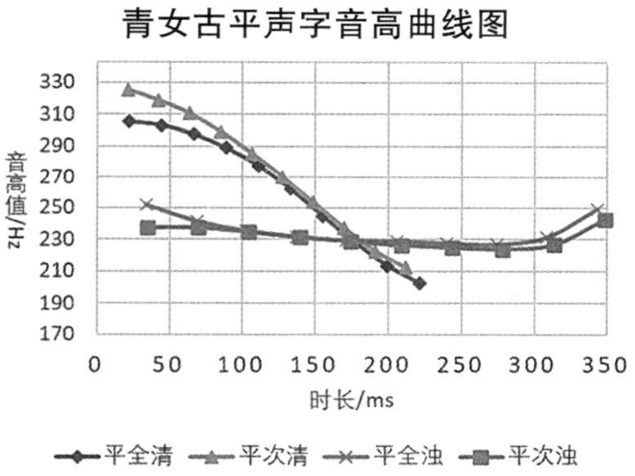

图2　青年古平声音高曲线图

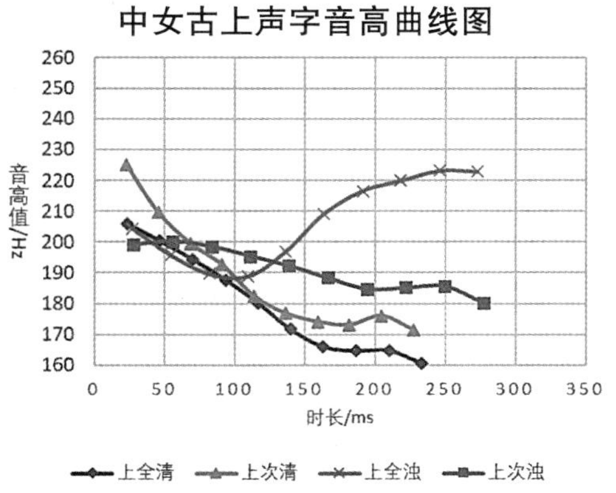

图3　中年古上声音高曲线图

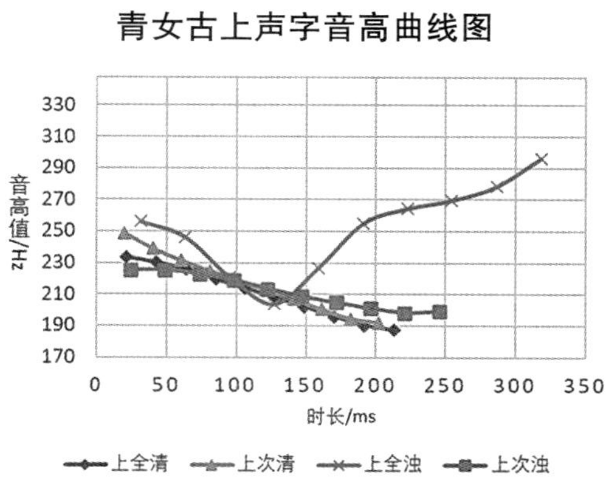

图4　青年古上声音高曲线图

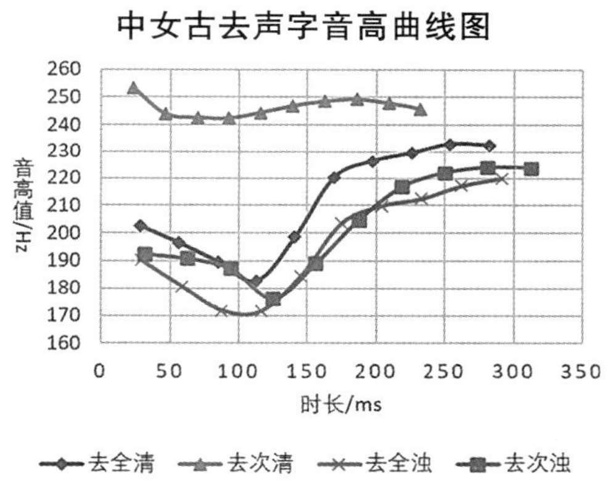

图5　中年古去声音高曲线图

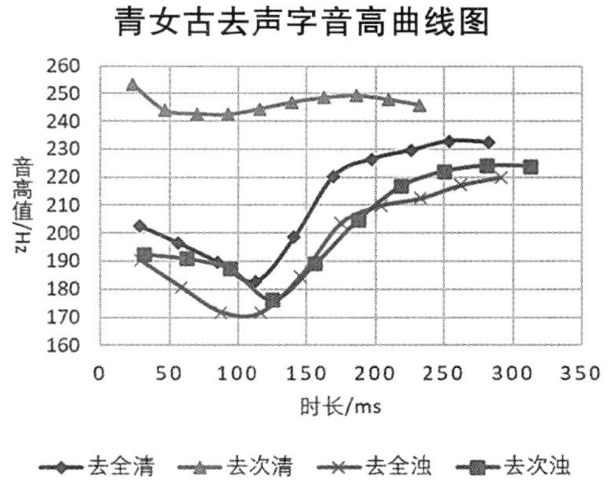

图6　青年古去声音高曲线图

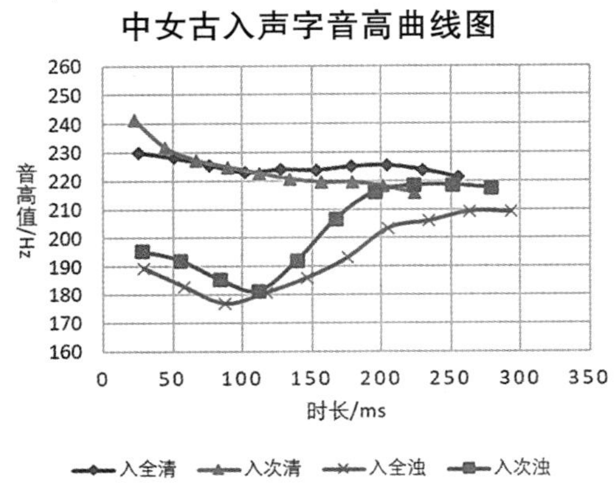

图7 中年古入声音高曲线图

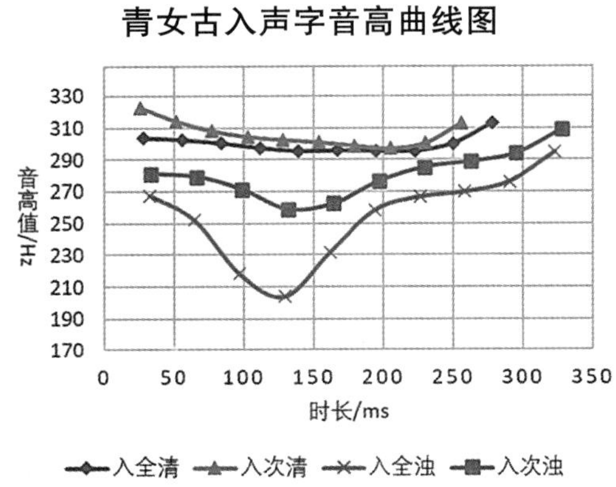

图8 青年古入声音高曲线图

观察两位发音人的音高曲线，可以看到两位发音人之间存在一定的音域差异，中年女性的音高在160—260Hz，而青年女性在170—330Hz，但这是由个人音域差异造成，并不影响声调的类型。即使在将发音人和字表同时视作实验变量的情况下，两次实验得出的音高模式也是一致的。根据图中的音高曲线，我们观察到如下现象：

（1）古平声字主要表现为两种调型：全清和次清是下降调型，全浊和次浊为中平调型；

（2）古上声表现为两种调型：全浊上为先降后升的曲折调型，前半段短而促，后半段低而缓升，非全浊上为中降调型；

（3）古去声表现为两种调型：古次清去声为高平调型，非古清去声呈先降后升的曲折调型；

（4）古入声主要表现为两种调型：全清和次清保持一致，为高平调型，全浊和次浊保持一致，为先降后升的曲折调型；虽然两位发音人次浊入音高曲线的曲折度不一样，但并不影响调类的基本特征，出现这种现象是由于次浊入有曲折调和高平调两种演变倾向，在以古调类为划分依据时中和了两种调型的特征。

3.2 古今调类对应关系

想要全面地展示遂川话的古今调类对应情况，就要从两种研究路径出发：一是以古调类为切入点，观察古调类的今读类型，探究其历时演变情况；二是从今调类出发，考察今调类的古调来源。为了进一步考察遂川话古调类分化和合并情况，了解古调类在演变过程中呈现出的离散性和聚合性，我们基于方言字表数据，通过汉语方言字音研究系统工具测算各个古音成分的分化系数和综合合并系数（具体计算方法请参考［17］）。

分化系数指的是古调类分化到不同调类的占比，用来说明古调类的分化程度，分化系数越大，也就意味着分化程度越高，分化到不同调类的数量就越多，反之则越少。合并系数指的是古调类之间发生合并的占比，用来说明古调类的合并程度，合并系数越大，合并的古调类就越多，反之则越少。除此之外，作为古调类分化系数的补充，我们还将古调类中任意两个调类组成一组对比对进行古音系数的两两比较，形成256组对比数据。

3.2.1 古调类的今读类型

表4是发音人古今数据对应关系。从表4可以看出，尽管主要分化路径的具体比值有所区别，但两位发音人在古调类今读的最主要类型上依然保持一致，这说明声调演化的规律是一致的。结合表中数据，我们将遂川话声调演化的主要规律总结如下：

（1）全清次清的古平声字今归“阴平”；

表4 遂川话古调类对应情况（中青年）

古音	主要今音类型	最主要类型	青年最大比	中年最大比
平次清	阴平；阳平；	阴平	92%	92%
平次浊	阳平；阴平；	阳平	91%	82%
平全清	阴平；	阴平	97%	93%
平全浊	阳平；阴平；	阳平	93%	89%
上次清	阴上；	阴上	89%	90%
上次浊	阴上；阳上；	阴上	86%	71%
上全清	阴上；	阴上	93%	96%
上全浊	去声；阳上；入声；阴上；	去声	43%	43%
去次清	入声；	入声	91%	93%
去次浊	去声；入声；	去声	72%	72%
去全清	去声；入声；阴平；	去声	63%	57%
去全浊	去声；入声；	去声	64%	77%
入次清	入声；阴平；	入声	78%	75%
入次浊	入声；去声；阴平；	入声	63%	42%
入全清	入声；阴平；	入声	79%	80%
入全浊	去声；入声；阳平；	去声	44%	68%

（2）全浊次浊的古平声字今归“阳平”；

（3）全浊的古上声字43%归“去声”，26%—37%归“阳上”；

（4）非全浊的古上声字今归“阴上”；

（5）古去声字和古入声字相混，古去声中有34%—36%的字归到入声，古入声中有14%—29%的字归为去声。

从古调类今读的调类分布来看，古平声符合“平分阴阳”的规律，按古声母清浊来分派调类，全清次清归阴调，全浊次浊归阳调。古上声中全浊上的主要演化为去声，符合“浊上归去”的规律，其次演化为阳上，这在赣方言吉茶片中是较为少见的。古次浊上随清上，今都归为阴上，路径较为统一。古去声的分化路径主要有两种，古全清去、古全浊去和古次浊去依然保留去声调，但次清去则主要演变为入声调，这就与古全清去的演化调类——去声区别开来。古入声最主要的演化路径为去声和入声，除全浊入归并到去声之外，其余的古全清入、古次清入、古次浊入则保留入声调。上述结论可从图9所示的分化系数中得到直观的观察。该系数由脚本生成。

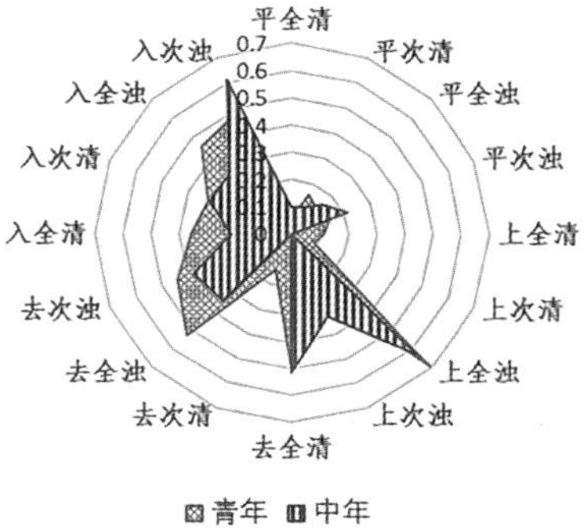

图9 遂川话古调类分化系数（中青年）

由图9可知，古平声的分化系数在所有调类中最低，在0.05—0.213。这说明古平声在遂川话中的分化程度最低，演变成的今调类在分布上较为集中。

古上声的分化系数也较为规律，除全浊上在0.6—0.7外，其余的全清上、次清上和次浊上的分化系数都远远低于全浊上，保持在0—0.35这一低区间内，分化程度较低。而古全浊上的调类分化较复杂，主要有去声、阳上、入声和阴上四种分化路径，而作为最主要今读类型的去声也只占例字总数的不到一半，这可以验证古全浊上在遂川话中的分化程度较高这一结论。

同样，古去声在调类分化程度中也呈现出内部差异。从图9中可以看出，次清去是古去声中分化系数最低，即分化程度最低的一类，中年发音人的分化系数甚至接近于0，这就意味着次清去今读调类的分化较为集中，主要演变为入声，例字数量占比都在90%以上。其余的全清去、全浊去和次浊去分化系数相差不大,在0.35—0.5左右,相对于次清去来说,分化路径更为复杂。

而古入声中分化系数最高的是次浊入,两位发音人的系数都保持在0.5—0.6,这在遂川话整个调类分化系统中都是较高的。这意味着古次浊入今读调类分布较为分散。其主要分化路径为去声和入声,中年发音人的数据中演变为去、入两声的数量相当,因此在分化程度上来说古次浊入较高。其余几类全清入、次清入和全浊入的分化系数在0.2—0.45,分化程度适中,主要还是去声和入声两条途径。

3.2.2 今调类的古音来源

如果说古声调的古今对应是以古调类为切入点考察声调分化途径的话,那今调类的今古对应便是从今读调类出发回溯过去,考察今调类的古音来源。

表5 遂川话今调类来源情况(中青年)

古音	主要古音类型	最主要类型	青年最大比	中年最大比
阴平	平全清;平次清;入全清;	平全清	66%	60%
阳平	平全浊;平次浊;入全浊;	平全浊	52%	56%
阴上	上全清;上次浊;上次清;上全浊;	上全清	49%	50%
阳上	上全浊;上次浊;	上全浊	33%	24%
去声	去全清;去全浊;去次浊;	去全清	34%	28%
入声	入全清;去全清;去次清;入次浊;入次清;	入全清	34%	28%

表5是遂川话今调类的古音来源情况。综合图5中两位发音人的数据,观察遂川话今调类的古调来源分布,我们可以得出如下结论:

(1)阴平的古调来源主要是古全清平和古次清平;

(2)阳平的古调来源主要是古全浊平和古次浊平;

(3)阴上的古调来源主要是古全清上、古次清上和古次浊上;

(4)阳上的古调来源主要是古全浊上和古次浊上;

(5)去声的古调来源主要是除次清去以外的古去声,其中又以全清去最多;

(6)入声的古调来源主要是古全清入、全清去和古次清去。

从今调类古音来源的调类分布来看,阴平、阳平、阴上和阳上都主要来源于相应的清声母或浊声母,符合古声清浊对应调类的规律——阴调源自古全清次清,阳调源自古全浊次浊。而去声由于不分阴阳,只有一个调类,大部分今读为去声的调类都来源于古去声调,而且其古音来源不受古声母清浊的影响。同时,今去声的古音来源还包括古全浊上和古浊入,但古全浊上在今读为去声的古调类中占比并不高,仅占6%—9%,所以在遂川话中,今去声最主要的古音来源不是古全浊上,而是除古次清去以外的古去声。入声最主要的古调类来源是古入声和古去声,这两类古调类大概占了入声来源的92%—93%左右。

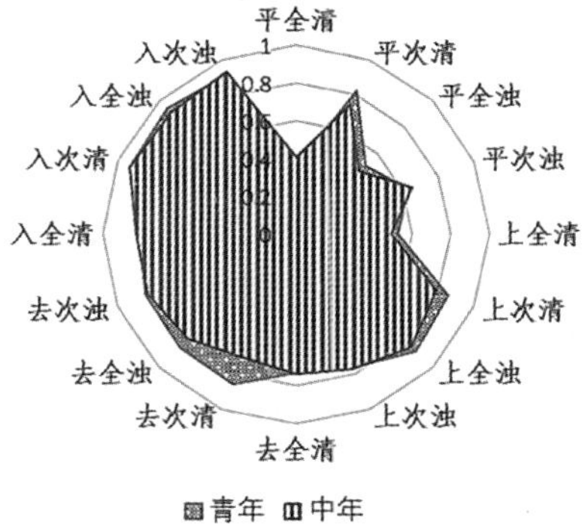

图10 中青年古调类合并系数

从两位发音人最主要今读调类古音来源所占的比例来看,占比最高的为阴平,大概占总数的60%左右，最低的为阳上，其次是去声和入声，三者相差无几，仅占30%左右。这也就意味着，今读为阴平的古调类来源较为简单，而阳上、去声和入声的古调类来源较复杂。

图10是两位发音人的古调类合并系数。从图中可以看出，相对于分化系数，合并系数在各个调类中分配得较为平均。除了全清平、全浊平、次浊平和全清上的系数在0.5左右之外，其余古调类型都在0.8上下浮动，保持在一个较高的水平。这意味着除上述四种古调类型较少与其他古调类发生合并，演变为同一类今读调类之外，其余几类的演化路径在调类之间更为趋同，与不同古调类有着相同的今读类型，即与这些古调类发生了合并。

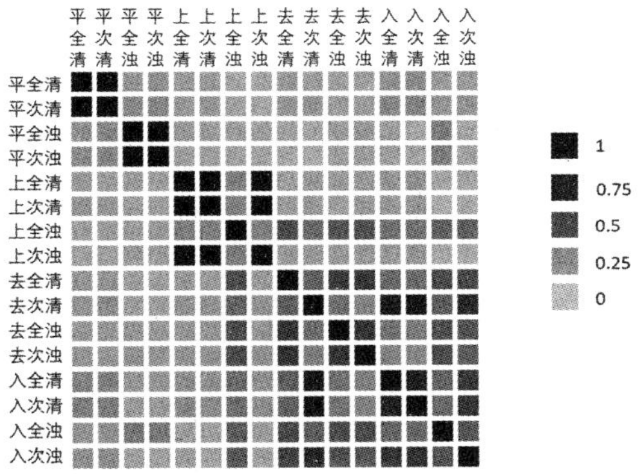

图11 青年古调类两两合并系数图

图11是古调类的两两合并系数图，共有16×16个小方格，以古调类和古声母清浊作为类别划分的标准，对应的方格代表的古调类作为本次两两对比的前后对比量，如第一行第二个方格代表全清平—次清平的合并系数，其他依此类推。每个方格的颜色代表合并系数的大小，颜色深，则合并系数大，两个古调类的合并程度就越高，反之则越低。

依据图11，我们可以观察到任意两个调类之间合并的情况。通过整理，归纳出以下几组合并程度较高（大于0.5）的调类组，所反映的规律与上述古调演变的语言事实相对应：

（1）全清平、次清平——归阴平

（2）全浊平、次浊平——归阳平

（3）全清上、次清上、次浊上——归阴上

（4）全浊上——归阳上

（4）全浊去、全清去、次浊去——归去声

（5）次清去、全清入、次清入、次浊入——归入声

4. 遂川话声调对应关系的主要特点

基于上述由汉语方言字音系统研究工具生成的各类关于遂川话古音演变的数据和图表，我们对遂川话古今声调演变的全貌有了基本的了解，可以概括出遂川话古调演变的规律，现归纳如图12。

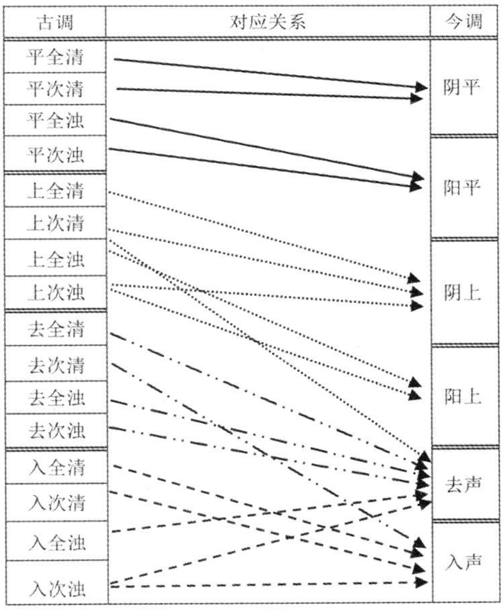

图12 遂川话古今声调对应关系

遂川话古平声符合按清浊分阴阳的规律，次浊上随清上归入阴上，全浊上归去声，这与赣语声调的主要演化趋势相符。但是遂川话中的声调演变也存在一些个性特征，如全浊上和部分次浊上保留了阳上调；清去按送气与否分成两个调类，次清归入声，全清与浊去仍为去声；入声中清

浊的演化路径有区别，全浊入与部分次浊入归去声，剩下的清入与部分次浊入仍为入声。

陈昌仪［4］认为赣语分区参考的声调演变标准主要为：（1）声母送气与否是否影响调类的分化；（2）全浊上声的分化；（3）去声的分化；（4）入声的分化及其调型。因此，本文从如上几个参考标准入手，讨论遂川话声调演变规律的特点。

首先，关于送气分调的情况。从本文的声调曲线和有关论述中可以看出，遂川话的古次清去与古全清去分化路径存在差异：古次清去归了入声，古全清去仍保留去声调。可见，遂川话调类的分化受到今声母送气与否的制约，即“送气分调”，最早是赵元任先生［19］调查吴语时发现的，后来不断有材料证明这一特征还广泛存在于赣语、湘语和平话中［12］。关于赣语遂川话的送气分调，先前也有学者注意到这一现象，陈昌仪［4］在《赣方言概要》中归纳吉茶片调类演变规律时提到：“（古今调类的演变），遂川县城受古清浊、今声母送气不送气制约”。刘纶鑫［8］归纳遂川话音系时也曾将阴去按声母送气与否一分为二。除此之外，昌梅香［2］、卢涌和占升平［9］还对遂川话的送气分调特征进行专文论述，归纳整理了遂川话送气分调的特点与形成原因。如在调类上只发生在古清去调；在调值上是次清调高而全清调低，与其他方言点不同；在发生的时间层次上是发生在浊上变去之前而非之后；在参与的声类上除了塞音、塞擦音之外还有部分擦音、边音、鼻音以及零声母字。送气分调是赣语调类分化的典型手段，但在不同方言点发展得并不平衡，如吉茶片中有送气分调现象的并不多，遂川是其中之一，但与遂川在地理位置上连成一片的万安、泰和就并未出现这一现象，这可能是内外因素综合导致的结果。送气分调的例字如下：

变/piẽn˧˩˦/ —— 片/pʰiẽn˥/

叫/tɕiɔ˧˩˦/—— 俏/tɕʰiɔ˥/

揍/tsɤ˧˩˦/ —— 凑/tsʰɤ˥/

卦/kua˧˩˦/ —— 胯/kʰua˥/

其次，古全浊上在遂川话中的分化较为复杂。结合上文的古今对应关系，可知古全浊上主要有四条演化路径——去声、阳上、入声和阴上，其中又以去声（43%）和阳上（25%—37%）占比最高。也就是说，遂川话的古全浊上一部分归入到了去声，一部分保留阳上调。古全浊上演变为去声符合“浊上归去”的语音演变规律，但是部分古全浊上归到了别的调类，这就使得遂川话古全浊上的演变规律较之其他调类更为复杂。在赣语吉茶片中，上声一般不分阴阳，大多数方言点阳上调并不独立，只有莲花、安福几个方言点存在上声调［3］。但是依据本文的实验结果，遂川话古全浊上中有26%—37%的例字读为阳上调，这与阴上调区别明显，理应单独划分为阳上调。而关于赣语古浊上的分派情况，王福堂［11］、李如龙和张双庆［7］、谢留文［13］、刘纶鑫［8］等学者都认为赣方言普遍存在浊上归阴去的情况。刘纶鑫［8］叙述吉茶片语音特征时提到“万安、永新、井冈山、吉水、永丰部分浊上字归阴平”，但在遂川话音系说明中又特别注明“全浊上字为阳上”，可见遂川话古全浊上的演变规律是较吉茶片大部分方言点不同的，遂川话的古浊上并不归阴平，没有受到临近客家话的影响［10］。昌梅香［3］也提出：“吉安赣方言中的古全浊上除了归到去声之外，并不是全部归到阴平，而是多方向地、无规律地归到各个调类”，但入声除外。她调查到的遂川话古全浊上的归并路径除去声外主要有三类：上声、变调和阴平，这与本文数据存在差异，上声归阴平的例子尚不能获得数据支撑，仅青年有1个例字（“辫”）读为阴平，不及总数的1%，因此，去声（43%）和阳上（25%—37%）才是遂川话古全浊上最主要的演化路径而非阴平。以下是古全浊上分别演化为去声和阳上的例字：

古全浊上归去声：道/t^{h}ɔ˨˩˦/　　像/ɕiɔŋ˨˩˦/

造/ts^{h}ɔ˨˩˦/　　倍/p^{h}e˨˩˦/

古全浊上归阳上：厚/hɤ˦˥/　　坐/ts^{h}o˦˥/

件/tɕ^{h}iε̃n˦˥/　　近/tɕ^{n}ĩn˦˥/

第三，去声演化问题。去声是否分阴阳也是赣方言声调的一个重要特征。吉茶片去声不分阴阳有两种情况，一是清去归阳平，如泰和、万安、永丰等地；二是去声只有一个调类，如永新、井冈山、新干等地［2］。如果从地理位置对这一特征进行划分的话，刘纶鑫［8］、昌梅香［3］认为“河西去声不分阴阳，河东去声多分阴阳”，熊燕［15］以具体的市县为例对这一特征进行了补充说明：“客赣方言在平江、奉新、万载、新余、吉安、上犹、于都、全南、瓮源、青平一线及此线以东为分阴阳去的方言，此线以西为不分阴阳去的方言”，而遂川位于此线以西，属于去声不分阴阳的一类。但陈昌仪［4］、谢留文［13］提出了不同的观点，他们认为遂川话的去声分了阴阳。根据本文的古今调类对应数据显示，遂川话古去声的演化路径主要有两类：古次清去与古清入为一类，今归为入声调，古全清去和浊去为一类，仍保留去声调。因此，以古音来源为参考标准的话，遂川话的去声只有一个调类，不分阴阳，符合“河西去声不分阴阳，河东去声多分阴阳”的规律。而关于赣语吉茶片古去声的分派，阴去与阳平合流是一个普遍趋势，如峡江、吉水、永丰、泰和、万安都是属于这种类型。但陈昌仪［4］提到，遂川话古清去声母今读入声，与浊声母字不同。观察本次实验的古今调类对应数据，古清去几乎没有演变为阳平的例子，仅青年发音人的古清去中有0.6%的字读为阳平，大部分字都归入到去声或入声，这明显不足以支撑“阴去与阳平合流”这一结论。因此，我们可以确定，遂川话古清去的演化路径与吉茶片其他方言点不同，大多数方言点阴去归阳平，而遂川话的阴去有两条演化路径，全清归去声，次清归入声。以下分别为全清去与次清去演化的例字：

全清去归去声：变/piε̃n˨˩˦/　　到/tɔ˨˩˦/

故/ku˨˩˦/　　架/ka˨˩˦/

次清去归入声：太/t^{h}æ˥/　　菜/ts^{h}uε˥/

怕/p^{h}a˥/　　抗/k^{h}ɔŋ˥/

第四，古入声演化的特色。入声的有无也是各方言点一个重要的语音特征。关于赣语吉茶片入声的情况，颜森［18］、陈昌仪［4］、刘纶鑫［8］、谢留文［13］等学者都在各自的著述中明确表示，吉茶片没有入声或大多数方言点没有入声，在这一点上已经达成了共识。但同时他们也都提出，还有少部分市县是存在入声的，刘纶鑫［8］、谢留文［13］注意到万安和永丰有入声调，但无入声韵。也有学者对遂川话进行过调查但在入声有无的问题上存在分歧。刘纶鑫［8］、谢留文［13］认为遂川话没有入声，古入声已经归入去声，但颜森［18］、陈昌仪［4］、辛世彪［14］、昌梅香［3］提出遂川有一个入声调，阴阳入不合并，且保留入声韵尾-ʔ。陈昌仪［4］在其著作中提到遂川话“古入声按清和全浊一分为二，其中之一仍读入声，另一部分则读去声”，在肯定遂川话有入声的同时明确了古入声的分派途径。那遂川话是否存在入声呢？这还要从古入声的演化途径入手。孙宜志［10］将遂川划分到清声母入声字与阴平合流、浊声母入声字与阳平合流一类，但是谢留文［13］、陈昌仪［4］则认为遂川话古全浊入今读去声，古清声母字与其他方言点不同，并不读阴平，而读去声或保留入声调。从上文古今调类对应数据可知，遂川话古入声的今读类型中占比最大的是去声和入声，仅有少部分例字读阴平，最大占比不超过1%。所以本文认为，在遂川话中，古浊入不与阳平合流，古清入不与古阴平合流，与陈昌仪［4］、谢留文［13］的观点一致。在赣语中次浊入的分化路径一直是学界讨论的焦点，辛世彪［14］、孙宜志［10］、李如龙［7］认为赣语的古次浊入两分，一部分跟清入走，一部分跟浊入走。这和客家话表现出一定的共性，客赣方言共同的语言特点之一是：次浊声母入声字有两个走向，或与清声母同调，或与全浊声母字同调。相对而言，客方言多数跟全浊走，赣方言多数跟清声母字走[7]。根据本文得出的数据，可以看到，古次浊入的演化的确较为复杂。在古今调类对应数据中，古次浊入在中年发音人处的演化情况是去声和入声各占总数的42%，在青年发音人处是有63%演化为入声，29%演化为去声。可见，去声作为古次浊入的第二演化路径是不可忽视的。依据青年人的发音数据可以印证李如龙先生的观点。作为赣语的遂川话，古次浊入主要还是与清声母字同调，归入声，其次和全浊声母字一起，归入去声，现举几个例子如下：

次浊入归入声：六/tio˥/　药/io˥/

密/miɛ˥/　纳/na˥/

次浊入归去声：灭/miɛ˧˩˥/　落/lo˧˩˥/

叶/iɛ˧˩˥/　玉/y˧˩˥/

5. 结语

本文在充分记录描写的基础上，依据熊子瑜博士研发的汉语方言字音系统实验研究工具对赣语遂川话声调的共时面貌和古今演变进行探讨，希望通过相对系统的实验研究，对方言声调研究中有疑问的现象进行实验分析。研究的结论在某种程度上也支持经典的方言研究的成果。就遂川话而言，在今调类的共时分布上，遂川话共有六个调类，平上各分阴阳，去入不分阴阳，区别于吉茶片的阳上调不独立且无入声调。在古调类的历时演变上，遂川话的上去入三声的演变规律都与赣语吉茶片其他方言点不同。遂川话的古全浊上除演变为去声外，还保留阳上调，而吉茶片古浊上普遍归阴平；古清去声与送气分调，在吉茶片中较为少见；去入两调互相混合，古次清去读入声，古全浊入和部分次浊入读去声，剩下的保留本调。此外，从方法论的角度来说，本文以遂川话的研究实例证明，这套工具能系统地观察方言中声调几乎所有可能出现的情况，方便全面地归纳和总结方言声调的演变规律，今后也可以用来对不同方言中的各种现象作较为系统、深入的探讨。

6. 致谢

本研究得到以下基金项目的支持：国家社科基金重大项目“汉语方言学大型辞书编纂的理论研究与数字化建设”（13&ZD135）；国家社科基金一般项目“广东粤、闽、客方言韵律特征研究”（18BYY187）。

参考文献

[1] Boersma，P. Weenink，D. 1992 – 2022. Praat：Doing phonetics by computer [Computer program]. Version 6.2.06.，retrieved 23 January 2022 from https：//www.praat.org.
[2] 昌梅香（2012）赣语遂川方言的送气分调，《方言》第 4 期，310—313 页。
[3] 昌梅香（2007）《吉安赣方言语音研究》，博士学位论文。
[4] 陈昌仪（1991）《赣方言概要》，江西教育出版社。
[5] 中国社会科学院语言研究所（2004）《方言调查字表》，商务印书馆。
[6] 江西省地方志编纂委员会（2005）《江西省方言志》，方志出版社。
[7] 李如龙、张双庆（1992）《客赣方言调查报告》，厦门大学出版社。
[8] 刘纶鑫（1999）《客赣方言比较研究》，中国社会科学出版社。
[9] 卢涌、占升平（2015）江西遂川方言声调的送气分化，《黔南民族师范学院学报》第 6 期，32—38 页。
[10] 孙宜志、陈昌仪、徐阳春（2001）江西赣方言语音的特点，《南昌大学学报（人文社会科学版）》第 4 期，122—127 页。
[11] 王福堂（1998）关于客家话和赣方言的分合问题，《方言》第 1 期，14—19 页。
[12] 徐越（2013）汉语方言中的气流分调现象，《中国语文》第 3 期，265—272 页。
[13] 谢留文（2006）赣语的分区（稿），《方言》第 3 期，264—271 页。
[14] 辛世彪（1999）赣方言声调的演变类型，《暨南学报（哲学社会科学）》第 3 期，17—28 页。
[15] 熊燕（2015）《客赣方言语音系统的历史层次》，世界图书出版公司。

[16] 熊子瑜（2018）汉语方言字音系统实验研究工具，https://pan.baidu.com/s/1lmiRJlAaHt5L1bYxE5sggg（提取密码为：8v5c）
[17] 熊子瑜：《基于汉语方言字音系统实验研究工具的合肥与北京话声母系统对比分析》，《中国语音学报》2021年第15辑，24—42页。
[18] 颜 森（1986）江西方言的分区（稿），《方言》第1期，19—38页。
[19] 赵元任（2011）《现代吴语研究》，商务印书馆。
[20] 中国社会科学院语言研究所、中国社会科学院民族学与人类学研究所、香港城市大学语言资讯科学研究中心（2012）《中国语言地图集（第2版）》，商务印书馆。

曾 玲 暨南大学文学院，硕士。主要研究领域为方言学、实验语音学。
Email：zengling20@163.com
余俊毅 暨南大学文学院，硕士。主要研究领域为方言学、实验语音学。
Email：yjy2021jnu@foxmail.com
刘新中 暨南大学文学院，博士，教授。主要研究领域为方言学、实验语音学。
Email：liuxinzhongjn@163.com

声调信息在单词视觉识别中的作用

李梦锐　吴建设　邱寅晨　郎建国

摘　要　在汉语词汇识别中，超音段信息所起的作用一直存有争议，且当前关于超音段信息的研究集中于听觉范式下单个词汇或语句研究，较少涉及视觉识别以及复合词的加工。针对这一现象，本研究通过控制首、尾字，基于两个实验探究视觉范式下超音段信息在汉语复合词识别与语义整合加工中的作用。实验采用掩蔽启动范式，2（音段）×2（声调）设计，共 4 个条件：音段声调完全匹配（S+T+）、音段匹配声调不匹配（S+T-）、声调匹配音段不匹配（S-T+）、音段声调完全不匹配（S-T-）。实验 1 结果显示在首字启动条件下，与声调匹配音段不匹配（S-T+）条件相比，被试在完全匹配（S+T+）条件下反应显著更快；与完全不匹配（S-T-）条件相比，被试在声调匹配音段不匹配（S-T+）条件下反应显著更慢，表明声调匹配信息在汉语复合词视觉识别中起抑制作用。实验 2 结果显示在尾字条件下，声调和音段加工没有发现任何显著差异，表明被试对声调和音段信息两者都不敏感。实验 1 和实验 2 表明声调信息参与了汉语复合词的视觉识别过程，且发挥比音段更为重要的作用；但这一作用更多体现于单词识别阶段，无论处于首字或尾字位置，声调信息的影响较为类似。

关键词　超音段信息，单词视觉识别，汉语复合词

The Role of Tonal Information in Visual Word Recognition

LI Mengrui　WU Jianshe　QIU Yinchen　LANG Jianguo

Abstract The role of suprasegmental information in Chinese word recognition has been controversial. Also the current research mainly focuses on the suprasegmental information processing within a single word or sentence in an auditory paradigm; little has been done on the visual recognition of compounds. Two experiments were conducted in this study to explore the role of suprasegmental information in the visual recognition and semantic integration of Chinese disyllabic compounds by controlling the initial and final characters. A masking priming paradigm and 2 (segment) ×2 (tone) design were adopted, leading to the following four conditions with the selected target word in disyllabic compounds being replaced with segment and tone matching (S+T+), segment mismatching but tone matching (S+T-), segment mismatching but tone matching (S-T+), and segment and tone completely mismatching (S-T-). Experiment 1 showed that the response for completely matching (S+T+) condition was significantly faster than tone matching but segment mismatching (S-T+) condition; meanwhile, the response for tone matching but segment mismatching (S-T+) condition was significantly slower than segment and tone completely mismatching (S-T-) condition, suggesting that tone information played an inhibitory role in visual recognition of Chinese compounds under the condition of initial word priming. However, no significant difference was observed in Experiment 2, suggesting that subjects were not sensitive to both tone and segment information under the condition of final word priming. Together, the results of both experiments indicated that tonal information was not only engaged in visual recognition of Chinese compounds, but also played a more important role than segment, a role which was mainly reflected in the stage of word recognition, regardless of whether it was located in the initial or final position of a compound.

Keywords Suprasegmental information, Visual word recognition, Chinese disyllabic compounds

1. 引言

与印欧语言不同，汉语是一门典型的声调语言，在普通话中包含四种声调：阴平、阳平、上声和去声。而汉语词汇中包含丰富的相同音节结构的汉字，而声调便是区分这些同音字的关键之一［22］。

为了揭示声调这类超音段信息在汉语单词识别过程中的作用，近十几年来，语言学家们对其进行了多维度、多层次的分析与研究［1，29］。总体来看，学者们对于声调信息是否参与单词识别过程仍持不同观点。部分研究认为，在汉语单词识别过程中，声调和音段（即声母韵母）信息被并行加工，且两者处于同等重要的地位［8，14，19，31］。而另外一些研究则认为，音段信息在单词听觉识别过程中更重要或最先被加工［6，22，28，31］。但也有少数研究认为声调信息在单词识别过程中更为重要［4，11，27］。

上述研究结果的不一致可能主要与研究者所采用的刺激呈现方式与实验任务相关。从实验范式来看，声调信息对听觉通道存在显而易见的依赖性，因而较为可能的是，与听觉实验、跨通道实验相比，视觉实验可能更容易受实验材料、实验任务的影响，从而影响研究结果；而从实验任务来看，与多数研究所采用的“词汇判断任务”不同，上述部分研究采取了“同音字判断任务”“Stroop 任务”。这明显强化了任务的冲突性，由此声调信息不仅可能需要参与单词的识别过程，还可能需要参与与冲突解决相关的整合与再分析过程。有鉴于此，本研究将基于视觉实验，采用与声调信息、音段信息非直接相关的实验任务，借助汉语复合词中首/尾共享汉字更好地控制了识别过程与再分析过程之间的可能互动，借此初步探讨了声调与音段信息在汉语单词视觉识别过程中的可能作用。

现有研究表明，在听觉实验下，尽管声母声调双匹配条件、韵母声调双匹配条件在不同研究结果中并不一致，但声调匹配条件总体上会出现不同程度的抑制效应，且一般会比音段匹配条件的启动效应更小。Sereno 等人［22］基于汉语单词判断任务与听觉启动实验（ISI = 250ms）在实验 1 中发现，完全匹配条件（如：ru4 – ru4）、音段匹配条件（如：ru3 – ru4）都产生了不同程度的启动效应，但声调匹配条件（如：sha4 – ru4）却没有。而在实验 2 中，声母声调双匹配条件（如：/re4/ – /ru4/）的反应时最长、错误率最高，而韵母声调双匹配条件（如：/pu4/ – /ru4/）次之，随后才是完全不匹配条件、完全匹配条件。而 Yip［28］基于粤语命名任务与听觉启动实验（ISI = 250 ms）发现，与完全无关条件相比，声母声调双匹配条件（如：chi2 – cho2）产生了抑制效应，但韵母声调双匹配条件（如：do2 – cho2）、音段匹配条件（如：cho1 – cho2）却产生了促进效应。而在 ERP 研究中，Zhao 等人［31］基于汉语“图片—听觉汉字呈现—图片”跨通道匹配任务发现，与完全匹配条件（如：“鼻” – bi2 – “耳”）相比，仅仅韵母声调双匹配条件（如：“鼻” – li2 – “耳”）、完全不匹配条件在 N400 成分（300—500ms）上显著更负（右侧前部/后部脑区），声母声调双匹配条件以及音段匹配条件与之相比却没有出现显著差异。

基于双字复合词的研究同样发现音段匹配条件更容易出现启动效应。Zhou 等人［33］采用跨通道语义启动范式，设置启动项为双字假词，控制条件下启动项与目标项语义无关（如：**护蝶**—后悔），对比条件下启动项两字音段与目标项的一个语义关联真词相同，并分以下情况：首字假词（即用近音字替换掉语义关联真词的首字）、尾字相同条件下，与控制条件相比，音段匹配且声调高相似条件（如：**椅**/yi3/憾—后悔）引发了启动效应，音段匹配且声调低相似条件（如：**易**/yi4/憾—后悔）则没有；而在首字相同、尾字假词（即用近音字替换掉语义关联真词的尾字）条件下，与控制条件（如：健**权**—后悔）相比，音段匹配且声调高相似条件（如：辛**寝**/qin3/—懒惰）、音段匹配且声调低相似条件（如：辛**沁**/qin4/—后悔）都引发了启动效应。与之类似，Cutler 等人［1］采用听觉实验，要求被试对所听到粤语双字目标词进行真假词判断。研究发现，在首字相同、尾字假字条件下，完全不匹配条件在反应时上最慢，韵母声调双匹配条件（如：bok8 – ji6，“博士”，粤语发音为：bok8 – si6）、声调匹配条件（如：bok8 – jy6）都显著慢于音段匹配条件（如：bok8 – si2），而声母声调双匹配条件（如：bok8 – sy6）加工最快。Liu 等人［11］采用听觉实验，要求被试判断所听到刺激是否为真词（如：**食**物，shi2 – wu4）、成语（如：饥不择**食**）或假词（如：**持**物，chi2 – wu4）、假成语（如：饥不择**持**），却在双字复合词、成语、句子条件下发现音段匹配条件与声母声调双匹配条件、韵母声调双匹配条件之间没有显著差异。而 Zhou 等人［33］则发现在首/尾字都为音段匹配条件（如：先进/“现金”—支票）时，它们与控制条件（如：估计—支票）相比也没有显著差异。

而在视觉实验中，声调匹配不再引起抑制效应，更多会诱发启动效应。但该效应总体上同样弱于音段匹配效应。Wang 等人［24］基于汉语命名任务与不同启动时间（SOA = 57ms、100ms、200ms）、不同启动方式（汉字、拼音）发现，在汉字启动范式下，无论在 57ms、100ms 抑或 200ms 启动时间下，只有语音完全匹配条件（如：**连**—怜）产生了显著启动效应；而在拼音启动范式下，语音完全匹配条件、音段匹配条件（如：**lian4**—怜）在不同启动时间下都出现了启动效应。但声调匹配条件（如：**cheng2**—怜）仅仅在 200ms 启动时间下出现启动效应。Li 等人［9］基于 Stroop 范式，要求被试判断目标字的颜色。除发现 Stroop 效应外，还进而在一致条件（如：“红”/红色字体；“洪”/红色字体）下观察到，颜色字（如：红）、语音完全匹配（如：洪）、音段匹配（如：轰）、声调匹配（如：瓶）条件与控制条件（如：牵）相比都产生了显著启动效应。但声调匹配条件的启动效应最弱。

值得注意的是，同样在视觉实验中，如果采用“同音字判断任务”、“语音相似项匹配任务”或基于 Stroop 范式不一致条件（如：“红”/蓝色字体）的实验任务，则常常会发现音段匹配条件的抑制效应强于声调匹配条件。Li 等人［10］使用长时启动范式与同音字判断任务（实验 1）、拼音与汉字匹配判断任务（实验 2）发现，与控制条件（如：**本/ben3**—市）相比，汉语母语者和汉语二语习得者在音段匹配条件（如：**时/shi2**—市）下显著更慢，而语音完全匹配条件（如：**事/shi4**—市）次之，然后是控制条件，声调匹配条件（如：**掉/diao4**—市）反而显著最快。Malins 等人［14］采用“图片—汉字”跨通道匹配任务（同时呈现四张图片选项，包括目标汉字图片、语音条件图片以及两张无关条件图片，然后呈现听觉刺激）与眼动研究发现，与控制条件相比，被试对音段匹配条件（如：chuang2 – chuang1）、近似完全匹配条件（如：chuang2 – chuan2）的注视时间显著更长，而声调匹配条件与控制条件并无显著差异。而 Winskel 等人［25］基于泰语的结果发现，同为 Stroop 实验，在一致条件下，其研究结果与 Li 等人［9］完全相同；但在不一致条件下，抑制效应由强到弱分别是：颜色字不一致条件（如：/kʰ.ã:w/，“白色”，但以绿色、橙色、灰色字体呈现）、音段匹配条件（如：/kʰà:w/，“新闻”）、声调韵母双匹配条件（如：/hã:w/，“打哈欠”）、声调匹配条件（如：/pʰõ:m/，“细、薄”）。这与一致条件下的启动效应顺序刚好相反。

在句子加工的脑电研究中，音段匹配条件则常常与声调匹配条件（不包括韵母声调双匹配条件）表现相似，会引发 N400 效应或 P600 效应，这表明音段匹配、声调匹配的近音词在句子理解过程中会导致加工困难。Schmidt 等人［21］采用听觉句子实验发现，与语音完全匹配条件（如：xia4 – **dan4**，“下蛋”）相比，被试听到音段匹配（如：xia4 – **dan3**）、声调匹配（如：xia4 – **qian4**）、双重违反（如：xia4 – **qian1**）条件的词都引发了更负的 N400。但仅仅音段匹配、声调匹配会引发更早、更负的波形。Zou 等人［34］基于汉语句子材料与听觉实验，要求被试判断所听到句子是否合理。研究发现音段匹配条件（如：众－肿/**zhong3**/）的错误率显著更高。与完全匹配条件（如：众/**zhong4**/）相比，声母声调双匹配条件（如：众－赚/**zhuan4**/）、双重违反条件（如：众－转/**zhuan3**/）会引发更负的N400。但音段匹配条件、声母声调双匹配条件同时会引发更正的P600，而音段匹配条件的波形较声母声调双匹配条件分别提前50ms出现、结束。但稍有不同的是，Ho 等人［4］基于跨通道范式，先向被试视觉呈现句子（如："我朋友的**家**/**虾**/**价**/**糖**很明亮。"），然后听觉重复呈现相同或相似句子，要求被试判断前后呈现的两个句子是否匹配。研究发现，与基线条件（如：家）相比，韵母声调双匹配条件（如：虾）、音段匹配条件（如：价）和完全不匹配条件（如：糖）在早期N400（300—400ms）、晚期N400（400—500ms）上都更负。而音段匹配条件在上述两个成分上比韵母声调双匹配条件、完全不匹配条件都更负，而韵母声调双匹配条件仅仅比完全不匹配条件更负。

而在口语单词产出音韵研究的综述中，刘帅等人［35］注意到重音信息、声调信息在拼音文字的语言与汉语中可能存在不同的提取、编码以及与音段信息的整合方式，但他们对于声调信息在视觉识别过程中与音段信息的互动则未予关注。

上述研究总体表明，音段匹配条件可能比声调匹配条件更能促进单词的识别。相比视觉单词识别，声调信息与音段信息在听觉单词识别中所发挥的作用更为明显；而相比一般单词判断任务，"同音字/词判断"此类实验任务会增加单词加工的冲突性并进而造成启动效应的反转。而在实验材料为句子时，可能由于实验条件所设计的错误单词导致句子语义不连贯，从而造成该实验条件单词难以与句子完成整合与再分析，因而句子研究中的音段匹配条件、声调匹配条件都常常会产生抑制效应。

鉴于研究范式、实验任务与实验材料都可能影响声调信息加工并进而对单词加工产生影响，对上述因素的严格控制至关重要。本研究选择视觉—掩蔽启动范式（SOA = 47 ms，避免策略性加工），采用与音段信息、声调信息无直接相关的隐性实验任务（食物名称判断任务），分别操纵汉语复合词的首字（实验1：例如，启动字为：**费**/fei4/；目标词为：**废**/fei4/料、**肥**/fei2/料、**木**/mu4/料、**史**/shi3/料）、尾字（实验2：例如，启动字为：圣/sheng4/；目标词为：名**胜**/sheng4/、名**声**/sheng1/、名**著**/zhu4/、名**言**/yan2/），最大程度减少实验条件与首字/尾字在整合过程中可能产生的冲突或干扰信息，试图探索、厘清声调作为超音段信息在汉语单词视觉识别/整合过程中的可能作用。具体研究问题如下：

（1）在单词视觉识别过程中，声调匹配条件与音段匹配条件的各自作用如何？

（2）在首/尾字不同位置上，声调匹配信息的作用是否发生改变？

2. 实验1：首字启动实验

2.1 被试

北京某高校研究生共22人参与本实验（女生20人，平均年龄为23.6岁）。为确保被试对汉字音段与声调信息具有高度敏感性，所有被试的母语为汉语且为北方人，并均获得国家普通话一级乙等或二级甲等证书。所有被试均为右利手，视力或矫正视力正常，无精神病史。参与实验者均获得一定报酬。其中2名被试（女生1人）数据因正确率较低（<0.90）而被剔除。

2.2 研究设计

本实验采取掩蔽启动范式。参考先前研究惯例以及 Zhou 等人［32］、Feldman 等人［2］、Tsang 等人［23］之研究建议，启动词呈现时间定为47 ms。实验采用2（音段）×2（声调）设计，分别构成四种不同匹配条件：音段声调完全匹配（S+T+）、音段匹配声调不匹配（S+T－）、声调匹配音段不匹配（S－T+）、音段声调完全不匹配（S－T－）。为避免音段与声调可能的交互作用，四种不同条件的材料在尾字上完全相同。

2.3 实验材料

本实验目标词均为名词，且未重复。实验材料在整词词频、单字字频、单字与整词笔画上都进行了匹配（$ps > 0.05$），并确保每组目标词首字或尾字相同。由于材料编制困难，本实验因而无法对声调调型、语义相似度进行控制。最终每组实验条件选取32组试次，四种条件共128个双字复合词作为目标词。为了保证被试（北方人）对实验材料确实具有极好的区分度，另有20名来自中国北方的被试分别就启动字—目标词首字在音段或声调上是否相同进行评定（“是/否”）（详见表1、附录1）。

表1　首字实验材料举例及特征信息

特征	S＋T＋	S＋T－	S－T＋	S－T＋	启动词
	废料	肥料	木料	史料	费
整词词频	3.53（3.45）	3.59（3.48）	3.64（3.52）	3.87（3.47）	/
首字字频	5.66（5.89）	5.79（5.89）	5.72（5.79）	5.61（5.59）	5.66（5.79）
尾字字频	5.68（5.59）	5.68（5.59）	5.68（5.59）	5.68（5.59）	/
整词笔画	16.63（4.18）	16.13（3.39）	16.88（4.13）	17.03（4.13）	/
首字笔画	8.09（2.68）	7.59（2.51）	8.31（2.83）	8.63（2.84）	7.97（2.37）
尾字笔画	8.41（2.90）	8.41（2.90）	8.41（2.90）	8.41（2.90）	/
音段相同度	1.00（0）	0.99（0.02）	0.003（0.02）	0.002（0.01）	/
声调相同度	1.00（0）	0.003（0.01）	0.99（0.02）	0.003（0.01）	/

注：词频与字频来自北语BCC语料库，数值转换为对数值，括号内数值为标准差。

此外，Zhou等人［32］认为词汇判断任务中的强制性按键反应可能会影响单词视觉识别，并可能激活语义加工。为弱化强制性按键反应的影响，本研究参考Federmeier等学者的系列研究（如：Laszlo等人［7］，采用隐性任务，选择食物名称判断任务。共选取了128个食物名称作为填充词。

实验材料按拉丁方交叉分成4个区组。每个区组包含所有实验条件，并进行伪随机平衡，确保每种条件不连续出现3次或以上，且每个区组中前6组皆为填充材料。

2.4 实验程序

实验使用E－Prime 2.0软件编程。实验首先在计算机屏幕中心呈现注视点“＋”（时间分别为1000—3500 ms），接着呈现掩码“#####”500 ms，然后呈现启动字47ms，启动字消失后再次呈现掩码“#####”20 ms与30 ms空屏，最后呈现目标词500ms。目标词消失后，被试有1500ms时间进行按键反应（详见图1）。

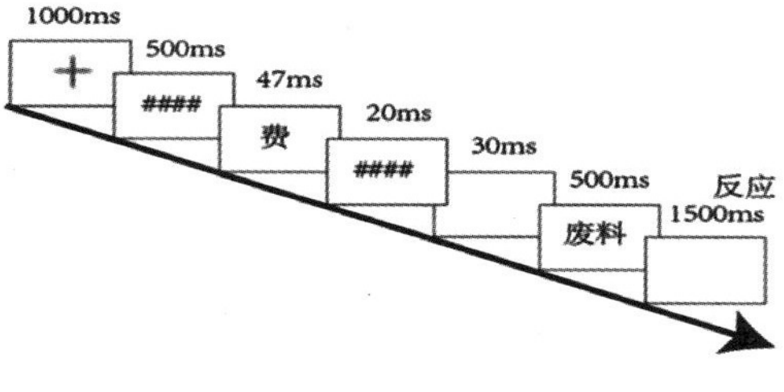

图1　实验1流程图

为避免物理刺激的重复效应，启动词字体设置为黑体，字号为70，目标词字体为宋体，字号为72。黑底白字。实验采用词汇判断任务，要求被试在看到目标词时，既快又准确地做出判断目标词是否为食物。是食物按“F”键，不是食物按“J”键，左右手按键在被试间平衡。程序同时记录被试在目标词上的反应时与正确率。实验前有练习阶段，使被试充分熟悉实验程序。实验过程中，被试可根据提示信息自主选择是否休息。整个实验约需15分钟。

2.5 数据处理与分析

在数据统计分析前，去掉数据中3个标准差之外的极端数值（少于2%）。使用SPSS 20.0进行重复测量方差分析，在必要时采用Greenhouse-Geisser校正，并在成对比较时进行Bonferroni校正。

2.6 实验结果

实验1的反应时与准确率见表2。

表2 首字不同条件的反应时（RT）和准确率（Acc）

启动条件	Acc（%）	RT（ms）	置信区间	启动量（ms）
S+T+	98（1.9）	590（81）	552，628	4
S+T-	97（2.2）	597（93）	553，641	-3
S-T+	98（2.3）	605（90）	563，647	-11
S-T-	95（1.9）	594（89）	552，635	--

注：括号内为标准差。

由表2可见，首字条件下，被试在完全匹配条件（S+T+）和声调匹配条件（S-T+）下正确率最高（Acc=98%），在音段匹配条件（S+T-）下次之（Acc=97%），而在完全不匹配条件（S-T-）下正确率最低（Acc=95%）。

就反应时而言，被试在完全匹配条件（S+T+）下的反应时最快（RT=590ms），在完全不匹配条件（S-T-）下次之（RT=594ms），然后是音段匹配条件（S+T-）（RT=597ms）、声调匹配条件（S-T+）（RT=605ms）（具体如图2所示）。

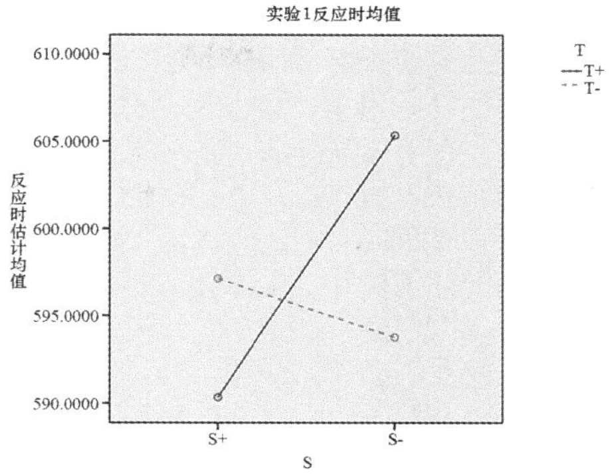

图2 实验1反应时均值

通过一般线性模型分析发现：就正确率而言，在首字条件下，声调主效应显著，[$F(1, 19)=27.053$，$p<0.001$，偏$\eta^2=0.587$]，声调相同较不同条件有更高的正确率；音段主效应达到边际效应显著[$F(1, 19)=4.278$，$p=0.053$，偏$\eta^2=0.184$]，反映为音段相同的启动项有正确率更高的倾向；声调与音段的交互作用不显著[$F(1, 19)=1.419$，$p=0.248$，偏$\eta^2=0.069$]。

就反应时而言，在首字条件下，声调主效应不显著[$F(1, 19)=0.311$，$p=0.584$，偏$\eta^2=0.016$]，音段主效应达到边际性显著[$F(1, 19)=3.738$，$p=0.068$，偏$\eta^2=0.164$]，但两者之间的交互作用显著[$F(1, 19)=4.669$，$p=0.044$，偏$\eta^2=0.197$]。进一步简单效应分析发现，在声调相同条件下，被试在音段相同条件下的反应时比音段不同条件下显著更短[$F(1, 19)=9.119$，$p=0.007$，偏$\eta^2=0.324$]。但在声调不同条件下音段效应不显著；而在音段相同条件下，声调效应不显著。但在音段不同条件下，被试在声调相同条件下的反应时比声调不同条件下显著更长[$F(1, 19)=4.187$，$p=0.055$，偏$\eta^2=0.181$]。

2.7 讨论

实验1研究结果总体表明，即使在单词视觉识别过程中，声调信息也明显介入并发挥了影响，但音段信息的作用仍难以确定。在正确率上，声调或音段不同的启动项都干扰了任务正确率。而在反应时上，交互作用存在，声调匹配相较不匹配所产生的效应，在音段相同的情况下产生不显著的促进作用，而在音段不相同的情况下则产生显著的抑制效应。从图2可见，事实上，在所有条件中，声调匹配（即S－T＋）的启动项引发了最大的反应时长，这一效应也远大于音段异同所引发的效应。

本研究所发现的声调匹配条件的抑制效应与先前视觉实验中所发现的启动效应明显不同，而与听觉实验中基于单音节汉字［22］、基于粤语单音节字［28］的研究结果较为接近。较为合理的解释是，本研究基于汉语双字复合词控制了尾字一致，减少了其他研究中整合过程所带来的可能冲突或干扰信息。由此本研究的结果更接近于那些基于听觉实验与单音字的研究。而Li等人［9］、Wang等人［24］在视觉实验中发现音段匹配条件的加工效应大于声调匹配条件，这似乎与本研究的结果相互冲突。但上述加工效应都为启动效应而非抑制效应。

值得注意的是，由于掩蔽启动范式一般被认为影响了单词加工的早期阶段，因而声调匹配信息极有可能在汉语复合词视觉识别的早期阶段即介入其中；而与之同时，实验1在正确率与反应时上也都存在音段效应。上述研究结果表明：声调匹配信息与音段匹配信息似乎都参与了视觉单词识别过程，但声调信息明显更为重要。实验1的研究结论与Ho等人［4］基于句子范式的结果并不完全相符，但由于缺乏相关研究，这一点仍有待将来研究的探索。

考虑到汉语复合词中首字与尾字作用可能有所不同，为了进一步了解声调信息与音段信息在复合词识别过程中的可能作用，本研究将控制首字信息，基于尾字启动设计，通过实验2来进一步考察。

3. 实验2：尾字启动实验

3.1 被试

参与本实验的被试与实验1相同。

3.2 研究设计

本实验采取的范式与实验1相同。在实验设计方面，本实验同样采用2（音段）×2（声调）设计。但与实验1不同的是，实验2操纵的是目标词的尾字，使其与启动项的单字在声调和音段上相同或不同，四种不同条件的材料在首字上完全相同。

3.3 实验材料

实验材料的编制过程同实验1（详见表3、附录2）。

表3　尾字实验材料举例及特征信息

特征	S＋T＋	S＋T－	S－T＋	S－T＋	启动词
	名胜	名声	名著	名言	圣
整词词频	3.63（3.52）	3.60（3.50）	3.58（3.40）	3.57（3.50）	/
首字字频	5.96（5.80）	5.96（5.80）	5.96（5.80）	5.96（5.80）	/
尾字字频	5.77（6.16）	5.71（5.73）	5.67（6.07）	5.69（5.73）	5.70（5.72）
整词笔画	15.88（4.36）	16.19（4.59）	16.88（4.13）	15.34（3.60）	/
首字笔画	7.34（2.35）	7.34（2.35）	7.34（2.35）	7.34（2.35）	/
尾字笔画	8.53（3.24）	8.84（3.74）	7.97（2.79）	8.00（2.38）	8.28（3.57）
音段相同度	1.00（0）	1.000（0）	0.003（0.02）	0.003（0.02）	/
声调相同度	1.00（0）	0.002（0.01）	0.99（0.02）	0.003（0.01）	/

注：词频与字频来自北语BCC语料库，数值转换为对数值，括号内数值为标准差。

3.4 实验程序

实验程序同实验1。

3.5 数据处理与分析

数据处理与分析方法同实验1。

3.6 实验结果

实验2的反应时与准确率见表4。

表4 尾字不同条件的反应时（RT）和准确率（Acc）

启动条件	Acc（%）	RT（ms）	置信区间	启动量（ms）
S+T+	99（2.2）	596（91）	553，638	-3
S+T-	94（3.9）	597（84）	557，637	-4
S-T+	99（2.5）	602（95）	557，646	-9
S-T-	96（4.2）	593（84）	554，633	--

注：括号内数值为标准差。

由表4可见，尾字条件下，与实验1相同，被试在完全匹配（S+T+）条件和声调匹配条件（S-T+）下正确率最高（Acc=99%）。但音段匹配条件（S+T-）正确率最低（Acc=94%）。

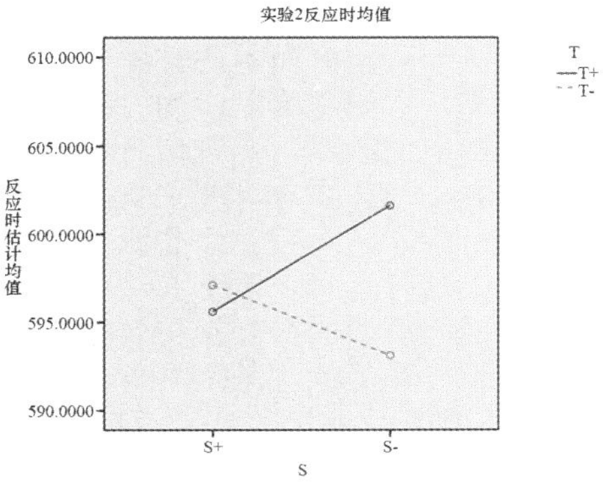

图3 实验2反应时均值

就反应时而言，被试在完全不匹配条件（S-T-）下的反应时最快（RT=593ms），在完全匹配条件（S+T+）下次之（RT=596ms），然后是音段匹配条件（S+T-）（RT=597ms）、声调匹配条件（S-T+）（RT=602ms）（具体如图3所示）。

通过一般线性模型分析发现：在尾字条件下，就正确率而言，声调主效应显著［$F(1, 19)=22.442$，$p<0.000$，偏$\eta^2=0.542$］，而音段主效应不显著［$F(1, 19)=1.723$，$p=0.205$，偏$\eta^2=0.083$］，且两者之间的交互作用不显著［$F(1, 19)=0.119$，$p=0.428$，偏$\eta^2=0.033$］。无论是在音段相同条件还是在音段不同条件，声调相同条件比声调不同条件的正确率显著更高。

就反应时而言，声调主效应不显著［$F(1, 19)=0.952$，$p=0.342$，偏$\eta^2=0.048$］，音段主效应不显著［$F(1, 19)=0.119$，$p=0.734$，偏$\eta^2=0.006$］，两者之间的交互作用呈边际显著效应［$F(1, 19)=3.069$，$p=0.096$，偏$\eta^2=0.139$］。但进一步简单效应分析并未发现任何显著差异。

3.7 讨论

上述研究结果总体表明，在正确率上，与实验1相同，无论音段是否相同，声调不同条件都干扰了任务正确率。而在反应时上，交互作用虽然依然存在，不过在实验2中仅仅达到边际效应。鉴于首尾字在复合词识别加工中具有可能不同的作用，这种作用可能进而造成被试在反应时上的交互作用有所弱化，虽然这仍需将来研究的进一步验证，但其机制仍然是可以理解的。

实验2的研究结果明显与Zhou等人［33］、Liu等人［12］的研究结果并不相同。他们的研究表明在首尾不同位置，声调匹配信息的作用会有所不同。其中Zhou等人［33］发现首字假词、尾字相同条件下，音段匹配且声调高相似条件引发了启动效应，音段匹配且声调低相似条件则没有；但在首字相同、尾字假词条件下，音段匹配且声调高相似条件、音段匹配且声调低相似条件都引发了启动效应。而实验2的结果倾向表明，尾字声调信息与音段信息在单词识别过程中与首字位置同样可能存在交互作用（边际效应），且交互模式与首字位置上的效应有相似性。较为可能的解释是，本研究采用了正常复合词（而非假词）作为材料，并且对首字信息进行了严格控制，确保了在尾字启动实验中首字相同，较好地避免了在复合词假词整合过程中语义冲突信息所造成的可能干扰，因而声调匹配信息仍在复合词的识别过程中发挥了显而易见的作用。

4. 总讨论

本研究基于实验1与实验2分别证实声调信息在汉语复合词视觉识别过程中的优先性与稳定性。研究发现声调与音段匹配信息在汉语复合词的首字、尾字不同位置下存在交互作用，且模式较为类似。但总体看来，在本研究中，声调匹配信息对单词识别过程影响更为明显。

本研究结果表明，在视觉识别范式下，声调信息同样影响了单词识别进程，在所有条件中，声调匹配（即S－T＋）的启动项引发了最大的反应时长，这一效应也远大于音段异同所引发的效应。因此本研究结果与Li等人［9］在视觉实验中基于Stroop任务的研究结果较为一致，也符合Wang等人［24］研究中的总体趋势。本研究总体倾向表明，声调信息在复合词的识别过程中具有优先加工地位。本研究的结果明显支持了Ye等人［27］、Liu等人［11］、Ho等人［4］等学者关于声调加工优先的结论。

但值得注意的是，本研究结果也明显不同于Winskel等人［25］在Stroop任务、Li等人［10］在语音匹配任务中的结果。正如先前讨论所提及那样，上述两项研究都涉及对整合过程中干扰信息的抑制。一种较为可能的推测是：声调信息更多参与了单词识别过程中语义记忆的提取过程，而音段信息则极有可能较大程度地参与了语义整合与分析过程。在听觉实验中基于单音节字的研究［14］、在听觉实验中基于复合词或成语的研究［1，11，27］同样与本研究结果不尽相同，上述研究都发现声调不匹配（音段匹配）条件下被试的反应显著更慢。但与Winskel等人［25］、Li等人［10］两项研究相似，它们所考察的单词识别过程也都不同程度地要求在整合过程中抑制干扰信息。而其他没有类似干扰信息的听觉实验研究则支持了本研究的结论。更直接的证据来自Zhao等人［31］、Hu等人［5］、Ho等人［4］、Zou等人［34］的ERP研究。这些研究总体发现，声调匹配（音段不匹配）条件在N400的波幅上显著负于完全匹配条件，而声母不匹配（声调匹配）条件在此阶段一般与完全匹配条件相比并无显著差异，但却常常在LPC、P600成分上与完全匹配条件显著不同。虽然有较多的研究支持上述推断，但由于目前关于视觉识别的相关研究仍然较少，仍有待将来更多研究的证实或证伪。

此外，本研究还清晰地表明，声调与音段信息之间存在交互作用，且它们在首字、尾字启动条件下的表现相似。本研究的结果明显不同于Zhou等人［33］、Liu等人［12］、Wong等人［26］等学者的研究结论。在上述研究中，都出现了明显的位置效应。较为可能的原因在于：由于上述研究都使用了假词，它们的位置效应极有可能源自假词的整合过程。由于本研究的四种条件都采用了正常复合词，并同时控制了首尾字启动条件下的各自尾字、首字信息的一致，因而本研究中不存在假词整合过程。本研究因而表明，首尾字所触发不同程度的声调与音段信息交互作用造成的交互作用，极有可能来自复合词中各汉字成分的识别过程，而非源自汉语复合词的语义整合过程。至于首尾字启动条件下，音段与声调的交互作用效应量有所不同，这或许是受到首尾字本身在单词识别过程的作用的调节。比如Zhang等人［30］的研究发现，汉语复合词首字为去声的加工要比它为阳平时更为困难。当然，由于本研究并未控制声调调型及语义相似度，启动词与目标词的声调调型、语义相似度亦有可能影响了实验的结果。在将来的研究中，还需要进而考虑在不同的实验条件下，如何严格控制声调的高低变化情况以及语义相似度的可能影响。此外，还有必要区分声调与音段信息在汉字成分本身、汉字成分之间的可能不同作用。

总体看来，交股模型（Cohort Model）[15] 强调“自左而右”（如从第一个音素/p/到第二个音素/ə/）的加工，临近激活模型（Neighbourhood Activation Model）[13] 则认为音段匹配的程度与相似性主导了单词的识别，而分布式交股模型（Distributed Cohort Model）[3]、Shortlist/MERGE 模型 [17，18] 以及 TRACE 模型 [16] 更多注重语音信息如何随着时间而展开。显而易见的是，上述模型都未能包含声调信息，因而无法较好地解释本研究的结果。虽然 O'Seaghdha 等人 [19] 提出的“合适单元假设”符合汉语特性，但他们认为音段才是基本识别单元，声调的作用是区分音段。而本研究结果表明在单词识别阶段，声调与音段信息存在交互作用，而声调匹配信息发挥着主导作用。由此可以推断，在首、尾不同位置上，由于相应语言信息在加工时间上存在先后之分，声调与音段信息在单词识别过程与语义整合中的作用可能有所不同。因而本研究的结果可能更加倾向支持考虑到时间因素的分布式交股模型、Shortlist/MERGE 模型、TRACE 模型。当然，由于此方面的研究有限，且本研究的实验设计为项目间设计而非项目内设计，虽然本研究尽量控制了各条件所使用词条的字频、笔画等特征，当前条件间差异亦有可能源自词汇差异。将来研究可以操控启动项，在目标词不变的基础上基于项目内设计进而验证本研究的结论。

5. 结论

本研究旨在探讨在视觉识别过程中声调（超音段）信息在汉语单词识别过程中的作用，并同时讨论了它在复合词整合过程中的可能作用。研究发现：

（1）声调信息参与了汉语单词的视觉识别过程，其作用较音段信息更为重要。

（2）声调信息的参与作用更多体现于单词识别阶段。无论处于首字或尾字位置，声调信息的影响较为类似。

参考文献

[1] Cutler, A., Chen, H. C. 1997. Lexical tone in Cantonese spoken-word processing. *Perception and Psychophysics* 59, 165－179.

[2] Feldman, L. B., Kostić, A., Gvozdencić, V., O'Connor, P. A., Moscoso del Prado, M. F. 2012. Semantic similarity influences early morphological priming in Serbian: A challenge to form-then-meaning accounts of word recognition. *Psychonomic Bulletin and Review* 19, 668－676.

[3] Gaskell, M. G., Marslen-Wilson, W. D. 2002. Representation and competition in the perception of spoken words. *Cogn. Psychol.* 45, 220－266.

[4] Ho, A., Boshra, R., Schmidtke, D., Oralova, G., Moro, A. L., Service, E., Connolly, J. F. 2019. Electrophysiological evidence for the integral nature of tone in Mandarin spoken word recognition. *Neuropsychologia* 131, 325－332.

[5] Hu, J. H., Gao, S., Ma, W. Y., Yao, D. Z. 2012. Dissociation of tone and vowel processing in Mandarin idioms. *Psychophysiology* 49, 1179－1190.

[6] Huang, X. J., Liu, X., Yang, J. C., Zhao, Q. W., Zhou, J. S. 2018. Tonal and vowel information processing in Chinese spoken word recognition: An event-related potential study. *Cognitive Neuroscience and Neuropsychology* 29, 356－362.

[7] Laszlo, S., Federmeier, K. D. 2007. Better the DVL you know: Acronyms reveal the contribution of familiarity to single-word reading. *Psychological Science* 18, 122－126.

[8] Lee, C. Y. 2007. Does horse activate mother? Processing lexical tone in form priming. *Language and Speech* 50, 101－123.

[9] Li, C. C., Lin, C. Y., Wang, M., Jiang, N. 2013. The activation of segmental and tonal information in visual word recognition. *Psychonomic Bulletin & Review* 20, 773－779.

[10] Li, C., Wang, M., Davis, J. A., Guan, C. 2019. The role of segmental and tonal information in visual word recognition with learners of Chinese. *Journal of Research in Reading* 1, 1－26.

[11] Liu, S. Y., Samuel, A. G. 2007. The role of Mandarin lexical tones in lexical access under different contextual conditions. *Language and Cognitive Processes* 22, 566 – 594.

[12] Liu, Y. N., Shu, H., Wei, J. H. 2006. Spoken word recognition in context: Evidence from Chinese ERP analyses. *Brain and Language* 96, 37 – 48.

[13] Luce, P. A., Pisoni, D. B. 1998. Recognizing spoken words: The neighborhood activation model. *Ear Hear* 19, 1 – 36.

[14] Malins, J. G., Joanisse, M. F. 2010. The roles of tonal and segmental information in Mandarin spoken word recognition: An eye-tracking study. *Journal of Memory and Language* 62, 407 – 420.

[15] Marslen-Wilson, W., Tyler, L. K. 1980. The temporal structure of spoken language understanding. *Cognition* 8, 1 – 71.

[16] McClelland, J. L., Elman, J. L. 1986. The trace model of speech perception. *Cogn. Psychol.* 18, 1 – 86.

[17] Norris, D., 1994. Shortlist: A connectionist model of continuous speech recognition. *Cognition* 52, 189 – 234.

[18] Norris, D., McQueen, J. M., Cutler, A. 2000. Merging information in speech recognition: Feedback is never necessary. *Behav. Brain Sci.* 23, 299 – 325.

[19] O'Seaghdha, P. G., Chen, J. Y., Chen, T. M. 2010. Proximate units in word production: Phonological encoding begins with syllables in Mandarin Chinese but with segments in English. *Cognition* 115, 282 – 302.

[20] Schirmer, A., Tang, S. L., Penney, T. B., Gunter, T. C., Chen, H. C. 2005. Brain responses to segmentally and tonally induced semantic violations in Cantonese. *Journal of Cognitive Neuroscience* 17, 1 – 12.

[21] Schmidt, S. B., Gonzalez, E. C. 2004. Who do you love, your mother or your horse? An event-related brain potential analysis of tone processing in Mandarin Chinese. *Journal of Psycholinguistic Research* 33, 103 – 135.

[22] Sereno, J. A., Lee, H. 2015. The contribution of segmental and tonal information in Mandarin spoken word processing. *Language and speech* 58, 131 – 151.

[23] Tsang, Y. K., Chen, H. C. 2014. Activation of morphemic meanings in processing opaque words. *Psychonomic Bulletin and Review* 21, 1281 – 1286.

[24] Wang, M., Li, C. C., Lin, C. Y. 2015. The contributions of segmental and suprasegmental information in reading chinese characters aloud. *PLOS ONE* 10, 1 – 20.

[25] Winskel, H., Ratitamkul, T., Charoensit, A. 2016. The role of tone and segmental information in visual-word recognition in Thai. *The Quarterly Journal of Experimental Psychology* 70, 1282 – 1291.

[26] Wong, A., Wang, J., Ng, T. Y., Chen, H. C. 2016. Syllabic encoding during overt speech production in Cantonese: Evidence from temporal brain responses. *Brain Research* 1648, 101 – 109.

[27] Ye, Y., Connine, C. M. 1999. Processing spoken Chinese: The role of tone information. *Language and Cognitive Processes* 14, 609 – 630.

[28] Yip, M. 2001. Phonological priming in Cantonese spoken-word processing. *Psychologia* 44, 223 – 229.

[29] Zhang, C. C. 2018. Online adjustment of phonetic expectation of lexical tones to accommodate speaker variation: A combined behavioural and ERP study. *Language, Cognition and Neuroscience* 33, 175 – 195.

[30] Zhang, C. C., Xia, Q. S., Peng, G. 2015. Mandarin third tone sandhi requires more effortful phonological encoding in speech production: Evidence from an ERP study. *Journal of Neurolinguistics* 33, 149 – 162.

[31] Zhao, J. J., Guo, J. J., Zhou, F. Y., Shu, H. 2011. Time course of Chinese monosyllabic spoken word recognition: Evidence from ERP analyses. *Neuropsychologia* 49, 1761 – 1770.

[32] Zhou, X. L., Marslen-Wilson, W. 1999. Phonology, orthography and semantic activation in reading Chinese. *Journal of Memory and Language* 41, 579 – 606.

[33] Zhou, X. L., Qu, Y. X. 2000. Lexical tone in the spoken word recognition of Chinese. In *The Proceedings of the 6th International Conference on Spoken Language Processing (ICSLP 2000, Volume II)*, October 16 – 20, 2000. Beijing.

[34] Zou, Y., Lui, M., Tsang, Y. K. 2020. The roles of lexical tone and rime during Mandarin sentence comprehension: An event-related potential study. *Neuropsychologia* 147, 107578.

[35]刘帅、王曼（2020）口语单词产出的音韵

编码过程研究。《中国语音学报》第1期，51—59页。

李梦锐 北京第二外国语学院，硕士。主要研究领域为心理语言学、二语习得。
Email：13083749627@163.com

吴建设 北京第二外国语学院，博士，教授。主要研究领域为神经语言学、二语习得。本文通讯作者。
Email：wujianshe@bisu.edu.cn

邱寅晨 北京第二外国语学院，博士，副教授。主要研究领域为翻译研究、心理语言学。
Email：qiuyinchen@bisu.edu.cn

郎建国 北京第二外国语学院，硕士，副教授。主要研究领域为词典研究、外语教育。
Email：ljg@bisu.edu.cn

附录 1

实验 1：首字实验材料

费	废料	肥料	木料	史料
乾	钱款	欠款	赔款	拨款
真	针线	阵线	专线	航线
必	币值	比值	案值	均值
借	戒律	节律	韵律	七律
淹	烟袋	眼袋	沙袋	睡袋
式	事例	实例	惯例	引例
抵	底层	低层	顶层	楼层
站	战区	展区	禁区	林区
掀	仙境	险境	边境	梦境
员	元气	怨气	毒气	杀气
止	纸条	枝条	柳条	信条
治	志向	指向	去向	偏向
县	限期	先期	末期	刑期
玉	寓意	语意	谢意	春意
院	愿景	远景	外景	盆景
附	副手	扶手	助手	枪手
防	房客	访客	常客	政客
移	遗物	异物	玩物	宠物
示	视点	时点	卖点	基点
彼	笔画	壁画	版画	图画
资	姿色	紫色	棕色	货色
思	丝路	死路	销路	套路
育	浴衣	雨衣	内衣	棉衣
逐	烛光	珠光	余光	亮光
积	激流	急流	车流	电流
立	历程	里程	射程	章程
舞	五味	无味	美味	怪味
屋	巫术	武术	医术	算术
互	户口	虎口	胃口	活口
细	戏服	西服	制服	礼服
忘	望族	王族	贵族	满族

附录2

实验2：尾字实验材料

圣	名胜	名声	名著	名言
官	城关	城管	城郊	城建
驾	花架	花甲	花样	花灯
排	门牌	门派	门牙	门厅
复	农妇	农夫	农具	农忙
爆	书报	书包	书柜	书评
腐	首府	首富	首领	首级
项	音像	音响	音讯	音符
搞	原稿	原告	原委	原型
目	字幕	字母	字句	字形
疾	特辑	特技	特权	特使
导	宝岛	宝刀	宝塔	宝剑
犯	风范	风帆	风浪	风云
同	神童	神通	神明	神社
试	宗室	宗师	宗庙	宗谱
眠	海绵	海面	海潮	海港
市	情势	情诗	情爱	情怀
嫁	身价	身家	身段	身板
办	夜半	夜班	夜大	夜晚
并	老病	老兵	老汉	老脸
割	表哥	表格	表征	表象
暑	亲属	亲疏	亲友	亲故
支	新知	新址	新欢	新月
利	定力	定理	定论	定局
致	皮质	皮脂	皮带	皮革
探	泥炭	泥潭	泥塑	泥坑
财	文才	文采	文集	文科
纪	心计	心机	心性	心田
仁	前人	前任	前台	前妻
艺	交谊	交椅	交道	交投
记	古迹	古籍	古训	古装
罚	军阀	军法	军团	军备

AN ACOUSTIC MODELING STUDY OF FRICATION LEVELS OF HIGH VOWELS IN CHINESE

XU Menghan, WU Bo

Abstract Frication of high vowels has three levels in auditory impression, including non-frication, low frication, and high frication. The aim of this study was to study the acoustic characteristics and social variability of the three levels via the method of multivariate statistical modeling. We estimated the weighting of each parameter by fitting the model of Boosted Logistic Regression to obtain the optimal parametric set. Pattern recognition then quantified the social variability with the optimal set. It showed that the acoustic characteristics of the vowel frication are mainly reflected in the formants, of which the second bandwidth ($B2$) plays the most prominent role in distinguishing the three levels. Three dimensional diagrams further illustrated that the high frication group has the greatest $B2$ value, with the smallest first formant ($F1$) and skewness, while the non-frication group is completely the opposite. Results of pattern recognition showed that the degrees of variation in age and gender are both close to 19%, where the higher the frication level is, the greater the variability is. This paper thus suggested that low frication variants should be treated as fricative approximants, instead of fricative vowels as reported in the literature.
Keywords High vowels, Frication levels, Acoustic modeling, Social variability

1. INTRODUCTION

In the production of vowel sounds, the articulators do not come very close together, and the passage of the airstream is relatively unobstructed [9]. Therefore, vowel is a speech sound produced with vibration of the vocal cords but without audible frication. There is, however, a fricative phenomenon of vowels in some Chinese dialects. The vocal tract is constricted to cause low or high audible frication, mainly appearing in (C) V syllables with high dorsal vowels /i, u, y/ and apical high vowels /ɿ, ʅ/. Representative dialects are Wu Chinese and its adjacent Jianghuai Mandarin distributed along the lower reaches of the Yangtze River. This phenomenon has been regarded as the sound change of fricativization in literature of Chinese dialectology, where fricative variants of vowels were defined as fricative vowels [25].

Although most of the previous discussions on fricative segments in Chinese focused on consonants [8, 14, 15, 21], vowel frication presents a special case in terms of sound change. Chao [23] first reported this kind of frication, who transcribed the fricative variant of /i/ with a subscript approximant as [i_j], and the fricative variant of /u/ following /f/ as [v]. So far, there have been no conventional diacritics for fricative vowels in the International Phonetic Alphabet.

Previous studies on vowel frication have mainly followed two research lines. One predominantly concerns with the process of historical sound change of apical vowels. These studies have regarded the frication in high vowels as the main motivation of the emergence of apical vowels [12, 22, 24]. Hu and Lin [7] further explained that the fricative high front vowel in Suzhou dialect is at an intermediate stage of vowel apicalization based on the acoustic and articulatory evidence.

The other line has paid attention to the phonetic characteristics of fricative vowels. Most of the studies have focused on the fricative variants of the high vowel /i/ during the past decades [7, 12, 19, 20]. Shi [12] proposed an order chain of fricative intensity based on auditory impression: non-frication (*N*) [i] (Beijing Mandarin) < low frication (*L*) [i_j] (Suzhou dialect) < mid frication (*M*) [j] (Changzhou dialect) < high frication (*H*) [ʑ] (Danyang dialect) < apical vowel [ɿ] (Xinghua dialect). According to this chain, the apical vowel /ɿ/ is characterized with the highest degree of frication.① The author therefore put forward the hypothesis of four fricative levels (*N*, *L*, *M* and *H*) both for apical vowels and dorsal high vowels. Wu [20] further studied the fricative variants of /i/ and argued for a three-level system in both perspectives of vowel perception and vowel production. On the one hand, the frication in Jianghuai Mandarin and Wu is concomitant and random, evidenced from pattern analysis using Support Vector Machine (SVM). On the other hand, vowel frication seems more widely distributed in speech of the young generation [20]. Besides, results of the Electromagnetic Articulographic (EMA) study by Hu and Lin [7] show that plain high front vowels, fricative high front vowels and apical vowels in Suzhou dialect distinguish in the active places of articulation.

Although there have been some discussions about the articulatory and acoustic characteristics of fricative vowels, no in-depth analysis has been made on their fricative levels, so that the acoustic characteristics of different fricative levels remain unclear. Also, little research effort has been made so far in quantifying the social variability of the levels caused by concomitant frication.

As mentioned above, there are two classifications on the fricative levels. One is the four levels of *N*, *L*, *M and H*, and the other is the three levels of *N*, *L and H*. As will be seen in the judgments of the 36 native speakers investigated in the current study, it is easier to distinguish the three levels of *N*, *L* and *H* rather than four levels. The present study thus accepted the three-level classification for the modeling analysis. Taking the word "姨 aunt" for example [20], Figure 1 shows the spectrograms of the same word in Standard Chinese, Suzhou dialect, Danyang dialect and Yangzhou dialect, respectively.

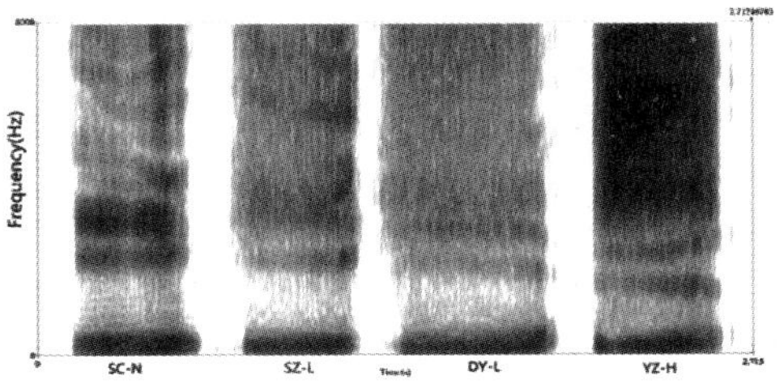

Figure 1 Spectrograms of the word "姨 aunt" in Standard Chinese (SC), Suzhou dialect (SZ), Danyang dialect (DY), and Yangzhou dialect (YZ). N for non-frication, L for low frication, and H for high frication.

As can be seen from the examples in Figure 1, *N*, *L* and *H* can be clearly differentiated in the spectrograms. The formant structure of *N* is normal vocalic, and there are obvious fricative noises in the frequency band above F1 of *L*. Nevertheless the spectrum of *H* is close to voiced fricatives (for more discussion, see Wu [20]).

This paper is a further study based on Wu [19, 20], aiming to further explore the acoustic differences of three fricative levels, and to quantify their social variability in age and gender. Objects of modeling include high dorsal vowels /i, u, y/ and the apical vowel /ɿ/.

---

① Wu [19], however, argued that the apical vowel /ɿ/ and the dorsal vowel /i/ are comparable in fricative intensity.

2. METHODS

2.1 Materials and subjects

Data of three dialects were collected from Suzhou dialect, Yangzhou dialect and Danyang dialect. Suzhou dialect is a typical vernacular of Wu Chinese. Yangzhou dialect is the representative of Jianghuai Mandarin. Danyang dialect is distributed in the transitional region between Wu Chinese and Jianghuai Mandarin. All these dialects exhibit systematic contrasts in the three fricative levels.

Target vowels included high dorsal vowels /i, u, y/ and the apical vowel /ɿ/. All target vowels were elicited in the (C)V syllable structure. Word lists were made for the three dialects respectively. In total, there were 101 monosyllabic words with different tones for Suzhou dialect, 102 for Danyang dialect and 47 for Yangzhou dialect.

Six male speakers (3 old and 3 young) and six female speakers (3 old and 3 young) of each dialect participated in the experiment. The mean ages of the old and young speakers were about 61 and 25, respectively, across dialects. Each participant read the materials three times in a different randomized order at each repetition.

Nine thousand tokens were recorded in total, including 3636 (101 words × 12 subjects × 3 repetitions) tokens from Suzhou, 3672 (102 words × 12 subjects × 3 repetitions) from Danyang, and 1692 (47 words × 12 subjects × 3 repetitions) from Yangzhou. With auditory inspection and acoustic spectrums of the samples of each dialect, 8601 tokens were judged as valid tokens.

These valid samples were further divided into three categories, namely non-frication (*N*), low frication (*L*) and high frication (*H*), according to Wu [20]. Each non-fricative vowel has free variants with low and high frication levels, for example, the vowel /i/ has a low fricative variant [i_j] and a high variant [ʑ]. Table 1 lists three fricative levels with four categories of vowels and variants (i.e., i-group, u-group, y-group and ɿ-group), and the proportions of valid tokens in each dialect were listed in Table 2.

Table 1 Number of valid tokens for different frication levels. As there are no diacritics for the fricative variants in IPA, this paper transcribes the low fricative variants as [i_j, u_v, y_j, $\text{ɿ}_{\text{ɹ}}$], and the high fricative variants as [ʑ, v, yʑ, z].

Non frication (*N*)	i	u	y	ɿ
	2697	1402	1062	801
Low frication (*L*)	i_j	u_v	y_j	$\text{ɿ}_{\text{ɹ}}$
	828	281	468	520
High frication (*H*)	ʑ	v	yʑ	z
	180	133	60	169

Table 2 Proportions of valid tokens of each level in the three dialects.

	Danyang	Suzhou	Yangzhou
Non frication (*N*)	0.604	0.760	0.738
Low frication (*L*)	0.302	0.197	0.222
High frication (*H*)	0.094	0.043	0.040

2.2 Acoustic analyses

All acoustic data were recorded in xRecorder developed by Xiong Ziyu from Chinese Academy of Social Sciences, at a 22050Hz sampling rate and 16-bit resolution in mono channel. All tokens were manually annotated in Praat [2].

A multivariate modeling analysis has been used in this study. First, we created a multivariate database of formants and spectral cues of the vowels and corresponding variants, by extracting the following 15-dimensional (15D) parameters:

(1) Formant frequencies (4D): $F1 \sim F4$.

(2) Formant bandwidths (4D): $B1 \sim B4$.

(3) Spectral moments (4D): $K1 \sim K4$.

The first moment ($K1$) and the second moment ($K2$) correspond to the mean and variance of spectral distribution, respectively. The third moment ($K3$) and fourth moment ($K4$) reflect the skewness and kurtosis of the distribution, respectively.

(4) Slope and curvature (2D). The slope and curvature were calculated through discrete cosine transformation (DCT). The first three coefficients ($DCT0$, $DCT1$, and $DCT2$) correspond to the mean, slope and curvature of the spectral envelope, respectively. There is a negative correlation between Slope and $DCT1$, and a positive correlation between curvature and $DCT2$ [17].

(5) Energy Ratio (1D). Logarithmic ratio reflects the spectral energy distribution between different frequency bands [6]. In this specific experiment, we calculated the energy ratio of frequency band of 1000 - 4000Hz to 4000 - 10000Hz.

2.3 Statistical analysis and modeling

To reduce the individual differences due to different dialects as much as possible, all raw acoustic data were first normalized into z-scores within each dialect. Further model fitting and pattern recognition were based on the normalized data in the following steps:

(1) Partitioning the data into the training set and the test set. To estimate the weighting of the predictors (i. e., the 15D acoustic parameters) in the classification of three frication levels (i. e., N, L, H), the training set was composed of 70% of the total tokens randomly selected, and the remaining 30% were the test set. For gender variation, the male data were used as the training set, and the female data as the test set. For age variation, the old group was the training set and the young group was the test set.

(2) K-fold cross-validation with 10 folds iteratively calculated each predictor of the training set. Model fitting of the K-fold training sets yielded the optimal model. By comparing 190 classification models [5, 16], this paper selected the Boosted Logistic Regression model (LogitBoost) due to its best result of prediction. The LogitBoost model of the training set then estimated the weighting scores of each predictor and automatically adjusted the optimal parameter sets depending on the result of prediction.

(3) The optimal parameter set served the pattern recognition of the age and gender variation. The hit rate (hr) of the pattern recognition quantified the social variability, i. e., the degree of variation (dv) equals to $1 - hr$. High hit rate means low variability, and vice versa.

All statistical analyses and modeling were carried out using the packages of emuR [18], wrassp [3], caret [5], plot3D [13], and caTool [16] in R [11].

3. ACOUSTIC OBSERVATIONS

3.1 Formants

Figure 2 shows the central tendencies of

formant frequencies ($F1 \sim F4$) and bandwidths ($B1 \sim B4$) of three fricative levels. On the $F1/F2$ plane (Figure 2a), the central tendency shows that F1 has an effect within each frication level, i. e., [ʐ] < [i_j] < [i], [yʐ] < [y_j] < [y], [z] < [ɿ$_ɹ$] < [ɿ], and the greater the frication is, the smaller F1 is. The group [v, u_v, u], however, does not conform to this tendency, where $F1$ of [v] and [u_v] are close. $F2$ differentiates the frication across four articulatory places, i. e., the high front i-group > the high front rounded y-group > the central ɿ-group > the back u-group. Both $F3$ and $F4$ (Figure 2b) show effects in distinguishing the rounded groups from the unrounded: [+rounded] < [+unrounded].

Among the four formant bandwidths, $B2$ has the most significant distinct effect across fricative levels, i. e., H [yʐ, ʐ, z, v] > L [y_j, i_j, ɿ$_ɹ$, u_v] > N [y, i, ɿ, u] (Figure 2c). The high frication groups were mainly differentiated with $B3$, while $B4$ mainly plays a role in the non-frication groups (Figure 2d).

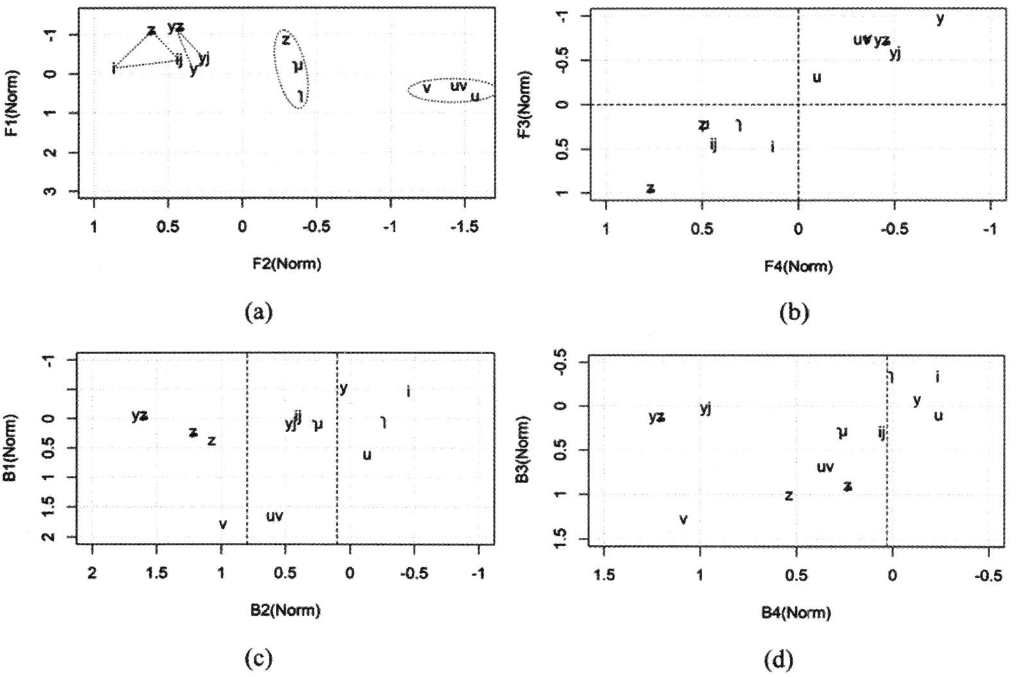

Figure 2 Central tendencies of formant frequencies ($F1 \sim F4$) and bandwidths ($B1 \sim B4$) of the vowels and corresponding variants of three fricative levels. (a): the tendency in the $F1/F2$ plane. (b): the tendency in the $F3/F4$. (c): the tendency in the $B1/B2$. (d): the tendency in the $B3/B4$.

3. 2 Spectrum

3. 2. 1 Energy ratio of frequency bands

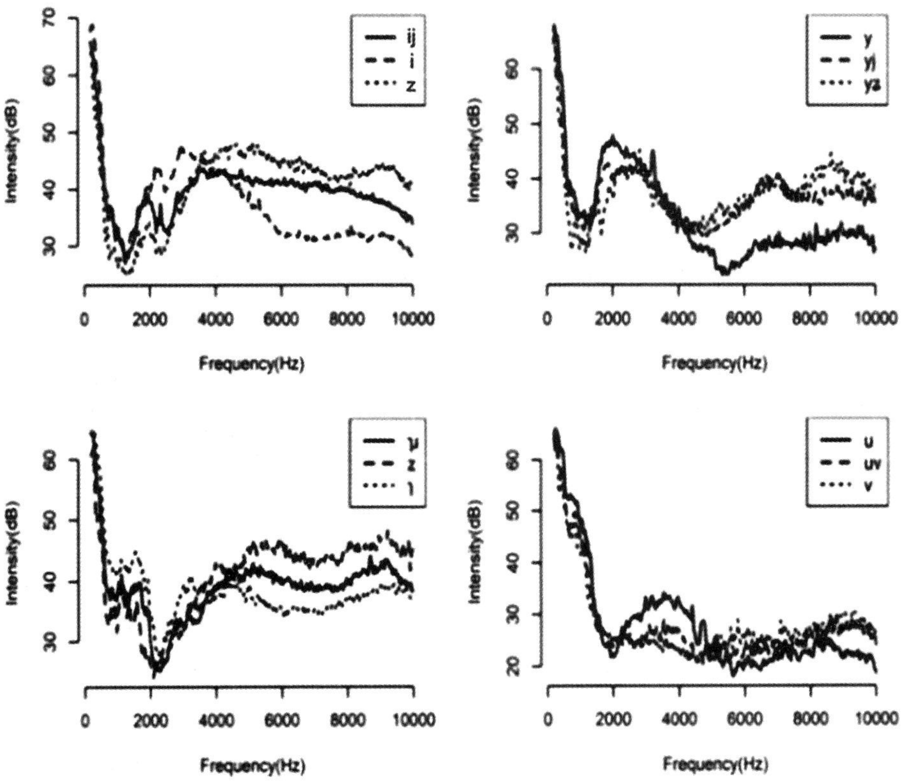

Figure 3 ***Top left*****: the spectrum of the i-group.** ***Top right*****: the spectrum of the y-group.** ***Bottom left*****: the spectrum of the ɿ-group.** ***Bottom right*****: the spectrum of the u-group.**

Figure 3 presents the 2D spectrums of the three groups. As can be seen from Figure 3, the levels were distinguished mainly in the band 4000 – 10000Hz. There is a positive correlation between the level and intensity, i. e. , the higher frication is, the greater intensity is. Differences within the u-group, however, are not clear enough because the high frication [v] is breathy.

Following Harrington [6], we further calculated a logarithmic ratio of spectral energy sum for the frequency band of 1000 – 4000Hz to 4000 – 10000Hz, as shown in the boxplots in Figure 4. Table 3 lists the median values of the ratios. The energy ratios of the two frequency bands rank as $H > L > N$. As frication enhances the energy of the high frequency band, the greater the ratio is, the higher the frication is for each group. Also, the rounded gesture seems to decrease the ratio.

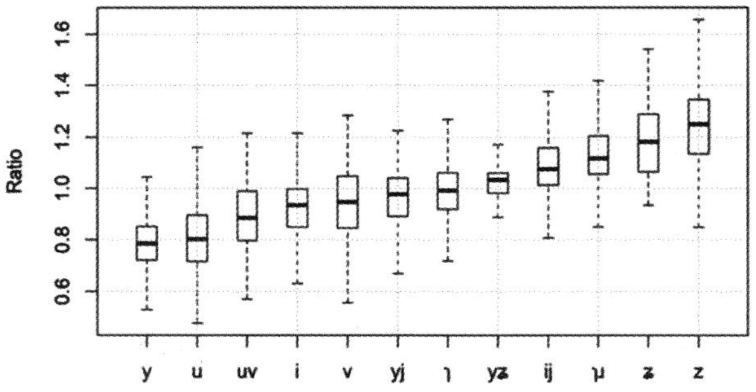

Figure 4 Energy ratios of frequency band [1000 – 4000Hz] to [4000 – 10000Hz] for each vowel and variant.

Table 3 Median values of the energy ratios of the vowels and corresponding variants. The table lists the values of each group from small to large (*H* > *L* > *N*), in order to make the frication more readable.

N	L	H	N	L	H
y	y_j	yʐ	i	i_j	ʐ
0.785	0.976	1.033	0.934	1.076	1.182
ɿ	$ɿ_ɹ$	z	u	u_v	v
0.991	1.118	1.249	0.802	0.884	0.946

3.2.2 Slope and curvature of the spectral envelope

Figure 5 presents the quantiles of *DCT*1 and *DCT*2 of the vowels and Table 4 lists the median values of them . We can see from the boxplots of Figure 5 that, in the three fricative levels, if the frication is high, the corresponding increase is of the curvature value, and the slope value relatively decreases except in the y-group. For example, the curvatures of [z] and [ʐ] are the largest while the slopes have the smallest absolute values; however, the lip rounding gesture also influences this characteristic. Median values in Table 4 also reflect that the slopes of the rounded are greater than those of the unrounded.

Table 4 Median values of *DCT*1 and *DCT*2 from small to large for each group.

*DCT*1	ʐ	i_j	i	z	$ɿ_ɹ$	ɿ	v	u_v	u	*yʐ*	y_j	*y*
	0.539	2.697	6.024	2.488	5.071	7.141	16.007	17.763	19.287	6.277	5.735	10.437
*DCT*2	i	i_j	ʐ	ɿ	$ɿ_ɹ$	z	u	u_v	v	y	y_j	yʐ
	6.930	8.439	10.576	2.819	6.550	8.977	1.835	3.137	3.309	1.459	4.263	5.950

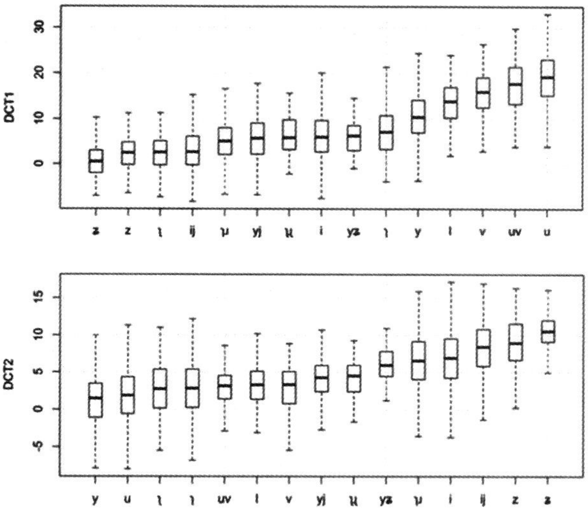

Figure 5 Boxplots of *DCT*1 and *DCT*2 of the vowels and corresponding variants of three fricative levels.

3.2.3 Spectral moments

Figure 6 and Table 5 present the 4D spectral moments of *K*1 – *K*4. The first moments (*K*1) of [z] and [ʐ] are the highest, and the rounded [u] [y] [u_v] [v] are the lowest. The rounded variants generally show a high degree of dispersion. The third moment (*K*3) reflects an overall negative skewness in the high frication excepting [v]. All of the four moments (*K*4) are negative so that the peaks are platy kurtosis, but *K*4 has no prominent effect on the levels. Comparatively, *K*1 increases with the frication, just as the opposite of *K*3.

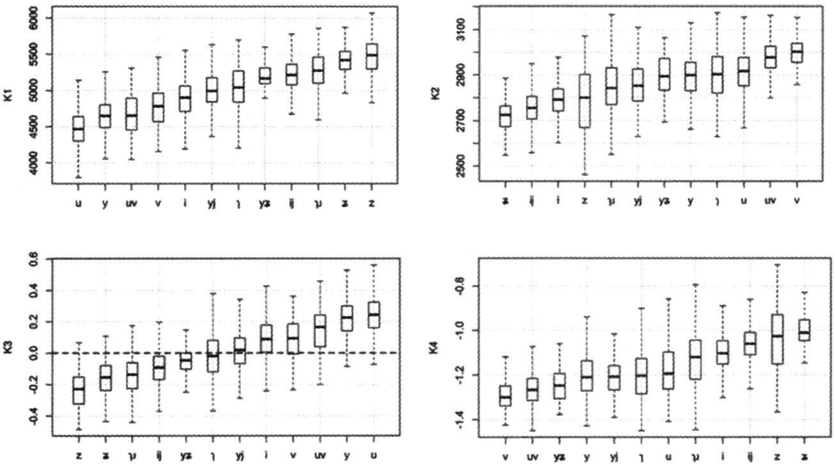

Figure 6 Boxplots of the 4D spectral moments of the vowels and corresponding variants. *K*2 has been converted into the spectral standard deviation by taking its square root. *Dotted line* in *K*3: the skewness of zero.

Table 5 Median values of the 4D spectral moments listed with different groups. *K*1, *K*2 and *K*3 have prominent effects on distinguishing the inner frication of each group. *K*1: *H* > *L* > *N*; *K*3: *H* < *L* < *N*.

*K*1 (Hz)	i	i_j	ʑ	y	y_j	yʑ	ɿ	ɿɹ	z	u	u_v	v
	4901	5214	5419	4649	4994	5166	5037	5273	5489	4464	4654	4783
*K*2 (Hz)	ʑ	i_j	i	y_j	yʑ	y	z	ɿɹ	ɿ	u	u_v	v
	2724	2755	2792	2852	2894	2900	2800	2843	2903	2918	2977	3002
*K*3	ʑ	i_j	i	yʑ	y_j	y	z	ɿɹ	ɿ	v	u_v	u
	-0. 228	-0. 153	-0. 137	-0. 092	-0. 047	-0. 019	0. 019	0. 089	0. 094	0. 165	0. 227	0. 243
*K*4	v	u_v	yʑ	y	y_j	ɿ	u	ɿɹ	i	i_j	z	ʑ
	-1. 300	-1. 266	-1. 247	-1. 211	-1. 208	-1. 203	-1. 194	-1. 12	-1. 103	-1. 06	-1. 026	-1. 011

4. STATISTICAL MODELING

As can be seen from the results of the current study, each parameter seems to play a certain role in distinguishing each group and each frication level. However, there are two further issues that need to be discussed.

1) How effective is each parameter in distinguishing three fricative levels?

2) According to the auditory impression, three levels of contrast often exhibit certain social variability. Sometimes, it is not easy to tell whether a fricative variant is high or low in frication levels, even for native speakers. Then how to quantify the variability?

4. 1 Weighting of acoustic parameters

4. 1. 1 Preprocessing of correlated predictors

Pearson correlation analyses between parameters show that there are very high correlations ($|r| > .7$) between Energy Ratio and *K*1 ($r = .84$), Energy Ratio and *K*3 ($r = -.87$), *K*1 and *K*3 ($r = .96$), *K*2 and *K*4 ($r = -.86$), *K*1 and *DCT*1 ($r = -.73$), respectively. Therefore, data of Energy Ratio, *K*1, and *K*2 were removed, so that only 12D parameters were remained as the predictors of further classification modeling.

4. 1. 2 Model fitting

After resampling by the K-fold cross-validation, we fitted the Boosted Logistic Regression model for the training set (70% of the data) to estimate the weighting of the 12D predictors in distinguishing three levels. Figure 7 and Table 6 illustrate the results.

Table 6 Importance scores of the predictors (scale: 0-100). All scores of the formant bandwidths are greater than 50. *F*4, *K*4, *F*2, and *F*3 are less than 20 (in italics).

	*B*2	*K*3	*B*3	*F*1	*B*4	*B*1	*DCT*2	*DCT*1	*F*4	*K*4	*F*2	*F*3
H	100	94. 31	85. 85	83. 36	70. 26	56. 97	56. 37	44. 77	*18. 69*	*17. 02*	*10. 99*	*0. 40*
L	61. 97	78. 85	49. 27	56. 90	46. 36	30. 43	33. 72	41. 18	*8. 86*	*10. 78*	*10. 90*	*0. 00*
N	100	94. 31	85. 85	83. 36	70. 26	56. 97	56. 37	44. 77	*18. 69*	*17. 02*	*10. 99*	*0. 40*

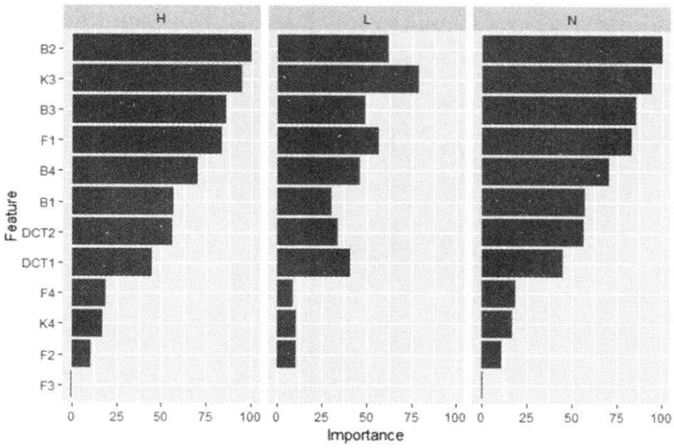

Figure 7 Importance of 12D predictors estimated by the Boosted Logistical Regression model. The *varImp* function in the *caret* package measures the importance scores. All measures of importance are scaled to have a maximum value of 100.

Multivariate model fitting shows that the most important predictors are the formant bandwidths, especially *B*2. The weighting scores of *B*2 are 100 in both the high and low frication groups. Score of *K*3 in the low frication group is higher than other predictors. Score of *F*1 is close to *B*3 in the high and the non-frication groups, while *B*3 is higher in the low frication group. Figure 8 plots the 3D diagrams of the mean values of *B*2, *K*3 and F1 for different vowel variants (left) and frication groups (right). In the right plot of Figure 8, the high frication group has the greatest *B*2 and the smallest *F*1 and *K*3 values, while the non-frication group is completely opposite; the low frication group falls in between. In terms of the projection of the normalized mean of *B*2, the high frication group is greater than 1, but in which [v] is slightly less than 1 because of its breathy phonation. B2 for the low frication group is in the range of 0.1 to 0.99, and the non-frication group is less than 0.1 (as also seen in Table 7). Therefore, it is appropriate to use *B*2 as an important cue to distinguish the levels.

Table 7 Mean values of *B*2 of the vowels and variants of three fricative levels. *B*2: H > L > N.

H				L				N			
yʑ	ʑ	z	v	u_v	y_j	i_j	$ɿ_ɹ$	y	u	ɿ	i
1.63	1.217	1.074	0.987	0.585	0.461	0.404	0.253	0.051	−0.132	−0.257	−0.454
mean: 1.227				mean: 0.426				mean: −0.198			

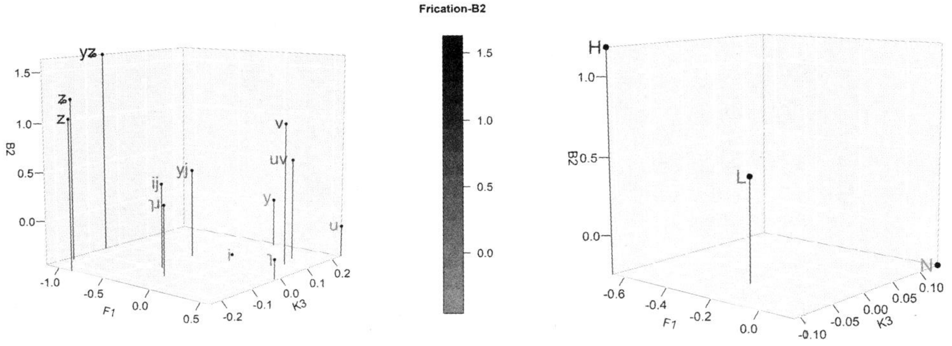

Figure 8 3D diagrams of the vowels and variants of three fricative levels. *Left*: mean values of each vowel and variants. *Right*: mean values of three levels. The strip of Frication – *B*2 shows the scale of frication.

4.2 Pattern recognition of social variability

Results of the model fitting of the acoustic parameters show that, the weighting scores of *F*2, *F*3, *F*4, and *K*4 are all below 20 (see the italics in Table 6). Consequently, the optimal parameter set consists of the predictors of above 20, including *B*2, *K*3, *B*3, *F*1, *B*4, *B*1, *DCT*2, and *DCT*1. Pattern recognition with the 8D optimal set further quantifies the social variability of three frication levels in age and gender. Note that all raw acoustic data were normalized with z-scores [10]. According to the discussion in [1], the z-normalization is optimal in studying the social variability in speech among others.

To analyze the age variation, the training set consisted of the old group, and the young group was used as for the test set. The fricative level (i. e., *H*, *L*, *N*) was the dependent variable and the 8D parameters were the predictors. LogitBoost model was carried out in the prediction procedure. The results in Table 8 show that the total hit rate of the three levels is about 81.3%, among which the non-frication group is relatively stable with the highest hit rate of 83%; the hit rate for the low frication group is about 75%, and that for the high frication group is 54.9%. Therefore, the total degree of age variation is about 18.7%, and the degrees from large to small are thus *H* (45%) > *L* (25%) > *N* (17%), where the higher the fricative level is, the greater the age variation is.

Similarly, to analyze the gender variation, the training set consisted of the male data, and the female data were used as the test set. Results of pattern recognition for gender are close to that for age. The differences are relatively prominent in the low frication group; the degree of the gender variation of 33.3% is about 8% higher than that of the age. Degrees from large to small are thus *H* (43%) > *L* (33%) > *N* (14%), where the higher the fricative level is, the greater the gender variation is.

Table 8 Results of the pattern recognition of the social variability of three levels in age and gender. The bold integers refer to the numbers of the matched samples between the training set and the test set. Others are the unmatched.

Age					Gender				
	H	L	N	Total hit rate		H	L	N	Total hit rate
H	**50**	59	37	0. 813	H	**83**	104	19	0. 816
L	37	**377**	515		L	55	**517**	260	
N	4	67	**2690**		N	14	210	**2285**	
Single hit rate	0. 549	0. 750	0. 830		Single hit rate	0. 566	0. 666	0. 857	

5. DISCUSSION AND CONCLUSIONS

Via statistical modeling, this paper explored the acoustic realization and social variability of vowels in three fricative levels. Based on the multivariate database, the model fitting estimated the weighting score of each predictor, in order to obtain the optimal parametric set. Pattern recognition further quantified the social variability with the optimal set. Prominent acoustic characteristics of vowel frication are the changes of bandwidths and frequencies of low frequency formants, in which *B*2 is the most significant cue in distinguishing three frication levels. Frication made *B*2 prominently wider. At the same time, other parameters, including *F*1, Energy ratio, Slope, Curvature, and Skewness (*K*3), also played important roles both within and across different frication levels. Results of the pattern recognition showed that the degrees of variation in age and gender are both close to 19%, where the higher the fricative level is, the greater the social variability is. Although the results have shown that there is a correspondence between acoustics and auditory impression regarding the three frication levels, further perception experiments with tuned parameters of the optimal set need to be done in the future.

This study thus contributes to the literature of Chinese vowel studies in two main aspects. First, previous studies on Chinese high vowels defined the low fricative variants as "fricative vowels"; however, this term contradicts the traditional vowel definition. This paper suggests that the variants of the low frication vowels are better named as "fricative approximant". The high frication vowels have the basic characteristics of voiced fricatives with the widest bandwidth (*B*2). This also indicates that pure vowels, pure consonants, and the transitional forms between them can act as the V in the (C)V context.

Second, there are two cases of phonological changes caused by vowel frication in Chinese dialects. Taking the high vowel /i/ for a typical example, it evolves into the low fricative variant [i_{j}] or even the high fricative variant [ʑ], with the significant changes of formant bandwidths and frequencies due to the fricative airflow. Besides, the vowel /i/ produces the apical vowel /ɿ/ for the forward articulatory gesture caused by the frication [7]. According to Wu [20], the vowel /i/ produced by the young generation has been in the process of disappearing in Nantong dialect of Jianghuai Mandarin, but replaced with the low fricative variant [i_{j}] and the apical vowel [ɿ] . In Changzhou dialect of Wu Chinese, the low fricative variant [i_j] and the non-frication [i] in the young generation, corresponding to [i] and [ɪ] in the old generation respectively, have formed a new phonemic contrast. This thus could be the evolutionary trend of fricative variants of high vowels in other Chinese dialects in the future.

6. ACKNOWLEDGEMENTS

The work was supported by the National Social Science Foundation of China (19BYY048) and the Major Program of the National Social Science Foundation of China (19ZDA307) . Thanks to Prof. XIONG Ziyu for the great work of developing xRecorder software.

REFERENCES

[1] Adank, P. , Smits, R. , van Hout, R. 2004. A comparison of vowel normalization procedures for language variation research. *Journal of the Acoustical Society of America* 116 (5), 3099 – 3107.

[2] Boersma, P. , Weenink, D. 2018. Praat: Doing phonetics by computer (6. 0. 40) . Retrieved March 11, 2018, from http: //www. praat. org.

[3] Bombien, L. , Winkelmann, R. , Scheffers, M. 2018. wrassp: an R wrapper to the ASSP Library (0. 1. 8) . Retrieved August 31, 2018, from https: //github. com/IPS-LMU/wrassp.

[4] Gries, S. T. 2013. *Statistics for Linguistics with R: A Practical Introduction* (2nd ed.) . Berlin: De Gruyter Mouton.

[5] Kuhn, M. 2018. caret: Classification and Regression Training (6. 0 – 80) . Retrieved May 26, 2018, from https: //github. com/topepo/caret/.

[6] Harrington, J. 2010. *The Phonetic Analysis of Speech Corpora*. Chichester: Wiley-Blackwell.

[7] Hu, F. , Lin, F. 2019. Fricative vowels as an intermediate stage of vowelapicalization, *Language and Linguistics* 20 (1), 1 – 14.

[8] Ladefoged, P. , Wu, Z. 1984. Place of articulation: An investigation of Pekingese fricatives and affricates. *Journal of Phonetics* 12, 267 – 278.

[9] Ladefoged, P. 2006. *A Course in Phonetics* (5th ed.) . Boston: Cengage Learning.

[10] Lobanov, B. M. 1971. Classification of Russian vowels spoken by different speakers. *Journal of the Acoustical Society of America* 49, 606 – 608.

[11] R Core Team. 2018. R: A language andenvironment for statistical computing (3. 5. 1) . Retrieved July 2, 2018, from https: //www. R-project. org.

[12] Shi, R. 1998. On the high frication in high vowels in Chinese dialects. *Yuyan Yanjiu* 1, 100 – 109. (石汝杰:《汉语方言中高元音的强摩擦倾向》,《语言研究》1998 年第 1 期, 100—109 页。)

[13] Soetaert, K. 2017. plot3D: Plotting Multi-Dimensional Data (1. 1. 1) . Retrieved August 28, 2017, from https: //CRAN. R-project. org/package = plot3D.

[14] Sun, R. 2011. A study of the fricative quality based on spectral principal components. *Acta Acustica* 4, 427 – 434. (孙锐欣:《基于频谱主成分分析的音素摩擦性音质研究》,《声学学报》2011 年第 4 期, 427—434 页。)

[15] Svantesson, J. O. 1986. Acoustic analysis of Chinese fricatives and affricates. *Journal of Chinese Linguistics* 14 (1), 53 – 70.

[16] Tuszynski, J. 2018. caTools: Tools: moving window statistics, GIF, Base64, ROC AUC, etc. (1. 17. 1. 1) . Retrieved July 20, 2018, from https: //CRAN. R-project. org/package = caTools.

[17] Watson, C. I. , Harrington, J. 1999. Acoustic evidence for dynamic formant trajectories in Australian English vowels. *Journal of the Acoustical Society of America* 106, 458 – 468.

[18] Winkelmann, R. , Jaensch, K. , Cassidy, S. , Harrington, J. 2018. emuR: Main Package of the EMU Speech Database Management System (1. 1. 1) . Retrieved November 12, 2018, from https: //github. com/IPS-LMU/emuR.

[19] Wu, B. 2013. A study of the types of apical vowels [ɿ] in Chinese dialects. *Yuyan Yanjiu Jikan* 10, 113 – 122. (吴波:《汉语方言舌尖元音 [ɿ] 的类型》,《语言研究集刊》2013 年第 10 辑, 113—22 页。)

[20] Wu, B. 2018. A study offricativization of vowel [i] in Northern Wu Chinese and Jianghuai

Mandarin. *Wuyu Yanjiu* 9, 151 - 158. (吴波:《北部吴语与江淮官话元音 [i] 的擦化》,《吴语研究》第 9 辑, 151—158 页。)

[21] Zhang, L. H., Chen, B., Qu, D. 2012. Method for fricative and affricate classification based on articulatory characteristic. *Jisuanji Kexue* 9, 211 - 214. (张连海、陈斌、屈丹:《基于发音特性的摩擦音和塞擦音分类算法》,《计算机科学》2012 年第 9 期, 211—214 页。)

[22] Zhao, R. 2007. [i] > [ɿ] in Chinese dialects. *Zhongguo Yuwen* 1, 46 - 54. (赵日新:《汉语方言的 [i] > [ɿ]》,《中国语文》2007 年第 1 期, 46—54 页。)

[23] Zhao, Y. R. 2011. *Studies in the modern Wu dialects*. Beijing: Commercial Press. (赵元任:《现代吴语的研究》,商务印书馆 2011 年版。)

[24] Zhu, X. 2004. Sound changes of high vowels in Chinese dialect. *Zhongguo Yuwen* 5, 440 - 451. (朱晓农:《汉语方言的高顶出位》,《中国语文》2004 年第 5 期, 440—451 页。)

[25] Zhu, X. 2010. *Phonetics*. Beijing: The Commercial Press. (朱晓农:《语音学》,商务印书馆 2010 年版。)

XU Menghan She is a graduate student of School of Humanities, Nanjing Normal University. Her research interests include speech production and perception. She is now working in Maigao Qiao middle school of Nanjing.
Email: 1245340157@ qq. com

WU Bo PhD. Corresponding author. He is a professor of School of Humanities, Nanjing Normal University. His research interests include speech production, comparative dialectology and Chinese traditional phonology.
Email: wubo1977@ 163. com

VOWEL CONTEXT, PLACE DIFFERENCE, AND THE PERCEPTUAL DISTINCTIVENESS OF SIBILANTS

LI Mingxing

Abstract Vowel contexts are shown to influence the perceived distinction of sibilants at different places, e. g. , with alveolar vs. palatal sibilants perceptually less distinct in the [_i] context than in the [_a] context. This study investigates if this pattern holds across different sibilant place contrasts, e. g. , an alveolar-palatal contrast vs. an alveolar-retroflex contrast. Twenty-four listeners completed a speeded-AX discrimination task in which the stimuli were the sound pairs [si – ɕi] [sa – ɕa] [si – ʂi] [sa – ʂa], which aimed to access the relative psychoacoustic distinction of these pairs. The [si – ɕi] pair turned out to introduce a lower accuracy and a longer response time than the other pairs, with no response time difference among the other three. Assuming a longer response time to indicate less perceptual distinctiveness, the results confirm the observation in the literature that a [si – ɕi] pair is perceptually less distinct than a [sa – ɕa] pair; the lack of difference in [si – ʂi] vs. [sa – ʂa] suggests that the [_i] context does not reduce the perceived sibilant place distinction across all places. There seems to be a trading relation between the effect of vowel context (e. g. , a reduced distinction in the [_i] context) and the relative acoustic difference between sibilants when evaluating the distinctiveness of a CV pair.
Keywords Sibilant, Contrast, Place of articulation, Vowel context

1. INTRODUCTION

Consonants differ in their places and manners of articulation and voicing, which correspond to different acoustic and perceptual properties. The sound systems of human languages are observed to prefer consonantal contrasts that are more distinct [4, 9, 10, 25]. When it comes to a particular consonant, its acoustic properties may differ to various extents when it appears in different vowel contexts, which usually translates into different qualities in relation to its perceptual cues [21, 22, 30].

The perceptual distinction of a particular pair of consonants can be influenced by vowel contexts such that the same two consonants are perceived to be less distinct in one context than in another [27, 28, 32, 33]. For fricatives at different places, experimental studies showed that a high-front vowel context such as [_i] may introduce a reduced perceptual distinction as compared with other vowel contexts, e. g. , [_a] [17, 19, 20]. The reduced perceptual distinctiveness in the [_i] context has been attributed to factors such as the similarity of the frication noise in the sibilants [13, 16, 34] and weakened formant transitions in the high front vowel context than in other vowel contexts [19]. In their experimental study of alveolar vs. palatal sibilants (e. g. , [s ts ts^h] vs. [ɕ tɕ $tɕ^h$]), [20] tested the perceptual distinction of the same pairs of sibilants in different vowel contexts, e. g. , [si – ɕi] [si – ɕi] [sou – ɕou]. The response time data from the speeded-AX discrimination experiment revealed that the [_i] context introduced a longer response time, corresponding to less perceptual distinction, as compared with the other vowel contexts. The experimental results are shown to be consistent with the typological pattern across Chinese dialects that contrasts such as [si tsi ts^hi] vs. [ɕi tɕi $tɕ^hi$] tend to be avoided [20].

Sibilant consonants widely exist across Chinese dialects [18]. The study in [20] focused on the place contrasts of alveolar vs. palatal sibilants and it did not involve other sibilant place contrasts. What remains unclear is if the vowel effect observed in [20], e. g., the same sibilant pair perceptually less distinct in the [_i] context, holds for sibilant pairs across different places. For example, for an alveolar-retroflex pair (e. g., [s – ʂ]), does the [_i] context introduce a smaller perceptual distinction than the [_a] context?

2. METHOD

The current study aims to investigate the relative psychoacoustic distinction of two sibilant pairs, [s – ɕ] and [s – ʂ] in two vowel contexts: [_i] and [_a], instead of the perceptual distinction of the pairs by listeners from a particular language background. Speeded AX discrimination experiment was initiated by [1, 11], which has been shown to be able to access the psychoacoustic distinction of sound pairs independent of the listeners' native sound systems [1, 11, 20]. In a speeded-AX discrimination task, a listener judges if two sounds are the same as quick as possible. In contrast to a traditional AX discrimination task, a speeded-AX discrimination experiment, as in [1, 11], is featured by (i) a short Inter-Stimulus-Interval (ISI) within a sound pair, such as 100 ms, to elicit judgment based on the acoustic difference of the two sounds, (ii) a time pressure such as encouraging the listeners to make a judgement within 500ms, to reduce the influence from the listeners' native sound systems, (iii) a feedback on response time and accuracy after each trial, to encourage the listeners to maintain a balance of speed and accuracy [23]. In a speeded-AX discrimination, a shorter response time to a different pair is assumed to indicate a larger perceptual distinctiveness of the two sounds and vice versa, as in a traditional AX discrimination task [29, 36].

2.1 Participants

Previous studies adopting the speeded-AX discrimination task [1, 11, 20] have established that participants with different native sound systems, e. g., English vs. Dutch or English vs. Mandarin, did not differ in their response patterns, suggesting that the setting in a speeded-AX discrimination task is able to access the relative perceptual distinction of sound pairs independent of the listeners' native sound systems. In this study, therefore, native English listeners' responses would be taken to be representative of general listeners' evaluation of the relative psychoacoustic differences of the sound pairs. Twenty-four native English listeners served as the subjects, all of whom were university students and none reported hearing or speaking impairments.

2.2 Stimuli

The stimuli were the four sound pairs [si – ɕi] [sa – ɕa] [si – ʂi] [sa – ʂa], involving two place contrasts, i. e., alveolar vs. palatal as in [s – ɕ] and alveolar vs. retroflex as in [s – ʂ], and two vowel contexts, i. e., [_i] vs. [_a]. The stimuli were created through the following steps.

2.2.1 Recording

While the sibilants [s] [ɕ] and [ʂ] widely exist across Chinese languages, the syllable [si] is absent in Mandarin Chinese (which has [sɹ̩] instead of [si]) and many other Chinese dialects. Even in dialects reported to have [si], the [s] might have undergone palatalization, e. g., under the influence of Mandarin Chinese. The syllable [ʂi] is even rare across Chinese dialects and reported only in a few Chinese dialects such as Qimen

祁门 [31] and Wuhua 武华 [35]. On the other hand, both [si] and [ʂi] exist in the sound system of Peking opera, which preserves many features of the sound system of Chinese languages in earlier centuries. Furthermore, actors of Peking Opera are trained to give accurate pronunciation of consonants and vowels thus they are suitable speakers to produce the stimulus syllables for the experiment.

The syllables in Table 1 were produced by a male actor of Peking opera, who is also a native Mandarin speaker. The target syllables (in Chinese characters) were read in the carrier sentence ['我说的是____这个字'] 'what I said was ____ this character'. The speaker read the target syllables in Column I and the carrier sentences as they are in the narrative style of Peking opera. He read those in Column II as in the normal speech Mandarin, because not all the relevant syllables are legal forms in Peking opera.

Table 1 Syllables for the stimulus recording

Onsets	I. [_i] context	II. [_a] context
s	si 西 'west'	sa 撒 'to release'
ɕ	ɕi 兮 'particle'	ɕa 瞎 'blind'
ʂ	ʂi 世 'world'	ʂa 杀 'to kill'

Two notes on the syllables in Table 1. First, all the syllables bear a high-level tone except that [ʂi] 世 'world' has a falling tone. The speaker was invited to produce it with a high-level tone as in other syllables. Second, the syllable [ɕa] as in Mandarin Chinese was conventionally presented as [ɕia] or [$ɕ^j$a] in the literature. The assumed on-glide [i/j], according to [15], was actually not different from the formant transition between a palatal consonant and a following vowel [a]. Thus, the syllable was represented as [ɕa] in Table 1.

The recording was done at a sampling rate of 44.1kHz. Six tokens were produced for each syllable in Table 1. Out of the six tokens, one was selected for further manipulation, whose acoustic properties were close to the mean values of the six tokens, e.g., the COG, dispersion, and intensity in the sibilant portion and the formants in the vowel portion.

2.2.2 Manipulation

The six selected tokens were manipulated through the following steps using Praat [5] before the formation of syllable pairs.

First, the durations of the fricatives were normalized to 125 ms, which is close to their typical length in normal-speed speech [7]. The durations of the naturally produced sibilants were all longer than 125 ms and the fricatives were generally shortened.

Second, the vocalic portions of the syllables were normalized to 120 ms to match the mean vowel durations in natural speech [7] with 50 ms for the consonant-vowel transition [6] and 70ms for the steady vowel. The vowel durations in the produced syllables were typically longer than 120 ms, thus the vowels were all shortened in the manipulation. For the syllable [ɕa] in particular, the interval from the onset of periodic waves to the onset of steady vowel formants was manipulated into 50 ms.

Third, across all the stimulus syllables, a level F0 of 200 Hz was superimposed onto the vocalic portions. As the syllables were all produced with a high-level tone, this manipulation did not lead to obvious distortion of the vowel quality.

Fourth, the root-mean-square intensities of the vocalic portions in the stimulus syllables, e.g., [i] in [si], were normalized to 72 dB, which was the mean intensity value across the vowel portions of all the naturally produced tokens. The amplitudes of the vowels faded out to zero within the last 20ms. The intensities of the sibilants, e.g., [s] as in [si], were manipulated to the mean values of the 6 repetitions in the speaker's production.

The acoustic properties of the manipulated syllables are presented in Table 2. For the sibilants, the COG, dispersion, and intensity were measured across the whole consonants; for the vowels, the F1 and F2 were measured at the mid-points. The F2 onsets were measured at the beginning of the vocalic portion, which have been shown to be useful in evaluating the formant transitions in the relevant syllables [20]. The measurement results are presented as Hz values together with corresponding values on the Bark scale. The waveforms and spectrograms of the stimulus syllables are provided in Figure 1.

Table 2 Acoustic properties of the manipulated stimulus syllables

a. Onset sibilant

Syllable	COG(Hz/Bark)	Dispersion(Hz)	Intensity(dB)
si	8119/19.80	1977	59
çi	4719/16.56	1374	62
ʂi	4230/15.91	2127	62
sa	6221/18.21	1383	58
ça	4588/16.39	1149	59
ʂa	3385/14.59	1363	59

b. Vocalic portion

Syllable	F1(Hz/Bark)	F2(Hz/Bark)	F2Onset(Hz/Bark)
si	321/3.07	2570/12.97	1895/11.20
çi	318/3.05	2590/13.01	2431/12.64
ʂi	315/3.02	2547/12.91	1982/11.46
sa	928/7.32	1392/9.47	1282/9.02
ça	933/7.35	1391/9.47	1908/11.24
ʂa	966/7.53	1392/9.47	1549/10.06

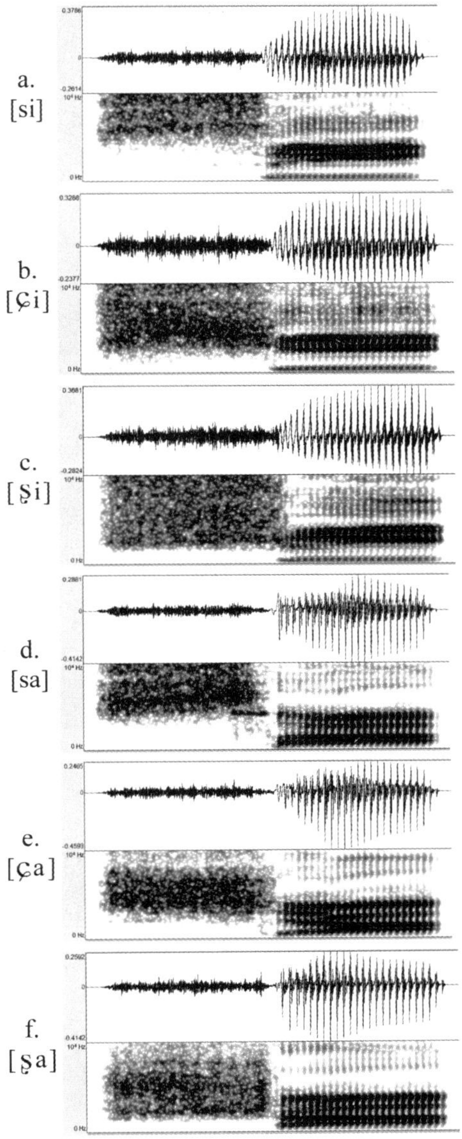

Figure 1 Waveforms and spectrograms of the stimulus syllables after manipulation

2.2.3 Pair formation

Four contrast pairs were formed using the six manipulated syllables, [si – çi], [sa – ça], [si – ʂi], and [sa – ʂa], involving an alveolar-palatal contrast (i. e., [s – ç]) and an alveolar-retroflex contrast (i. e., [s – ʂ]) in two vowel contexts (i. e., [_i] vs. [_a]).

For each contrast pair (e. g., [si – çi]), four stimulus pairs were formed: two different pairs (e. g., [si – çi] [çi – si]) and two identical pairs (e. g., [si – si] [çi – çi]). Thus, a total of 16 pairs were formed.

Within each stimulus pair, the Inter-Stimulus-Interval (ISI) was set as 100 ms to facilitate responses based on the psychoacoustic difference of the two sounds [1,11,29,36], instead of perceptual difference based on the sound system of a listener's native language.

2.3 Procedure

The experiment was programmed using the software Paradigm (Perception Research Systems 2007). On hearing a sound pair, a participant judged if the two sounds are the same by pressing 'same' or 'different' on a button box. The listeners were all right-handed and the same button box layout was used, with 'same' appearing on the left and 'different' on the right.

The main experiment was preceded by a practice session, in which the stimuli were 16 sound pairs such as [di – du] and [di – di]. In the practice session and the main experiment, the participants were instructed to give a response as quick as possible, with a response time goal of 500 ms [1,11]. After a decision was made, a feedback screen would appear informing a participant of (i) the accuracy of his/her response to the sound pair (Correct vs. Incorrect), (ii) the accumulated accuracy of their judgments (e.g., 90% correct), and (iii) his/her response time for the current pair in terms of whether it was below 500 ms or not.

3. RESULTS

3.1 Accuracy

The 24 participants gave a total of 576 responses to the four sound pairs, with an overall accuracy rate of 95%, i.e., an acoustically different pair judged as different, across all the pairs and all the listeners. Table 3 provides the accuracy rates of the four pairs in terms of their percentages of correct responses. Of the four pairs, [si – ɕi] has a relatively lower accuracy as compared with the other pairs.

Table 3 Accuracy of CV Pairs

CV Pairs	% of correct responses
[si – ɕi]	92%
[si – ʂi]	97%
[sa – ɕa]	94%
[sa – ʂa]	98%

3.2 Response time

For a different pair in an AX discrimination experiment, a longer response time is assumed to indicate more difficulty in distinguishing the two sounds, which corresponds to a smaller perceptual distinction of the two parts in the sound pair; conversely, a shorter response time in judging two sounds as different indicate a larger perceptual distinction of the two.

For each stimulus pair, the response time was calculated from the onset of the sibilant in the second syllable, e.g., the starting of frication noise of [ɕ] in a [si – ɕi] pair. The twenty-four listeners' raw response times (RT) to the different pairs, the distribution of which is usually skewed towards the smaller values on the scale, were log transferred (LogRT) to facilitate statistical analyses. To exclude outliers in the LogRT data, for each participant, the data points below and above 2.5 standard deviations from the mean LogRT were trimmed off.

The LogRT data were submitted to Linear Mixed Effects Models using the "lmer" function in the R package lme4 [2,3] and the *p*-values were determined by the R package lmerTest [14]. The dependent variable is LogRT and the predicting variable is CVPair (i.e., the four pairs [si – ɕi], [sa – ɕa], [si – ʂi], [sa – ʂa]), and the random factors are Participant (i.e., the 24 participants) and Participant: CVPair (i.e., the four pairs in each participant). A null model with Participant and Participant: CVPair as the random factors was compared with a superset model including CVPair as the predicting variable. The addition of CVPair improved the model although the *p*-value is slightly above the usually adopted cutoff level of 0.05 ($X^2 = 7.74$, $df = 3$, $p = .052$). Therefore, the superset model including Onset was taken as the model for the participants' responses. Then, the model was checked with different sound pairs alternatively as the baseline to find out the difference among the four pairs. The results are summarized in Table 4, including the *t* values and *p* values.

Table 4 Pairwise comparisons in the results: *t* values with *p* values

	[sa – ɕa]	[si – ʂi]	[sa – ʂa]
[si – ɕi]	-1.99(0.047)	-1.94(0.053)	-2.64(0.009)
[sa – ɕa]		0.07(0.945)	-0.64(0.526)
[si – ʂi]			0.71(0.476)

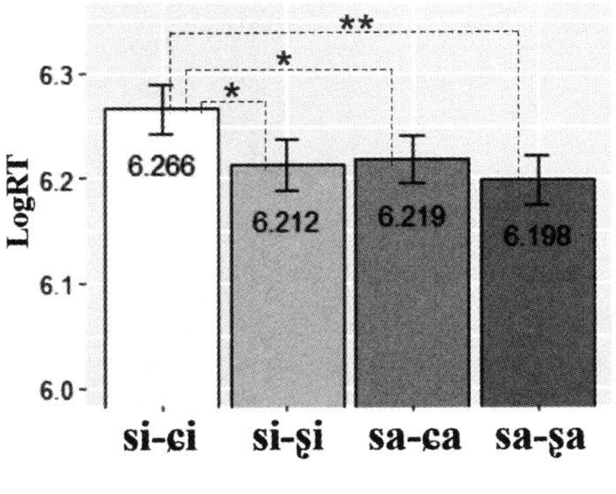

Figure 2 Results of Mean LogRT across the four stimulus pairs

Incorporating the results of pairwise comparisons in Table 4, Figure 2 presents the mean LogRTs of the four pairs [si – ɕi], [sa – ɕa], [si – ʂi], [sa – ʂa], with standard errors illustrated by the short lines. The dotted lines illustrated the differences between sound pairs whose *p* values turned out to be lower or extremely close to 0.05. Simply put, the results in Figure 2 show that the [si – ɕi] pair led to a longer response time than the pairs [sa – ɕa], [si – ʂi], [sa – ʂa], with no significant difference among the latter three.

4. Discussion

4.1 Vowel effect in different sibilant pairs

This study examines if the reduction of sibilant place distinction in the [_i] context holds across sibilant contrasts at different places of articulation. Assuming a longer response time to indicate a smaller perceptual distinction, the results of the speeded AX-discrimination as in Figure 2 suggest that

(1) the [si – ɕi] pair is perceptually less distinct than the pairs [sa – ɕa], [si – ʂi], [sa – ʂa];

(2) the three pairs [sa – ɕa], [si – ʂi], [sa – ʂa] have similar perceptual distinctiveness.

It needs to be noted that the results of the accuracy are also consistent with the above. As shown in Table 3, the [si – ɕi] pair introduced a lower accuracy than all the other three pairs, which is likely to suggest that it is the most confusable pair among the four.

The pattern (i) confirms the observation in [20] that alveolar vs. palatal sibilants are perceptually less distinct in the [_i] context than in a vowel context such as [_a]. The pattern (ii), however, shows that [si – ʂi] is not perceptually less distinct than [sa – ʂa]. In other words, for the place contrast in an alveolar [s] vs. a retroflex [ʂ], the vowel context [_i] does not introduce a reduced perceptual distinctiveness as compared with the vowel context [_a].

Referring to the research question raised in this study, the results in Table 2 shows that the reduction of sibilant place distinction in the [_i] context, as observed in [20], does not hold across all sibilant contrasts at different places of articulation, e. g., not applicable to the contrast of an alveolar [s] vs. a retroflex [ʂ].

4.2 Interaction of different properties in perceptual distinction

To examine the role of acoustic properties in the observed results, the acoustic differences of the sibilants and those of the vowels in the stimulus syllables are laid out in Table 4, referring to the measurements in Table 2. In Table 5, a difference value (e. g., a ΔCOG as 3400 Hz or 3.24 in Bark for the [si – ɕi] pair) was obtained as the absolute value of the difference of the two sibilants in a pair (e. g., 8119 Hz in [s] vs. 4719 Hz in [ɕ]). For vowel formant difference, an additional percentage value (e. g., a ΔF1 as 3 Hz for the [si – ɕi] pair) was calculated by dividing the formant difference (e. g., |ΔF1| of the [si – ɕi] pair) by the lower of the two formant values involved (e. g., 318 Hz of the F1 in [ɕi]).

An examination of the acoustic difference in Table 5 suggests that the reduced perceptual distinctiveness of [s] vs. [ɕ] in the [_i] context, as compared with the [_a] context, is unlikely to be rooted in the acoustic differences of the sibilant onsets, which is consistent with [20]. More specifically, referring to the acoustic differences in Table 5, the [si – ɕi] pair has a larger difference (ΔCOG = 3400 Hz or 3.24 in Bark) than the [sa – ɕa] pair (ΔCOG = 1633Hz or 1.82 in Bark), which is in a different direction from the relative smaller perceptual difference of [si – ɕi] than [sa – ɕa]. Neither is the vowel effect likely to be rooted in the steady vocalic portions, because the formant differences in both [si – ɕi] and [sa – ɕa] are below the Just Noticeable Difference (JND) of formant differences, which was reported to be 3% – 5% of the reference formant frequency [8, 12, 26] and, for vowels in consonantal contexts, 60 Hz for F1 and 176 Hz for F2 [24]. In terms of Bark values, similarly, the difference in F1 and F2 are quite small, all smaller than 0.06, as shown in Table 5. As proposed in [20], a potential explanation is that the F2 Onset difference in the [si – ɕi] pair (ΔF2Onset = 536 Hz or 1.44 in Bark) is smaller than that in the [sa – ɕa] pair (ΔF2Onset = 626 Hz or 2.22 in Bark), which translates to a smaller difference in the consonant-to-vowel formant transitions in the [si – ɕi] pair than in the [sa – ɕa] pair. Assuming this to be the case, the reduced perceptual distinction of [s] vs. [ɕ] in the [_i] context can be attributed to their smaller formant transition difference in the [_i] context, which overrides the larger acoustic difference in the sibilants when the participants listen to a CV syllable as a unit.

Table 5 Acoustic differences of the manipulated stimulus syllables

a. Onset difference

Syllable	|ΔCOG| (Hz/Bark)	|ΔDispersion| (Hz)	|ΔIntensity| (dB)
si – ɕi	3400/3.24	603	3
sa – ɕa	1633/1.82	234	1
si – ʂi	3889/3.89	150	3
sa – ʂa	2836/3.62	20	1

b. Vocalic difference

Syllable	|ΔF1| (Hz &%/Bark)	|ΔF2| (Hz&% /Bark)	ΔF2Onset(Hz&% /Bark)
si – ɕi	3 (1%) / 0.02	20 (1%) / 0.04	536 / 1.44
sa – ɕa	5 (1%) / 0.03	1 (<1%) / < 0.01	626 / 2.22
si – ʂi	6 (2%) / 0.05	23 (1%) / 0.06	87 / 0.26
sa – ʂa	38 (4%) /0.21	<1(<1%) / < 0.01	267 /1.04

The larger perceptual distinction of [si – ʂi] than [si – ɕi] seems to suggest a trading relation between the acoustic difference in the sibilants and the influence of formant transition difference in the perceived distinctiveness of CV pairs. Based on the measurements in Table 5, for example, [si – ɕi] has a smaller COG difference (ΔCOG = 3400 Hz or 3.24 in Bark) than [si – ʂi] (ΔCOG = 3889 Hz or 3.89 in Bark), consistent with the larger perceptual distinction in [si – ʂi]; on the other hand, [si – ɕi] has a larger formant transition difference (ΔF2Onset = 536 Hz or 1.44 in Bark) than [si – ʂi] (ΔF2Onset = 87 Hz), which contradicts the larger distinction in [si – ʂi]. Thus, the observed larger distinction of [si – ʂi] than [si – ɕi], as in Figure 1, seems to suggest that a larger acoustic difference in the onset sibilants may override a smaller formant transition difference when perceiving the distinctiveness of a CV pair.

The lack of a significant difference in the perceptual distinctiveness of [sa – ɕa] vs. [sa – ʂa] also seems to suggest a balancing of different acoustic properties when evaluating the perceptual distinction of a CV pair. As illustrated in Table 5, [sa – ɕa] has a smaller COG difference in the onset sibilant (ΔCOG = 1633 Hz or 1.82 in Bark) than [sa – ʂa] (ΔCOG = 2836 Hz or 3.62 in Bark) while [sa – ɕa] has a larger formant transition difference (ΔF2 Onset = 626 Hz or 2.22 in Bark) than [sa – ʂa] (ΔF2 Onset = 87 Hz or 0.26 in Bark). This seems to suggest that a balance was struck, for example between the COG difference in the sibilants the formant transition difference in the vowels, when evaluating the perceptual distinctiveness of a CV pair.

5. Conclusions

This study examines the relative perceptual distinctiveness of sound pairs involving different vowel contexts ([i] vs. [a]) and different place contrasts of sibilants ([s – ɕ] vs. [s – ʂ]). Results from the speeded-AX discrimination experiment confirmed the observation in the literature, i. e., the alveolar vs. palatal sibilants are perceptually less distinct in the [_i] context than in the [_a] context. On the other hand, the alveolar vs. retroflex sibilants, e. g., [s] vs. [ʂ], turned out to be equally distinct in the [_i] context and the [_a] context, when compared with the perceptually weak contrast [si – ɕi].

For sibilant place contrasts, experimental studies in the literature [19, 20] observed that the [_i] context may reduce the perceptual distinctiveness. This lent support to the contention that the emergence of apical vowels in Mandarin is likely to be relevant to the enhancement of sibilant place contrast, e. g., a perceptually less distinct /si – ɕi/ contrast is phonetically realized as a perceptually more distinct [sɹ̩ – ɕi] pair [20]. In the results of the current study, the difference in [si – ɕi] vs. [sa – ɕa] confirm the observation in [19, 20]. On the other hand, the lack of difference between [si – ʂi] and [sa – ʂa] suggests that [_i] context may not reduce the perceptual distinction of sibilant difference across all places. In other words, the reduced perceptual distinction in the [_i] context may occur only to two sibilants that are close enough on certain dimensions. The examination of the acoustic properties of the sibilants and vowels in the current study suggests a trading relation between the influence of vowel contexts and the differences in sibilant places, by which the acoustic difference in the sibilants and the vowels interact in a delicate way and contribute to the perceptual distinction of a CV pair.

It needs to be noted that the discussions in this study are based on a minimal number of sound pairs and a small number of aspects of acoustic properties and are thus suggestive. The more detailed interaction of different acoustic properties of sibilants and vowels when listeners evaluating the perceptual distinctiveness of a CV pair awaits more sophisticated investigation in future research.

6. ACKNOWLEDGEMENTS

I would like to thank Profs. Jie Zhang, Allard Jongman, Joan Sereno, Annie Tremblay, Crispin Williams, and The University of Kansas Phonetics & Psycholinguistics Laboratory (KUPPL), for the support and help. Thanks to the two anonymous reviewers for their valuable advice. The research is partially supported by Hong Kong Baptist University Research Committee's Start-up Grant for New Academics and Hong Kong Baptist University Faculty Research Grant (FRG) Category II (No. FRG2/17 – 18/076).

REFERENCES

[1] Babel, M., Johnson, K. 2010. Accessing psychoacoustic perception with speech sounds. *Journal of Laboratory Phonology* 1, 179 – 205.

[2] Bates, D., Maechler, M., Bolker, B., Walker, S. 2015a. lme4: Linear mixed-effects models using Eigen and S4. R package version 1.1 – 9, https://CRAN.R-project.org/package = lme4.

[3] Bates, D., Maechler, M., Bolker, B., Walker, S. 2015b. Fitting Linear Mixed-Effects Models using lme4. ArXiv e-print; *Journal of Statistical Software*, http://arxiv.org/abs/1406.5823.

[4] Boersma, P., Hamann, S. 2008. The evolution of auditory dispersion in bidirectional constraint grammars. *Phonology* 25, 217 – 270.

[5] Boersma, P., van Heuven, V. 2001. Praat, a system for doing phonetics by computer. *Glot International* 5(9/10), 341 – 345.

[6] Delattre, P. C., Liberman, A. M., Cooper, F. S. 1955. Acoustic loci and transitional cues for consonants. *The Journal of the Acoustical Society of America* 27, 769 – 773.

[7] Feng, L. 1985. Beijinghua yuliu zhong shengyundiao de shichang [Duration of consonants, vowels and tones in colloquial Beijing Mandrain]. In Lin, T., Wang, L. (eds) *Beijing Yuyin Shiyan Lu* [*Experimental Studies in Beijing Mandarin*]. Beijing: Peking University Press.

[8] Flanagan, J. L. 1955. A difference limen for vowel formant frequency. *The Journal of the Acoustical Society of America* 27, 613 – 617.

[9] Flemming, E. 2004. Contrast and perceptual distinctiveness. In Hayes, B., Kirchner, R., Steriade, D. (eds) *Phonetically Based Phonology*, 232 – 276. Cambridge: Cambridge University Press.

[10] Flemming, E. 2005. Speech perception and phonological contrast. In Pisoni, D. B., Remez, R. E. (eds) *The Handbook of Speech Perception*, 156 – 181. Oxford: Blackwell.

[11] Johnson, K., Babel, M. 2010. On the perceptual basis of distinctive features: Evidence from the perception of fricatives by Dutch and English speakers. *Journal of Phonetics* 38, 127 – 136.

[12] Kakusho, O., Kato, K. 1968. Just discriminable change and matching range of acoustic parameters of vowels. *Acustica* 20, 46 – 54.

[13] Keyser, S. J., Stevens, K. 2006. Enhancement and overlap in the speech chain. *Language* 82, 33 – 63.

[14] Kuznetsova, A., Brockhoff, P. B., Christensen, R. H. B. 2015. lmerTest: Tests in linear mixed effects models. R package version 2.0 – 20.

[15] Ladefoged, P., Maddieson, I. 1996. *The Sounds of the World's Languages*. Blackwell Publishers Ltd.

[16] Lee, C. – Y., Li, Z. 2003. Enhancement of phonological contrast: Acoustics of apical and retroflex vowels in Mandarin Chinese. Poster Presentation on *The 34th Annual Meeting of the North Eastern Linguistic Society*. Stony Brook, NY.

[17] Lee, G., Jongman, A. 2014. Cue integration in the perception of fricative-vowel coarticulation in Korean. Presentation on *The 168th Meeting of the Acoustical Society of America*, Indianapolis, Indiana, USA: Oct 27 – 31, 2014.

[18] Lee, W. – S., Zee, E. 2014. Chinese phonetics. In Huang, C. – T. J., Li, Y. – H. A., Simpson, A. (eds) *The Handbook of Chinese Linguistics*. Malden, MA, USA: Wiley-Blackwell.

[19] Lee-Kim, S – I. 2014. Contrast neutralization and enhancement in phoneme inventories: Evidence from sibilant place contrast and typology. Ph. D. dissertation, New York University.

[20] Li, M., Zhang, J. 2017. Perceptual distinctiveness between alveolar and palatal sibilants in different vowel contexts and its implications for phonological contrasts. *Laboratory Phonology* 8 (1), 18.

[21] Liberman, A. M. , Delattre, P. , Cooper, F. S. 1952. The role of selected stimulus-variables in the perception of the unvoiced stop consonants. *The American Journal of Psychology* 65, 497 – 516.

[22] Mann, V. A. , Soli, S. D. 1991. Perceptual order and the effect of vocalic context on fricative perception. *Perception and Psychophysics* 49, 399 – 411.

[23] McGuire, G. 2010. A brief primer on experimental designs for speech perception research. Manuscript. UC Santa Cruz.

[24] Mermelstein, P. 1978. Difference limens for formant frequencies of steady-state and consonant-bound vowels. *The Journal of the Acoustical Society of America* 63, 572 – 580.

[25] Mohr, B, Wang, W. S. – Y. 1968. Perceptual distance and the specification of phonological features. *Phonetica* 18, 31 – 45.

[26] Nord, L. , Sventelius, E. 1979. Analysis and prediction of difference limen data for formant frequencies. *Quarterly Progress Status Report* 3 – 4. 60 – 72. Stockholm: Speech Transmission Laboratory, Royal Institute of Technology.

[27] Padgett, J. 2001. Contrast dispersion and Russian palatalization. In Hume, E. , Johnson, K. (eds) *The Role of Speech Perception in Phonology*. Academic Press.

[28] Padgett, J. 2003. Contrast and post-velar fronting in Russian. *Natural Language and Linguistic Theory* 21, 39 – 87.

[29] Pisoni, D. 1973. Auditory and phonetic codes in the discrimination of consonants and vowels. *Perception and Psychophysics* 13, 253 – 260.

[30] Sereno, J. A. , Baum, S. R. , Marean, G. C. ; Lieberman, P. 1987. Acoustic analyses and perceptual data on anticipatory coarticulation in adults and children. *The Journal of the Acoustical Society of America* 81, 512 – 519.

[31] Shen, T. 1989. Qimen fangyan de yüyin tedian [The phonetic properties of Qimen dialect]. *Fangyan* [*Dialects*] 1, 30 – 39.

[32] Steriade, D. 1999. Alternatives to syllable-based accounts of consonantal phonotactics. In Fujimura, O. , Joseph, B. D. , Palek, B. (eds) *Proceedings of LP '98: Item Order in Language and Speech*. Prague: Charles University and Karolinum Press.

[33] Steriade, D. 2008. The phonology of perceptibility effects: The P-map and its consequences for constraint organization. In Hanson, K, Inkelas, S. (eds) *The Nature of the Word: Essays in Honor of Paul Kiparsky*, 151 – 180. Cambridge: The MIT Press.

[34] Stevens, K. , Li, Z. , Lee, C. – Y. , Keyser, S. J. 2004. A note on Mandarin fricatives and enhancement. In Fant, G. , Fujisaki, H. , Cao, J. , Xu, Y. (eds) *From Traditional Phonology to Modern Speech Processing*, 393 – 404. Beijing: Foreign Language Teaching and Research Press.

[35] Wei, Y. 1997. Wuhua fangyan tongyinzihui [The syllables and homophones in Wuhua dialect]. *Fangyan* [*Dialects*] 3, 206 – 219.

[36] Werker, J. F. , Logan, J. S. 1985. Cross-language evidence for three factors in speech perception. *Perception and Psychophysics* 37, 35 – 44.

LI Mingxing PhD He is an Assistant Professor in Department of English Language and Literature at Hong Kong Baptist University. His research interests include phonetics, phonology, speech perception, second language/phonology.
Email: mingxingli@ hkbu. edu. hk

维吾尔族大学生汉语普通话单元音习得研究：基于共振峰相似度的对比分析

古力努尔·艾尔肯　艾斯卡尔·艾木都拉

摘　要　为了进一步了解汉语普通话学习者的发音状况、发音方式并满足学习者语音识别上高精度的实际应用需求，本文研究了维吾尔语为母语的大学生学习汉语普通话元音产出的共振峰模式及相似度。当人们在学习一门语言的语音的时候，他们通常会调整其发音方式和位置以达到一种有效或正确的模式，即构成一个发音空间。二语语音的学习过程实质上是在母语发音空间的基础上构建一个新的区别于母语的发音空间，但这个新的发音空间一定程度上受到母语发音空间的制约。基于以上考虑，本研究中先是通过计算出在不同普通话学习阶段（初、中以及高级）的学习者和标准普通话母语者的元音共振峰结构之间的距离，并进行了对其声学特征的对比实验，从而获得了代表初、中、高级学习者元音发音差异性的特征。此实验结果有利于为学习者提供教学相关的有效参考信息，为计算机辅助语言教学系统（CALL）提供可靠、正确的参数和发音评估，也有利于提高多民族汉语普通话语音识别的精度。

关键词　普通话，单元音，学习者，共振峰特征，对比分析

Acquisition of Mandarin Monosyllabic Words by Uyghur College Students: A Comparative Analysis Based on Formant Similarity

ARKIN Gulnur　HAMDULLA Askar

Abstract This paper studies the vowel formant patterns of Mandarin Chinese learners who are native speakers of Uyghur, and the degree of similarity to native speakers of Mandarin, in order to further understand patterns and manners in the speech of learners of Mandarin Chinese, and to meet the needs for high - precision practical applications in learners' speech recognition systems, When people learn pronunciations of a language, they usually adjust their place and manner of articulation to reach an effective or correct mode of pronunciation, leading to a new pronunciation space. The process of second language speech learning is essentially to construct a new pronunciation space different from, but constrained by that of the mother tongue. Based on the above considerations, this study first calculated the distance between the vowel formant structures of Mandarin learners at different proficiency levels (beginning, intermediate, and advanced) and native Mandarin speakers. The experimental results could be a good resource for Mandarin learners, providing reliable and correct parameters and pronunciation evaluations for CALL systems, and improving the accuracy of multi - ethnic Mandarin speech recognition systems.

Keywords Mandarin, Monophthong, Learners, Formant characteristics, Comparative analysis

1. 引言

汉语普通话是我国通用语言，国家通用语言教学在我国各少数民族区域广泛开展。有关语音的教学质量仍待进一步提高，学习者语音水平也有很大的提升和发展空间。国内有不少探讨外国学习者对汉语普通话学习的实证研究［8］，尤其是关于美国、日本学习者的汉语普通话语音习得的研究比较多。［4］曾经对美国留学生学习汉语普通话时在三类复合元音上的偏误进行分析。［9］在语言学习模型（Speech Learning Model，SLM）的基础上对美国学习

者的汉语一级元音的习得情况进行了比较深入的研究。[10]采用跟踪调查的方法,研究得出日本学习者汉语舌尖后元音的发展轨迹等。[5]通过测试,分析了初、中、高水平的越南留学生汉语声母感知和产出两个方面的偏误。然而,整体来看,针对少数民族学生的汉语学习方面的定量研究不多。这使得针对性教学指导无法开展;另一方面,对于少数民族学习者来说,他们在具体的汉语语音合成和识别方面需要借助计算机辅助[1],但目前多民族汉语语音处理技术也有待提高。所以,本研究借助实验语音学方法,深入分析并定量对比高级水平、中级水平和初级水平学习者普通话与普通话母语者单元音的声学特点,以期为上述问题提供帮助。

第二语言习得(Second Language Acquisition,SLA)研究是20世纪60年代末新兴的学科领域,该领域主要研究第二语言习得的本质和习得的过程[2]。在国外由于SLA理论的不断发展,更由于语音学和音系学近几十年来所取得的丰硕成果,二语语音习得的研究近年来也取得了长足的进步。而在国内,虽然近年公开发表的二语语音习得论文数量有所增加,但与国际上的研究相比,在研究方法和理论上仍存在着差距。在这样的大环境下,相对于以汉语为母语的二语语音习得研究,关于少数民族以普通话为第二语言语音习得的研究数量少,方法滞后。在这当中,研究有关少数民族普通话语音习得静态性的语音习得偏误的居多,而他们语音习得的发展过程则鲜有探究[3],因此使用新的研究方法来探究少数民族的二语语音习得的动态过程很有意义,它可以推动少数民族的二语语音习得动态过程相关研究的发展。

而本研究就是以学习者二语习得的动态过程为研究对象,通过分析不同普通话水平的学习者在普通话元音的学习过程中表现出的声学上的动态发展变化的特征,深入了解其语音习得轨迹,探究其原因,以期能有效地为少数民族的普通话学习者的教学提供一些相关的参考数据。本研究也通过实验验证了二语习得中的一些重要理论,例如中介语(学习者的第二语言)动态地趋于目标语言的特性。

2. 实验说明

2.1 实验对象

本实验共有60名被试,其中有50名维吾尔族人(25男,25女),他们都是新疆大学学生,年龄均为20—26岁(平均年龄23岁)。他们的母语是维吾尔语,不存在语言和听力方面的问题,父母都是维吾尔族,日常交际使用维吾尔语;普通话是他们的第二语言,学习普通话时间均超过十年,他们的汉语MHK(少数民族汉语水平考试)口试成绩均在45以上。另外10名是汉族人(5男,5女),来自北京,他们的普通话属于标准普通话,平均年龄是23岁。

表1　　被试分组情况

被试者水平	性别	被试人数	MHK平均分
初级水平组(UCB)	男	6	57
	女	6	55
中级水平组(UCI)	男	10	65
	女	10	67
高级水平组(UCA)	男	9	83
	女	9	82
标准组(MC)	男	5	—
	女	5	—

我们需要研究的是维吾尔族人学习普通话元音的发展轨迹,也就是研究维吾尔族人的普通话元音在不同的普通话学习阶段的习得情况,发音差异,以及受母语的影响程度。因此我们根据这50名学习者的普通话熟练程度将其分成三组,作为处在不同学习阶段的被试。普通话学习者50个人中普通话熟练分数范围是45到90分,他们的分数类似一个正态分布,其平均分是69分,标准差是11,因此我们在分组的时候,选取了在平均分上下二分之一的标准差作为分界点,将50人分成男、女各3组。最后的分组情况是:初级水平组

(UCB)MHK 得分区间是(45,60],中级水平组(UCI)得分区间是(61,75],高级水平组(UCA)是(76,90]。详细的分组情况见表1。

2.2 语音采集

语音数据在专门的录音室中采集,使用设备有笔记本、外置声卡、麦克风。使用外置声卡能达到调节声量大小、降噪声、监控爆破音情况等。使用 Matlab 编写录音程序。采集频率是 16kHz。发音材料是单音节词,每个被试需要录 500 个汉语单音节词,维吾尔族学生另需录 512 个标准维吾尔语单音节词。其中,汉语单音节词包括普通话中/i, y, u, a,o,ɤ, ɿ, ʅ/八个单元音,维吾尔语词包括维吾尔语中/a, ɛ,e, i, ɔ,Ø,u,y/八个单元音。

2.3 数据处理

首先,根据已标注的(标准组和非标准组)单音节语音,我们提取出元音的声学数据。一个元音的音色在很大程度上是由第一和第二共振峰决定的。因此我们用 PRAAT、Matlab 工具,在元音相对稳定段提取元音 F1 和 F2 频率数据。其次,为了接近实际的听感距离,并且去除一些不可控因素对于发音人的影响(如发音者的心情、录音时段的影响等),F1 和 F2 的频率值分别被转化为 Bark 值[11],转化公式如下:

$$\text{Bark} = 7.0 \times \log\left(\frac{f}{650} + \sqrt{\left(1 + \left(\frac{f}{650}\right)^2\right)}\right) \quad (1)$$

其中,f 代表共振峰频率。随后对比标准普通话者和学习者(初,中,高)的声学参数。

3. 实验结果:初、中、高级水平学习者与标准普通话者共振峰对比

3.1 共振峰值对比

因为男女声发音在声学上有很大的不同,所以本研究将分别对比分析男女声发音。实验得出的具体数据见下表,表2 和表3 分别代表维吾尔族学习者女声与汉语普通话母语者女声的单元音第一、第二共振峰平均 Bark 值。

表2 不同水平学习者与标准普通话者第一共振峰均值对比(女性、F1)(Bark)

元音	MC-女	UCA-女	UCI-女	UCB-女
a	5.65	5.64	5.57	5.73
o	4.26	4.20	4.35	4.16
ɤ	4.16	4.01	4.10	4.08
u	3.18	3.29	3.44	3.58
y	2.98	2.66	2.89	3.14
i	2.47	2.36	2.45	2.48
ɿ	3.30	3.18	3.27	3.44
ʅ	3.51	3.55	3.66	3.95

表3 不同水平学习者与标准普通话者第二共振峰均值对比(女性、F2)(Bark)

元音	MC-女	UCA-女	UCI-女	UCB-女
a	7.58	7.54	7.66	7.73
o	6.27	6.19	6.51	6.22
ɤ	7.29	7.01	7.24	7.26
u	8.46	8.67	8.34	8.43
y	9.92	9.81	9.94	9.86
i	11.04	10.94	11.05	11.07
ɿ	7.84	7.95	7.98	7.76
ʅ	9.18	9.14	9.20	8.92

表2 和表3 显示,初级水平女性学习者与女性标准普通话者在单元音产出方面可能存在系统性差异,从数值上看,在 F1,除了/u/和/ʅ/外,初级水平女性学习者普通话单元音的数值均比汉语母语者普通话小,在 F2, 除了/u,ɿ/,初级水平女性学习者其他单元音的数值均比汉语母语者小。

就/ɤ,y,i/而言,初级水平女性学习者的 F1、F2 平均值比汉语普通话母语者的 F1、F2 平均值稍微低,由此可以推断,学习者元音产出的舌位偏高且前。通过单因素方差分析,检验两组被试者的舌位是否差异显著。元音/ɤ/上的差异最为明显($p_{F1}<0.05$,$p_{F2}<0.05$)。另外,就元音/y/(p_{F1}

>0.05,$p_{F2}<0.05$)和元音/i/而言($p_{F1}>0.05$,$p_{F2}<0.05$),两组显著差异体现在F2上,第一共振峰数据未能体现出具体统计意义的差别,说明初级女性学习者主要区别在于舌位前后。对于元音/a,o,u,ɿ,ʅ/($p_{F1}>0.05$,$p_{F2}>0.05$)而言,两组产出的频率值在F1、F2上无显著性差异。

对中级水平女性学习者来说,从数值上看,除了元音/o,u,ʅ/外,中级水平女性学习者普通话单元音的F1均比汉语母语者普通话小;除/ɤ,u/外,中级水平女性学习者其他单元音的F2均比汉语母语者大。统计检验显示,对元音/o,y,ɿ/,两组舌位前后无差异($p_{F1}>0.05$),但学习者的舌位比母语者显著偏高($p_{F2}<0.05$)。对/a,u/而言,F1差异显著而F2不显著($p_{F1}<0.05$,$p_{F2}>0.05$),表现为学习者相较母语者,/a/舌位明显偏低,/u/舌位偏高。/ɤ,i,ʅ/($p_{F1}>0.05$,$p_{F2}>0.05$)差异不显著。

对高级水平女性学习者来说,大致上看,除了元音/ɤ,o/外,高级水平女性学习者普通话单元音的F1均比汉语母语者普通话数值大,而除了/a,i/外,学习者F2均比汉语母语者小。统计结果表明,对元音/a,y/,学习者比母语者的舌位偏前($p_{F2}<0.05$),舌位前后无差异($p_{F1}>0.05$);而两组在/o/($p_{F1}>0.05$,$p_{F2}<0.05$)的区分主要体现在学习者舌位较前、而普通话母语者则较后。另外,/i/($p_{F1}<0.05$,$p_{F2}>0.05$)的组间差异在于学习者舌位明显偏低,舌位的前后无差别。高级水平女性学习者对比母语者在/ɤ,u,ɿ,ʅ/上无明显差异($p_{F1}>0.05$,$p_{F2}>0.05$)。

表4和表5显示,在F1,除了元音/u,i,ʅ/外,初级水平男性学习者普通话单元音的F1平均值均比汉语母语者普通话小。在F2,除了/ʅ/,初级水平男性学习者其他单元音的F2数值均比汉语母语者小。从统计上看,/ɤ/上存在差异,初级学习者舌位偏高偏前($p_{F1}<0.05$,$p_{F2}<0.05$)。元音/a/主要学习者比母语者舌位偏高($p_{F1}<0.05$,$p_{F2}>0.05$)F1差异显著。而/ʅ/上的差异体现在于F2($p_{F1}>0.05$,$p_{F2}<0.05$),F1差异不显著。/o,i,ɿ/的F1、F2差异不显著($p_{F1}>0.05$,$p_{F2}>0.05$)。

对中级水平男性学习者来说,中级水平男性学习者普通话单元音的F1除元音/u/外均比汉语母语者普通话小,F2除/ʅ/外均比汉语母语者小。统计结果显示,学习者的元音/i,ɿ/的产出与母语者差异显著($p_{F1}<0.05$,$p_{F2}<0.05$),学习者/i/的发音舌位偏高偏前,/ɿ/的发音舌位偏高偏后。不仅如此,中级学习者/y/的舌位偏高,在舌位前后无明显差异($p_{F1}<0.05$,$p_{F2}>0.05$);学习者/ɤ/的发音舌位明显偏后,F2有显著差异,舌位高低即F1无显著差别($p_{F1}>0.05$,$p_{F2}<0.05$);学习者/ʅ/的发音舌位偏高,F1有显著差异,前后无显著差别($p_{F1}<0.05$,$p_{F2}>0.05$)。

对高级水平男性学习者来说,在F1上,除了元音/u,y,i/外,高级水平男性学习者普通话单元音均比汉语母语者普通话小;在F2上,除/ɿ,ʅ/,高级水平男性学习者单元音均比汉语母语者小。统计显示,/o,ʅ/上学习者与普通话母语者差异最为明显($p_{F1}<0.05$,$p_{F2}<0.05$),/o/舌位偏低偏前,/ʅ/舌位偏后。对于元音/ɤ/,学习者的差异在于舌位偏高,舌位前后无显著差异($p_{F1}<0.05$,$p_{F2}>0.05$),但元音/u/($p_{F1}>0.05$,$p_{F2}<0.05$)的产出则表现出完全相反趋势。两组在/a,y,i,ɿ/上舌位基本重合,产出差异不显著。

表4 不同水平学习者与标准普通话者第一共振峰均值对比(男性、F1)(Bark)

元音	MC-男	UCA-男	UCI-男	UCB-男
a	4.55	4.45	4.44	4.46
o	4.00	3.93	3.87	3.93
ɤ	3.86	3.58	3.57	3.52
u	2.85	2.94	3.27	3.43
y	3.08	2.72	2.95	3.12
i	2.45	2.56	2.41	2.54
ɿ	3.47	3.36	3.11	3.39
ʅ	3.38	3.54	3.35	3.38

表5　不同水平学习者与标准普通话者第二共振峰均值对比(男性、F2)(Bark)

元音	MC－男	UCA－男	UCI－男	UCB－男
a	7.30	7.18	7.06	6.93
o	8.25	7.80	7.63	8.06
ɤ	8.08	7.46	7.38	7.34
u	8.08	7.70	7.54	7.92
y	9.64	9.44	9.50	9.62
i	10.45	10.23	10.17	10.41
ɿ	8.41	8.17	7.73	8.19
ʅ	8.20	8.42	8.33	8.60

我们又进一步计算了不同水平学习者和母语者的共振峰差异,计算方式为(f 为共振峰 bark 值):

$$差值 = |(f_{标准普通话者} - f_{学习者})| / f_{标准普通话者} \quad (2)$$

当共振峰的离散度大于10%时,在听觉上可以认为是另一个元音[6],因此下文以10%作为参考值讨论。

表6　不同水平学习者与标准普通话者第一共振峰差值(女性、F1)

	F1－女　(Differences %)		
元音	MC－UCA	MC－UCI	MC－UCB
a	0.14	1.41	1.47
o	1.56	2.11	2.23
ɤ	3.61	1.44	1.83
u	3.56	8.17	12.72
y	10.89	3.02	5.27
i	4.54	0.81	0.46
ɿ	3.70	0.90	4.30
ʅ	1.24	4.27	12.44

从表6和表7可知,高水平女性学习组(UCA)单元音/y/,初级女性组(UCB)的单元音/u/的F1与标准普通话的差异较大,差值均大于10%,其余均在10%以内。而初(UCB)、中(UCI)、高(UCA)水平学习者的单元音F2的差值都在10%以内。

表7　不同水平学习者与标准普通话者第二共振峰差值(女性、F2)

	F2－女　(Differences %)		
元音	MC－UCA	MC－UCI	MC－UCB
a	0.46	1.05	1.98
o	1.37	3.82	0.74
ɤ	3.80	0.68	0.40
u	2.52	1.41	0.30
y	1.03	0.20	0.57
i	0.96	0.09	0.32
ɿ	1.40	1.78	1.00
ʅ	0.37	0.21	2.80

从以下表8和表9显示,高级水平男性学习组(UCA)单元音/y/,中级水平男性组(UCI)的/u/、/ɿ/,初级男性组(UCB)的单元音/u/的F1与标准普通话的差异较大,差值大于10%,其余均在10%以内。而无论是初、中、高级水平男性学习者(UCA,UCI,UCB)普通话单元音的F2与标准普通话差值都在10%以内,此模式与女性学习者相似。

表8　不同水平学习者与标准普通话者第一共振峰差值(男性、F1)

	F1－男(Differences %)		
元音	MC－UCA	MC－UCI	MC－UCB
a	2.17	2.42	1.97
o	1.81	3.25	1.83
ɤ	7.09	7.51	8.84
u	3.23	14.74	20.18
y	11.79	4.22	1.39
i	4.31	1.63	3.86
ɿ	3.15	10.37	2.30
ʅ	4.78	0.89	0.11

表9 不同水平学习者与标准普通话者第二共振峰差值(男性、F2)

	F2 – 男 (Differences %)		
元音	MC – UCA	MC – UCI	MC – UCB
a	1.65	3.29	5.04
o	5.43	7.52	2.34
ɤ	7.71	8.66	9.11
u	4.62	6.68	1.98
y	2.06	1.45	0.17
i	2.05	2.68	0.37
ɿ	2.88	8.09	2.59
ʅ	2.71	1.59	4.88

3.2 共振峰相似度对比

在这里我们使用F1、F2构建声学空间,通过计算声学空间中学习者的音素和本族者的音素之间的欧式距离,将这种距离作为衡量学习者第二语言语音的正确度,也就是学习者的L2(Second Language)的语音体系和标准的目标语音体系之间的差异。

$$ED = \sqrt{(x_2 - x_1)^2 + (y_2 - y_1)^2} \quad (3)$$

在此公式中,(x_1, y_1)、(x_2, y_2)代表声学元音图中的两点。其中,x的值为F2的Bark值,y的值为F1的Bark值。

这个差异越小,即声学距离越小,代表着学习者的第二语言语音越是接近标准的语音(本族人的语音)。M为男性发音人,F为女性发音人。

表10 不同水平学习者与标准普通话者陌生元音距离

发音人 \ 元音	o	ɤ	ɿ	ʅ
$ED_{UCA-MC/M}$	0.45	0.68	0.27	0.27
$ED_{UCI-MC/M}$	0.63	0.76	0.77	0.13
$ED_{UCB-MC/M}$	0.21	0.81	0.24	0.40
$ED_{UCA-MC/F}$	0.11	0.32	0.16	0.06
$ED_{UCI-MC/F}$	0.25	0.08	0.14	0.15
$ED_{UCB-MC/F}$	0.11	0.09	0.16	0.50

表11 不同水平学习者与标准普通话者相似元音距离

发音人 \ 元音	a	u	y	i
$ED_{UCA-MC/M}$	0.16	0.39	0.41	0.24
$ED_{UCI-MC/M}$	0.26	0.68	0.19	0.28
$ED_{UCB-MC/M}$	0.38	0.60	0.04	0.10
$ED_{UCA-MC/F}$	0.04	0.24	0.34	0.15
$ED_{UCI-MC/F}$	0.11	0.28	0.10	0.01
$ED_{UCB-MC/F}$	0.18	0.41	0.16	0.03

相似音素是指学习者母语发音和目标语发音声学上有差异[7]。维吾尔语和普通话有四个相似元音/a, i, u, y/。对于普通话学习者来说,普通话中的/ɿ, o, ʅ, ɤ/属于陌生元音,根据音系对比,它们和普通话/ɤ, ɿ, ʅ/的声学特征相差较大。根据对比分析假说(CHA),学习者在学习普通话时可以很好地掌握相似元音/a, i, u, y/,而掌握/o, ɿ, ʅ, ɤ/的发音时有困难。与此相反,语音学习模型(SLM)的等值归类机制预测学习者更容易习得陌生元音/o, ɿ, ʅ, ɤ/。

据表10和表11,按照与标准发音人的元音距离,不同水平学习者的普通话单元音排序(从小到大)如下:

(1)女性高级水平学习者:/a, ʅ, o, i, ɿ, u, ɤ, y/。

(2)女性中级水平学习者:/i, ɤ, y, a, ɿ, ʅ, o, u/。

(3)女性初级水平学习者:/i, ɤ, o, y, ɿ, a, u, ʅ/。

(4)男性高级水平学习者:/a, i, ɿ, ʅ, u, y, o, ɤ/。

(5)男性中级水平学习者:/ʅ, y, a, i, o, u, ɤ, ɿ/。

(6)男性初级水平学习者:/y, i, o, ɿ, a, ʅ, u, ɤ/。

总的来说,不同水平的学习者产出相似音素/a, i, y/较好,声学距离较小。不同水平学习者也各有一些发音较好的陌生音素。图1和图2直观表现了学习者产出相似元音和陌生元音与母语者的距离。

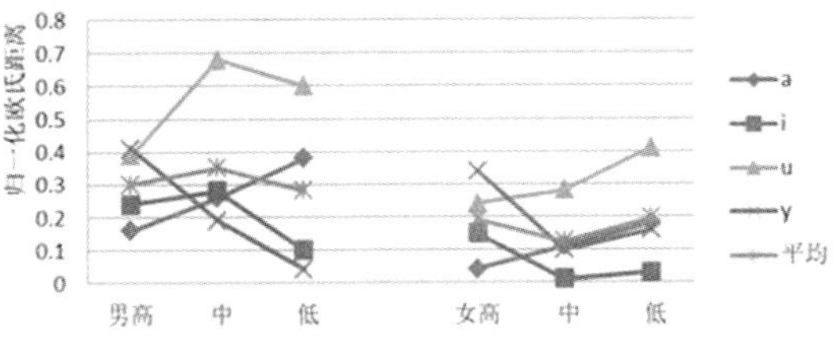

图 1　不同水平学习者与标准普通话者相似元音距离

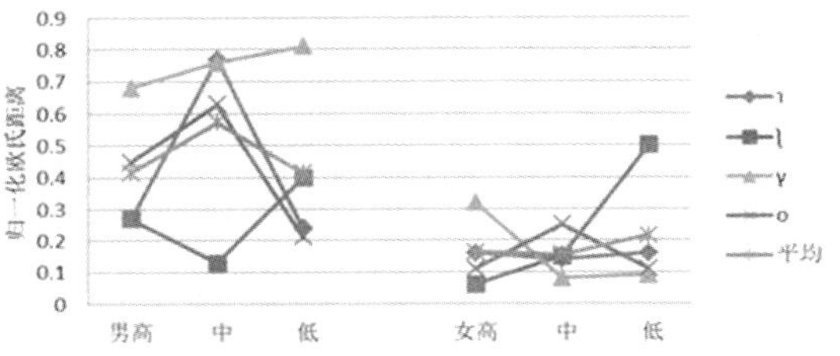

图 2　不同水平学习者与标准普通话者陌生元音距离

4. 讨论与结论

为了进一步了解新疆地区维吾尔族学习者汉语普通话发音状况,本文主要对不同水平的(初、中、高级)学习者产出的普通话元音与普通话母语者元音进行声学参数对比,并描述了发展轨迹。

我们的结果显示,无论男女,初级水平学习者在多个相似元音上发音较好,但在经过一段时间学习成为高级水平学习者后,这些元音的发音并没有更明显的提升。而对于一开始发音较不标准的相似元音,学习后都有了一定改进。陌生元音的习得则总体起点一般,且发展轨迹显示,提升效果不理想,男性学习者只有在/ɤ/、女性学习者只有在/ʅ/上逐渐习得了更好的发音。我们认为,结果总体与"对比分析假设"的预测较接近,即相似元音较易习得,陌生元音较难习得。但该假设无法解释初级学习者为何在几个陌生元音上有较好的产出,反而"语音学习模型"对这几个个例有更好的解释。

本研究结果对学习者提供教学参考,也为少数民族普通话学习自然度语音合成与高精度语音识别技术的发展提供数据,为计算机辅助语音系统提供可靠、正确参数和发音评估。

5. 致谢

本文研究得到了国家民委民族研究项目"推广普及国家通用语言文字与促进各民族交往交流交融——以南疆地区为例"(2021 - GMD - 081);新疆财经大学校级科研基金项目"深度神经网络背景下国家通用语言学习者声调自动检测研究"(2022XGC023)的经费支持。

参考文献

[1] Fant, G. 1960. *Acoustic Theory of Speech Production*. The Hague: Mouton, 118 - 120.

[2] Flege, J. 1995. Second language speech learning: Theory, findings, and problems. *Speech Perception and Linguistic Experience: Issues in Cross-language Research*. 233 - 277.

[3] Zhao, L., Feng, H. 2014. Acoustic features of Mandarin monophthongs by Tibetan speakers. *International Conference on Asian Language Processing*, 147 - 150.

[4] 邓丹:《美国学习者汉语复合元音的偏误分析》,《第九届中国语音学学术会议论文集》2010 年。

[5] 傅氏梅、张维佳:《越南留学生的汉语声母偏误分析》,《世界汉语教学》2004 年第 2 期,第 69—80 页。

[6] 呼和:《蒙古语元音声学分析》,《民族语文》1999 年第 04 期,第 58 - 65 页。

[7] 王韫佳:《跨语言语音对比与 L2 语音习得》,《第八届中国语音学学术会议暨庆贺吴宗济先生百岁华诞语音科学前沿问题国际研讨会——CAH、PAM 和 SLM 述评》2008 年,第 1—5 页。

[8] 温宝莹:《美国学生汉语元音习得的实验研究》,《汉语学习》2010 年第 7 卷第 3 期,第 95—104 页。

[9] 温宝莹:《汉语普通话元音习得的实验研究》,博士论文,南开大学,2006 年。

[10] 谢小丽:《日本学习者汉语普通话舌尖后音习得研究》,博士论文,中山大学,2006 年。

[11] 赵璐、冯卉、王慧霞、党建武:《藏语背景大学生普通话单元音的声学实验研究》,《第十一

届中国语音学术会议论文集》2014年。

古力努尔·艾尔肯 新疆财经大学公共管理学院讲师,博士。主要研究领域为实验语学、L1 & L2语音习得。
Email: gulnur407@163.com
艾斯卡尔·艾木都拉 新疆大学信息科学与工程学院教授,博士。研究领域包括自然语言处理、语音识别、语音合成和实验语音学。
Email: 2219658263@qq.com

绵阳安州话“儿尾”和“儿化”词缀的声学分析

张哲璇　吴君如

摘　要　绵阳安州话中“儿”词缀可以表现为独立成音节的卷舌“儿尾”，也可以表现为前一音节的卷舌“儿化”，两者可能反映了儿缀合音构词演变的先后两个不同阶段。本研究通过语言游戏实验进行诱导，采集了68名安州话发音人对34个带儿缀的安州话词汇的自发发音，研究了安州话儿尾和儿化的音系表征、词汇变异，并在此基础上通过第一、二共振峰（F1、F2）声学元音图比较了两者的声学特征，并讨论了其与开口度及发音前后的关系。研究发现，绵阳安州话中“儿”词缀的儿尾和儿化形式在音系表征上分别处于儿缀合音构词演变的“儿”独立音节阶段和合音长度正常的特殊合音单音节阶段。两者作为词汇变体的分布呈现出典型的词汇扩散模式。两者声学表征的主要区别在于F1最高点（开口度最低点）附近，此处儿尾的共振峰轨迹有较为一致的减速段，而儿化的共振峰轨迹的速度则相对较为均匀。但是，从安州话儿尾和儿化的共振峰轨迹看，两者在动作的轨迹方向以及轨迹中旋转的次数上都表现出较为丰富的变异，我们据此对于儿缀的语音演变机制做了相应讨论。

关键词　儿尾，儿化，合音，声学元音图，词汇扩散

An Acoustic Analysis of the Syllabic Suffix Er and Retroflexed Suffixation in the Anzhou Dialect of Mianyang

ZHANG Zhexuan　WU Junru

Abstract In the Anzhou dialect of Mianyang, Er-suffix has two alternative realizations, an independent retroflex syllable (Er Wei) or a retroflexed suffixation to its preceding syllable (Er Hua). The two forms may reflect two different stages of synaeresis in the word formation process. This study used a linguistic game to elicit 68 natural productions of the Anzhou words that contain the morphological suffix Er. We then compared the phonological realizations and lexical variations in the data of the syllabic and retroflexed suffixations. We analyzed acoustic realizations of the two forms by calculating and plotting F1 – F2 formants for the recorded samples. We found that, the syllabic and retroflexed forms of the Anzhou Er-suffix can be characterized, respectively, as being one independent syllable, and being a synaeresis syllable of the normal length with retroflexed rhymes. The lexical distribution of the two types of lexical variants showed a typical lexical diffusion pattern. Their acoustic realizations differ primarily in the speed of vowel trajectories. Around the maximal point of F1 (when the mouth is at its most open position), syllabic Er-suffix tend to involve deceleration at a relatively consistent speed, while retroflexed suffixation tends to involve a relatively smoother transition in its whole trajectory. However, the vowel trajectories of both Er-suffix forms showed extensive variations, pointing to individual differences regarding the direction and number of the movements. Accordingly, the mechanism of the phonetic evolution regarding the Er-suffix was discussed.

Keywords Syllabic suffix-Er, Retroflexed suffixation, Synaeresis, Vowel chart, Lexical diffusion

1. 引言

“儿化”和“儿尾”是汉语中“儿缀”常见的两种语音形式。其中，“儿尾”是自成音节的“儿缀”，“儿化”是“儿”韵附着在前一语素上并与前一语素融合成一个音节的“儿缀”［7，16］。汉语儿化音的来源主要是“里”“日”“儿”“了”等有限的几个字的音变［7，10］。除温州话等南方方言的儿尾为自成音节的［ŋ˞］之外，北方方言“儿”字单念的读音通常

用［ɚ］表示，不过吴宗济等学者通过实验发现“儿”是有很小的动程的，并据此认为它是复合元音［24，25］。

关于“儿”单字的语音表现目前仍有争议，而且关于“儿化”的语音表现的研究目前也还比较少。王理嘉、贺宁基［22］通过听辨实验为北京话归纳了［ar］、［ɛr］、［ər］、［ur］四类儿化韵。石锋［17］利用F3的升降区别、舌位动程的方向和速率，并结合声学元音图把北京话的“儿化韵”分为了融合型“儿化韵”、拼合型“儿化韵”以及鼻化型“儿化韵”这三类。

值得注意的是，刘振平［12］通过分析北京话儿韵和儿化韵语图中前三个共振峰的变化特点发现，“儿韵”的发音方式有两种，既可以先卷舌再发音，也可以逐渐卷舌；“儿化韵”的卷舌音色的载体是一个单纯的音素而非音丛；“儿化韵”与“儿韵”的“儿”音相同。北京话“儿韵”及“儿化韵”的声学变异或许与北方方言中儿缀读音演变的历史渊源有关。

从音系演化的角度来看，“儿化”和“儿尾”可能是“儿缀”语音演变的先后两个不同阶段。王洪君［21］提出，汉语北方话的儿化合音分为六个阶段：第一阶段为两音节阶段，也就是还没有开始合音的阶段；第二阶段为一个半音节阶段，后字经历轻声弱化，这是开始合音的第一步；第三阶段为长音节阶段，两个音节融合成一个长音节；第四阶段属于长度正常的特殊单音节阶段，其中又可以根据“-儿”的特征在前字音节中的扩展位置分为两类，分别是音节的末位置和韵腹位置；第五阶段也属于长度正常的特殊单音节阶段，但是这一阶段“-儿”的特征扩展到了前字音节的介音；第六阶段为正常的单音节阶段，“-儿”完成合音构词。丁崇明、荣晶［6］等进一步从聚合系统的角度提出，儿化韵的历时演变有三种状态：儿化韵数目增加、儿化韵整合以及儿化韵衰落。

“儿尾”和“儿化”形式在某些汉语方言中可以共存，例如湖北英山话［4］、河北顺平话［11］，以及晋语的平遥、太原、娄烦等方言［8］都有成音节的“儿尾”和不成音节的“儿化”共存的现象，其音系表现各有差异。本研究引入另一种“儿尾”“儿化”共存的方言，西南官话绵阳安州话作为研究对象，利用音系和语音方法考察两者的声学表现，并对相应的语音演化问题做出讨论。

2. 安州话儿缀的自然语料采集

2.1 被试

通过安州区社区活动中心的工作人员介绍，我们邀请了候选被试，并请被试填写了语言背景调查问卷的网页版或纸质版。我们根据候选被试的语言背景筛选出语言习得关键期［1］12岁及以前一直定居在安州区（事实上参与本研究的所有被试16岁以前都定居在安州区）、无语言障碍、以安州话为母语的本地人作为被试，参与命名实验。

本研究根据年龄段、性别将被试分为六组。两名被试由于忘记实验程序未能完成实验，因此其实验结果未列入本研究的有效数据库。顺利完成实验和数据采集的被试共68人，其中青年女性13人，青年男性11人，中年女性11人，中年男性11人，老年女性11人，老年男性11人，男女比例和年龄比例基本持平（青年组年龄范围18-39岁，中年组年龄范围40-59岁，老年组年龄60岁以上）。

2.2 实验材料

我们结合安州话语料和《汉语方言词汇调查手册》［18］、《成都话方言词典》［13］、《成都方言词典》［9］、《四川方言词典》［23］等资料，选取了34个词作为绵阳安州话儿尾和儿化变异的实验词。

2.3 实验过程

本研究采用语言游戏范式采集被试对实验词语的口头命名（verbal naming）数据。采用了笔记本电脑（ThinkPad X260）、外接声卡（SOUNDDEVICES USB-Pre 2）、话筒（AKG C544L）等硬件设备，以及实验生成软件E-Prime（version 3.0）。

实验时E-Prime（version 3.0）为不同被试以不同的随机顺序呈现实验刺激，并对被试的回答进行录音，录音设置为单声道，采样频率为16kHz，时长为5秒。在进行语音分析时，采用的软件为Praat（version 4.4.30）。

实验刺激采用音频与视频同步播放的方式，被试看到一个表示实验词的图片，并听到一个用绵阳安州话表述的句子作为指示语，这个句子对目标词进行了描述，要求被试根据上述提示说出图片表示的词。具体而言，我们为每一个实验词制作了一条指示语，该指示语说明实验词表示的事物或动作的种类和特征，并询问被试如何为之命名。指示语尽量避免说出与该事物或动作的名称相同或相似的内容干扰被试，并且每一条指示语的长度尽量接近。指示语由研究者（安州话青女使用者）以正常语速、语调用安州话平静地念出并录制，由E－prime实验生成程序调用，在实验时配合实验图片为被试自动播放与实验词对应的指示语。播放设备为笔记本电脑（ThinkPad X260）的内置喇叭。

（语音播放）一种动物，咯咯咯地叫，要吃米吃虫，还要下蛋，这是啥？

图1 实验刺激示例

3. 安州话儿缀的音系分析

绵阳安州话的儿缀可以表现为独立成音节的儿尾或融入前一音节的儿化。

安州话的儿尾单独成音节，大多数安州人发儿尾时读音与“儿”单字读音近似。

安州话的儿化韵归并与成都、重庆、自贡等地的方言基本一致，儿化韵系统按开口、齐口、合口、撮口四呼归并为四个卷舌儿化韵。本研究经过调查总结的绵阳安州话儿化韵系统如表1。（短横表示读该韵母的语素无儿化形式）

表1 绵阳安州话儿化韵表

韵母	儿化韵	例词
ɿ	ɚ	果汁R ko55tsɚ33
i	ɚ/iɚ	滴滴R（表示少量）ti45tɚ 55 花生米R fa45sən55miɚ53
u	ɚ	指拇R tsɿ55mɚ33
y	yɚ	蛐蛐R tɕ^{h}y22tɕ^{h}yɚ22
a	ɚ	尾巴R uei55pɚ33
ia	iɚ	豆芽R təu21iɚ 42
ua	uɚ	地瓜R ti21kuɚ45
e	ɚ	模特R mo22t^{h}ɚ21
ie	iɚ	柳叶R liəu55iɚ51
ue	——	——
ye	yɚ	噘R（叫声）tɕyɚ21
o	ɚ	一颗R i45kɚ53
io	iɚ	麻雀R ma22tɕ^{h}iɚ 21
ai	ɚ	口袋R k‘əu55tɚ 53
iai	——	——
uai	uɚ	冰块R pin45k^{h}uɚ53
ei	ɚ	酒杯R tɕiəu55pɚ 33
uei	uɚ	酸味R suæn45uɚ 53
au	ɚ	火炮R xo55pɚ 53
iau	iɚ	蒜苗R suæn21miɚ 42
əu	ɚ	红豆R xoŋ22tɚ 21
iəu	——	——
æn	ɚ	脸蛋R liæn55tɚ 53
iæn	iɚ	冒烟R mau21iɚ45
uæn	uɚ	吸管R ɕi22kuɚ 31

续表

韵母	儿化韵	例词
yæn	yɚ	汤圆 R t^{h}ɑŋ45yɚ $\underline{53}$
ən	ɚ	搽粉 R ts^{h}a22fɚ53
uən	uɚ	滚滚 R（轮子）kuən55kuɚ $\underline{51}$
in	iɚ	苍蝇 R ts^{h}ɑŋ45iɚ55
yn	yɚ	短裙 R tuæn55tɕ^{h}yɚ $\underline{51}$
ɑŋ	ɚ	胖胖 R（胖子）p^{h}ɑŋ21p^{h}ɚ45
iɑŋ	——	——
uɑŋ	uɚ	网网 R uɑŋ55uɚ $\underline{51}$
oŋ	ɚ	封封 R（方形袋子或盖子）foŋ45fɚ55
ioŋ	——	——

注：声调中的下划线表示发音短促，此为轻声的特点，与入声无关，R 代表韵母儿化，全文同。

安州话儿化韵系统简化后主要有/－ɚ，－iɚ，－uɚ，－yɚ/这四个儿化韵，以/i，u，y/为介音的韵母以及单元音/i，y/单独充当的韵母，儿化后原韵母仅保留介音或/i，y/，再加上卷舌元音/－ɚ/；在其他情况下（包括韵母是单元音/u/的情况），儿化后原韵母整体丢失，韵母直接变为/－ɚ/。可以看到，安州话的儿化主要处于王洪君所述的第四阶段之后，比北京的儿化更推进了一步，已经失去了韵腹的对立，但还能保留部分介音的差异。

安州话的变调系统较为复杂，有左控式和右控式平行的两套，变调实现受构词等因素的影响，本文从略，但其在儿尾和儿化中的表现在词汇音系演化上具有一定意义，以下作简要介绍。（1）考察发现，安州话的两字组加儿尾构成三字组可以实现的变调情形有 14 种，其中前两字变调模式所遵循的规则均可从两字组的连读变调规则中得到解释。单字加儿尾的特殊两字组也遵循了常规两字组的连读变调规律，或保留变短变轻的本调。有时候运用不同的变调规则还可以表示不同的意思，例如“花儿”读 45＋55 表示烟花，读 45＋$\underline{53}$ 表示植物的繁殖器官。这说明，安州话的儿尾基本处于王洪君所说的第一和第二阶段，具有较强的独立性。（2）安州话后字儿化的两字组（加上“儿”共三字）可以实现的变调情形有 36 种，与常规两字组的变调模式高度重合，只有两种特有的变调情形，即 A＋BR 由“21＋53”和“21＋213”变为“22＋22”，如“凉粉 R”和“媳妇 R”，可能显示了“儿”的声调影响的残余。这说明，从变调看，安州话的儿化基本失去了“儿”的本字声调，这也符合王洪君所说的第四阶段之后的情况。

4. 安州话儿缀的词汇变异

值得注意的是，绵阳安州话儿缀的音系总体上表现呈现出较大的词汇和社会变异。

表 2　绵阳安州话“儿尾”合音构词过程中的“词汇扩散”表

U	V	C
鸡儿（男性生殖器官）		
	花儿（烟花）～花 R（烟花） 花儿（植物的繁殖器官）～花 R（植物的繁殖器官） 画儿～画 R 碗儿～碗 R 猫儿～猫 R 奶娃儿～奶娃 R 肚脐儿～肚脐 R 踢毽儿～踢毽 R 毛梨儿～毛梨 R	
		尾巴 R 豆芽 R 抓子 R（一种游戏） 凉粉 R

注：U ＝未变（仅表现为儿尾形式），V ＝ 变异（儿尾、儿化形式均存在），C ＝ 已变（仅表现为儿化形式）

首先，尽管绝大多数安州人将“儿”单字以及儿尾音节读为卷舌元音/-ɚ/，也有少数安州人将“儿”缀实现为平舌韵，还有极少数安州人的“儿”音在卷舌韵和平舌韵之间切换。这种情况较为特殊，但与红安话类似［5］。根据我们的深入调查，在安州话中出现的平舌儿化韵一共有三种语音形式：/-ɯ/，类似兰州话［23］和陕西户县话［19］；/-ə/，类似昆明话的“儿”字音/ə/［20］；以及-/e/，类似红安话的小称变韵［14，15］。以下仅考虑常见形式。

更重要的是，安州话发音人在表示具体词汇时对于儿尾和儿化形式的选用也有较大的变异。若将儿尾和儿化看作演变的不同阶段，那么可以看到，绵阳安州话儿缀合音构词过程中儿尾和儿化两类词汇变体的分布在发音上是离散的，而在词汇上是连续的，显示出了典型的“词汇扩散”式音变的特点［3］。

5. 安州话儿尾和儿化的声学表现

从实验结果来看，在三十四个实验词中，有九个词处于变异（V）阶段，在安州话中既有儿尾形式，又有儿化形式，分别是“画、碗、猫、花（烟花）、花（植物的一种繁殖器官）、奶娃、肚脐、踢毽、毛梨（猕猴桃）”。这九个词的儿化韵又有三种情形：①儿化后韵母完全丢失直接变为卷舌元音［-ɚ］，如“猫、画、花（烟花）、花（植物的一种繁殖器官）”这四个词，“猫R”读为［mɚ45］，“画R”读为［fɚ213］，“花R（烟花）”和“花R（植物的繁殖器官）”都读为［fɚ45］；而儿尾韵则保留原韵母，“猫儿”读为［mau45ɚ55］，“画儿”读为［fa21ɚ45］，“花儿（烟花）”读为［fa45ɚ55］，“花儿（植物的繁殖器官）”读为［fa45ɚ53］。这些词的词根都不含介音。②儿化后保留了原韵母的介音再加上卷舌元音［-ɚ］构成儿化韵，如“碗、奶娃、踢毽”三个词儿化后分别读为［uɚ53］［lai55uɚ21］［tʰi22tɕiɚ213］；而这些词的儿尾韵也保留原韵母，“碗儿”读为［uæn55ɚ21］，“奶娃儿”读为［lai55ua52ɚ21］，“踢毽儿”读为［tʰi22tɕiæn21ɚ45］。③如“肚脐、毛梨（猕猴桃）”这两个词，主元音为高元音，它们的儿化韵与儿尾韵都保留了词根音节的韵母，再加上卷舌元音［-ɚ］，不过在“儿”是否成音节上，“肚脐”的儿化形式读为［tu21tɕʰiɚ42］，儿尾形式读为［tu21tɕʰi42ɚ21］，“毛梨（猕猴桃）”的儿化形式读为［mau22liɚ22］，儿尾形式读为［mau22li22ɚ22］。

前两种情形的六个词儿化以后韵母有不同程度的丢失，其儿化韵与完整保留了原韵母的儿尾在词根末字韵母构成上存在差异。而“肚脐”和“毛梨（猕猴桃）”这两个词的儿化形式和儿尾形式由相同的元音组合结尾，都为［i］+［ɚ］，更能对比得出相近的语音条件下词缀“儿”的语音区别表现。因此我们以25毫秒的窗长提取了韵母段的共振峰F1、F2的轨迹数据，用Praat做了“肚脐”和“毛梨（猕猴桃）”这两个词的儿尾和儿化变体的词形样本的F1、F2声学元音轨迹。根据语音的量子理论［2］，F1与开口度正相关，F2数值越大，发音越靠前。F3数据亦做了提取，但因其意义不够明确，本文暂时仅针对意义相对明确的F1、F2声学元音轨迹加以讨论。

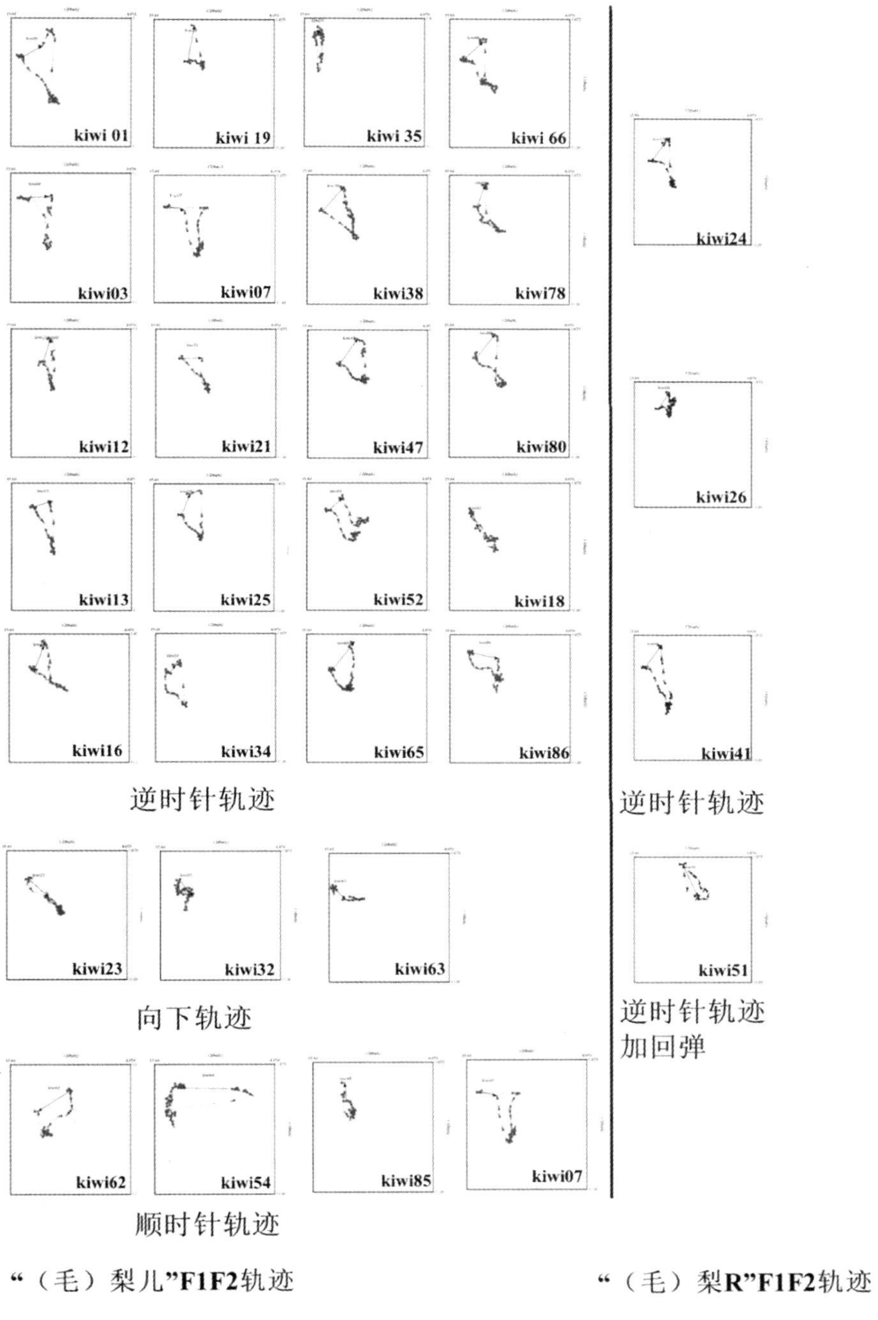

图2　“毛梨（猕猴桃）”的词干韵母加儿缀部分的共振峰变化轨迹。横轴 F2，纵轴 F1，单位为 Bark。**左栏图幅轨迹：“毛梨儿”中“梨”字的韵母加上儿尾的共振峰轨迹；右栏图幅轨迹：“毛梨 R”中“梨 R”的儿化韵母的共振峰轨迹，左右栏用垂直直线隔开。连接圆圈的小箭头：声学动程细节。实心大箭头：声学运动起始位置到终点位置的向量。**

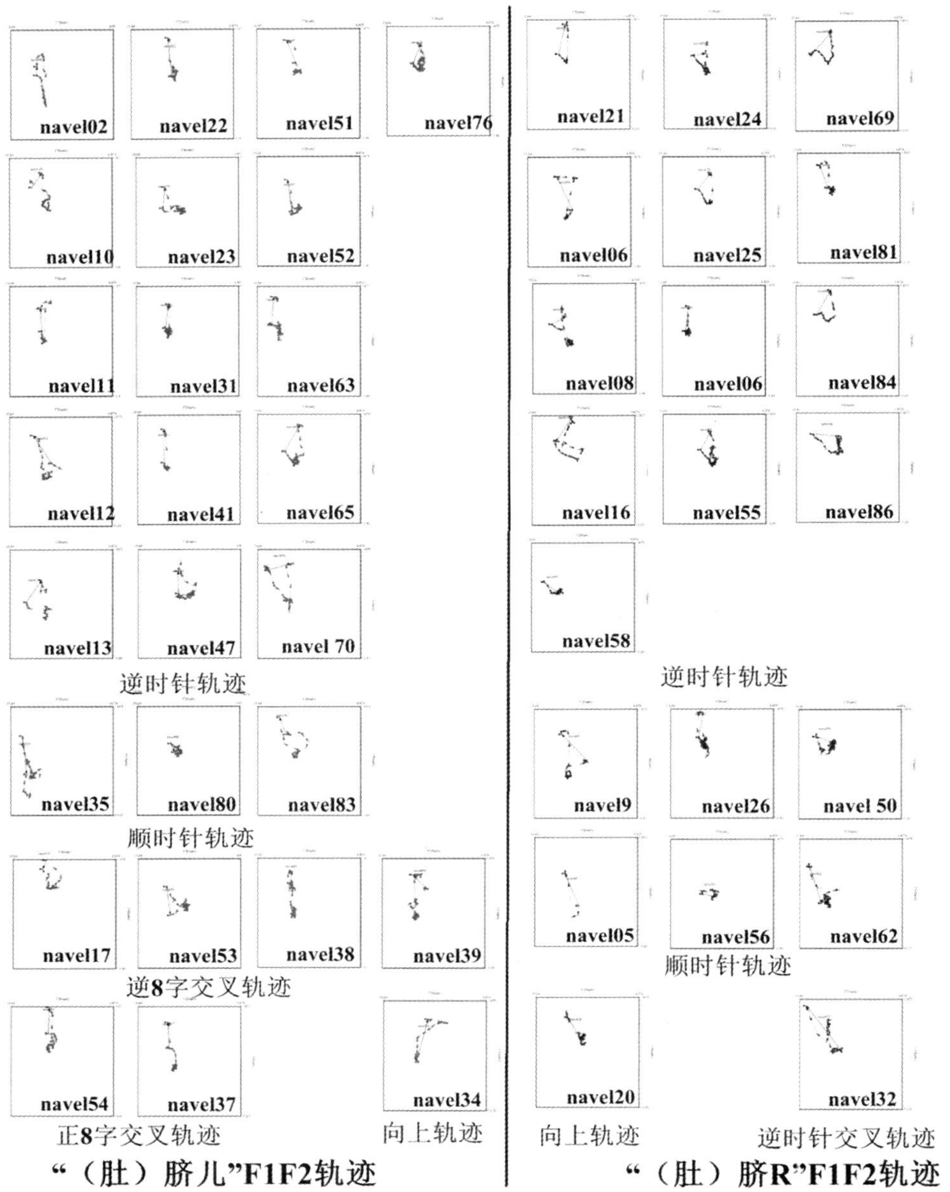

图 3 “肚脐”的词干韵母加儿缀部分的共振峰轨迹。横轴 F2，纵轴 F1，单位为 Bark。左图轨迹：“肚脐儿”中“肚”字的韵母加上儿尾的共振峰轨迹；右图轨迹：“肚脐 R”中“脐 R”的儿化韵母的共振峰轨迹，左右栏用垂直直线隔开。连接圆圈的小箭头：声学空间中动程细节。实心大箭头：声学运动起始位置到终点位置的向量。

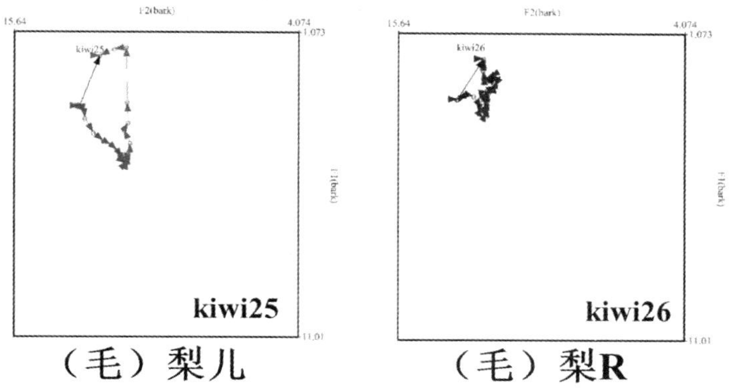

图4　25号与26号发音人所发“毛梨（猕猴桃）”的词干韵母加儿缀的共振峰轨迹。横轴F2，纵轴F1，度量Bark。左图轨迹：25号发音人发“毛梨儿”中“梨”字的韵母加上儿尾的动程轨迹；右图轨迹：26号发音人发“毛梨R”中“梨R”儿化韵母的共振峰轨迹。连接圆圈的小箭头：声学动程细节。实心大箭头：声学运动起始位置到终点位置的向量。

在图2和图3的F1、F2动态变化轨迹图中，纵坐标表示F1，反映开口大小，横坐标表示F2，反映发音舌位位置的前后。为更直观地反映“儿尾”和“儿化”变体的听感距离，我们用Praat提取的Bark作为横、纵坐标的单位而不用Hz。Bark与Hz的转化公式为：$Bark = 7\ln\{(f/650) + [(f/650)^2 + 1]^{1/2}\}$。因各个发音人的共振峰变化轨迹彼此差异非常大，为每个发音人单独作一幅声学元音图。图中连接圆圈的小箭头的轨迹代表动程，从儿缀之前一个音节的韵母开始提取到整个词结束，每100毫秒绘制一个箭头，也就是说，对于儿缀实现为儿化的词形样本，绘制范围覆盖词末的儿化音节及其前一个音节的韵母；对于儿缀实现为儿尾的样本，绘制范围覆盖词末的儿尾音节及其前一个音节的韵母。考察的关注点在F1、F2所构成的声学空间中箭头的疏密变化，某个声学空间内的箭头越密集代表移动单位声学距离所用的时间越长，即速度越慢。实心大箭头方向标示在声学空间中的起始到终点位置的向量。因篇幅限制，图2和图3图幅较小，仅作轨迹及箭头密度展示，绘制细节参见图4大图案例。实验词英文加编号代表实验词及被试，如“kiwi01”代表01号被试说“毛梨（猕猴桃）”一词的情况。

通过比较上述两例前字词根韵母为/i/的例词中儿尾与儿化的共振峰声学表现可以看到，从F1参数的变化轨迹来看，无论采取儿尾还是儿化形式，绝大多数被试的F1先增大后减小，图中表现为不规则的V字形，但F1参数的起点和终点位置在被试中存在较大差异，有的起点小于终点，有的终点小于起点。F1参数的变化趋势反映被试的开口度可能有先开后合的过程，舌位经历了“高→低→高”的变化过程，而开口度相对位置在被试之间可能具有较大的变异。

然而，从F2参数的变化轨迹来看，不同被试的F2参数呈现出多样的变化趋势。多数被试的F2起始值大于结束值（结合F1变化趋势在图2、图3中呈逆时针变化轨迹），少数被试的F2起始值小于结束值（结合F1变化趋势在图2、图3中呈顺时针变化轨迹），另外还有个别发音人发儿尾形式时F2起始值与结束值几乎没有差异。F2参数的变异反映大部分被试在发/i/韵卷舌音时舌位从前往后变化，但也存在舌位起始点在后而终点位置靠前，或仅仅改变开口度舌位前后变化不明显的情况。

此外，还有些发音人的 F2 值不仅仅单调增大或减小，而是在 F1 值最大点附近发生小幅逆向变化后再重新增大或减小，在图 2、图 3 中表现为 8 字形或逆 8 字形交叉轨迹，即图中小箭头的方向变化与书写“8”的笔顺相似或相反。这反映出这些发音人可能会在开口度较大时小幅逆向调整舌位的前后变化方向。

从变化速度来看，“毛梨（猕猴桃）”和“肚脐”的儿尾形式倾向于在 F1 变化的拐点即“V”形轨迹的 F1 最大点附近速度减慢（图中箭头更密集），而儿化形式的箭头密集段不如儿尾形式明显，也就是说，儿化形式的共振峰变化较儿尾形式更稳定。由此可见，在可能的开口度最大点，儿化形式的发音动程可能较儿尾形式更稳定。本文认为这与“儿”缀在儿尾词和儿化词中实现的音节地位有关。在儿尾词中“儿”缀实现为独立音节，“儿”与词根末音节的界限较为明显，而儿化词中的“儿”缀已与词根末音节融合，因此在发音时儿尾形式（词根末音节与“儿”组成）内部会有共振峰变化的显著减慢段，这可能标记着音节的边界。

但是，值得注意的是，不同发音人发儿化时 F1、F2 参数的速度变化的变异很大。有的发音人在轨迹中段会有一个明显的变化加速段，例如图 2 右上（24 号）发音人发儿化韵“（毛）梨 R”的共振峰速度变化模式与其他人发词根末音节加儿尾“（毛）梨儿”（图 2 左栏）的共振峰速度变化模式很相似，也可以在 F1 最大值附近观察到明显的减速过程（表现为箭头的聚集）。而有的发音人，例如图 2 右中（26、41 号）两名发音人的整个儿化发音过程中 F1、F2 参数的变化相对缓慢匀速，缺少明显的加速或减速段，类似于刘振平［12］所描述的北京话匀速卷舌儿化。还有个别发音人，如图 2 右下（51 号）发音人，在 F1 匀速增大又减小，F2 减小的逆时针轨迹完成之后，还紧接着一个快速的 F1 增大的变化，反映其后续还有向下张口或降低舌位的动作。值得注意的是，不论上述哪种儿化发音，过程中声带一直振动，中间没有中断，因此没有严格对应于刘振平所描述的北京话“先卷舌再发音”的情况。

总之，根据“毛梨”和“肚脐”不同发音变体在 F1 – F2 声学空间中的共振峰动态变化轨迹蠡测儿尾与儿化的语音区别，主要发现了二者在声学参数的运动变化速度上存在一定差异，即儿尾形式与儿化形式相比具有更明显的减速段。

6. 讨论与总结

本文通过诱导自然词汇产出，对绵阳安州话儿缀的儿尾与儿化形式进行音系及声学语音分析，我们在其词汇层面和语音层面都观察到了丰富的变异。

在词汇音系层面，安州话的儿缀词的儿尾与儿化形式处于词汇合音音变的不同阶段，其词汇分布符合词汇扩散模型，一些儿缀表现为儿尾，处于未变状态，另一些儿缀表现为儿化，处于已变状态，还有一些儿缀和儿尾变体都有，呈现出词汇变异状态。词汇扩散在安州话语言社团中也有体现，有些发音人倾向于使用儿尾，另一些倾向于使用儿缀，个别人同一个词有两种发音。该发现从词汇领域进一步验证了王洪君对于儿缀语音演变的看法，并提供了相应过程的细节案例。

尽管声调表现以及母语者（本文第一作者）的听感都可以清晰地区分安州话儿缀词的儿尾与儿化形式，但是元音共振峰声学分析提示，安州话儿尾和儿化在发音上还是有一定的过渡性的。例如，从发音人的声学共性上可以看出，安州儿尾和儿化的主要区别在于，带儿尾的音节倾向于在 F1 最大值附近，即推测“V”形轨迹的开口度最低点附近参数变化速度减慢，之后又重新加速，而儿化形式则往往缺少剧烈的速度变化，F1、F2 参数的变化相对缓慢均匀。然而，从个体的变异上可以看出，个别发音人尽管发的是儿化变体，但也会在共振峰轨迹上呈现一个明显的加速段，轨迹与儿尾变体十分相似。这提示我们，或许在安州话的儿尾和儿化的语音实现上也有一定的过渡性质。相应的语音演变过程或许是以词汇扩散为主，连续音变为辅的演变模式。

值得注意的是本研究的声学分析结果只是基于安州话一个韵母/i/后加儿缀/ɚ/时的声学表现得出的，而安州话其他韵母后加儿缀时则涉及儿尾形式和儿化形式不同的韵母变化，是否可以在其他韵母后得到类似的规律，仍有待进一步的验证。

还有一点值得注意。安州话儿尾和儿化的共振峰轨迹方向非常多样，尽管逆时针“V”形轨迹占据主流，也有不少发音样本的共振峰声学元音图轨迹是顺时针的“V”形，或者根本就不是“V”形，有的直接在两个稳定的目标之间快速直线移动，有的出现了出现了F1、F2参数向量的反复来回变化的交叉轨迹。甚至还有安州人所说的“儿”是不卷舌的，呈现出关中方言的特点。我们认为，这可能与安州的地理位置以及老蜀语、新蜀语［26］，乃至安州与周边湖广、关中地区的人口流动和语言接触有关，毕竟语言接触中最容易产生干扰的是词汇，而语音则容易保存底层的特点。安州儿缀的这些个体变异与刘振平对于北京儿化的观察也是能够相互印证的。由此可见，不论在北京话还是其他方言中，“儿”的声学表现都可以是多样的，其中蕴涵着向各种不同方向演变的潜力，而其最终的演变方向，可能还是要受到标准语的影响，并以社会经济因素为其继续演变的关键动因。

7. 致谢

本文的部分内容改写自第一作者所撰硕士学位论文《绵阳安州话“儿尾”和“儿化”构词的音系及语音研究》（华东师范大学中文系，2020，第二作者为指导教师）。本项研究还得到了上海市哲学社会科学规划一般课题“普通话—上海话双语词汇语音接触心理机制实验研究”（2017BYY001）的经费支持。

参考文献

［1］Lenneberg, E. H. 1967, *Biological Foundations of Language*. New York: Wiley, 1967.

［2］Stevens, K. N. 1989, On the quantal nature of speech. *Journal of Phonetics* 17 (1－2), 3－45.

［3］Wang W. S. Y. 1969, Competing Changes as a Cause of Residue. *Language* 45 (1), 9.

［4］陈淑梅:《英山方言的儿尾》,《语言研究》1989年第2期，22－31页。

［5］陈章太、李行健:《普通话基础方言基本词汇集》，语文出版社1996年版。

［6］丁崇明、荣晶:《汉语方言不同阶段的儿化及儿化韵的整合》,《语文研究》2011年第2期，18—22页。

［7］董少文:《语音常识》文化教育出版社1955版。

［8］蒋平、沈明:《晋语的儿尾变调和儿化变调》,《方言》2002年第4期，289—298页。

［9］李荣:《成都方言词典》，江苏教育出版社1998年版。

［10］李思敬:《汉语“儿”［ɚ］音史研究（增补）》，商务印书馆1994年版。

［11］刘淑学:《河北顺平方言的语音特点》，全国汉语方言学会年会第十一届年会会议论文，2001年西安未出版。

［12］刘振平:《儿韵和儿化韵的实验分析》,《汉语学习》2008年第6期，73—78页。

［13］罗韵希:《成都话方言词典》。四川省社会科学出版社1987年版。

［14］钱曾怡:《论儿化》,《中国语言学报》1995年第5期，124－141页。

［15］钱曾怡:《汉语方言官话研究》，齐鲁书社2010版。

［16］沈明:《山西方言的小称》,《方言》2003年第4期，335－351页。

［17］石锋:《北京话儿化韵的声学表现》,《南开语言学刊》2003年第00期，11—19页。

［18］Simmons R V N、顾黔、石汝杰:（2006）《汉语方言词汇调查手册》中华书局2003年版。

［19］孙立新:《户县方言研究》，东方出版社2001年版。

［20］王福堂:《汉语方言语音的演变和层次》，语文出版社2005年版。

［21］王洪君:《汉语非线性音系学》，北京大学出版社2008年版。

［22］王理嘉、贺宁基:《北京语音实验录》中华

书局1985年版。
[23] 王文虎、张一舟、周家筠:《四川方言词典》,四川人民出版社2018年版。
[24] 赵元任:《汉语口语语法》。吕叔湘译,商务印书馆1979年版。
[25] 周殿福、吴宗济:《普通话发音图谱》商务印书馆1963年版。
[26] 周及徐:《传播与演变——明代以来四川方言形成概述》,《语言历史论丛》2020年第14辑,73—85页。

张哲璇 上海民办浦东交中初级中学教师。华东师范大学中文系硕士。
Email: victoriawithsun@163. com

吴君如 华东师范大学中文系语言认知与演化实验室,博士,副教授。主要研究领域为语言接触的心理及词汇语音机制。
Email: jrwu@zhwx. ecnu. edu. cn

鼻音/m/的话者间频谱差异及其在声纹鉴定中的应用初探

耿浦洋　卢启萌　郭　弘　曾锦华　施少培

摘　要　本研究以汉语普通话鼻音声母/m/为例，考察了/m/的 11 个频谱特征在话者间的差异性和话者内的稳定性。研究结果显示：/m/的前四个共振峰（F1、F2、F3 和 F4）和带宽（B1、B2、B3 和 B4）以及共振峰间距（F2 - F1、F3 - F2、F4 - F3）具有显著的话者间差异；F1、F2、B1、B3、B4 和 F2 - F1 具有较好的话者内稳定性；除 F3 - F2 外，佩戴口罩对于/m/的频谱特征无显著影响。此外，基于/m/的 11 个频谱特征，使用随机森林模型进行话者自动判别的正确率为 43.82%。上述研究结果说明，/m/的频谱特征具有较好的话者间差异性，对于声纹鉴定中的话者同一判别具有一定参考价值。本研究不仅增进了对汉语普通话产出特征的认识，对于声纹鉴定的理论研究和实践技术也具有一定的价值。

关键词　鼻音，频谱特征，话者间差异性，话者内稳定性，口罩语音，随机森林，声纹鉴定

A Preliminary Study on the Inter-speaker Variance of Spectral Features of /m/ and Its Implication for Forensic Voice Comparison

GENG Puyang　LU Qimeng　GUO Hong　ZENG Jinhua　SHI Shaopei

Abstract The present study aims to investigate the inter-speaker variance and intra-speaker stability of the eleven spectral features of nasal consonant /m/ in Mandarin Chinese. The results showed that the first four formants of /m/ (F1, F2, F3, and F4), their bandwidths (B1, B2, B3, and B4), and the formant dispersions (F2 - F1, F3 - F2, and F4 - F3) exhibit significant differences across the speakers; F1, F2, B1, B3, B4 and F2 - F1 of /m/ exhibit good intra-speaker stability; wearing mask has no significant effect on all spectral features of /m/ except for F3 - F2. Furthermore, based on the eleven spectral features of /m/, an accuracy rate of 43.82% for speaker classification was acquired using the random forest model. These results suggested that the spectral features of /m/ could be valuable to forensic voice comparison. The current research not only enhanced the understanding of Mandarin speech production, but also contributed to the theory and practices of forensic voice comparison.

Keywords Nasal consonant, Spectral feature, Inter-speaker variance, Intra-speaker stability, Face mask speech, Random Forest model, Forensic voice comparison

1. 引言

鼻音，是口腔内成阻，同时软腭下降形成咽腔—鼻腔通路，浊音声源经鼻腔共鸣后由鼻孔辐射而形成的。在频谱上，鼻音具有较为明显的特征，比如第一共振峰（F1）能量最强、第二共振峰（F2）和第三共振峰（F3）接近、共振峰带宽（bandwidth）较宽、在宽带语图上出现"断层"现象等［17］。

由于人类的鼻腔形状是基本固定的，王英利［19］提出鼻音的共振峰模式反映了个体特征以及人际间差异。其他也有学者对此持相同观点，认为"鼻音的音色是因人而异的"［17］。

然而，目前对于上述观点的实证研究仍显不足。张翠玲［20］对 11 名发音人产出的/na/和/ni/进行分析发现，/n/的话者间差异大于单元音，具有较强的个体间

差异性。Amino 和 Arai [1] 的研究发现，鼻音（即/m/、/n/和/ɲ/）的能量曲线斜率存在较好的话者间差异性，且优于其他音素（如/t/、/d/、/s/、/ʃ/等）。另外，Enzinger 和 Zhang [6] 基于 MFCC、LPCC 等参数对鼻音的话者间区分度进行考察发现，/m/的相关参数对于话者识别率的提高优于/n/的相关参数。然而，其他学者也有不同的发现，如 Yim 和 Rose [16] 对日语和粤语的研究发现，鼻音的频谱特征对于话者识别具有一定效果（即日语：$C_{llr}s = 0.5$，粤语：$C_{llr}s = 0.8$），但并未优于其他音素；Hoffmann [8] 对 Hakha Chin 语（一种缅甸西部使用的缅藏族语言）的研究发现，清化鼻音（voiceless nasals）的时长和口鼻气流特征在话者间和话者内的差异都具有显著性。

此外，王英利 [18] 对10名发音人的汉语普通话鼻韵母共振峰特征进行分析，发现主元音共振峰走向、主元音与鼻韵尾时长比例等特征存在明显的话者间差异，并且这些特征具有一定的话者内稳定性；庄琳 [21] 对捏鼻语音的声学参数（即基频、振幅和共振峰等）进行分析，发现10名发音人的个体间差异大于个体内差异。

综上所述，可以发现：(1) 目前对于“鼻音是否反映个体特征，且具有较高话者间差异”问题的研究仍处于探索阶段；(2) 已有研究的结论尚存分歧。因此，基于前人研究的启示，本文以汉语普通话的鼻音声母/m/为例，对/m/频谱特征的话者间差异性和话者内稳定性进行了统计分析，并基于随机森林模型（Random Forest）考察了相关特征用于话者自动判别的效果。最后，本研究对鼻音频谱特征在声纹鉴定中的应用进行了探讨。本研究的结果不仅有利于增进对汉语普通话语音产出模式的认识，对于声纹鉴定的技术实践也具有一定应用价值。

2. 研究方法

2.1 实验被试

本研究共招募了30名汉语普通话发音人（15男15女）。所有被试说标准普通话，都是右利手，都没有言语听觉损伤的历史。

其中，男被试平均年龄26.7岁，平均身高177.0 cm（标准差为4.3cm）；女被试平均年龄24.1岁，平均身高163.3 cm（标准差为6.1cm）。

2.2 语料采集

录音材料为《北风与太阳》，含5个以/m/为声母的字，文本参见附录1。

考虑到新冠肺炎疫情形势下人们日常佩戴口罩的要求，本文还采集了发音人佩戴口罩时的语音产出，旨在考察口罩对于/m/频谱特征的影响。

录音实验在安静的录音室内进行，使用 Zoom H5 专业录音机进行录音。录音机置于发音人面前30—40cm处。采样率为48.0 kHz，量化精度为16 bit。录音开始前，要求被试提前熟悉并试读材料。然后，要求被试不佩戴口罩朗读录音材料2遍，要求被试佩戴口罩朗读录音材料1遍。最终，共采集5（音节数）×3（遍）×30（发音人）=450个/m/音节。

2.3 特征提取

目前，在司法声纹鉴定的实践中，共振峰是声谱测量环节最重要的特征之一。因此，为结合声纹鉴定的实践需要，本文选取前四个共振峰（F1、F2、F3、F4）和带宽（B1、B2、B3、B4），以及四个共振峰的间距（F2－F1、F3－F2、F4－F3）共11个频谱特征用于统计分析和话者自动判别分析。

首先，使用 Montreal Forced Aligner 软件 [14] 对2.2节采集的语料进行了自动标注，并由一名具有丰富标注经验的人员对自动标注的内容进行了手动校正。然后，使用 Praat 软件 [3] 对语料中/m/前四个共振峰及带宽进行了数据提取，每个/m/音节提取10个点（首末点+8个9等分点）的数据。最后，对共振峰间距进行了计算。

3. 统计分析

3.1 话者间差异性

30名发音人/m/的频谱特征的统计数据（即均值和标准差）详见表1。30名发音人前四个共振峰、带宽和共振峰间距的均值分布情况，如图1—图3所示。

表1 /m/频谱特征的统计数据（单位：Hz）

频谱特征	均值	标准差
F1	519.34	296.95
F2	1499.93	366.52
F3	2583.5	245.26
F4	3647.6	349.88
B1	224.14	144.63
B2	351.81	248.8
B3	313.25	223.91
B4	349.79	240.25
F2 - F1	980.59	340.22
F3 - F2	1083.57	416.27
F4 - F3	1064.09	395.02

使用R语言［15］，以/m/的11个频谱特征为因变量分别建立线性混合模型（Linear Mixed-Effects Model，LMM）［2，9］。每个模型中，发音人为固定效应，朗读遍数和性别为随机效应①。

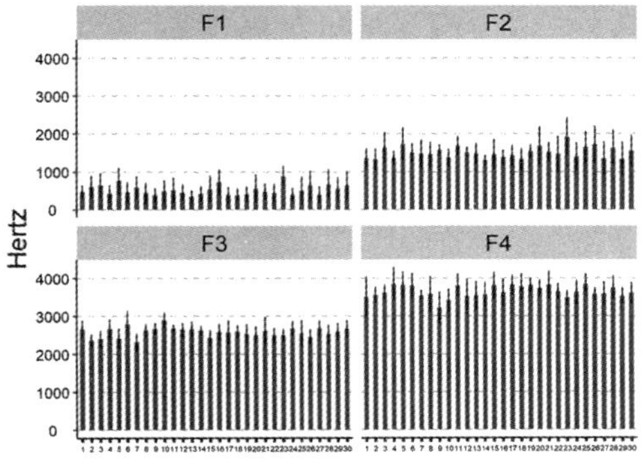

图1 30名发音人/m/的共振峰F1至F4均值

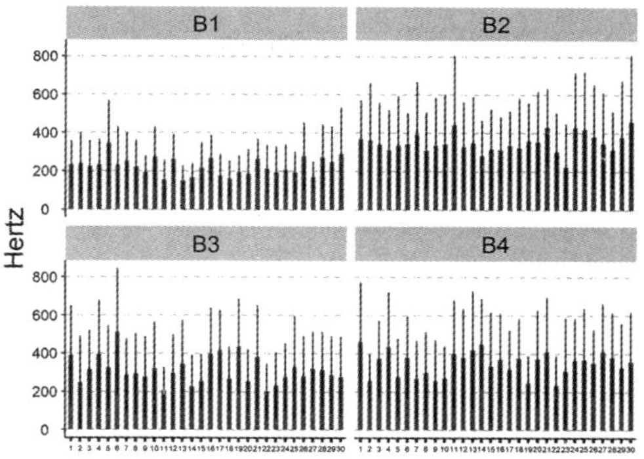

图2 30名发音人/m/的带宽B1至B4均值

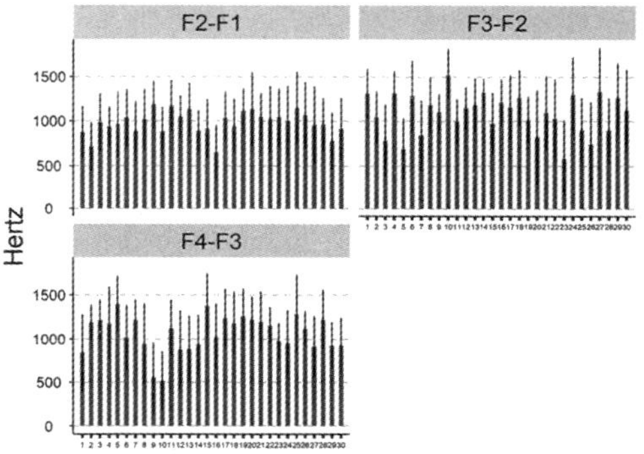

图3 30名发音人/m/的共振峰间距（F2 - F1、F3 - F2和F4 - F3）均值

LMM模型的统计结果如表2所示，/m/的11个频谱特征在不同话者间的差异都具有显著性（即 $p < 0.001$）。

表2 /m/频谱特征的话者间差异性LMM统计结果

频谱特征	*F* 值	*p* 值
F1	33.25	**<0.001**
F2	28.31	**<0.001**
F3	52.89	**<0.001**
F4	34.56	**<0.001**

① R代码：model < - lmer (feature ~ speaker + (1 | gender) + (1 | repetition), data = data)。

续表

频谱特征	F 值	p 值
B1	16.94	**<0.001**
B2	6.29	**<0.001**
B3	16.57	**<0.001**
B4	11.09	**<0.001**
F2 - F1	24.30	**<0.001**
F3 - F2	57.70	**<0.001**
F4 - F3	60.40	**<0.001**

3.2 话者内稳定性

通过 3.1 节的结果可以发现，30 名发音人产出的/m/在共振峰、带宽及共振峰间距上都具有显著的话者间差异。进一步，为了探索/m/的频谱特征的话者内稳定性，对/m/的 11 个频谱特征分别建立 LMM 模型。每个模型中，朗读遍数为固定效应，发音人和性别为交互随机效应①。然后，对模型中的显著效应进行 Tukey 事后检验②［10］。

表 3　/m/频谱特征的话者内稳定性 LMM 统计结果

频谱特征	F 值	p 值
F1	1.09	0.34
F2	1.60	0.20
F3	4.97	**0.007**
F4	4.51	**0.011**
B1	1.22	0.30
B2	8.42	**<0.001**
B3	0.30	0.74
B4	1.67	0.19
F2 - F1	1.05	0.35
F3 - F2	5.11	**0.006**
F4 - F3	4.77	**0.009**

LMM 模型的统计结果如表 3 所示，/m/的 F1、F2、B1、B3、B4 和 F2 - F1 在三次朗读中具有稳定性（$p > 0.05$）；F3、F4、B2 以及高次共振峰间距（即 F3 - F2 和 F4 - F3）在三次朗读中的差异显著（$p < 0.05$）。

然后，对具有显著差异的特征进行 Tukey 事后检验，结果显示：（1）对于 F3，第一遍朗读与第二、第三遍③差异均不显著（$p > 0.05$），而第二遍与第三遍之间存在显著差异（$\beta = 24.5$，$SE = 7.81$，$z = 3.14$，$p = 0.005$）；（2）对于 F4，第一遍与第二遍、第二遍与第三遍差异均不显著（$p > 0.05$），而第一遍与第三遍差异显著（$\beta = 34.1$，$SE = 11.6$，$z = 2.93$，$p = 0.009$）；（3）对于 B2，第一遍与第三遍差异不显著（$p > 0.05$），而第一遍与第二遍（$\beta = 35.9$，$SE = 8.96$，$z = 4.00$，$p < 0.001$）、第二遍与第三遍（$\beta = -25.1$，$SE = 8.98$，$z = -2.80$，$p = 0.014$）差异均具有显著性；（4）对于 F3 - F2，前两次朗读的差异不显著（$p > 0.05$），而第一遍与第三遍（$\beta = 32.1$，$SE = 13.1$，$z = 2.46$，$p = 0.037$）、第二遍与第三遍（$\beta = 39.3$，$SE = 13.1$，$z = 3.00$，$p = 0.008$）差异显著；（5）对于 F4 - F3，仅第一遍与第二遍差异显著（$\beta = 37.6$，$SE = 12.3$，$z = 3.05$，$p = 0.006$）。

3.3 口罩对/m/频谱特征的影响

通过 3.2 节的结果可以发现，对于/m/的 F3、F4、B2 和 F3 - F2 特征，第三遍朗读（即佩戴口罩）均和前两遍（即不佩戴口罩）存在一定差异。那么，这是否是口罩造成的影响呢？为了回答这个问题，对/m/的 11 个频谱特征分别建立 LMM 模型。每个模型中，是否佩戴口罩为固定效应，朗读遍数为随机效应，发音人

① R 代码：model < - lmer（feature ~ repetition +（1 | speaker：gender），data = data）。

② R 代码：emmeans（model，pairwise ~ repetition，adjust = “tukey”）。

③ 本研究中，第一遍和第二遍朗读未佩戴口罩，第三遍朗读佩戴口罩。

和性别为交互随机效应①。

/m/的 11 个频谱特征在不佩戴和佩戴口罩时的数据分布如图 4 所示。

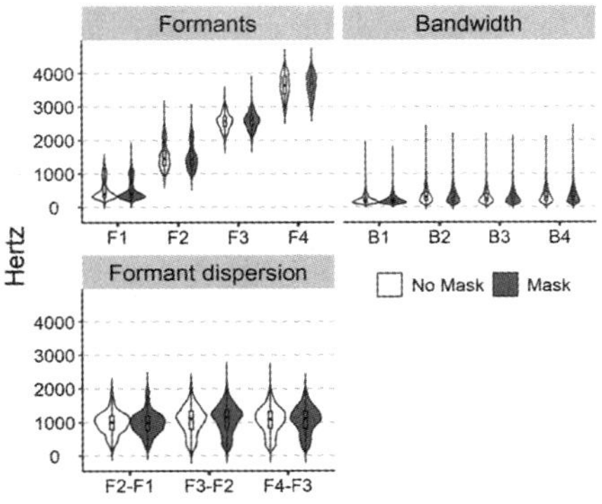

图 4　/m/频谱特征在不佩戴口罩（No Mask）和佩戴（Mask）时的数据分布

LMM 模型的统计结果如表 4 所示，是否佩戴口罩仅对 F3 – F2 具有显著效应。Tukey 事后检验结果显示，佩戴口罩时第二和第三共振峰间距升高 35.6 Hz（β = 35.6，SE = 11.3，z = 3.15，p = 0.002）。

表 4　/m/频谱特征是否佩戴口罩的 LMM 统计结果

频谱特征	F 值	p 值
F1	0.17	0.75
F2	2.88	0.09
F3	2.01	0.39
F4	1.22	0.47
B1	1.27	0.46
B2	0.05	0.86
B3	0.48	0.49
B4	0.05	0.86
F2 – F1	1.78	0.18
F3 – F2	9.91	**0.002**
F4 – F3	0.02	0.90

4. 随机森林模型分析

本研究选取随机森林模型（random forest model）进行话者自动判别分析，其优点是可以克服决策树过拟合问题，对噪声和异常值有较好的容忍性，以及可以同时进行分类和回归分析。

使用 R 语言的 randomForest 包［11］建立随机森林模型。本研究数据集共包含 11 个频谱特征，每个特征 30（发音人）×15（/m/音节）×10（数据提取点）= 4500 行数据。将所有数据按 7:3 的比例随机分为训练集和测试集。模型内，决策树的数量（ntree）设为默认值 1000。同时，为最小化 OOB（out-of-bag）预测错误率，使用 randomForest 包中的“tunTF”功能，将 mtry 参数最优化为 4，训练集的 OOB 预测错误率为 55.73%

随机森林模型结果显示，话者判别的正确率为 43.82%。测试集判别结果的混淆矩阵如附录 2 所示，每一列代表了预测类别，每一行代表了数据的真实归属类别，黑体表示真实数据被预测为该类的数目。

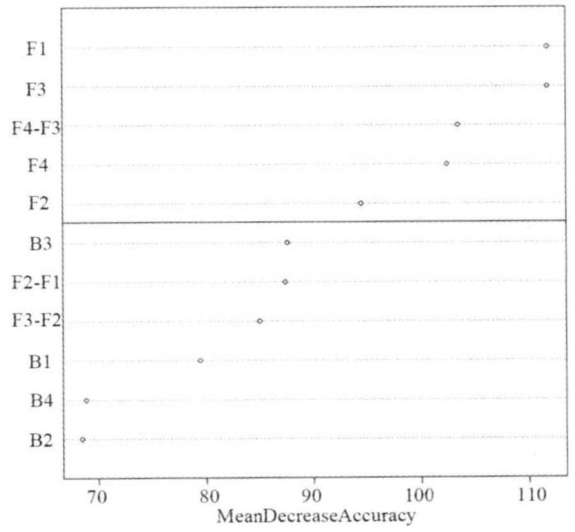

图 5　/m/的频谱特征对话者判别的贡献度

① R 代码：model < – lmer (feature ~ mask + (1 | repetition) + (1 | speaker: gender), data = data)

以正确率降低程度（Mean Decrease Accuracy）为标准，对11个频谱特征对话者判别的贡献度进行排序。如图5所示，对话者判别正确率影响较大的参数（即黑色实线以上）包括：前四个共振峰和F4－F3。

5. 讨论

本文对汉语普通话鼻音声母/m/的11个频谱特征进行了研究。统计分析发现：/m/的前四个共振峰（F1、F2、F3和F4）和带宽（B1、B2、B3和B4）、以及共振峰间距（F2－F1、F3－F2、F4－F3）均具有显著的话者间差异；F1、F2、B1、B3、B4和F2－F1具有较好的话者内稳定性。同时，除F3－F2之外，佩戴口罩对/m/的频谱特征影响不显著。最后，通过随机森林模型分析发现，/m/的11个频谱特征用于话者判别的效果一般（即平均判别正确率43.82%）。

本研究统计分析（线性混合模型）的结果发现，/m/的频谱特征具有显著话者间差异性。这一发现在一定程度上证明了前人的观点，即鼻音反映了个体差异［17，19］。这样的发现对于声纹鉴定的声谱测量具有一定启示，即共振峰、带宽和共振峰间距特征对于话者同一判别具有一定的参考价值。从生理语音学角度，Lu和Dang［12］提出鼻腔通道结构复杂且具有较大的个体差异，因此鼻音的声学特征能够反映较多的话者生理信息；Fitch［7］的研究则发现共振峰间距与声道体积、体型具有显著的相关性。上述内容说明，鼻音的话者间差异性研究对于话者识别具有较大意义和价值，需要在未来开展更深入的声学和生理实验加以探索。例如，梨状窝作为声道分支在语音产出过程中会导致4k—5k Hz范围内产生零点（即反共振anti-resonances）［12］，而梨状窝作为个体生理上的稳定特征，在语音产出过程中变化极小，可能是话者识别中的重要特征［5］，未来可针对相关参数进行专门的声学和生理研究。

对于/m/频谱特征的话者内稳定性，本文结果和前人研究［18］的结果基本一致。值得注意的是，尽管本文发现F3、F4、B2、F3－F2和F4－F3的话者间差异具有显著性，但这五个频谱特征的话者内稳定性却较差，因此其作为区分特征进行话者同一判别的有效性和价值仍有待商榷，在声纹鉴定实践中也应格外注意。

此外，本文发现佩戴口罩对/m/的频谱特征影响并不显著。前人对英语［13］、意大利语［4］的研究发现，佩戴口罩并不会显著影响基频、音强、HNR等声学参数。本文结果与已有研究观点一致，认为佩戴口罩对于声学特征并无显著影响。这一发现对于新冠肺炎疫情防控常态化时期的声纹鉴定具有较高的实践意义，即佩戴和未佩戴口罩的语音信号具有稳定性和可比性。

最后，本文发现基于/m/的频谱特征，尽管使用随机森林模型进行话者自动判别的整体正确率并不理想。但从附录2随机森林模型判别结果的混淆矩阵来看，每名发音人的判别中大部分结果是正确的（如附录2中黑体标示）。因此，鼻音/m/的频谱特征可能是潜在的话者自动识别的有效特征，这也说明了未来需要尝试其他机器学习算法、进一步提炼特征的必要性。对于频谱特征的贡献度，具有较高贡献度的特征主要为前四个共振峰及第三和第四共振峰间距。这一结果也与本文统计分析的发现较为吻合。

本文对/m/频谱特征的话者间差异进行了初步的研究，仍有许多不足值得改进，例如：（1）需要增加语料数量，考察文本对于/m/频谱特征的影响，验证本文结果的可推广程度；（2）需要测试其他机器学习算法（如SVM、GMM等模型）对基于/m/频谱特征的话者识别的效果如何；（3）本研究对于声纹鉴定实践的应用效果尚不得而知，需要未来开展更多的实践应用研究。

6. 结论

本文发现，鼻音声母/m/的频谱特征具有较好的话者间差异性和话者内稳定性，并且佩戴口罩并不会显著影响/m/的频谱特征。上述结果说明，/m/的频谱特征对于声纹鉴定中的话者同一判别具有较高的参考价值。本研究不仅对于声纹鉴定具有一定的理论价值和实践意义，同时也可以为计算机自动声纹识别技术提供一些研究基础。

7. 致谢

感谢匿名审稿人对本文提出的宝贵意见。本文研究得到了国家社会科学基金青年项目“毒品成瘾人群的言语产出及感知特征研究”（21CYY011），上海市科委技术标准项目“人像司法鉴定标准关键技术研究”（21DZ2200100），以及中央级科研院所公益研究基金（GY2021G－9、GY2019G－2、GY2018G－4）的经费支持。

参考文献

[1] Amino, K. Arai, T. 2009. Speaker-dependent characteristics of the nasals. *Forensic Science International* 185 (1－3), 21－28.

[2] Bates, D., Fishbein, M., Bolker, B., Walker, S., Christensen, R. H. B., Singmann, H. 2015. lme4: Linear Mixed-effects Models using Eigen and S4. R package. Retrieved from https://CRAN. Rproject. org/package = lme4.

[3] Boersma, P., Weenink, D. 2016. Praat: Doing Phonetics by Computer [Computer program]. Retrieved from retrieved 1 January 2019 from http://www. praat. org/.

[4] Cavallaro, G., Di Nicola, V., Quaranta, N., Fiorella, M. L. 2021. Acoustic voice analysis in the COVID－19 era. *Acta Otorhinolaryngologica Italica* 41 (1), 1.

[5] Dang, J., Honda, K. 1997. Acoustic characteristics of the piriform fossa in models and humans. *The Journal of the Acoustical Society of America* 101 (1), 456－465.

[6] Enzinger, E., Zhang, C. 2011. Nasal spectra for forensic voice comparison. In *Paper at Special Session on Forensic Acoustics*, *162nd ASA Meeting*, San Diego.

[7] Fitch, W. T. 1997. Vocal tract length and formant frequency dispersion correlate with body size in rhesus macaques. *The Journal of the Acoustical Society of America* 102 (2), 1213－1222. https://doi. org/10. 1121/1. 421048

[8] Hoffmann, M. 2018. Inter-and intra-speaker variability in the production of voiceless nasal consonants. *The Journal of the Acoustical Society of America* 143 (3), 1968－1968.

[9] Kuznetsova, A., Brockhoff, P. B., Christensen, R. H. B. 2017. lmerTest package: tests in linear mixed effects models. *Journal of Statistical Software* 82 (13). https://doi. org/10. 18637/jss. v082. i13

[10] Lenth, R. 2018. Package ‘lsmeans’. *The American Statistician* 34 (4), 216－221.

[11] Liaw, A., Wiener, M. 2018. Random Forest: Breiman and Cutler's Random Forests for Classification and Regression (R Package Version 4. 6－14). Retrieved from https://CRAN. R－project. org/package = randomForest.

[12] Lu, X., Dang, J. 2008. An investigation of dependencies between frequency components and speaker characteristics for text-independent speaker identification. *Speech Communication* 50 (4), 312－322.

[13] Magee, M., Lewis, C., Noffs, G., Reece, H., Chan, J. C., Zaga, C. J., Paynter, C., Birchall, O., Azocar, S. R., Ediriweera, A. 2020. Effects of face masks on acoustic analysis and speech perception: Implications for peri-pandemic protocols. *The Journal of the Acoustical Society of America* 148 (6), 3562－3568.

[14] McAuliffe, M., Socolof, M., Mihuc, S., Wagner, M., Sonderegger, M. 2017. Montreal Forced Aligner [Computer program]. Retrieved from 17 January 2017 from http://montrealcorpustools. github. io/Montreal-Forced-Aligner/

[15] R Core Team. (2018). R: A Language and Environment for Statistical Computing. *R Foundation for Statistical Computing*, Vienna, Austria. Retrieved from https://www. R-project. org/.

[16] Yim, A. C. S., Rose, P. 2012. Are nasals better? Likelihood ratio-based forensic voice comparison with segmental cepstra from Cantonese and Japanese syllabic/mora nasals. In *Proceedings of the 14th Australasian International Conference on Speech Science and Technology* (pp. 5－8).

[17] 鲍怀翘、林茂灿：《实验语音学概要（增订

版)》2014年版。
[18] 王英利:《利用鼻韵母共振峰特征进行声纹鉴定的研究》,第七届中国语音学学术会议暨语音学前沿问题国际论坛,2006年。
[19] 王英利:《声纹鉴定技术》2013年版。
[20] 张翠玲:《法庭语音技术研究》2009年版。
[21] 庄琳:《捏鼻语音的声纹鉴定研究》,《中国人民公安大学学报(自然科学版)》,2010年16卷第04期,1-7。

耿浦洋 司法鉴定科学研究院,博士,助理研究员。主要研究领域为实验语音学、声纹鉴定、特殊人群语音。
Email: gengpy@ssfjd.cn

卢启萌 司法鉴定科学研究院工程师。研究领域包括声纹鉴定和刑事技术。
Email: luqm@ssfjd.cn

郭　弘 司法鉴定科学研究院正高级工程师。研究领域为刑事技术。
Email: guoh@ssfjd.cn

曾锦华 司法鉴定科学研究院高级工程师。博士。研究领域为刑事技术。
Email: zengjh@ssfjd.cn

施少培 司法鉴定科学研究院正高级工程师。研究领域包括声纹鉴定和刑事技术。
Email: shisp@ssfjd.cn

附录1:《北风与太阳》文本(下划线标示含/m/的音节的字)

有一天,北风跟太阳在那里争论谁的本事更大。说着说着,来了一个走路的人,身上穿了一件厚袍子。他们(men)俩就商量好了,说谁能叫这个走路的人把他的袍子脱下来,就算谁的本领大。于是,北风就卯(mao)足了劲儿,拼命(ming)地吹呀吹呀。可是,他吹得越厉害,那个人就把他的袍子裹得越紧。到了最后,北风没(mei)辙了,只好就算了。一会儿,太阳出来一晒,那个人马(ma)上就把他的袍子脱了下来。所以,北风不得不承认,还是太阳比他的本领大。

附录 2: 随机森林模型的判别结果混淆矩阵

话者	1	2	3	4	5	6	7	8	9	10	11	12	13	14	15	16	17	18	19	20	21	22	23	24	25	26	27	28	29	30
1	**22**	0	0	0	1	4	1	4	0	3	0	1	0	0	1	4	0	1	1	0	1	0	0	0	0	0	0	0	0	0
2	0	**18**	0	0	3	0	4	0	0	0	0	0	0	4	1	0	1	0	1	0	0	4	1	0	0	4	0	2	1	0
3	0	1	**16**	1	1	1	4	0	0	0	0	1	0	0	0	1	1	1	2	1	0	1	2	0	0	1	1	2	3	0
4	2	0	0	**18**	0	2	0	0	0	0	0	0	2	1	0	2	1	1	0	0	1	0	0	2	0	0	1	2	0	1
5	0	0	3	0	**20**	0	0	0	0	0	0	1	0	0	5	0	1	0	0	1	0	1	3	0	3	1	0	3	0	2
6	1	0	0	2	0	**12**	0	0	1	1	0	1	3	0	0	0	1	1	5	0	1	0	0	0	0	0	0	0	0	1
7	0	6	3	0	2	1	**26**	0	0	0	0	0	0	0	4	2	0	0	2	2	1	1	0	0	1	2	1	1	2	1
8	1	1	0	0	3	0	0	**14**	2	0	1	1	3	2	0	1	0	4	0	1	0	0	0	1	1	0	1	2	0	2
9	1	0	0	2	0	0	0	2	**25**	2	1	1	5	0	0	0	0	1	1	0	0	0	0	0	0	0	0	1	0	1
10	4	0	0	0	0	1	0	0	0	**36**	1	0	0	1	0	0	0	1	0	0	0	0	0	1	0	0	1	0	0	0
11	2	0	0	0	2	3	0	0	3	1	**25**	2	1	1	0	0	1	1	0	0	2	0	0	1	0	0	1	0	0	0
12	4	0	0	1	0	4	0	6	1	0	3	**16**	3	0	0	2	2	2	0	0	2	1	0	1	1	0	0	0	0	1
13	1	0	1	3	0	2	0	0	1	2	2	1	**19**	3	0	0	1	1	0	0	0	0	0	2	1	0	0	0	0	3
14	2	0	0	6	0	0	4	2	1	0	1	1	0	**25**	2	1	0	1	0	0	0	3	0	2	1	0	0	0	3	2
15	0	1	0	0	3	0	0	0	0	0	1	0	0	0	**10**	0	1	2	1	1	0	1	0	1	6	0	0	3	0	1
16	2	2	2	3	1	1	0	2	0	1	0	2	0	2	2	**27**	0	2	1	1	4	0	0	1	0	0	1	1	0	0
17	0	1	1	3	2	2	0	1	0	0	0	1	1	0	3	1	**16**	0	4	2	1	0	0	0	3	0	3	1	0	1
18	1	0	0	1	0	0	0	2	0	0	0	0	3	2	1	1	2	**18**	1	0	1	0	0	3	0	0	0	1	1	1
19	0	0	2	0	0	0	1	2	3	0	0	2	1	0	0	0	6	3	**25**	0	2	1	0	1	0	1	1	1	1	1
20	0	0	2	0	2	0	0	0	0	0	0	0	0	0	2	0	1	1	0	**15**	0	3	4	4	1	4	0	4	0	2
21	5	0	2	2	0	6	1	0	0	4	0	3	0	0	1	0	0	0	2	0	**26**	0	2	1	0	1	0	1	0	0
22	0	6	0	1	1	0	3	0	0	0	0	0	0	1	0	0	0	1	1	2	0	**20**	0	1	0	1	1	0	0	1
23	0	1	1	0	0	0	1	0	0	0	0	0	0	0	0	0	0	0	0	0	0	0	**12**	0	0	3	0	2	0	0
24	1	0	0	0	0	0	0	1	0	1	0	1	1	2	1	1	0	2	1	0	1	0	0	**8**	0	0	1	0	1	3
25	2	0	0	0	0	1	1	1	0	0	0	0	1	0	5	2	1	0	0	4	0	0	0	2	**13**	0	0	4	1	0
26	1	2	0	0	2	0	4	0	0	0	1	0	0	0	0	0	0	0	0	1	1	3	5	0	2	**16**	0	1	5	1
27	1	0	1	1	0	1	0	2	0	0	0	0	0	0	1	2	3	3	0	4	0	0	0	2	2	0	**31**	1	1	0
28	0	0	1	0	4	2	1	0	0	0	2	0	1	0	4	1	1	1	0	0	0	1	2	1	3	1	1	**10**	2	2
29	0	2	1	1	0	0	3	2	0	0	0	0	0	2	2	1	3	4	0	1	1	1	2	1	0	1	3	0	**25**	0
30	1	0	1	1	1	1	2	0	1	0	0	2	0	1	0	1	0	0	0	4	1	3	1	5	3	0	1	1	6	**21**

母语、二语以及言语障碍人群言语加工中产出与感知的关系

胡 伟 崔程洋 吴梦瑄

摘 要 深入探索言语感知与产出的关系问题，理解已有研究结论中存在的矛盾，对揭示言语感知机制的本质大有助力，对母语获得的机制探索、第二语言的学习与教育、言语障碍人群的言语干预与矫治也有一定的启示。据此，本文将从母语、二语、言语障碍人群这三个言语使用群体出发，综述已有研究进展并探讨言语产出与言语感知的关系问题。在综合分析的基础上，尝试指出未来该领域潜在的研究方向。

关键词 言语产出，言语感知，言语产出与言语感知的关系

The Relationship between Speech Production and Perception in Native Speakers, L2 Speakers, and Individuals with Speech Impairment

HU Wei CUI Chengyang WU Mengxuan

Abstract Investigating the relationship between speech production and perception, along with a better understanding of salient issues in the empirical studies, greatly facilitates research into the mechanisms to speech perception. Moreover, such an effort also serves to generate works in language acquisition of native speakers, L2 learning and education, and the intervention and treatment of individuals with speech impairment. This article reviewed relevant studies and discussed the relationship between speech production and perception in native speakers, L2 speakers and individuals with speech impairment. Based on a comprehensive analysis, the authors attempted to suggest potential future research directions.

Keywords Speech production, Speech perception, The relationship between speech production and perception

1. 引言

在语音加工领域，一系列理论和实证研究都试图回答该领域的一个基本问题，即言语产出（Speech production）与言语感知（Speech perception）是否存在联系？存在的话，两者的关系模式具体是怎样的？探索言语产出与感知之间的关系问题，可以帮助揭示言语感知的预测机制，可以帮助教育者制订更为有效的言语训练方法，提升口语学习与交流的效率。

早在 20 世纪中叶，就有研究［18，49］发现，听者要根据不同的语音背景（Context）调整合成音位的声学参数，才能得到稳定的音位感知。可见，对同一个音位的感知，对应着不同的声学特征。这说明声学信息并不足以稳定预测音位感知。研究者据此推测，言语产出相对更为稳定，有可能更适合与言语感知建立解释与被解释关系。此后，针对不同的言语使用群体（母语者和二语者），研究者陆续提出了针对性的言语加工理论来解释言语产出与言语感知的关系问题，例如，动觉理论（Motor theory）［47，50，51］、一般方法（General Approach）［22，23，24，25，42，43］、直接实在论的知觉理论（Direct Realism）［6，8，9，30，31，32］，语音学习模型（Speech Learning Model）［27］、感知同化模型（Perceptual Assimilation Model）［10］等等。此外，对于存在不同程度言语障碍的特殊人群，其

言语感知与言语产出的联系是否与正常人群存在差别，这也是检验言语产出与感知关系实质的一个重要切入点。此领域尚未形成成熟的理论，但也进行了相当程度的探索［1，60，62］。本文对上述理论和实证研究进行了综述和简要分析，以期深入了解言语产出与感知联系在不同语言使用群体中的具体关系模式。

2. 母语言语加工中言语产出与感知的关系

在母语语音获得领域，已有理论对于言语产出与感知是否存在联系并没有严重的分歧。无论是以 Liberman 为代表的发音姿态（articulatory gestures）观点，还是以 Diehl 等人为代表的心理物理/一般听觉加工的观点［3，24，25］，都认为言语产出与言语感知之间存在紧密的联系。但两类观点对于言语产出与言语感知的具体关系模式存在分歧，本文将在下文中结合实证研究结论进一步阐述、对比并简评。

2.1 发音姿态（Articulatory gestures）观点下的言语产出与感知关系

在发音姿态观点中，理论提出者认为，听者（listeners）要想正确理解说者（speakers）的言语，说与听的过程中必须存在一个共有的“一般等价物”，该等价物的作用类似黄金在货币流通中的作用，即确保言语交流中信息在产出和感知过程中被有效传递。理论提出者将该等价物定义为发音姿态（Gestures)，也就是说，发音姿态是言语的基本单元。在此基础上，动觉理论［47，50，51］提出，语音产出就是与发音动作相关的神经冲动支配发音器官形成一系列发音姿态的过程；而感知的过程，就是逆向解码语音产出的过程，也就是通过言语信息逆向解码并加工发音姿态信息的过程。这保证了说者产出的语音信息和听者感知到的语音信息，都是发音姿态。

上述观点得到了一系列实证研究的支持。Liberman 等人［47］展示的合成音节/di/和/du/的语谱图中，第一共振峰过渡的频谱信息只能表明这两个音节中的辅音是一个浊化的爆破音（例如，可能是/b/、/d/、或/g/），而第二共振峰过渡的频谱信息的变化则提供了辅音/d/被识别的关键信息。具体为：第二共振峰过渡的上升段频谱信息帮助听者识别了/di/中的辅音/d/，而第二共振峰过渡的下降段频谱信息帮助听者识别了/du/中的辅音/d/。同样被感知为/d/，却对应不同的声学特征，研究者据此认为声学线索是不稳定的，易受环境影响的，并不适合来解释言语感知。Macdonald 与 McGurk［53］通过视听跨通道范式考察英语辅音感知。结果发现，与听觉通道加工相比，说话者口唇运动的视觉信息在感知中起到了更重要的作用。这也暗示言语感知的过程更倾向于加工口腔、嘴唇的发音姿态而非单纯声音信号。Newman［56］通过记录被试的辅音/p/的发音模仿任务和典型性评价任务考察了言语感知和产出之间的关系。研究者发现，被试发音的响音起始时间（voice onset time，VOT）与那些典型性评价成绩较高的发音的 VOT 之间存在显著的相关关系。也就是说典型性评价越高，在产出中也往往有较长的 VOT。Perkell 等人［59］通过考察英语母语者对元音产出准确性和感知准确性的联系，也发现说话人越准确地辨别出元音间的差异，其产出准确性就越明显。

上述研究都发现言语产出与感知联系紧密，那么两者的具体联系是怎样的呢？动觉理论认为，“言语感知的过程，就是逆向解码言语产出的过程”。在某种程度上，对言语产出的编码决定了言语能否被正确解码并理解。也就是说，言语产出影响了言语感知。一部分研究支持了这一结论，举例来说，Cooper 等［19］要求说者说出一个重复的音节序列（由/bæ/、/mæ/、/væ/组成），然后再去识别合成音节/bæ/－/dæ/－/gæ/连续统。结果发现，随着重复产出/bæ/、/mæ/、/væ/越来越多，说话者对/b/－/d/的辅音范畴边界越来越趋近于/b/，对辅音/b/的识别时间也越来越短。Bell－Berti 等［4］同样先进行产出实验，要求说话者产出元音/i/、/

I/、/e/和/ε/，并记录舌头的肌电图数据。然后对从/i/到/I/共七个合成元音组成的连续统进行识别实验，每个合成元音出现的概率相同。为了锚定第一个合成元音/i/，将其出现的概率增加为其他元音的四倍。产出结果发现，有些被试主要根据舌头的高度来区分不同的元音发音；另外的被试则根据舌头的肌张力来区分；感知结果发现，所有被试对/i－I/元音范畴边界都向/i/移动。而那些使用舌头高度作为发音策略的被试，范畴边界的变化幅度大于使用舌头肌张力来区分这些元音的被试。Franken 等［33］应用多元回归分析，将基于产出的两个指标（元音内部的离散程度和元音音位之间的语音距离）作为预测变量，元音辨别分数作为因变量，考察了元音产出能力对于感知的预测。结果发现，元音间的语音距离是元音感知的良好预测指标。元音间距离越大，元音感知越好。元音内部的离散程度则对元音感知影响不大。

上述结果都说明言语产出影响了言语感知，然而，这个结论却并不适合解释早期的言语发展，婴儿很早就具备了辨别语音的能力，而其产出语音的能力却远未建立。母语发展中，儿童的言语感知一般也较言语产出更先达到成人水平［2］。从这个角度来看，是言语感知“引导”并影响了言语产出［27］。这一结论在成人的实证研究中也获得了支持。Cooper 和 Lauritsen［20］要求被试在重复听一个选定音节之后立即产出给定的辅音和元音音节。听的过程中，要求他们不能发声，并将舌头夹在牙齿和嘴唇之间，以保证被试只听不复述。实验 1 要求被试重复感知/i/、/pi/和/bi/70 次后，产出 /pi/ 和/bi/。对/pi/语音分析结果表明，被试对/pi/的发音 VOT 值显著下降。实验 2 则要求被试重复感知/i/、/pi/和/bi/70 次后，产出/ti/或/di/。结果发现被试对/ti/的发音 VOT 值显著下降。该结果一方面说明感知经验的累积确实导致了产出的变化；同时还说明产出的变化并不体现在特定的辅音上，还有可能体现在某些发音特征上。因为在上述研究中，/pi/和/ti/都有 VOT 变化，这很可能是因为重复感知导致了/p/和/t/共享的一些发音特征的变化。

上述研究范式都是先重复感知，完成后再测试产出；或者先重复产出，再测试感知。也有研究通过设置感知和产出“同步”以探索产出和感知在发生时间上的关系。Porter 与 Castellanos［61］针对录音材料/aba、apa、ama、aga、aka/设计了不同的“影子跟读”任务。在选择反应任务中，被试被要求准确地重复听到的话语，清晰地产出首元音和辅音；在简单反应 ABA 任务中，被试被要求在首元音/a/出现时立即开始发音，但在辅音开始时不管听到什么辅音，都固定地直接发出/ba/音。可见，在这样的实验设计中，选择反应任务中被试需要先正确识别，才能正确重复其发音。而在简单反应 ABA 任务中，被试并不需要注意听到的音节。在两个任务中被试都被要求和录音尽量“同步”，不要等到话语完成后才开始反应。同时，记录被试的言语感知选择以及发音反应时。实验结果发现，选择反应任务中的正确率都很高，且选择反应重复任务和简单反应 ABA 任务中，被试完成发音任务的反应时都非常短（仅 170—240 毫秒），且无显著差别。这说明，选择反应任务中，对听到音节的感知并未显著影响（延长）被试的发音反应时。此外，需要指出的是，“影子跟读”任务并不是一种自然发音方式，研究者是在用一种非常规的方式探索言语产出与感知的关系。

综上可见，不管是动觉理论还是实证研究，都指出言语产出与感知之间存在紧密联系。而产出和感知的关系模式，也就是谁如何影响了谁的问题，则受研究范式的影响很大。研究范式中的重复效应指出言语经验调整着言语产出与感知之间的联系。同时，这种联系，可能并不基于音位层级，而是基于某些关键的发音特征。

2.2 一般方法（General approach）视野下的言语产出与感知关系

Diehl 等［24］综合一系列类似理论之后，提出了一般认知加工观点指导下的关于言语感知的一般方法。与动觉理论不同的是，一般方法认为听者可以直接对声音信号中的语音信息进行感知，而非感知发音姿态。它假设言语是通过一般听觉和学习机制来感知的，而并不是通过特异化的语言加工机制。在言语感知和产出的关系这一问题上，该理论同样认为两者存在紧密关系，但对其关系的解释则不同于发音姿态观点。一般方法通过分散原则［23，52］和听觉增强假说［22，25，42，43］来解释言语产出与感知的关系。其认为言语系统倾向于满足一个分散的原则，即在可用的语音空间内使语际距离最大化，以提高言语的可理解性，而这一原则是通过听觉增强假说实现的。听觉增强假说指说话者通过增强单个音位的某个特定的核心声学特征来增强听觉效果。举例来说，元音/u/，区别于其他元音的声学特性是低频F2。当说话者需要清楚地说话时（例如，在有背景噪音的情况下），他们通常会通过突出嘴唇，收缩唇口，缩回和抬高舌体、通过向前移动舌根扩大咽腔、抬高软腭、降低喉部来产出/u/。这些姿态中的每一个都独立地有助于降低第二共振峰（F2）的频率，以形成一个最具辨识度的/u/，即一个在听觉上与其他元音差异最大的/u/。这说明，要得到较好的感知，必须突出声学信号的关键特征，而这个声学信号是与说者的发音姿态相联系的。所以，好的感知得益于说者的清晰的发音姿态。

一般方法将言语感知置于一般听觉加工的认知体系中，这使得言语产出与感知的联系受到的影响更为复杂，因为可能受到来自于更高阶认知加工的调节。举例来说，Candia［17］通过检测西班牙语中辅音近音的产出和感知，考察了辅音弱化。产出任务中，首先要求完成单词表、短文和半引导式对话三个启发任务。单词表由84个单词和51个无意义单词组成，每个辅音近音与5个元音和3种重音模式组合，随机分组后分成二十个项目，要求被试尽可能自然地朗读并对其录音；其次要求被试在熟悉后大声朗读两篇类似新闻文章的短文并对其录音；最后一个任务是一个半引导式对话，由受过语音训练的研究人员和参与者进行。这项任务从一个关于爱好的对话开始，然后发展到参与者感兴趣的其他主题，直到至少连续10分钟的对话被记录下来。研究最终记录了西班牙语辅音中/b、d、g/的弱化范围。感知任务中，通过不同的听觉和语义线索条件下的音位监测（phoneme monitoring）、识别（identification）和辨别（discrimination），调查了听者如何解决语音处理中潜存的歧义。在音位监测任务中呈现VCV和VV序列（例如mega和mea），要求被试在听一段语音序列时判断给定的辅音是否存在。在识别任务中，被试被告知他们会听到VCV或VV序列，他们通过按键来完成识别任务。在辨别任务中，被试会听到3个项目的声音序列，并判断第三个项目与第一个和第二个项目中哪个相同。结果发现，在产出任务中/b、d、g/的发音近似值、省略变体非常常见；但在感知实验中，当被试听到辅音被省略的刺激时依然可以完整地感知音节。这说明影响感知任务成绩的不仅仅是听者可获得的声音线索，听者的产出经验也在感知中发挥作用。正是因为听者经常在发音中省略辅音，类似经验的累积形成了认知加工定势或原型，所以在感知类似的情况时才不会因辅音的弱化而发生感知错误。这也说明，高阶认知加工在某种程度上调节了言语产出与感知的关系。

综上，一般方法认为声学线索与感知之间存在直接联系，而言语产出与感知之间的联系是间接的，是以声学线索作为中介的。好的言语感知，可以通过说者清晰的发音姿态，突出声学信号的关键特征来获得。此外，该方法认为言语产出与感知间的联系受到一般认知加工体系中更高阶认知过程的调节，即受到“自上而下加工”的影响。

综合以上两个主要观点可以发现，对于言语产出与感知的关系，两者的核心结论并无重大差别，都认为言语产出与感知相互紧密联系，两个理论的差异主要体现在对言语产出和感知关系的关系模式、经验对此关系的作用以及感知的基础三个方面。（1）关系模式：两个理论对言语产出和感知关系解释的侧重点不同。发音姿态观点给出的解释更为直接，即言语感知就是逆向解码言语产出。发音姿态及其对应的神经运动过程在口语交流的认知加工中占据了更为重要的位置。这是因为，如果言语感知要逆向解码言语产出，言语产出就要贡献最初的知识表征编码，而言语感知是在这一基础上完成的。一般方法的观点的侧重点则在于解释外界刺激（声学信号）与感、知觉加工之间是如何建立联系的。其主要结论是，要获得好的言语感知，必须突出声学信号的某个核心特征，这一核心特征在感知觉的识别和区分中起着关键作用。可是，因为声学信号与发音姿态是存在联系的，所以言语产出同样影响了言语感知。总结来说，对言语产出与感知的关系这一科学问题的回答，发音姿态观点认为两者的关系是直接的，而一般方法的观点认为言语产出与感知需要以声学信息作为中介。(2) 经验的作用：发音姿态观点认为，随着言语产出和感知经验的增加，两者分别调节和影响着彼此。一般方法的观点认为，言语产出与感知的联系还受到高级认知加工（例如，长时记忆表征）的影响，而经验的累积是在长时记忆中完成的。(3) 感知的基础：发音姿态的观点认为言语感知的基础在于基于发音姿态的知识表征，而一般方法的观点则倾向于认为言语感知的基础在于声学信息。对于感知的基础，前者更强调（相对于听者的）远端信息，后者更强调近端信息。(4) 两方面的观点也都受到了一定程度的质疑。对动觉理论的主要质疑来自于 Ohala［57］。他列举了三类反例：①音系数据表明，语音的声学/听觉属性（而不是发音姿态）是人类行为的主要决定因素；②婴儿和人类之外的其他物种可以区分人类语言中的某些语音对比，但他们却几乎不可能推断出产生语音的声道运动；③人类可以分辨出许多非言语声音（例如，鸟的叫声），但却不可能还原这些声音的发声机制。对一般方法的质疑则主要来自于支持发音姿态观点的科学家。Liberman 和其在 Haskins 实验室的同事在一系列研究中［46，48，49］指出，“两个不同的发音动作，可能会发出声学特征相似的语音，却对应不同的感知结果；两个相似的发音动作，可能发出声学特征相异的语音，却对应相似的感知结果”。上文已有相关的文献介绍，在此不做赘述。

3. 第二语言言语学习中言语产出与感知的关系

与母语的语音获得不同，第二语言的语音学习是个体在已经习得了母语之后，重新学习的第二种语音。也就是说，在发展上，第二语言的语音学习是晚于母语的语音获得的（本文主要探讨先习得母语，后学习二语的情况，此情况在整个二语学习中占较大比例）。在此种情况下，若探讨第二种语言的言语感知与产出的关系，则需要考虑母语语音经验的影响。

3.1 语音学习模型对第二语言言语产出与感知关系的解释

Flege 提出的语音学习模型（Speech Learning Model，SLM）［27］最初是用来解释第二语言发音问题（外国腔）与起始学习年龄的关系。此外，该模型也解释了二语语音与母语语音的联系，并进一步解释第二语言学习中言语感知与言语产出的联系。该模型认为，语言学习者以相同的方式进行母语和第二语言的学习，使用相同的学习机制，经历类似的言语学习过程。母语发展中，儿童的言语感知一般较言语产出更先达到成人水平。据此，Flege 认为，二语语音感知同样“引导”了二语语音产生。要获得准确的二语语音，需要准确的言语感知标准来指导二语语音的感觉运动学习。而准确的二语言语感知，则取决于二语语音和相似母语语音的语音（phonetic）区别。语音区别越大，则二语语音更容易被识别。

一系列二语语音感知和产出相关的实证研究证实了上述观点。Flege 和 Hillenbrand［28］发现法、英双语者产出的法语/t/的 VOT 值约为 55ms，这通常是法语和英语单语者对/t/产出时观察到的中间值。研究者认为双语者在感知上判断法语和英语的/t/是相同的，这种感知判断影响了他们对法语/t/的感知目标，并最终影响了他们对该辅音的产生。Flege［26］考察了意大利出生，后移民加拿大并开始学英语的意大利语母语者，对英语元音的产出和可理解性任务。结果发现被试到达加拿大的年龄越早，其产出的英语元音就更准确，对英语元音的理解也更准确。这可能表明早期双语者，即在更小的年龄学习二语的双语者会以一种学习母语的方式学习第二语言元音。这符合 SLM 提出的母语与二语使用同一种学习机制，且二语语音产生的准确性受到其感知准确度的限制。

此外，还有研究者从学习的角度着手，以语音训练作为手段，试图通过记录纵向数据探索二语言语感知与产出的因果联系。Bradlow 等［15］通过对日语母语者进行英语辅音识别能力训练，考察了二语学习中对言语感知的训练是否会影响言语产出。实验的前测刺激为不同语音环境下的包括/r/和/l/的英语音节。后测阶段，受试者被呈现三组刺激：原始的前测刺激，加上两组迁移刺激。第一组迁移刺激由额外的 96 个单词组成，这些单词将/r/或/l/放在一个新的说话者（不同于前测）所说的五个不同的语音环境中。第二组迁移刺激由与前测相同的说话者产出不同于前测的包含/r/－/l/的单词。训练中使用的语音刺激包含了前测刺激，要求被试对其中的辅音/r/－/l/进行识别。结果显示由于感知训练使得后测中日语母语者对英语/r/－/l/识别能力显著提高并迁移到了其他未训练过的语音环境和说话人的条件中，同时提高的还有其产出的包含英语/r/和/l/的单词的可理解度。

Fouz－González［29］训练西班牙母语者学习英语辅音。训练包括 4 个阶段，第一个阶段被试得到一个关于目标特征（英语辅音某个难于学习的发音特征）的解释。这包括目标发音的位置和发音方式，这些发音最常见的拼写，为什么它们对西班牙语为母语的英语学习者有挑战，以及如何纠正可能的发音错误的技巧。第二阶段为输入阶段，要求被试听一个三分钟的语音片段，并找到至少 10 个包含目标音的单词，以及是否在语音片段中听到了难于学习的发音特征。第三阶段为输出阶段，要求被试录制一段包含大量目标音的录音。第四阶段要求被试对其他被试录音中的特定语音进行评分。实验的前、后测都是测量被试对目标特征的感知和产生。结果显示即使没有经过针对目标发音特征的产出训练，感知训练同样可以帮助二语学习者提高对难于掌握的二语发音特征的产出。

针对韩语母语者对英语音节韵尾的学习困难，Huensch 和 Tremblay［39］设计了针对性的音节韵尾感知训练程序。其要求韩语为母语的英语学习者进行一系列的韵尾音（例如，edge-edgy，catch-catchy）感知训练，对照组则接受包含/æ/－/ɛ/，/i/－/ɪ/，/oʊ/－/ʊ/的一系列单音节假词（不包含韵尾音）的无关感知训练。训练任务都是要求被试通过迫选完成对单元音和包含目标元音的单词的识别任务。在前、后测阶段，被试完成了包含目标元音的迫选识别任务和大声朗读产出任务。结果发现，针对性训练提高了韩语母语者对英语音节韵尾的感知，且促进了二语者的产出准确性。这表明对二语元音发音困难的针对性感知训练可有效地改善二语元音的产出水平。此外，研究者还发现产出水平的训练提升和感知水平的训练提升之间并不存在显著地线性相关。这提示二语言语产出与感知同样存在紧密联系，但并不像动觉理论认为的那样调用相同的表征。

上述研究发现训练二语者的言语产出，可以有效提高其言语感知。然而，同样有研究发现了相反的结论，也就是训练二语者的言语感知可以有效提升其言语产出水平。Kartushina 等［41］对法语母语者进行了丹麦语元音产出训练，探索二语语音产出训练是否能提高二语者的二语元音感知能力。在训练前后对被试的英语语音产出与感知水平进行评估。感知任务应用 ABX 范式，要求被试指出第三个刺激与第一个还是第二个更相似（即 /e/－/ɛ/、and /y/－/ø/）。产出评估要求被试分别重复/e/、/ɛ/、/y/、and /ø/，并通过计算产出值与 F1－F2 空间中对应的母语元音分布之间的马氏距离（Mahalanobis distance）分析英语元音产出的准确性。训练阶段有五次 45 分钟的训练，对每个元音（/e/、/ɛ/、/y/、/ø/）进行相同量的训练并给予反馈。对每个被试在训练前和训练后测试表现的变化进行了数据分析，发现只要 1 小时的训练，就可以有效地提高非母语元音的发音准确率，即马氏距离减小。同时，产出训练还显著提高了二语者元音区分的准确率。这表明，训练外国元音的发音，不但可以改善二语者的发音，还可以调整对这些元音的感知。然而，进一步的相关分析同样发现，产出能力的提高和感知能力的提高之间缺乏强有力的相关性，这表明二语者的二语产出和感知的提升并没有直接的联系。与 Huensch 和 Tremblay ［39］ 的研究结果相似，该研究也发现二语言语感知与产出间并不是同步提升的，缺乏直接的对应关系。

此外，也并不是所有研究都发现了二语语音产出与感知的联系。Hattori 和 Iverson ［36］ 研究了日语母语者对英语辅音/r/ − /l/的感知与产出的关系。在感知实验中，被试需要完成识别、辨别和最佳范例搜索（best exemplar search）三个任务。识别任务中要求被试匹配听到的辅音与电脑上呈现的包含辅音的对应选项。辨别任务要求被试听到一对辅音刺激并判断它们相同与否。在最佳范例搜索任务中被试在电脑屏幕上看到一个目标辅音，然后听到一个句子，并用 7 点评价（1：最差；7：最好）评定句子中辅音的典型性。在产出实验中要求被试产出 19 对包含辅音/r/ − /l/的单词并录音，然后测量每个辅音的 F2、F3 的相对频率值。通过分析感知实验结果和产出结果的相关性发现，只在识别任务和产出结果之间发现了中等强度的相关，其他感知任务与辅音产出的共振峰频率之间并未发现显著相关。据此认为二语的语音感知和产生过程可能涉及相对独立的表征。Peperkamp 和 Bouchon ［58］ 的研究也发现了类似的结果。在其研究中，要求法、英双语者对/i/和/I/进行辨别以及产出。辨认任务采用 ABX 范式。产出任务则要求双语者朗读英语句子并对其录音，然后由英语母语者对句子进行外国口音评分，并由英语母语者对句子中包含/i/ − /I/的音节进行元音识别判断。对产出任务中的外国口音评分和元音识别判断分别与感知任务中的错误率进行线性相关分析，结果都没发现存在显著相关。研究者将这一不相关解释为 ABX 任务中 ISI（Inter − Stimulus Interval，刺激间隔时间）时间窗口过短（300 毫秒），导致被试无法完成语音环路的加工，从而中断了语音产出和感知的联系。

综合上述理论与实证研究可见，第二语言言语产出与感知是紧密联系的，但已有研究对其关系模式并未达成一致。这可能是因为尚未将母语语音经验的影响纳入整个模型中。因为，言语学习模型中提到的“母语的语音范畴与二语的语音范畴应用了同样的语音学习体系”，这说明两者是存在相关联系的。依据这一假设，随着二语语音范畴的逐渐发展，相似的母语语音范畴也会受到相应的影响。举例来说，法语母语者，如果其产出的英语辅音/t/一直被认为是法语/t/的语音范畴，那么其母语语音/t/的表征可能在 VOT 上会逐渐延长。而要测量这种跨语言的语音相互影响，就必须测量跨语言语音距离。目前一般从语音［40］和感知［16，38，45］两个维度来测量。但目前并未出现学界一致接受的比较稳定有效的测量指标。所以导致较难将母语经验的影响加入二语言语产出和感知的关系讨论之中。可见，探索二语言语感知与产出的联系，不单单要直接测量两者的关系，还需要额外考虑来自于母语的产出和感知经验的影响。此外，二语语音感知与产出在训练/学习模式下并不总是同步改善的。这也说明，两者可能并不是简单的“一对一”关系，该关系受到的影响机制较为复杂。未来需要更全面的研究设计来支撑。

3.2 直接实在论（Direct Realism）观点对第二语言言语产出与感知关系的解释

直接实在论观点认为，感知并不与感知对象的表征直接联系，也不与感知对象的物理特征直接联系，而是通过整合了运动和知觉的感知体系，以人类感知事物的具体行为（acts）直接加工（pick up）感知对象的物理信息。在该理论体系中，感知系统真正加工的是人类加工物理信息的具体行为。对应到言语加工领域，该理论同样强调发音姿态［34，35］。

在二语语音学习领域，研究者发现不同的语言间大量音段在发音姿态和音系空间的分布（distribution of phonological space）上会有相当程度的重叠。从这一现象出发，感知同化模型［9，10］应用直接实在论观点，从母语音段和第二语言音段的发音姿态组合的共性和差异性来预测第二语言语音感知的难易。该模型最基本的假设是，第二语言音位和母语音位发音姿态组合间的相似性决定了听者是否将第二语言音位在感知上同化为母语音位类别。具体来说，如果听者察觉出母语和二语音位在发音姿态上非常相似，那么，二语音位可能被相似的母语音位类别同化，被感知为与该母语音位类别相同；反之，如果听者从发音姿态中察觉出母语和第二语言音位的不同，那么，该二语音位将不会被同化为母语音位类别，其可能被感知为二语音位，也可能被感知成非言语声音。据此可知，感知同化模型将二语言语产出和感知的关系解释为前者影响并预测了后者［9，10］，具体为：

TC 型同化（Two-Category Assimilation）：两个二语语音分别与两个母语音位发音姿态相似，它们将在感知上被同化为这两个母语音位类别。此种情况下，听者很容易区分这两个二语语音。

CG 型同化（Category-Goodness Difference）：两个二语语音在感知上被同化为同一个母语音位类别，但它们与母语音位的发音姿态相似度不太一样（一个更像，一个没那么像）。此种情况下，听者很容易区分这两个二语语音。

SC 型同化（Single-Category Assimilation）：两个二语语音在感知上被同化为同一个母语音位类别，且它们与母语音位的发音姿态的相似度一样。此种情况下，听者较难区分这两个二语语音。

UU 型同化（Both Uncategorizable）：两个二语语音都是无法在感知上被母语音位同化的言语音段（发音姿态不相似）。这种情况对这两个二语语音的区分难度介于容易和困难之间。

UC 型同化（Uncategorized versus Categorized）：两个二语语音，一个可以被同化，另一个无法被同化。这种情况很容易区分这两个二语语音。

NA 型同化（Nonassimilable）：两个二语语音的发音姿势特征与所有母语音位都有很大差异，此时其被感知为无法同化的非言语声音。这种情况下，对这两个声音的区分取决于两者之间的感知差异。

一系列研究支持了感知同化模型的具体预测。举例来说，在对非母语辅音的感知中，祖鲁语的双爆破发音和除阻姿态与任何英语语音发音姿势皆不同，因此，按照感知同化模型的预测，英语母语者会将祖鲁语中的一系列非鼻化的吸气辅音对立对感知为非言语声音。结果显示，尽管英语母语者几乎没有这类吸气辅音的言语经验，但其对这些辅音对照的识别和区分都比较好［12］。类似的结果还有：祖鲁语中的边擦音浊化辅音对立对被同化成两个不同的英语辅音范畴（TC 型），软腭清送气音与爆破音对立对被同化为英语辅音/k/（CG 型），浊双唇爆破音与内爆破音被同化成英语辅音/b/（SC 型或者弱 CG 型）［7］。此外，将埃塞俄比亚语中的喷音对立对/p'/－/t'/呈现给英语母语听者时，听者无一例外地将其同化成了英语辅音/p/和/t/，并且对其区分水平相似（TC 型）［13］。

在对非母语元音的感知中，英语母语者在对挪威语圆唇元音与不圆唇高前元音对立对的感知中，发生了 SC 型同化以及较差的感知区分。另外，在对挪威语高前不圆唇元音与圆唇元音的对立对、法语高圆唇与中前元音对立对的感知中，两对元音都被同化成 TC 型，并且很容易区分。还有，在对法语中前圆唇与中央元音对立对、法语后圆唇元音与鼻化后圆唇元音对立对，以及泰语高后不圆唇元音与中后不圆唇元音的感知中，则表现出混合的同化模式，从 TC 到 CG 到 UC 再到 SC 型的转化［11］。

综上，感知同化模型与其支撑数据都支持言语产出行为与感知的联系。同时，该模型强调发音姿态在言语感知中的重要作用，认为跨语言发音姿态间的差异可以预测第二语言言语感知的难易程度，并指出了具体的预测模式。然而，该模型并不是以变量控制的实验研究作为基础，更多是对言语现象的诠释和解读。

综上对比两种观点可见，两个模型都认为言语产出与感知存在联系，且都考虑了母语语音对二语语音的影响。两个模型都认为母语与二语间的某些差异决定了二语语音的学习难度。两者的区别在于：第一，语音学习模型认为，语音差异决定了二语感知的难易，而感知同化模型认为决定学习难易的决定因素是发音姿态的跨语言差异。第二，语音学习模型一方面强调二语言语感知引导了语音产出，另一方面又认为跨语言语音差异是正确感知的基础。可以说，该模型并未真正回答两者的关系模式，或者，二语言语感知与产出的联系并不是该模型关注的重点问题。知觉同化模型则不同。首先，知觉同化模型与动觉理论相似，都认为发音姿态是言语感知的基础（与动觉模型的细微不同是，感知同化模型秉承直接实在论观点，认为言语感知的基础是现实中发音姿态（actual gestures），而不是发音姿态的表征形式（Intended Gestures in Motor Theory））。其次，该模型认为二语语音与母语语音发音姿态的相似性决定了该二语语音是否能被相似母语语音类别同化，进而决定了其是否容易被感知。也就是说，在二语言语产出与感知的关系中，该模型认为言语产出起到了更为决定性的作用。此外，通过回顾文献，我们发现二语言语感知与产出关系的实证研究主要应用训练的方法探究两者的因果关系。而谁作为自变量，谁作为因变量，主要取决于理论假设。通过综述我们发现，不同的理论假设对应不同的实验设计，并导致了相反的结论。因此，对于因果关系的探讨，可能需要研究方法方面的进一步创新。最近一篇［55］研究英语为母语的晚期法语学习者对法语元音对立/u/－/y/的感知和产出研究中，研究者通过聚类分析，证明了良好的感知是良好产生的先决条件。可见，方法的更新有可能是解决目前二语言语感知与产出关系问题的突破口之一。

4. 言语障碍群体言语加工中言语产出与感知的关系

一系列生理疾病都与言语加工有关，本部分从不同言语障碍群体出发，探索不同生理诱因下言语障碍中产出与感知的关系，有利于以与正常人群不同的研究角度来理解言语产出与感知的关系内涵。以下我们将从几个常见的会导致言语加工异常的生理疾病群体出发，以进一步了解在特殊群体中言语产出与感知的关系模式。

体感和运动控制障碍（somesthetic perception and motor control impairment）：患者表现出难以保持平衡、运动时肢体难以启动、调节以及维持精细动作的特点。该类型障碍一般由脑卒中引起，中枢神经下行性传导通路受损，进而导致运动单位放电率变慢，造成平衡与运动控制障碍［67］。由于言语与运动控制联系紧密，产出与感知的联系在这一特定群体中存在着特殊的模式。举例来说，在 MacNeilage 和 Roots［54］的研究中，一名患有体感和运动控制障碍的17岁女性患者，表现出严重的吞咽、咀嚼、言语困难，对其进行了包括朗读大量单音节、双音节和一些多音节词在内的产出测验，以及音位识别与辨别测验。结果发现，其正确产出了约80%的元音，但其产出的辅音错误较多。浊塞音全错，清擦音和流音几乎全错，鼻音与清塞音正确率较高，达到80%以上。同时，其在识别和辨别语音任务中与正常人并无显著差别。可以发现，虽然患者的语音感知与常人无异，但其辅音产出问题表现明显，而元音产出问题则受影响不大。这提示感觉运动障碍的问题切断了辅音产出和感知的联系，却对元音影响不大。

失语症（aphasia）：失语症一般是因大脑损伤所导致的获得性言语障碍。多种脑部疾病都有可能引起失语症，尤其是脑血管病，约三分之一的急性卒中患者会发生失语［64］。与上文提到的体感和运动障碍相比，在言语产出能力上，失语症患者的言语产出能力丧失得更为彻底。从行为表现上来看，患者的言语产出与言语感知的联系也分离得更为彻底。Blumstein 等［14］对16例左脑损伤的失语症病人进行单音节中元音/d/－/t/的识别与辨别以及产出测试。结果发现：总体感知成绩中，失语症组略差于对照组。失语症患者如果识别任务成绩差，其辨别任务也必然差；但反过来则非必然。这说明失语症患者并不是不能觉察音位间的一系列发音特征的区别，而是缺乏将这些特征以语言加工的形式整合起来的能力。另外，产出实验中，失语症患者表现出浊音和清音之间的重叠，这表明他们在发音程序上有缺陷。也就是说，存在发音动作序列编程缺陷。研究同样未在患者的感知能力缺陷与产出能力缺陷之间发现直接对应的关系。

人工耳蜗植入（Cochlear Implants）：人工耳蜗是一种人工假体，用以替代人体感觉器官，主要作用机制是将环境中的声信号转换成为电信号，并传入耳蜗，对螺旋神经节细胞以及听神经产生刺激，继而促使患者重新产生听觉［68］。大部分人工耳蜗植入的儿童的母语并未习得，所以存在术后建立母语语音表征的过程。有研究［44］比较了植入人工耳蜗儿童语音感知和产出发展的层次结构。他们选取了35名语前听力受损儿童，任务为图片命名与跟读以及语音对立的听觉迫选任务。研究结果发现：人工耳蜗植入儿童的言语感知在术后4—6年后达到正常儿童76%水平。语音特征产出与感知的层次结构是平行发展的：都是先发展元音，然后发展辅音，最后（术后2—3年后）发展浊音化。该结果表明，在行为水平，人工耳蜗植入儿童的言语感知与产出在发展阶段上存在同步性。

帕金森症（Parkinson's Disease）：帕金森病是一种常见的老年神经系统退行性疾病，主要特征表现为动作迟缓、静止性震颤和肌张力增高等。运动减少性构音障碍是帕金森病的主要言语障碍，主要表现为声音嘶哑、粗糙声、气息音、声音震颤等［66］。De Keyser 等［21］比较了14名帕金森病患者和14名听力和认知正常的健康对照者的言语产出（语音清晰度评估、声学分析和语音强度测量）和言语感知（总体估计、强度估计、强度模仿）成绩，并考察两者的关系。研究患者对自身录音中言语特征的判断成绩与其各项声学分析指标，结果并未发现任何显著联系。

言语失用症（Apraxia of speech）：言语失用是一种与言语符号的组织与编程相关的神经性疾病，患者一般并不存在发声结构或肌肉功能损失。言语失用有时是脑损伤后患者的主要言语表现，并明显影响患者的口语恢复［70］。在一项言语失用症的个案研究中［63］，一名因左半球缺血性中风而导致言语失用症的患者，其临床言语特征表现为频繁的语音错误。初步分析发现，其图片命名错误率高达52%和口语单字重复错误率高达33%。进一步测试发现，对于非词中的语音，该患者在语音辨别任务中表现出正常的范畴边界，但在识别任务中不能识别或标记。同时，该患者却可以正常标记真词中的语音。研究者据此推断：非词中语音的识别可能涉及语音运动系统，但语音的辨别不需要运动系统。当词汇语义线索不可用时，可能需要运动过程来识别语音输入中的音位类别。然而，也有研究［37］发现了不同的结果，在其研究中，研究者探讨了言语失用症患者的产出VOT（“bees”和“peas”）以及合成语音连续统（通过调整VOT获得）中的/b/－/p/识别。结果虽然发现患者存在识别和产出问题，但并未发现其对VOT的感知和产出之间存在相关。

功能性构音障碍（Functional articulation disorder）：一般指发音器官无结构、形态及功能方面的异常，并且语言发育已达4岁水平以上，听觉功能正常，但出现有规律的发音错误［69］。有研究［5］探索了功能性构音障碍儿童言语产出与感知的联系。研究选取了33名患有不同构音障碍的儿童，并确定其不存在语言障碍或存在解剖和形态学改变等共病，同时排除听力障碍。研究者使用图片命名任务考察了构音障碍儿童的辅音发音，并使用辅音识别任务考察其语音感知。结果发现：构音障碍儿童产出平均成绩为 74.97%，感知平均成绩为 87.41%。其言语感知成绩显著高于言语产出成绩，且两者成绩呈正相关。研究还考察了言语产出错误与言语感知错误之间的关联，结果只在摩擦辅音上发现了显著相关，在爆破音和响辅音上则未发现关联。该结果表明，构音障碍儿童，其言语产出与感知之间存在联系，该联系可能受到音位范畴的影响。据此，研究者认为，言语产出与感知之间存在联系，但这种联系并不是一对一的对应关系。也就是说，并不是对某一个音位的产出好，对其感知就好。

此外，在本文作者最近一项关于（因咽喉癌）声道切除的病人（平均年龄 60 岁左右，汉语母语，共采集了 4 个人的数据。这类患者整个发音器官都被切除，完全无法发声，也就是说其语音产出能力为零）的研究中，在患者术后 3—6 个月进行汉语语音感知测试发现，其语音识别（元音、辅音、声调）和句子言语理解能力达到了天花板效应。在该研究中，病患的语言产出与感知之间的联系被完全切断，但其言语感知能力仍未受影响。该结果也提示了言语感知与产出的分离。当然，该结果尚不稳定，有可能受诸多因素影响。例如，采样人数较少，术后时间较短，并未测试其学习新词的能力等，只可作为参考。

综上可见，不管什么类型的言语障碍导致的言语产出困难，基本都未观察到一一对应的言语感知困难。也就是出现了言语产出与感知的分离。这与动觉理论的“感知是对产出的逆向解码”的核心观点是不一致的。对于上述患者，言语产出对于言语感知似乎并不是必需的。在正常人群中，这一结论则并不常见。这可能是因为正常人的产出与感知的表征存在联系（或者应用了同样的表征，动觉理论），其表现出来的产出行为和感知能力是可以被分别有效测量的。而对于上述病患，当产出行为发生问题，其对应的产出表征是否受到破坏，该如何进行测量，并与感知表征进行相关分析，目前都是未知的。据此，有必要重新考虑动觉理论的适用范围。此外，上述言语障碍都是由神经中枢的问题直接或间接导致的。行为与功能、神经基础与功能之间，都存在联系［65］。言语障碍人群的障碍特征的神经基础特点，提示在考虑言语产出与感知的联系时，有可能需要将神经基础作为中介或调节变量。如能针对此进行实验设计，或许可以获得关于言语产出和感知关系的更全面的数据。

5. 综合讨论

本文一直围绕一个问题“言语产出与言语感知的关系”，也就是言语产出和感知，谁在先，谁在后，谁如何影响了谁。通过综述分析后发现，对这个研究问题，不同的群体、不同的发展阶段、不同的研究范式，带来了不一致的研究结果。也就是说，言语产出与言语感知的关系可能在不同发展阶段上、不同的群体和研究范式中都存在差异。对于母语群体，虽然也存在认为言语感知引导了言语产出的理论和实证数据，但主流的理论观点（例如，动觉理论）更倾向于认为言语产出是言语感知的基础。同时，主流观点也都指出，随着感知和产出经验的累积，两者之间存在显著的相互影响。此外，两者的联系可能并不是发生在音位水平，而有可能发生在更为细节的发音特征水平。对于二语群体，跨语言语音差异和跨语言发音姿态，究竟谁是二语语音感知好坏的基础，目前的理论和实证研究并未达成一致。同时，已有研究在考虑二语语音学习中言语产出和感知的关系时，不但考虑了两者的直接联系，还考虑了母语语音经验对二语语音学习的影响。事实上，可能正是因为二语语音学习的影响因素来源复杂（来自于母语和二语），而导致了二语语音感知的基础难以确定。而言语障碍群体，或多或少都观察到了言语产出与感知的分离。也就是产出行为受损，而感知能力全部或部分保持良好。目前，由于行为上的产出障碍，很难直接测量并分析言语产出行为与感知能力之间的关联。而对于产出表征的测量及其与感知表征间的关联，还有待进一步探索。

本文对后续的同类研究、教育训练与临床干预都产生了一定的启示。首先，从机制层面，这可能说明言语感知与产出的关系并不稳定，需要在明确发展阶段、群体和研究范式的情况下去认识两者的关系，以期发展出更为全面、更具解释力和预测力的模型。其次，从应用层面，对于语音训练以及言语障碍的干预，都需要根据其发展阶段、所属群体进行针对性的训练与干预，以期得到较好的效果。最后，言语产出与言语感知的关系并不是一个可以轻易下结论的科学问题。它不但涉及语言科学与心理科学的交叉融合，还涉及回答一些分支问题，例如言语感知与产出的关系是否依赖于不同水平的语言材料？如果是，那么是在哪一级的语言加工中，两者建立了联系？言语经验的累积是否以及如何影响了两者的联系？等等。这些问题交织在一起，让解答其中任何一个问题都变得复杂。要深入挖掘其中任何一个科学问题，都要具备全局意识。从研究领域的整体出发，不但要通过具体研究范式回答某个特定问题，还要考虑其与相关问题的交互，以避免“头痛医头、脚痛医脚”的孤立式研究。

本文存在一定的局限。首先，本文主要综述了言语的产出表现与感知能力之间的关系，而未考虑神经基础在这一关系中的角色，未来还需要在脑、行为与认知功能三者关系的范围内，进一步探讨言语产出与感知的关系。并且，本文主要以成人数据作为实证论据，对于儿童言语感知与产出的数据参考较少，未来还需要从发展的角度进一步发掘该问题。此外，本文在综述分析时并未考虑具体的音系环境，而是将对不同语言的言语产出与感知关系的结果统统放在一起考虑。未来进一步的综述分析中，或可将音系作为一个自变量，考察不同音系环境中，言语产出与感知的联系是否存在不同。

6. 结论

（1）对于母语语音使用群体，言语产出是言语感知的基础。随着语音经验的累积，言语产出和言语感知之间彼此相互影响。

（2）对于二语语音学习群体，考察言语产出和言语感知之间的关系，不但需考察两者的直接联系，还需分别考察母语语音产出和感知对二语语音产出和感知的分别影响。

（3）对于言语障碍群体，言语产出与言语感知一般存在行为水平上的分离。也就是产出表现受损，而感知能力全部或部分保持良好。

7. 致谢

本研究得到了天津市教委科研计划专项任务项目（心理健康教育）“言语障碍儿童的语音产出困难与其情绪行为适应能力的关系研究”（2021ZDGX12）的经费支持。

参考文献

[1] Allen, M. C., et al. 1998. Speech intelligibility in children after cochlear implantation. *The American Journal of Otology* 19 (6), 742 – 746.

[2] Allott, R. 2005. The child and the world: How children acquire language. In: *The Child and the World: How the Child Acquires Language How Language Mirrors the World. Able* Publishers, 1 – 48.

[3] Aslin, R. N., Pisoni, D. B., Jusczyk, P. W. 1983. Auditory development and speech perception in infancy. In: Mussen, P. H. (eds), *Handbook of Child Psychology: Formerly Carmichael's Manual of Child Psychology*. New York: Wiley, 573 – 687.

[4] Bell-Berti, F., Raphael, L. J., Pisoni, D. B., Sawusch, J. R. 1979. Some relationships between speech production and perception. *Phonetica* 36 (6), 373 – 383.

[5] Berti, L. C., et al. 2021. Speech production and speech perception in children with speech sound disorder. *Clinical Linguistics & Phonetics*, 1 – 20.

[6] Best, C. T. 1984. Discovering messages in the medium: Speech perception and the prelinguistic infant. In: Fitzgerald, H. E., Lester, B. M., Yogman, M. W. (eds), *Theory and Research in Behavioral Pediatrics*. Boston: Springer, 97 – 145.

[7] Best, C. T. 1990. Adult perception of non-native contrasts differing in assimilation to native phonological categories. *The Journal of the Acoustical Society of America* 88 (S1), S177 – 178.

[8] Best, C. T. 1993. Emergence of language-specific constraints in perception of non-native speech: A window on early phonological development. In: de Boysson-Bardies, B., de Schonen, S., Jusczyk, P., McNeilage, P., Morton, J. (eds), *Developmental Neurocognition: Speech and Face Processing in the First Year of Life*. NATO ASI Series, 69. Dordrecht: Springer, 289 – 304.

[9] Best, C. T. 1994. The emergence of native-language phonological influences in infants: A perceptual assimilation model. In: Goodman, J. C., Nusbaum, H. C. (eds), *The Development of Speech Perception: The Transition from Speech Sounds to Spoken Words*. Cambridge: MIT Press, 167 – 224.

[10] Best, C. T. 1995. A direct realist view of cross-language speech perception. In: *strange, w. (ed) Speech Perception and Linguistic Experience: Issues in Cross-language Research*. Timonium: New York Press, 171 – 204.

[11] Best, C. T., Alice F., et al. 1996. Assimilation of non-native vowel contrasts to the American English vowel system. *The Journal of the Acoustical Society of America* 99 (4), 2602 – 2603.

[12] Best, C. T., McRoberts, G. W., et al. 1988. Examination of perceptual reorganization for nonnative speech contrasts: Zulu click discrimination by English-speaking adults and infants. *Journal of Experimental Psychology: Human Perception and Performance* 14 (3), 345 – 360.

[13] Best, C. T., McRoberts, G. W., et al. 1990. Infant and adult perception of nonnative speech contrasts differing in relation to the listener's native phonology. Infant Behavior and Development. *International Conference in Infant Studies*.

[14] Blumstein, S. E., et al. 1977. The perception and production of Voice-Onset Time in aphasia. *Neuropsychologia* 15 (3), 371 – 383.

[15] Bradlow, A. R., et al. 1999. Training Japanese listeners to identify English /r/and /l/: Long-term retention of learning in perception and production. *Perception & Psychophysics* 61 (5), 977 – 985.

[16] Browman, C. P., Goldstein, L. 1990. Gestural specification using dynamically-defined articulatory structures. *Journal of Phonetics* 18 (3), 299 – 320.

[17] Candia, F. 2016. *Lenition in the Production and Perception of Chilean Spanish Approximant Consonants: Implications for Lexical Access Models*. Doctoral dissertation, University College London.

[18] Cooper, F. S., et al. 1952. Some experiments on the perception of synthetic speech sounds. *The Journal of the Acoustical Society of America* 24 (6), 597 – 606.

[19] Cooper, W. E., et al. 1975. Articulatory effects on speech perception: A preliminary report. *Journal of Phonetics* 3 (2), 87 – 98.

[20] Cooper, W. E., Lauritsen, M. R. 1974. Feature processing in the perception and production of speech. *Nature* 252 (5479), 121 – 123.

[21] De Keyser, K., et al. 2016. The relationship between speech production and speech perception deficits in Parkinson's disease. *Journal of Speech, Language, and Hearing Research* 59 (5), 915 – 931.

[22] Diehl, R. L., Molis, M. R., et al. 2001. Adaptive design of sounds systems: Some auditory considerations. In: Hume, E., Johnson, K. (eds), *The Role of Speech Perception in Phonology*. Academic Press, 123 – 139.

[23] Diehl, R. L., et al. 2003. *Increasing Realism of Auditory Representations Yields Further Insights into Vowel Phonetics*.

[24] Diehl, R. L., Andrew J. L., et al. 2004. Speech perception. *Annual Review of Psychology* 55 (1), 149 – 179.

[25] Diehl, R. L., Kluender, K. R. 1989. On the objects of speech perception. *Ecological Psychology* 1 (2), 121 – 144.

[26] Flege, J. E. The relation between L2 production and perception. 1999. *Proceedings of the XIVth International Congress of Phonetics Sciences* 2, 1273 - 1276.

[27] Flege, J. E. 1995. Second language speech learning: Theory, findings, and problems. In: Strange, W. (eds), *Speech Perception and Linguistic Experience: Issues in Cross-language Research*. Balti more: York Press, 233 - 277.

[28] Flege, J. E., Hillenbrand, J. 1987. Differential use of closure voicing and release burst as cue to stop voicing by native speakers of French and English. *Journal of Phonetics* 15, 203 - 208.

[29] Fouz-González, J. 2019. Podcast-based pronunciation training: Enhancing FL learners' perception and production of fossilised segmental features. *ReCALL* 31 (2), 150 - 169.

[30] Fowler, C. A. 1986. An event approach to the study of speech perception from a direct-realist perspective. *Journal of Phonetics* 14 (1), 3 - 28.

[31] Fowler, C. A. Auditory perception is not special: We see the world, we feel the world, we hear the world. *The Journal of the Acoustical Society of America* 89 (6), 2910 - 2915.

[32] Fowler, C. A. 1989. Real objects of speech perception: A commentary on Diehl and Kluender. *Ecological Psychology* 1 (2), 145 - 160.

[33] Franken, M. K., et al. 2017. Individual variability as a window on production-perception interactions in speech motor control. *The Journal of the Acoustical Society of America* 142 (4), 2007 - 2018.

[34] Gibson, J. J. 1996. The problem of temporal order in stimulation and perception. *The Journal of Psychology* 62 (2), 141 - 149.

[35] Gibson, J. J. 1979. *The Ecological Approach to Perception and Action*. London: Houghton Mifflin.

[36] Hattori, K., Iverson, P. 2010. Examination of the relationship between L2 perception and production: An investigation of English /r/ - /l/ perception and production by adult Japanese speakers. *Interspeech Workshop on Second Language Studies: Acquisition, Learning, Education and Technology*.

[37] Hoit-Dalgaard, J., et al. 1983. Voice onset time production and perception in apraxic subjects. *Brain and Language* 20 (2), 329 - 339.

[38] Hu, W., et al. 2019. Distinctiveness and assimilation in vowel perception in a second language. *Journal of Speech, Language, and Hearing Research* 62 (12), 4534 - 4543.

[39] Huensch, A., Tremblay, A. 2015. Effects of perceptual phonetic training on the perception and production of second language syllable structure. *Journal of Phonetics* 52, 105 - 120.

[40] James, A. R. 1984. *The Suprasegmental Context of Segmental Variation in Second Language Pronunciation Performance*. University of Leeds, Department of Linguistics and Phonetics. PhD dissertation.

[41] Kartushina, N., et al. 2015. The effect of phonetic production training with visual feedback on the perception and production of foreign speech sounds. *The Journal of the Acoustical Society of America* 138 (2), 817 - 832.

[42] Kingston, J., Diehl, R. L. 1994. Phonetic knowledge. *Language* 70 (3), 419 - 454.

[43] Kingston, J., Diehl, R. L. 1995. Intermediate properties in the perception of distinctive feature values. In: Connell, B., Arvaniti, A. (eds), *Phonology and Phonetic Evidence: Papers in Laboratory Phonology IV (Papers in Laboratory Phonology)*. Cambridge: Cambridge University Press, 7 - 27.

[44] Kishon-Rabin, L., et al. 2002. Development of speech perception and production in children with cochlear implants. *Annals of Otology, Rhinology Laryngology* 111 (suppl), 85 - 90.

[45] Hillenbrand, J., Getty, L. A., Clark, M. J., Wheeler, K. 1995. Acoustic characteristics of American English vowels. *The Journal of the Acoustical Society of America*, 97 (5), 3099 - 3111.

[46] Liberman, A. M. 1957. Some results of research on speech perception. *The Journal of the Acoustical Society of America* 29 (1), 117 - 123.

[47] Liberman, A. M., et al. 1967. Perception of the Speech Code. *Psychological Review* 74 (6), 431 - 461.

[48] Liberman, A. M., et al. 1954. The role of consonant-vowel transitions in the perception of the stop and nasal consonants. *Psychological Monographs: General and Applied* 68 (8).

[49] Liberman, A. M., et al. 1952. The role of selected stimulus-variables in the perception of

the unvoiced stop sonsonants. *The American Journal of Psychology* 65 (4), 497.

[50] Liberman, A. M., Mattingly, I. G. 1985. The motor theory of speech perception revised. *Cognition* 21 (1), 1-36.

[51] Liberman, A. M., Mattingly, I. G. 1989. A specialization for speech perception. *Science* 243 (4890), 489-494.

[52] Liljencrants, J., Lindblom B. 1972. Numerical simulation of vowel quality systems: The role of perceptual contrast. *Language* 48 (4), 839-862.

[53] Macdonald, J., McGurk, H. 1978. Visual influences on speech perception processes. *Perception & Psychophysics* 24 (3), 253-257.

[54] MacNeilage, P. F., et al. 1967. Speech production and perception in a patient with severe impairment of somesthetic perception and motor control. *Journal of Speech and Hearing Research* 10 (3), 449-467.

[55] Melnik-Leroy, G. A. et al. On the relationship between perception and production of L2 sounds: Evidence from Anglophones' processing of the French /u/-/y/ contrast. *Second Language Research* 2021, 1-25.

[56] Newman, R. S. 2003. Using links between speech perception and speech production to evaluate different acoustic metrics: A preliminary report. *The Journal of the Acoustical Society of America* 113 (5), 2850-2860.

[57] Ohala, J. J. 1996. Speech perception is hearing sounds, not tongues. *The Journal of the Acoustical Society of America* 99 (3), 1718-1725.

[58] Peperkamp, S., Bouchon, C. 2011. The relation between perception and production in L2 phonological processing. *In Twelfth Annual Conference of the International Speech Communication Association.*

[59] Perkell, J. S., et al. 2004. The distinctness of speakers' productions of vowel contrasts is related to their discrimination of the contrasts. *The Journal of the Acoustical Society of America* 116 (4), 2338-2344.

[60] Platt, L. J., et al. 1980. Dysarthria of adult cerebral palsy: I. Intelligibility and articulatory impairment. Journal of Speech, Language, and Hearing Research 23 (1), 28-40.

[61] Porter, R. J., Castellanos, F. X. 1980. Speech-production measures of speech perception: Rapid shadowing of VCV syllables. *The Journal of the Acoustical Society of America* 67 (4), 1349-1356.

[62] Shelton, R. L., McReynolds, L. V. 1979. Functional articulation disorders: Preliminaries to treatment. *Speech and Language*, 2, 1-111.

[63] Stasenko, A., et al. 2015. A causal test of the motor theory of speech perception: A case of impaired speech production and spared speech perception. *Cognitive Neuropsychology* 32 (2), 38-57.

[64]董瑞国、高素荣:《失语症》,《医师进修杂志》2003年第6期第26卷,9—12页。

[65] 李其维:《心理学的立身之本——"心理本体"及心理学元问题的几点思考》,《苏州大学学报(教育科学版)》2019年。

[66] 李淑华、陈海波、苏闻、蔡晓杰、王新德:《帕金森病的工作记忆检查结果分析》,《诊断学理论与实践》2004年第2期第3卷,23页。

[67] 廖麟荣、廖曼霞:《脑卒中患者运动控制障碍的原因与特征》,《中国康复》2016年第4期31卷,309—311页。

[68] 曲学华、刘俊微、赵倩、李慧:《语前聋人工耳蜗植入患儿佩戴人工耳蜗装置的康复疗效》,《哈尔滨医科大学学报》2021年第3期55卷,311—314页。

[69] 于萍:《儿童言语和语言障碍的研究现状》,《中华耳科学杂志》2013年第3期11卷,408—408页。

[70] 袁永学:《言语失用的言语特征评价及机制探讨》,《中国康复理论与实践》2014年第7期20卷,637—640页。

胡 伟 天津师范大学心理学部,博士,助理研究员。主要研究领域为母语与二语的言语感知、言语产出与感知的关系。系本文通讯作者。
Email: jykxhuwei@ tjnu. edu. cn.

崔程洋 天津师范大学心理学部,硕士研究生在读。
Email: 1501456929@ qq. com.

吴梦瑄 德克萨斯大学言语、语言与听力科学系,博士研究生在读。
Email: mengxuan. wu@ utexas. edu.

胡以鲁：中国现代语音学理论之先声

王继超

摘　要　胡以鲁《国语学草创》是中国学者系统引介西方现代语音学理论的第一本著作。胡以鲁把西方现代语音学理论和中国传统音韵学理论紧密结合，以章太炎成均图的阴声韵部为音值依托，结合Hellwag的“元音三角形”理论阐释汉语元音的发音机制，运用西方现代语音学理论重新解读成均图的阳声韵韵尾音值并修订成均图各韵部的排列次序，深入探讨成均图旁转、对转的本质，为我们进一步认识章太炎成均图的理论内涵及其二十三韵部的具体音值提供了新视角。
关键词　胡以鲁，现代语音学，罗马字母标注，解读，成均图

Hu Yilu: Pioneer of Chinese Modern Phonetics Theory

WANG Jichao

Abstract Hu Yilu's *Guoyuxue Caochuang*«国语学草创»is the first book to introduce the theory of the modern western phonetics to China. Drawing on insights from the western modern phonetics and the traditional Chinese phonology, Hu developed a new interpretation for the articulatory mechanisms in the Chinese vowels, based on discussions of the Yin rhymes in Zhang Taiyan's Cheng Yun Tu (成均图) and the perspective of Hellwag's theory of Vowel Triangle. Then he reinterpreted the Yang rhymes by providing phonetic values to their endings, rearranged their order, and explored the properties of Pang Zhuan (旁转) and Dui Zhuan (对转). By doing so, Hu offered new perspectives into understanding the theoretical framework of the Cheng Yun Tu, and the phonetic values of the 23 rhymes.
Keywords Hu Yilu, Modern phonetics, Phonetic notation by Roman alphabets, Interpretation, Cheng Yun Tu

1. 引言

1939 年岑麒祥的《语音学概论》［4］最早谈到西方现代语音学在中国的引介和发展史，他在第一章第四节“语音学之历史”中指出：

> 我国音韵之研究，由来已久；《尔雅》《方言》《释名》诸书，已启其端。汉后佛教东渐，梵语音学，输入中土，国人受其影响，创为反切，治音韵学者，代有其人，韵书群出，蔚为大观，惜所用多属旧法，离近代之语音学尚远。政变以还，国人因感于国音之不能统一，乃有采用近代语音学之原理，创为国音。学者对于古音之研究，亦渐知运用历史语音学之方法。

林焘［14］在《中国语音学史》序中也提到，在 20 世纪以前，中国语音学史实际上只是一部传统音韵学的历史，到了 20 世纪初，西方语音学理论和方法传入中国，才摆脱汉字的羁绊，开始从揭示汉语的语音特性入手研究语音。然而，岑氏只是谈及中国近代语音学引介的大致时间，“政变以还”即民国成立以后，并没有谈及具体的学者及其著作。《中国语音学史》第一章第九节“走向现代化道路的重大转折”中指出：

> 1919 年爆发的五四运动彻底摧毁了旧文化堡垒，建立起了适应新时代

> 要求的新文化。中国语音学也开始系统地接受西方先进的理论和方法，呈现出生气勃勃的崭新面貌。……五四以后国语的推行和席卷全国的白话文运动密切地结合在一起，形成了很有声势的国语运动。为了配合国语运动，出版了一些“国音学”的概论性著作，试图用西方语音学知识介绍“国音”的发音原理，其中以汪怡《新著国语发音学》（1924）影响较大。

《中国语音学史》认为西方现代语音学理论的引介始于1919年的五四运动，时间界限的划定上更加具体，并且交代了引介的历史背景、代表学者以及主要著作。

李永宏等［13］认为，中国的现代语音学研究可以认为起始于刘复先生1924年在北京大学国文系建立“语音乐律实验室”，它标志着现代语音学在中国进入了系统科学的研究阶段。

实际上，就中国现代语音学理论的引介史而言，1913年胡以鲁的《国语学草创》［22］是中国学者系统引介西方现代语音学理论的第一本著作。2014年，山西人民出版社重印出版了该书，正文之前新附“作者简介”：

> 胡以鲁，语言学家。字仰曾，浙江省宁波人。曾留学日本，初于日本大学学习法政，获法学士学位，后又就学日本帝国大学博言科，学语言学，获文学士学位。回国后曾任教于北京大学，著有《国语学草创》一书。该书是作者唯一的一部语言学著作，也是我国第一部普通语言学著作。他是把西方语言学理论系统引进中国的第一人，他的《国语学草创》第一次为汉语的研究搭建了普通语言学的间架。

李无未［11］认为，虽然《国语学草创》在近现代中国语言学史上的地位十分显赫，可以和《马氏文通》相提并论，但长期以来，学者们并不重视对《国语学草创》的研究，相关论著很少见到。王继超［22］考证指出，直到最近十年才开始有学者重视对《国语学草创》的文本进行剖析式研究，沈国威专门研究了该书的词汇［17］，海晓芳研究了该书的语法［9］，李无未先后研究了该书的方言地理分区和三十六字母罗马字标注谱系［11，12］。

《国语学草创》不仅是我国的第一部普通语言学著作，同时也是中国学者系统引介西方现代语音学理论的第一本著作。胡以鲁不仅用罗马字母为成均图二十三韵部标注了具体音值，而且立足现代语音学理论重新排列成均图各韵部的次序。章太炎为《国语学草创》作序说：

> 尝为声韵对转之图，撰次二十三部，补东原、抝约所未备，而仰曾综贯大秦驴唇之书，时时从余讲论，独有会悟，今见其书，乃为比合音理，别其弇舒，音有难喻，以珊斯克列及罗甸文参伍相证，令古今华裔之声奄然和会，斯治语学者所未有也。

“比合音理，别其弇舒”指的是胡以鲁引介Hellwag的“元音三角形”理论；“综贯大秦驴唇之书”“以珊斯克列及罗甸文参伍相证”指的是胡以鲁以梵语的卷舌辅音（按：胡以鲁称之为“里音Zerebral”）标注三十六字母的知组，以罗马字母标注成均图各韵部的具体音值；“独有会悟”“令古今华裔之声奄然和会”则是指胡以鲁的音值标注是准确的；“斯治语学者所未有也”则说明胡以鲁是利用西方语音学理论标注并解读成均图的第一人。

2. 成均图阴声韵部的音值解读

胡以鲁用罗马字母为成均图二十三韵部标注了具体音值：

> 孔氏《诗声类》以鼻音收声为阳声，以纯音收声为阴声，列为上下两行，发对转旁转之例。吾师章炳麟更图示而昌明之。抄其图而拟以罗马音

标如下。

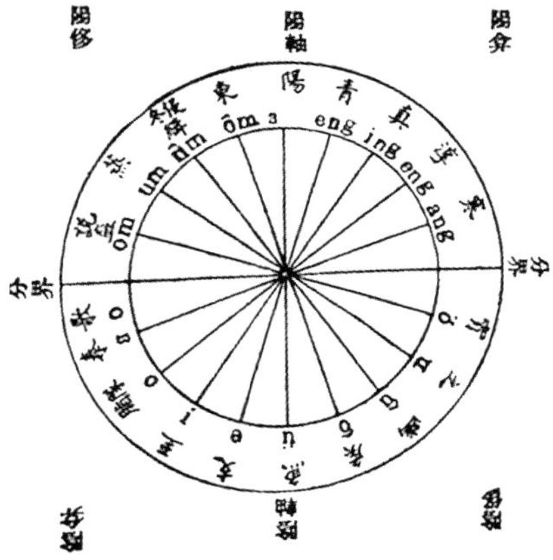

图1　胡以鲁标注《成均图》音值

王力［20］曾评价说："直到章太炎才用中国汉字去描写二十三部的音值，虽没有国际音标那样正确，但我们由此可知他所假定的古代韵值的大概。由此看来，章氏是知道注重韵值的第一人。"虽然章太炎没有使用罗马字母或国际音标标注成均图二十三部的音值，但是他用汉字描写的二十三部音值是具体的，而不是"大概"。胡以鲁之所以能够用罗马字母标注成均图二十三部，前提肯定是各韵部具有具体的音值。1934年钱玄同［16］的《古韵二十八部音读之假定》明确指出：章太炎师始言"钟""冬"音读之异，他以为"钟"部（东部）古音当如今吴越间《广韵》的"江"韵之音，即［òng］，"冬"部古音当如今读《广韵》的"东""冬""钟"诸韵之音，即［ong］（此亦吴越间读法）。章太炎［25］自己也说："盖自戴、王得其事证，而鄙人始撢其声势也。"与其说章氏是知道注重韵值的第一人，不如说他是拟定具体韵值的第一人。

章太炎之所以能够为古韵部拟定具体的音值，与他的考证古音的方法有关。其1924年的《与汪旭初论阿字长短音书》［25］一文提到考证古韵音值的具体纲领：

> 往昔顾、段诸公未知泰、夬与脂、微、齐、皆、灰异类，东原、石渠考迹周秦有韵之文，知其不同矣。乃所以不同之故，二公亦未能著言之。盖以去声祭、泰、夬、废，入声曷、末、黠、月、屑、薛，声音凌杂，莫由得其纲领故。纲领云何？以吴越音相证。其呼介、疥、芥、界、带、泰、快、外、蔡、败、拜、赖、癞等字，皆作阿字长音，正如中原之呼麻部去声者。中原呼大、话等字，音亦然也。其在入声，戛、獭、达、撻、闥、乞、空、牵、豁、昏、叡、殺、轢、刷、蔡、拔、跋、橃、髮、發、伐、刺，通语皆为阿字长音之促已。

无论是吴越音、通语，还是各地方言，都是现代语音材料。为了表述清楚古音的具体音值，章太炎不但借助现代语音材料作为音值的载体，而且把现代语音材料的特征作为古音特征的依据。朱右白［28］指出，成均图纯论音理，由声音之开合弇侈，而成旁、通、对转，成均图所论音声之通转，皆有直接证据，即以今人之音整理古音。唐作藩［19］也指出，章氏运用了现代方音材料做佐证，如云："古之泰部如今中原呼麻。"又说："今吴越间呼泰，则与地方呼麻者同。"此说比顾炎武所谓"麻音来自西域，非中原旧读"的看法则较合乎实际，因而是进了一步，但章氏没有讲出个道理来。

胡以鲁依据章太炎对成均图各韵部音值的解说为成均图标注罗马字母，因此，他标注音值的纲领同样也是"以吴越音相证"，兼以各地方言。他说：

> 如"穷"在冬部，然《诗》"不宜空我师"，《传》以"空"为"穷"，则所谓冬、东旁转也。今之语音自湖南、江西、安徽等外，冬、东之别亦复不存，"穷乏""空乏"韵虽异而音则同矣。时地方音之差盖若是也。此种类例章先生《国故论衡》

举之甚多。别无所见不更述。

胡以鲁用现代语音学理论阐释汉语元音的发音机制，但结合了成均图的阴声韵部的音值，实际上把阴声韵部和元音在概念上直接对等：

> 元音之种别，高下为之。元音之高下，则口腔之大小。即舌头向口盖隆起之差也。隆起舌之后部而发音为“泰”。稍前为“队”。更出而突起其前部为“支”为“至”。此等元音古所谓韵，亦如纽然。以之作叠韵之代表耳。音之所以为音处，无从知也。兹欲分析而得其元音，亦惟以其所为翕之音，表以罗马音标。以 a e ĕ i 等当之。由 a 及 i 唇舌渐前隆，口腔空处渐小渐前渐后向，音乃渐就明锐。次圆撮其两唇，舌渐后隆，发上四音，则为“歌”“侯”“之”即 o ǒ u 是也。此时音渐后响而圆笼，乃渐就沉钝。又以两唇作椭圆而嘘声，为闭口之“鱼”音［ü］。以 i 及 u 与 ê 及 ô 之折中位置而发两者中和之音，则为“幽”“宵”，略如 û ö。所谓韵者，如是而已。

胡以鲁的元音理论正是 Hellwag“元音三角形”的基本原理。Hellwag 原本是德国医生，其全名是 Christoph Friedrich Hellwag（1754—1835），胡以鲁译为海尔华尔胥，岑麒祥译为嚇尔哇格（见下文）。Pfitzinger & Niebuhr［3］指出，Hellwag 在他的博士论文［1］中首次选择使用三角形来排列元音，引入经典的“元音三角形”（Vowel Triangle）。［a］在倒立三角形的底尖，以显示元音长度之间的关系以及相应的舌位。后来又经过了两次改进，进一步完善了“元音三角形”，成为今天元音梯形（vowel trapezium）或定位元音（Cardinal vowel）系统的前身，二者在垂直区间的高度划分上是一样的。改进之后的“等距舌位元音三角形”（Vowel triangle with equidistant tongue height positions by Hellwag 1783）如下：

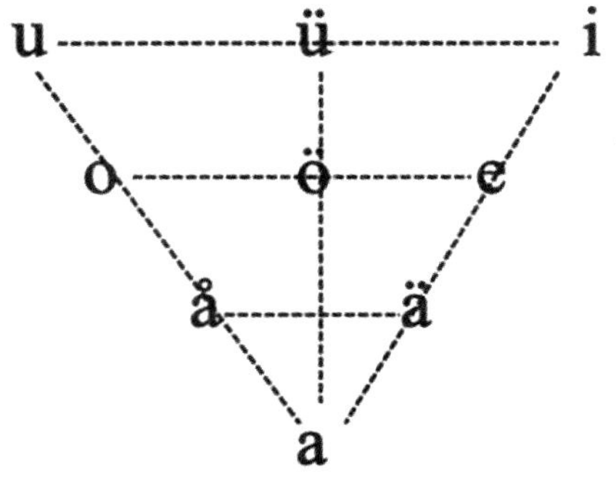

图2　Hellwag“等距舌位元音三角形”（1783）

1939年岑麒祥的《语音学概论》［4］也提到 Hellwag“元音三角形”理论，并且用国际音标转写了原图中的德语字母标注：

> 吾人既明各母音之性质，若就其近似之处加以类别，是为母音之分类。十九世纪语音学家曾作母音之分类者，可以德国嚇尔哇格（Hellwag）及英国贝尔①二人为代表。嚇氏曾就各母音之音色及发音法绘成三角形如下：
>
> i　　y　　u
> e　　　　o
> ɛ　　œ　　ɔ
> a
>
> 以 a 为出发点，ɛ e i 为前母音，发音时口腔逐渐闭合，舌部逐渐向前移动；ɔ o u 为后母音，发音时口腔亦逐渐闭合，惟舌部逐渐向后收缩；y œ 则为 i ɛ 之圆唇音。图内所列母音虽极不完备，而对于母音发音时各发音机关之动作颇能表出，故现代语音学家多沿用之。

岑麒祥对元音发音机制的阐述和胡以

---

① 艾约瑟（1876）最早引介贝尔的视话法理论，可参看艾约瑟发表在《益智新录》上的两篇文章：《方言得形新法考》（1876）和《方言得形新法（附图）》（1877）。

鲁的元音理论基本一致，都旨在说明“元音之种别，高下为之。元音之高下，则口腔之大小”，而且元音的排列顺序也基本一致。但二者之间也存在一些细节上的不同，首先是音值的标注方式不同，胡以鲁使用德语字母标注，而岑麒祥则使用的是国际音标。另外，胡以鲁指出“以 i 及 u 与 ê 及 ô 之折中位置而发两者中和之音，则为‘幽’‘宵’，略如 û ö”，岑氏无此论；岑氏指出“œ 为 ɛ 之圆唇音”，胡氏无此论。

比较而言，胡以鲁的元音理论更加接近 Hellwag 的理论原型。据海晓芳［9］考证，胡以鲁 1909 年入日本东京帝国大学言语科（按：语言学系）学习言语学（按：语言学），师从藤冈胜二。柿木重宜［18］指出，藤冈胜二，师从东京帝国大学文科大学博言学科教授上田万年，1901 年藤冈到德国留学，回国后不久从上田万年手中接过东京帝国大学文科大学言语学专业。所以胡以鲁的元音理论更加接近 Hellwag 的理论原型。岑运强［5］指出，岑麒祥 1931 年入法国巴黎大学，师从巴黎大学语言研究所主任房德里耶斯学习普通语言学，从语音研究所主任傅舍学习语音学。岑氏精通国际音标，1937 年商务印书馆出版了他的《国际音标用法说明》。虽然他们的标注工具不同，但音值上是对等的，例如：Hellwag“元音三角形”的德语的 ä，胡氏标注为“队（侈口 e)”，岑氏标注为［ɛ］，实际音值一样。

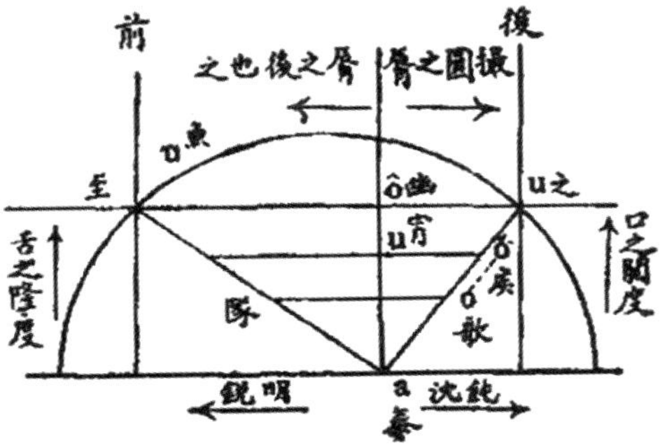

图3　胡以鲁所作元音三角形（同图1）

岑麒祥先罗列 Hellwag“元音三角形”然后再解说元音的发音机制，而胡以鲁则先解说元音的发音机制然后再罗列 Hellwag 的“元音三角形”：

> 为作音表如下。右表利用海尔华尔胥 Hellwarg 三角形图参酌之案也。按图索之，庶几知音之位置性质乎。

或许是排版印刷上的失误，上图的标注存在几点问题：（1）队 e、支 ê、至 i 的标注信息不全。（2）原文中“支”和“侯”的标注不统一，原文中既标注为 ĕ 和 ŏ，也标注为 ê 和 ô，Hellwag 标注为 ä 和 å，德语的 ä 实际上对应于法语的 ê，所以我们统一标注为 ê 和 ô。（3）上图中“幽”和“宵”的标注和原文的解说不一致，“幽”应标注为 û，“宵”应标注为 ö。

Hellwag“元音三角形”的七个定位元音的音值是确定的，和国际音标舌位图的定位元音的音值一致。比照岑麒祥的国际音标标注，我们可以首先确定胡以鲁所标注的七个定位元音（Cardinal vowel）的音值分别为：泰 a［a］、队 e［ɛ］、支 ê［e］、至 i［i］、歌 o［ɔ］、侯 ô［o］、之 u［u］。

接下来，我们结合章太炎《二十三部音准》，进一步验证胡以鲁罗马字母标注的合理性。

董婧宸［7］指出，就韵部系统而言，章太炎早年在《论语言文字之学》（1906）和《新方言·音表》（1909）中，分别提出过古韵二十二部、二十三部的分部构想，只不过从古韵框架来看，此时主要是以段玉裁古音十七部为基本格局。在《国故论衡·成均图》（1910）中，章太炎吸收孔广森之说，以对转作为古韵系统的基础，立九类二十三部。据陈平原［6］考证，1910 年《国故论衡》初版由东京秀光舍印刷发行，第二、三版分别于 1912 年 12 月和 1913 年 4 月由上海大共和日报馆印行，封面及正文完全相同。1915 年上海右文社铅印本《章氏丛书》中的《国故论衡》，删去《古今音损益说》，增《音理论》和《二十三部音准》，各文多有修正。

依据胡以鲁的音值标注和他所说的"时地方音之差盖若是也。此种类例章先生《国故论衡》举之甚多。"我们认为《二十三部音准》(1915)的理论基础仍然是《国故论衡》(初版)的二十三部古韵理论，虽然有所修订，但考证古音的纲领不变。例如："泰"，胡以鲁标注为 a [a]，对应《二十三部音准》所说的"古之泰部如今中原呼麻"；"队"标注为 e [ɛ]，对应"其声满口而幎呼"；"支"标注为 ê [e]，对应"敁、迟、企……右九十六字，今读横口，乃支部正音"；"至"标注为 i [i]，对应"至部古音如今音"；"歌"标注为 o [ɔ]，对应"古歌部如今音"；"侯"标注为 ô [o]，对应"侯音稍穹口呼之"；"之"标注为 u [u]，对应"每、媒、梅等十四字如江南音，今读纵口，乃之部正音"。

章氏以"横口"描写 [e]，以"纵口"描写 [u]，再比如章太炎 [26] 对古泰部的音变描写：

> 古之泰部如今中原呼麻，自麻部变为张口，而泰部乃有横口、纵口音矣。

赵元任 [27] 调查指出，现代吴语里，一部分泰韵字在"d 系""g 系""h 系"作声母时音值为 [a] 和 [e]，一部分泰韵字在"d 系"作声母时音值为 [ɯ] 和 [u]。"泰部乃有横口、纵口音矣"，即泰部由 [a] 演变为 [e] 和 [u]。

综上对比可知，胡以鲁的音值标注基本符合章太炎《二十三部音准》的理论界定。

现在我们讨论其他三个韵部的音值。胡以鲁说："以两唇作椭圆而嘘声，为闭口之'鱼'音 [ü]"，结合图3，线的右边表示"唇之圆撮"，即"鱼 ü"是"至 i"对应的圆唇音，可以确定"鱼 ü"的音值就是 [y]，即德语的 ü。

尽管胡以鲁指出"以 i 及 u 与 ê 及 ô 之折中位置而发两者中和之音，则为'幽''宵'，略如 û ö"，但我们并不能仅凭此就能确定 û 和 ö 的具体音值。1906 年冈仓由三郎在《发音学讲话》[8] 中详细介绍了 Hellwag "元音三角形"的发音原理：

> 如果把舌头放在イ的位置，嘴唇放在ウ的位置，就会发出一种与イ和ウ不同的中间音，即德语的 ü 的音。然后，把舌头放在オ处，把嘴唇的形状做成エ时的话，就会发出德语的 ö 的音。

由此可知，胡以鲁所说的"折中位置而发两者中和之音"其实可以理解为：û 是 i 的舌位 u 的唇形，ö 是 ô 的舌位 ê 的唇形。首先"宵 ö"的音值基本可以确定，即为德语的 ö [ø]。问题在于，i 的舌位 u 的唇形发音应该为德语的 ü，而胡以鲁却标注为 û，显然胡以鲁的标注和德语原文是矛盾的，而解决这一矛盾的一个基本假设就是：ü 和 û 的音值虽然不同，但二者非常接近。

要考定"幽 û"的具体音值，我们仍然需要借助章太炎拟定古音的纲领。章氏 [26] 指出，"幽部古音如今音，齐齿而直，故与侯殊"依据"以吴越音相证"，胡以鲁是宁波人，宁波方言 [10] 幽字的韵母是 [iɤ]。现代吴语 [27] 里面"幽"韵字在"g、h、tz 系"作声母时的音值包括 [iɯ]、[ɤ] 和 [y]。因为鱼部的音值为 [y]，所以首先排除 [y]，再考虑到 û 是 i 和 u 的"中和之音"，而且在三角形图中排在"唇之圆撮"的一面，所以 û 是圆唇音，故而排除 [iɯ]。又舌位图上的标注点位只代表单元音，因此，胡以鲁所标注的"幽 û"的音值最有可能是 [ɤ]。而这一音值恰好能够满足之前的假设。

3. 旁转、对转的形成机制

胡以鲁按照"音声学之原理"把阴声韵部的音值分为两大类，包括七个"纯粹元音"(包括之 u、侯 ô、支 ê、至 i、脂队

e、泰a、歌o）和三个“变徵之音”（包括宵ö、幽û、鱼ü）。

> 未经调节之音，所谓口腔大小之差者，乃凡用有节言语 Articulated speech 者所大同。所不同者，o、a、e、i、u之外拗杂之音耳。如吾国语音中之 û ü ö 是也。然既曰变徵，已非纯粹元音。乃为元音所杂糅者矣。实则所谓二重音三重音者此也。吾国古昔语中多二重音三重音，不难想象。即如“泰”音，上古殆发如 tai、如 taei 无疑。后则单节语得势乃同化于单音 a 而为去声耳。晚近且有由入声而转为去声者，去声音语益多，乃又有延长而为二重音三重音者矣。今之北京语其显著者也。“鱼”“幽”“宵”等音表以 ü û ö（··）（∧）等音符，固昔日之独立一音而渐摩翕合者也。观今日“宵”之北京读音已析而为 iao，逆而推之，所谓变徵之音，上古皆曾为二重三重者，未可知也。
>
> 要之，音之中泰（a）队（侈口e）支（弇口e）至（侈口i）与歌（侈口o）侯（弇口o）之（侈口u）纯粹元音也。鱼（ü）幽（û）宵（ö）则所谓变徵之音，殆即二重音三重音之上翕 Steigende（按：德语，叠加）也。

尽管成均图中十类阴声韵的音值都是单元音，但从历史语音学的角度来看，“鱼”“幽”“宵”三个韵部在上古很可能是双元音或三合元音，经过“二重音三重音之上翕 Steigende”演变为单元音，所以称其为“变徵之音”。萨默斯［2］指出，古阿拉伯语使用的是 ai 和 au 而不是 e 和 o，希腊语和拉丁语中，Καισαρ 演变为 Cœsar，θανμα 在爱奥尼亚方言（Ionic dialect）① 里面演变为 θωμα，它们和汉语里面发生的语音演变非常类似，这一点在“汉语方言对照表”（the Comparative Table of Dialects）中一目了然。法语单词 lait、mais、aussi 的今天读法也反映了这一事实，另外德语的 auch 演变为 ōch 亦是如此。萨默斯从类型比较的角度论证汉语中也存在双元音演变为单元音的情况，汉语方言比较可以作为例证。胡以鲁认为，汉语不仅存在双元音演变为单元音的可能，也存在单元音再次演变为双元音的可能。例如“泰”，上古发音为 tai 或者 taei，后来由于单节语（按：单元音）得势，tai 或者 taei 被“同化”为单元音 ta，并且变为去声，晚近，一些入声字变为去声字，去声字增加，为了避免因同音字过多而造成的交流障碍，单元音又延长为双元音或三合元音。

也就是说，胡以鲁所解读的成均图的各韵部的音值并非都是上古音。《二十三部音准》是对成均图的进一步阐释，其中提到：鱼部古音皆合口，如乌、姑、枯、吾。其撮口如於、居、祛、鱼者，后世之变也。从是开口则近歌，从是齐齿则近支，此鱼部所以常与歌、支相转。“从是”即“后世之变”以后，“鱼部所以常与歌、支相转”。因此，鱼部的古音应该拟音为［u］，但成均图中鱼部的音值“撮口如於、居、祛、鱼者”，所以胡以鲁将其标注为德语的 ü［y］。因此，成均图既有“如今音”的古歌部，也有“后世之变”的鱼部，即使章氏指出的“古之泰部如今中原呼麻”，按照胡以鲁的观点，［a］也未必就是泰部的上古音。因此，胡氏所标注的成均图各韵部音值并非都是上古音，只是为了能够从音理上说明各韵部之间的旁转、对转的关系而已。胡以鲁指出：

> 凡是展转而又同音者，发起之时地不同，所谓方音之差也。如《尚书》与《诗》时世不同，《诗经》中更有诸风之差，汇萃之于一书，乃义同而音差，有所谓对转、旁转者矣。表中所据虽为《唐韵》，不得便谓之古音。然就一时世为观察点而论其差，固有法有则若是也。

“旁转、对转”形成机制主要有两个：

① 爱奥尼亚方言，几种古希腊方言中的一种，大约公元前1000年在亚洲的爱奥尼亚使用。

一个是“时世不同”，另一个是“方音之差”。尽管成均图二十三部的划分依据的是《唐韵》，但“不得便谓之古音”，因为“所谓旁转、对转者，音声学理所应有，方音趋势所必至也”。“音声学理所应有”是谈语音的历时演变；“方音趋势所必至”是谈语音的共时演变。这也就是为什么章太炎的成均图理论既谈古音的历时演变，也谈现代方言的比较。“就一时世为观察点而论其差，固有法有则若是也”，历史上任何一个时间段的方言差异都能使成均图中旁转、对转的关系成立。王宁、黄易青［23］也谈到，运用成均图所阐释的语音学原理和所表现的语音关系，不但可以合理地解释古代发生过的历史音变和方音变化，更可以深入地理解上古音系统的结构。

4. 成均图阳声韵的音值解读

章太炎［26］指出：

> 然鼻音有三孔道：其一侈音，印度以西皆以半“摩”字收之，今为谈、蒸、侵、冬、东诸部，名曰撮唇鼻音；其一弇音，印度以西皆以半“那”字收之，今为青、真、谆、寒诸部，名曰上舌鼻音；其一轴音，印度以“姎”字收之，不待撮唇上舌，张口气悟，其息自从鼻出，名曰独发鼻音。

王宁、黄易青［23］解读为，阳侈收唇鼻音［－m］，阳弇收舌鼻音［－n］，阳轴的阳部收舌根鼻音［－ŋ］。也就是说，谈、蒸、侵、冬、东四部的鼻音韵尾为［－m］；青、真、谆、寒四部的鼻音韵尾为［－n］；阳部的鼻音韵尾为［－ŋ］。

胡以鲁以“音声学之理”对成均图阳声韵鼻音韵尾的音值解说认为：

> 在对转也，撮唇之音转为唇内，弛唇后向之音转为喉内，闭口引唇之音转为舌内，此诚音声学之理也。

首先，依据“鼻音ng、n、m亦有以之收声者：以m收者曰唇内鼻音；以n收者曰舌内鼻音；以ng者曰喉内鼻音”，确定胡以鲁标注的成均图阳声韵鼻音韵尾包括［－m］、［－n］、［－ŋ］三个。

然后，依据“由a及i声渐后向，舌渐前隆，口腔空处渐小渐前，音乃渐就明锐”，确定“弛唇后向之音”即泰a、队e、支ê、至i；依据“次圆撮其两唇，舌渐后隆，发上四音，则为歌侯之，即o ǒ u是也”，确定“撮唇之音”即歌o、侯ô、之u；依据“以两唇作椭圆而嘘声，为闭口之鱼音［ü］”，确定“闭口引唇之音”即鱼ü。由于幽部和宵部排在侯部和之部之间，以“撮唇之音”视之。

综上，泰a、队e、支ê、至i对转的寒、谆、青、真四部的鼻音韵尾为［－ŋ］；侯ô、宵ö、幽û、之u对转的东、谈（盍）、冬（侵、缉）、蒸四部的鼻音韵尾为［－m］；鱼ü对转的阳部的鼻音韵尾为［－n］。胡以鲁即以此标注成均图的音值如下：

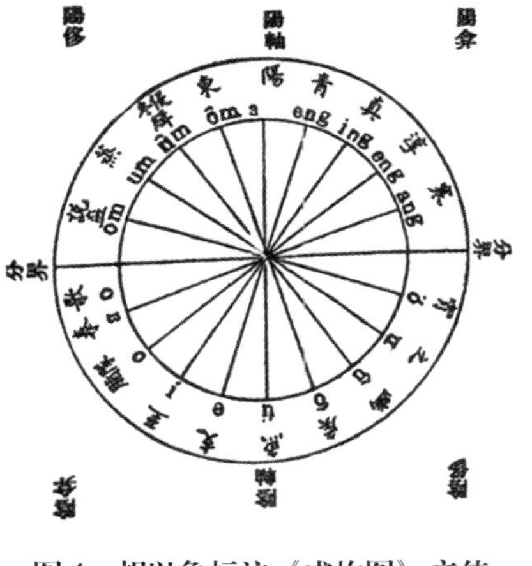

图4 胡以鲁标注《成均图》音值

上图中存在两个问题：（1）歌部虽然附在泰部的旁边，但歌ɒ没有对转的阳声韵；（2）阳部的音值只标注了a，在另一张成均图里面标注为am，也即并没有按照解说把阳部标注为［an］。而更大的矛盾在于，章太炎拟定的青、真、谆、寒四部的鼻音韵尾为［－n］，而胡以鲁却认为这四部的鼻音韵尾为［－ŋ］。原因很可能是在宁波方言里面，前鼻音韵尾往往读为后鼻音韵尾。胡氏给出的理由比较简单：此诚音声学之理也。按照胡以鲁的标音，我们把成均图九个阳声韵部的音值转写如下：

寒 ang［aŋ］、谆 eng［ɛŋ］、真 ing［iŋ］、青 ěng［eŋ］、阳 an［an］、东 ŏm［om］、冬 ûm［ɤm］、蒸 um［um］、谈 öm［øm］。

胡以鲁依据“音声学之理”不但重新解读成均图阳声韵的鼻音韵尾，而且重新修订成均图各韵部的排序：

> 虽然先生之图，作圆转之则，诚尽美矣。然所谓音转果一如图序配列与否，犹不能无疑也。其在对转也，撮唇之音转为唇内，弛唇后向之音转为喉内，闭口引唇之音转为舌内，此诚音声学之理也。然其他旁转、次旁转得非顺序颠倒否。敢据音声学之理，拟之如下，以乞教于先生。

图5　胡以鲁重排成均图各韵部排序

如果我们把上图顺时针旋转45°，再与“胡以鲁所作元音三角形”对比，就会发现成均图阴声韵的排列次序与“元音三角形”的排位基本一致。二者比较如下：

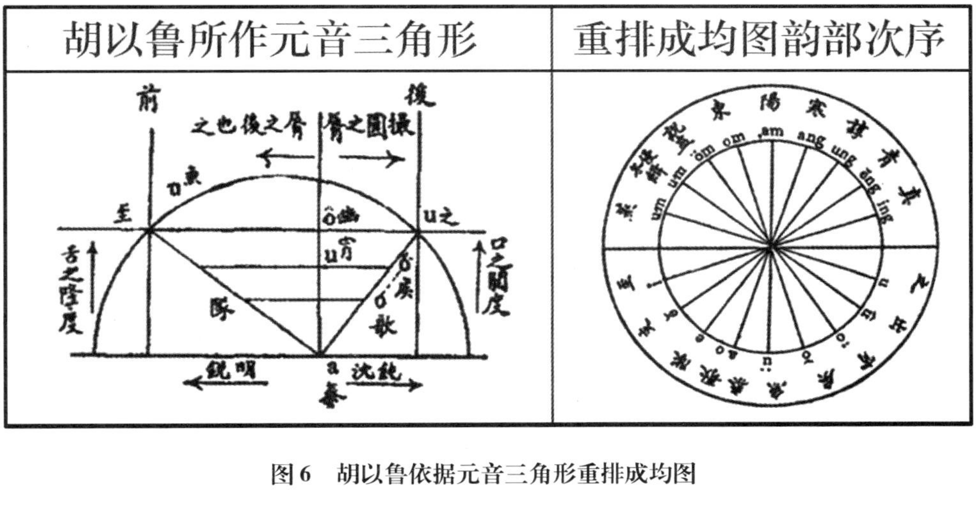

图6　胡以鲁依据元音三角形重排成均图

右图中的鱼部和阳部仍然作为成均图的阴轴和阳轴，分别隔开“阴侈”“阴弇”和“阳侈”“阳弇”。先看鱼部的左边，虽然歌部和泰部仍然作为一部，如果我们暂不考虑歌部，就会发现从下到上的排序为：泰、队、支、至；鱼部的右边，从下到上的顺序为：侯、宵、幽、之。成均图各韵部重新排序之后和“胡以鲁所作元音三角形”中的次序以及排位基本一致。

王宁、黄易青［23］指出，这种以韵部次第来显示古音关系、说明古声流转相通渠道的做法，发明于段玉裁的“合韵说”。韵部次第安排的根据，首先是古人用韵、谐声、异文、异体、读若所表现的声音关系，以及建立在对古音材料理解之上的语音学理论。而胡以鲁对成均图韵部排序的认识并没有和古音材料很好地结合，单纯从现代语音学理论的角度重新审视成均图，实际上把舌位图和成均图混淆为一体，这是胡氏的不足之处。

5. 余论

王力［21］批评说：胡以鲁在他的《国语学草创》中，一方面介绍西方的语言学说，另一方面也介绍了他的老师章炳麟的语言学。但是，“中西合璧”是做不好的，正如刘复所嘲笑的“风琴与洞萧合奏”一样，显得十分不和谐。不可否认，胡以鲁的理论存在一定的不足之处，例如他对成均图二十三部的理解过于偏重西方现代语音学理论，和传统古音材料结合不足。但“中西合璧”本身并没有不好，关键是能够真正做到把中西完美结合。

《中国语音学史》［14］以钱玄同《文字学音篇》（1918）开始使用音标标注汉语音系标志中国传统音韵学开始向现代音韵学转变。而钱氏《论注音字母》［15］一文中用罗马字母标注宋人三十六字母仍然以《国语学草创》的标注为参照：

> 这表中标“知”“徹”“澄”“娘”“微”“匣”六纽的罗马字母，用亡友胡仰曾君所著《国语学草创》所标。

因此，尽管胡以鲁对成均图的阐释存在一定的不足，但我们不能因此就对《国语学草创》的学术价值予以全盘否定。作为中国学者第一本系统引介西方现代语音学的著作，它仍然具有十分重要的学术史价值。作为标注并解读章太炎成均图二十三韵部的第一人，胡以鲁运用西方现代语音学理论解读章太炎的成均图，为我们进一步考证成均图各韵部的具体音值提供了新视角。

《国语学草创》不仅是中国学者系统引介西方现代语音学理论的第一本著作，也是中国传统音韵学向现代音韵学开始转变的标杆。因此，作为中国现代语音学史的开端，胡以鲁《国语学草创》的学术史地位及其价值需要重新审视和评估。

6. 致谢

本文研究得到了国家社科基金冷门绝学研究团队项目“东亚汉语音韵学史文献发掘与研究”(21VJXT014）的支持。

参考文献

［1］Hellwag，C. F. 1781. *Dissertatio Inauguralis Physiologico Medica de Formatione Loquelae*. Ph. D. thesis，Tübingen.

［2］Summers，J. 1863. *A Handbook of the Chinese Language*. Oxford：Oxford University Press.

［3］Pfitzinger，H.，Niebuhr，O. 2011. Historical development of phonetic vowel systems—The last 400 Years. *Proceedings of the 17th ICPhS*，Hong Kong，160－163.

［4］岑麒祥（1939）《语音学概论》。上海：中华书局。

［5］岑运强（1997）岑麒祥传略。《文教资料》第02期，3—7页。

［6］陈平原（2002）《国故论衡》导读。载《国故论衡》，上海：上海古籍出版社，2003年。

［7］董婧宸（2020）章太炎《文始》的成书与版本考。《民俗典籍文字研究》第02期，25—36页。

［8］冈仓由三郎（1906）《発音学講話》。东京：有朋堂。

［9］海晓芳（2014）《文法草创时期中国人的汉语研究》。北京：商务印书馆。

［10］李荣 主编（1997）《宁波方言词典》。南京：江苏教育出版社。

［11］李无未（2019）胡以鲁《国语学草创》汉语方言分区理论及“原型”。《语文研究》第2期，8—16页。

［12］李无未（2019）《国语学草创》36字母罗马字标音理论及“原型”。《古汉语研究》第2期，2—17页。

［13］李永宏、孔江平、于洪志（2008）现代语音学仪器及生理语音学研究。《生命科学仪器》第6卷第09期，54—58页。
［14］林焘 主编（2010）《中国语音学史》。北京：语文出版社。
［15］钱玄同（1918）论注音字母。《新青年》第4卷第1期。
［16］钱玄同（2011）《钱玄同文字音韵学论集》。上海：上海古籍出版社。
［17］沈国威（2013）双音节化与汉语的近代演进：胡以鲁“汉语后天发展论”的启示。《或问》第24号，139—154页。
［18］柿木重宜（2017）近代「言語学」成立事情——言語学者藤岡勝二の役割を中心として。《関西外国語大学研究論集》第105号，5—10页。
［19］唐作藩（2017）《汉语语音史教程》。北京：北京大学出版社。
［20］王力（1956）《汉语音韵学》。北京：中华书局。
［21］王力（1981）《中国语言学史》。太原：山西人民出版社。
［22］王继超（2021）重审胡以鲁《国语学草创》版本信息。《宁波大学学报（人文科学版）》第34卷第2期，88—93页。
［23］王宁，黄易青（2010）章太炎先生成均图的结构及其元音系统。载《中国语言学（第二辑）》，济南：山东教育出版社，40—50页。
［24］吴宗济（2001）普通话语音合成中有关自然度的韵律变量问题。载《新世纪的现代语音学——第五届全国现代语音学学术会议》（蔡莲红、周同春、陶建华主编），北京：清华大学出版社，291—294页。
［25］章太炎（1924）与汪旭初论阿字长短音书。《华国》第1卷第5期，44—49页。
［26］章太炎（2010）《国故论衡》。北京：商务印书馆。
［27］赵元任（1956）《现代吴语的研究》。北京：科学出版社。
［28］朱右白（1940）成均图与广韵通转表。《说文月刊》第1期，124—128页。

王继超　厦门大学人文学院中文系博士研究生。研究方向为中外汉语音韵学史研究。
Email：wangjichao0105@foxmail.com

湘乡方言①

曾 婷

摘 要 湘乡（[ɕjaŋ⁴⁴ɕjaŋ⁴⁴]）方言为汉语方言之一，主要分布于中国湖南省中部的湘乡城区（行政区划代码：CN-430381），使用人口约为 88 万 5552 人［27］。该方言归属于汉语十大方言之一的湘方言（[ɕjaŋ⁴⁴]，ISO：639-3：[hsn]）［39］②。湘方言可分为老湘语和新湘语［36，40］，而湘乡方言常被认为是老湘语的代表点［27，40］。③ 此处"老"和"新"并不表示时间维度的先后，而指如今使用者保留湘方言历史变体的多寡。以往研究对湘乡方言的声韵调进行了基于印象的语音描写，如赵元任和吴宗济［38］、曾少达［37］和蒋军凤［27］等。

基于作者的博士论文数据［20］，本文对湘乡方言语音系统进行转写与归纳，以期呈现湘乡城区方言的语音表现。数据材料来自作者本人，女性，在湘乡生长至 18 岁后于异地求学，能流利使用湘乡方言。录音时年三十五岁上下，与父母进行日常交流时仍使用湘乡方言。本文的声调转写使用赵元任的五度标记法，即 1 为音高最低值，5 为最高值［3］。

The Xiangxiang Dialect of Chinese

ZENG Ting

Abstract Xiangxiang ([ɕjaŋ⁴⁴ɕjaŋ⁴⁴]) is a Chinese dialect spoken by a population of 885,552 in the urban area of Xiangxiang (CN-430381), a city located in the centre of Hunan Province, China [27]. It belongs to Xiang ([ɕjaŋ⁴⁴], ISO: 639-3: [hsn]), which is one of the ten major dialect groups of Chinese (LAC 2012). Xiang has two main subgroups, New Xiang and Old Xiang (36,40), and Xiangxiang is often cited as a representative dialect of Old Xiang [22,27]. Rather than denoting different historical stages, 'old' and 'new' reflect more and less conservative varieties among contemporary Xiang dialect speakers. Some impressionistic descriptions of the sounds and tones of Xiangxiang dialect will be found in Chao & Wu[38], S. Zeng [3] and Jiang [27]. The current tran-

---

① 编者按：本文为曾婷博士生前代表作，英文原文"The Xiangxiang dialect of Chinese"发表在国际语音协会会刊 JIPA 第 50 卷第 2 期［Zeng, T. (2020) The Xiangxiang dialect of Chinese. *Journal of the International Phonetic Association* 50 (2), 258－281. International Phonetic Association 2019, published by Cambridge University Press (Reprint with permission)］。中文由曾婷的三位学生闻欣怡、巫紫萱、邓凤妮翻译。感谢凌锋博士对翻译文稿的校对。在国际语音协会主席 Michael Ashby 教授、JIPA 主编 Marija Tabain 教授等支持下，《中国语音学报》得到本文的中文出版授权，编辑部以此向曾婷博士对中国语音学的贡献表示致敬，同时感谢国际语音协会和 JIPA 的支持。

② 不同学者就中国境内方言种类的数量存在不同观点，有五种［35］、七种［26，28，36］、九种［10］、十种［39］之说。本文参考中国语言地图集［39］的观点将汉语主要方言分为十种：官话，晋语、吴语，闽语，客家话，粤语，湘语，赣语，徽语，平话和当地土话。中国语言地图集［39］基于汉语方言主要语言特征的基本事实（尤其是近 20 年大量有影响力的前沿研究）对汉语方言的分类和分布进行了全面且前沿的陈述。

③ 除湘乡方言外，双峰方言也常被视作老湘语的代表点（如［36］），这是因为老湘语的语言特征在两地都很显著［23］。事实上，双峰方言也被认为是湘乡方言的一个次方言点，因为（i）1951 年前，双峰在行政规划上属于湘乡；（ii）这两地方言的语音系统有大量的相似之处［23，24］。

scriptions and generalizations, which are based on the data gathered for T. Zeng [20], present a variety of the Xiangxiang dialect that is typical of the city of Xiangxiang. The recordings accompanying this Illustration are from the author, who is a fluent female speaker of the dialect variety. She was born and grew up in the city of Xiangxiang, residing there for 18 years until she moved to attend college. She was in her mid-thirties at the time of recording and still uses Xiangxiang in daily communication with her parents. Throughout this article, Chao tone numbers are used to transcribe the tones, whereby 1 denotes the lowest pitch and 5, the highest [3].

1. 辅音

本节对辅音的概括和讨论基于作者博士论文[20]中三个实验的结果,即(1)六位发音人(三男三女)的腭位和舌位研究;(2)十位发音人(五男五女)浊阻音的声学研究;以及(3)七位发音人(六男一女)鼻音的气流研究。发音人皆为湘乡方言母语者,录音时年龄在 45 至 55 岁之间。

湘乡方言共有九个爆发音,呈现出清不送气/p t k/(如/pa^{34}/"八"、/ta^{34}/"达"、/ka^{44}/"街")、清送气/p^{h} t^{h} k^{h}/(如/p^{h}a^{25}/"派"、/t^{h}a^{24}/"塔"、/k^{h}aʊ^{55}/"敲")和浊音/b d g/(如/ba^{24}/"牌"、/daʊ^{24}/"桃"、/gi^{24}/"骑")的三元对立。两个非唇爆发音/ta^{34}/"达"和/ka^{44}/"街"发音的腭位图及舌位图如图 1 所示。

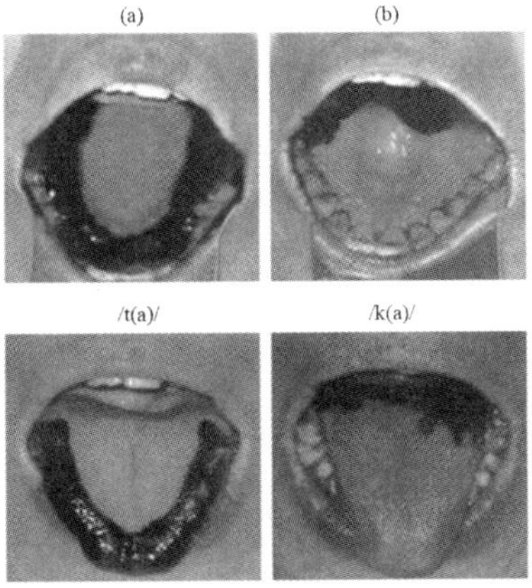

图 1 (a)/ta^{34}/"达"和(b)/ka^{44}/"街"的腭位图和舌位图

爆发音/t t^{h} d/的发音部位位于舌尖—舌叶(apico-laminal)以及齿—龈—龈后(denti-alveolo-post-alveolar)。以图 1a 为例,/ta^{34}/"达"发音时,舌尖和舌叶与口腔顶部接触,范围从上前牙到齿槽后部。

辅音表

	双唇	齿	龈	龈后	龈腭	硬腭	软腭
爆发音	p p^{h} b	t t^{h}d					k k^{h}g
塞擦音		ts ts^{h}dz		tʃ tʃ^{h}dʒ	tɕ tɕ^{h}dʑ		
鼻音	m		n				ŋ
擦音		s		ʃ	ɕ		
近音	w	ɹ				j ɥ	x ɣ

六位发音人的/k k^{h} g/基本一致,为舌背软腭爆发音(dorsal velar plosives),如图 1b 的/ka^{44}/"街"所示,发音时舌背后部与软腭接触。

湘乡方言还具有三组咝音(sibilants)的四元对立,即/ts ts^{h} s dz/(如/tsɹ̩^{44}/"资"、/ts^{h}ɹ̩^{25}/"刺"、/sa^{34}/"杀"、/dza^{24}/"柴"),/tʃ tʃ^{h} dʒ ʃ/(如/tʃɹ̩^{34}/"侄"、/tʃ^{h}ɹ̩^{24}/"尺"、/dʒɹ̩^{24}/"时"、/ʃɹ̩^{44}/"诗")以及/tɕ tɕ^{h} dʑ ɕ/(如/tɕi^{34}/"积"、/tɕ^{h}i^{34}/"七"、/dʑi^{24}/"齐"、/ɕi^{34}/"习")。图 2 为六位发音人发清塞擦音/ts tʃ tɕ/与清擦音/s ʃ ɕ/的腭位图和舌位图。

/ts ts^{h} dz s/为齿—龈音(denti-alveolar),发音时舌尖(如图 2d 的/s/)或舌叶(如图 2a 的/ts/)向口腔顶部中切牙(central incisors)至齿槽区域上抬,从而收窄声道。

/tʃ tʃ^{h} ʃ dʒ/在以往文献中通常写作卷舌音/tʂ tʂ^{h} ʂ dʐ (ʐ)/(如[27])。然而如图 2b 中的/tʃɹ̩^{34}/"侄"与图 2e 中的/ʃɹ̩^{44}/"诗"所示,该组辅音为舌叶龈后音(laminal post-alveolar sounds),发音时舌叶向齿槽后部抬升。这说明它们的调音不同于 Ladefoged

和 Maddieson[7]所讨论的两种典型的卷舌元音的调音:一个涉及舌尖的向后和向上卷曲,如泰米尔语(Tamil)和托达语(Toda)的舌尖下硬腭音(sub-apical palatal);另一个舌尖微微向上卷起,与齿龈后部产生接触,如印地语(Hindi)和柏语(Bzyb)的舌尖龈后音(apical post-alveolar)。因此,湘乡方言的龈后咝音应转写为/tʃ tʃʰ ʃ dʒ/(严式标音为/tʃ tʃ̺ʰ ʃ̺ d ʒ̺/),而非/tʂ tʂʰ ʂ dʐ/。

非音节化辅音										音节化辅音				
p	pa^{34}	八	t	ta^{34}	达	k	ka^{44}	街		m̩	m̩^{22}	妈		
pʰ	pʰa^{25}	派	tʰ	tʰa^{24}	塔	kʰ	kʰaʊ^{55}	敲		n̩	n̩^{21}	你		
b	ba^{24}	牌	d	daʊ^{24}	桃	g	gi^{24}	骑		ŋ̍	ŋ̍^{21}	我	ŋ̍^{34}	黄
m	ma^{34}	埋	ts	tsɹ̩^{44}	资	ŋ	ŋa^{34}	鸭		ɹ̩	tsɹ̩^{44}	资	tʃɹ̩^{34}	侄
w	wa^{34}	袜	tsʰ	tsʰɹ̩^{25}	刺	x	xa^{34}	瞎			dzɹ̩^{24}	瓷	dʒɹ̩^{24}	时
			dz	dza^{24}	柴	ɣ	ɣa^{24}	鞋						
			tʃ	tʃɹ̩^{34}	侄									
			tʃʰ	tʃʰɹ̩^{24}	尺									
			dʒ	dʒɹ̩^{24}	时									
			tɕ	tɕi^{34}	积									
			tɕʰ	tɕʰi^{34}	七									
			dʑ	dʑi^{24}	齐									
			n	nan^{34}	农									
			s	sa^{34}	杀									
			ʃ	ʃɹ̩^{44}	诗									
			ɕ	ɕi^{34}	习									
			j	ja^{34}	热									
			ɥ	ɥa^{34}	月									

/tɕ tɕʰ dʑ ɕ/同样为典型的舌叶龈后音(post-alveolar),如图 2c 中的/tɕi^{34}/"积",和图 2f 中的/ɕi^{34}/"习"。相应地,它们的严式标音需要使用"舌叶化(laminal)"的附加符号(t̻ɕt̻ɕd̻ʑɕ̻)。

尽管/tʃ tʃʰ dʒ ʃ/和/tɕ tɕʰ dʑ ɕ/仍可依靠舌体形状进行区分。比较图 2b 和图 2c 以及图 2e 和图 2f 时可见,/tɕ tɕʰ dʑ ɕ/比/tʃ tʃʰ dʒ ʃ/在腭面和舌体有着更宽的边缘接触面,说明在/tɕ tɕʰ dʑ ɕ/的产出过程中,舌叶和舌体都位于口腔高位,从而形成了相对较长和平整的收紧点。

/tɕ tɕʰ dʑ ɕ/、/ts tsʰ dz s/和/tʃ tʃʰ dʒ ʃ/这三组音呈现互补分布。具体而言,/tɕ tɕʰ dʑ ɕ/仅出现在前高元音或滑音前(/i y j ɥ/),/tʃ tʃʰ dʒ ʃ/仅出现在相同发音部位的音节化近音/ɹ̩/前,但/ts tsʰ dz s/不出现在上述环境,因此可以合理推断/tɕ tɕʰ dʑ ɕ/为另外两组的音位变体。但是,由于/tɕ tɕʰ dʑ ɕ/与另外两组在听感上存在明显差异,本研究仍然将其认为是独立的音位,标记为与"龈后音"相近的"龈腭音(alveolo-palatal)"(可参考 Lee & Zee[9]、Chen & Gussenhoven[4]、Li 等[11]对该组音的类

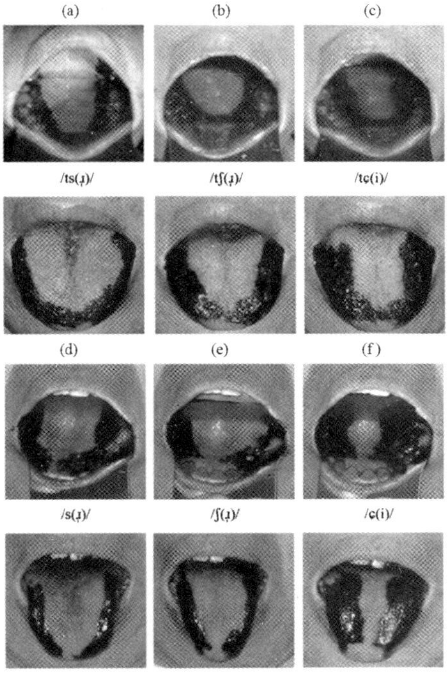

图2 (a)/tsɹ̩^{44}/“资”、(b)/tʃɹ̩^{34}/“侄”、(c)/tɕi^{34}/“积”、(d)/sɹ̩^{44}/“丝”、(e)/ʃɹ̩^{44}/“诗”、(f)/ɕi^{34}/“习”的腭位图和舌位图

似处理)。在很多汉语方言中,[tɕ tɕʰ ɕ]都会与[ts tsʰ s]、[tʃ tʃʰ ʃ]、[k kʰ x]中的一组甚至多组阻塞音呈互补分布,因此龈腭音是否能作为独立音位一直存在争议。例如,北京话中的[tɕ tɕʰ ɕ]与上述三组都呈互补分布。但在许多研究中,它们仍被处理为单独的音位,如 Li[12],以及 Lee 和 Zee[9]。对此更深入的讨论可见 Lin[13]。

值得注意的是,三组咝音的调音存在一定变体。例如,/ts tsʰ dz s/组有时可发为龈音(alveolar)或齿—龈—龈后音(denti-alveolo-post-alveolar)。在少数情况下,它们的调音也涉及舌尖及舌叶的更大区域。部分发音人的/tʃ dʒ tɕ dʑ/会涉及更大的舌中部区域,即齿龈和龈后部两个相邻的调音区域。本文不涉及对上述咝音发音变体的全面讨论,相关细节可见[20]。

对/dz dʒ dʑ/的进一步观察显示,三个音位的语音实现为擦音或塞擦音。图3分别为/dzu^{22}/ [zu^{22}]“坐”(a)、/dzo^{24}/ [dzo^{24}]“茶”(b)和/dzo^{22}/ [zo^{22}]“茬”(c)的波形和频谱图,其中图3a由一位女发音人发音,3b和3c来自另一位女发音人。图3a中辅音无除阻爆破阶段,且在摩擦间存在持续的浊音段,因此为一个典型的浊擦音[z]。图3c的擦音存在部分浊音段,该浊音段仅在摩擦开始之后出现。而图3b则为一个存在部分浊音的塞擦音([dz]),其有明显的除阻爆破,在持阻阶段形成浊音,但浊音并不持续到摩擦部分。此外,上述三组塞擦音同样存在发音变体(即[dz] ≈ [z],[dʒ] ≈ [ʒ],[dʑ] ≈ [ʑ]),这些变体在不同的发音人之间,甚至同一位发音人对同一个音的不同重复中都有发现。这说明[dz dʒ dʑ]和[z ʒ ʑ]在音节首并不严格对立。基于此发现,以及湘乡方言中塞擦音为上述音位的主要语音实现[20],本文推断/dz dʒ dʑ/应为其底层形式。

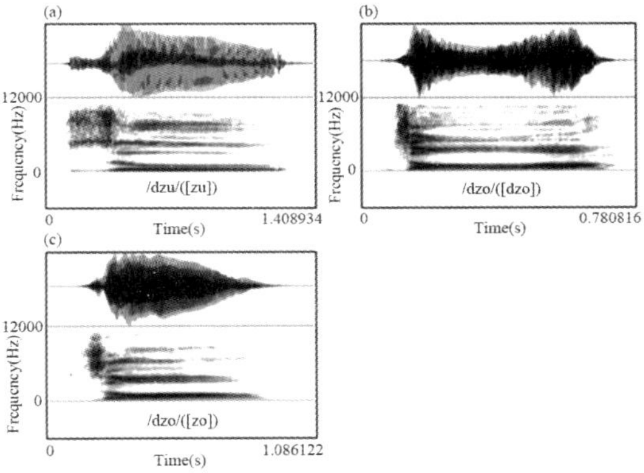

图3 (a)/dzu^{22}/ [zu^{22}]“坐”、(b)/dzo^{24}/ [dzo^{24}]“茶”、(c)/dzo^{22}/ [zo^{22}]“茬”的波形和频谱图

湘乡方言还存在两个非咝音擦音/x ɣ/,如/xa^{34}/“瞎”和/ɣa^{24}/“鞋”,语音表现为舌背软腭擦音(dorsal velar fricatives),发音时舌背向软腭靠近。

湘乡方言中存在三个鼻音/m n ŋ/。/m/的语音实现为双唇鼻音[m],如[ma^{34}]/“埋”。/n/有多种语音实现形式,如图4所示的/nẽ^{22}/ [nẽ^{22}]“练”(4a)、

/naɪ^{34}/ [nãĩ^{34}]"来"(4b)、/naɪ^{21}/ [laɪ^{21}]"篓"(4c)和/nu^{34}/ [l̃ũ^{34}]"露"(4d)。图中虚线双箭头为鼻气流基线,实线双箭头则指元音鼻化的时长①。如图所示,如果后续的韵母存在鼻韵尾或鼻元音,/n/会实现为[n](如图 4a 的/nẽ^{22}/ [nẽ^{22}]"练",存在大量鼻气流而无口腔气流)。如果韵母为纯粹的口元音,/n/则会呈现其自由变体,如/nai^{21}/ [lai^{21}]"篓"的[l](4c),/nu^{34}/ [l̃ũ^{34}]"露"中鼻化的[l̃](4d),或/nai^{34}/ [nãĩ^{34}]"来"中的[n](4b)。

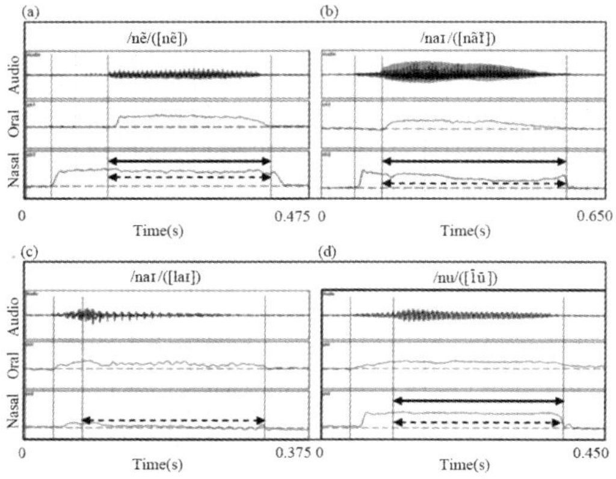

图 4 (a)/nẽ^{22}/ [nẽ^{22}]"练"、(b)/naɪ^{34}/ [nãĩ^{34}]"来"、(c)/naɪ^{21}/ [laɪ^{21}]"篓"、(d)/nu^{34}/ [l̃ũ^{34}]"露"的口鼻气流图(airflow traces)。小图中的三条竖线依次表示辅音起始时间、元音起始时间和音节结束时间。

值得注意的是,[l̃]是与[n]和[l]不同的语音变体。[n]在其全部时段内存在高原状的鼻气流曲线,并且无气流从口腔流出(4a,4b),而[l̃]同时具备鼻气流和口腔气流(4d),这一点与[l]更相似(4c)。但是,[l̃] 仍然在两个方面不同于[l]。第一,[l̃]的鼻气流水平高于[l];第二,[l]的轻微鼻气流无法触发其后元音的鼻化,而[l̃]后的元音则有不同程度的鼻化,这一点与[n]后接的元音类似。在图 4a,4b 和 4d 中,元音的鼻气流水平均高于对应的鼻气流基线,说明元音都被完全鼻化。但从音位的角度来说,图 4b 和 4d 的元音[ãĩ]和[ũ]仍被转写为口元音,即/aɪ/和/u/,这是由于它们仅在鼻音环境下被鼻化。而图 4a 的/ẽ/可出现在鼻辅音或口辅音后,因而无论是语音还是音位转写,都可以写作鼻元音。

六位发音人的数据显示,/n/常常实现为舌尖—龈鼻音(apico-alveolar nasal)或边音,如图 5a 的/ni^{34}/ [ni^{34}]"离"和图 5b 的/na^{34}/ [la^{34}]"蜡"。[n]同样存在发音变体。从腭位图可知,舌体与上腭的接触面可以向前延伸到牙齿,向后延伸到齿龈后区。而舌体的接触位置则涉及舌叶区域,在极少数情况下还涉及舌背的前部。

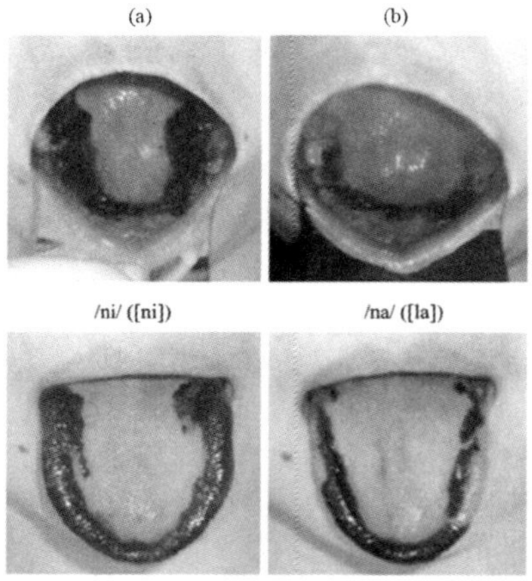

图 5 (a)/ni^{34}/ [ni^{34}]"离"和(b)/na^{34}/ [la^{34}]"蜡"的腭位图和舌位图

由于/n/和/l/在历史上存在对立,一些研究把/n/和/l/处理成独立的两个音位,如曾少达[37]和蒋军凤[27]。鉴于没有共时证据表明它们之间存在音位对立,且[n]出

① 鼻气流基线是纯口音环境下(pure oral contexts)口元音的固有鼻气流水平,通过计算(C)V 音节中的口元音平均鼻气流速率确定。对鼻元音或 C(V)N 音节中的口元音来说,其鼻化的起止时间分别为鼻气流高于基线和低于基线的时间点。基线水平取决于元音性质和发音人个体。

现的语音环境多于[1],它们也会被分析为/n/的两个音位变体,如赵元任和吴宗济[38]。

/ŋ/在除一种环境外的所有环境中都实现为舌背—软腭鼻音[ŋ](dorso-velar nasal),发音时舌背后部与软腭完全接触,如/ŋa^{34}/[ŋa^{34}]“鸭”(如图6a)。当其后接前高元音或滑音时,舌背后部则同硬腭后部与软腭接触(如图6b)。这种鼻音被中国境内的语言学家转写为龈腭鼻音[ȵ](如[37]),该符号在汉语方言学界常被用于转写在相似环境里出现的鼻音。然而,比较图6b的鼻音与图2c的龈—硬腭擦音/ɕ/时可发现,它们的调音部位完全不同(图6a为硬腭—软腭位置,图2c的/ɕ/则为齿龈后部),收紧点的位置也存在差异(图6a位于舌背,而/ɕ/则位于舌叶)。因此,湘乡方言该环境下/ŋ/的变体并不能描述为[ȵ]。

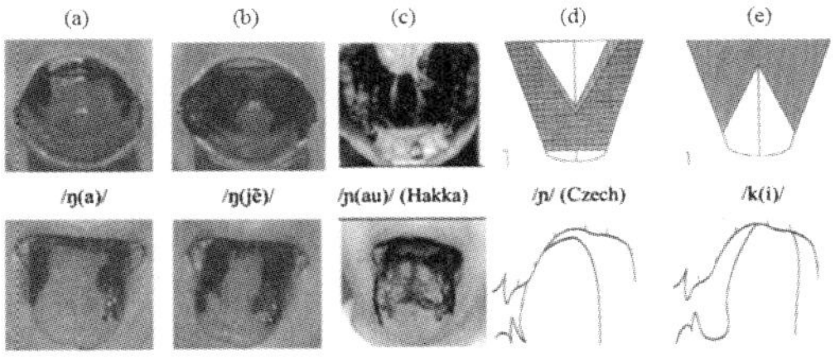

图6 湘乡方言的(a)/ŋ(a)/和(b)/ŋ(jẽ)/、客家方言的(c)/ɲ(au)/[19]、捷克语的(d)/ɲ/[15]、(e)/k(i)/[15]的腭位图和舌位图

此外,根据匿名审稿人的建议,此鼻音在前高元音或滑音前的语音实现形式也不宜用硬腭鼻音[ɲ]来描述,尽管该鼻音在发音时同样涉及了硬腭,但还是处理为前软腭鼻音和/ŋ/的变体为佳。首先,从类型学的角度来说,一种语言很少只有硬腭鼻音而没有硬腭爆发音或擦音。例如,在捷克语、匈牙利语、阿伦特语(Arrernte)和瓦尔皮瑞语(Warlpiri)(后两者均为澳大利亚境内语言)中存在硬腭鼻音,但也同时存在硬腭爆发音和擦音。另外在一些汉语方言里,这三种硬腭音也同时存在,如浏阳方言(赣方言的次级方言)。而湘乡方言里并不存在硬腭爆发音或硬腭擦音。

该鼻音变体不能用[ɲ]来描述的第二个原因是,湘乡方言中该鼻音的调音与其他语言的/ɲ/也有所不同,如图6c的客家方言[19]和图6d的捷克语[15],这种不同至少体现在两个方面。一是声道上部表面接触位置的不同。客家方言和捷克语的/ɲ/为齿龈后区到硬腭区域完全且持续的接触,这比湘乡方言硬腭—软腭鼻音(如图6b)的接触位置更加靠前。二是下部发音器官的差异。Recasens[15]指出/ɲ/的发音主要涉及舌背前端,尽管有时也涉及舌背中部,在极少数的情况下还涉及舌叶和舌背的后部。如图6b至d所示,客家方言和捷克语的/ɲ/主要涉及舌背前端,而湘乡方言的硬腭—软腭鼻音则涉及舌背后部。

Recasens[15]将辅音按所涉及硬腭的空间分为四组:龈腭音(alveolopalatals),前硬腭音(front palatal),中硬腭音(midpalatals)和后硬腭音(backpalatals)。客家方言和捷克语中的鼻音为典型的前硬腭音,而湘乡方言的则更接近后硬腭音,这和图6e的前软腭音类似(即前元音前的软腭音/k(i)/)。此外,考虑到它在湘乡方言里与/ŋ/呈互补分布,且仅出现在前高元音或滑音前,此种环境下辅音很容易出现硬腭化的情况,因此该鼻音可以描述为硬腭化的软腭鼻音,为/ŋ/的变体(如/ŋjẽ^{34}/[ŋʲjẽ^{34}]“泥”)。

湘乡方言中存在三个滑音/j w ɥ/,出现于音节首(如/ja^{34}/“热”、/wa^{34}/“袜”、/ɥa^{34}/“月”),或与前接辅音一同出现(如/kja^{34}/“格”、/kwa^{34}/“刮”、/ɕɥa^{34}/“雪”)。湘乡方言的音节化鼻音只出现在以下四个字中:/m̩^{22}/“妈”、/n̩^{21}/“你”、/ŋ̩^{21}/“我”和/ŋ̩^{34}/“黄”。音节化近音/ɹ̩/出现在/ts tsʰ s dz tʃ tʃʰ ʃ dʒ/后,并且调音位置随前接辅音而改变。具体来说,当近音位于/ts tsʰ s dz/后时,通常实现为舌尖或舌叶齿—龈近音(apical/laminal denti-alveolar approximant);而当其在/tʃ tʃʰ ʃ dʒ/后时,则实现为舌叶龈后近音(laminal post-alveolar approximant)。在以往的汉语研究中,这两类音节化近音通常被分别转写为舌尖元音[ɿ]和

[ʅ],例如/dzɹ̩^{24}/“瓷”和/dʒɹ̩^{24}/“时”会被分别转写为[dzʅ^{23}]和[dʐʅ^{23}][37]。

湘乡方言最显著的特征是具备清浊阻塞音的对立,而其他多数汉语方言不具备该对立情况。处于音节首的爆发音,擦音和塞擦音可呈现不同的清浊形态[21]。

湘乡方言的浊爆发音有两种发声模式。一种存在前置浊音(pre-voicing),即除阻前声带就已开始振动,另一种则无此现象。两种模式出现的情况在浊爆发音中占比分别为 59% 与 41%。

浊擦音有三种发声模式,分别为“完全浊(complete voicing)”、“部分浊(incomplete voicing)”和“不浊(no voicing)”。“完全浊”指整个擦音持续时间内都存在声带振动;“部分浊”指声带仅在部分时段内振动;而“不浊”则指擦音持续时间内完全无声带振动。三种模式的出现情况占比分别为 10%(“完全浊”)、80%(“部分浊”)和 10%(“不浊”)。

湘乡方言的浊塞擦音也存在三种发声模式。第一种为“完全浊(fully voiced)”,在口腔持阻阶段就已出现声带振动,并且延续到之后的元音;第二种为“部分浊(incomplete voicing)”,声带仅在塞擦音的部分时段内振动,且浊音段仅在摩擦阶段而非持阻阶段出现;第三种为“不浊(no voicing)”,即完全没有声带的振动。以上三种模式的出现情况占比分别为 21%(“完全浊”)、70%(“部分浊”)和 9%(“不浊”)。

综合上述浊音的模式可知,首先,59% 的浊爆发音,21% 的浊塞擦音和 10% 的浊擦音全程存在持续的声带振动。此外,80% 的浊擦音和 70% 的浊塞擦音实现为部分声带振动。整体而言,仍有 70% 左右的浊阻塞音存在声带振动,说明浊阻塞音仍是湘乡方言的一个显著特征。

阻塞音的清浊对立在其他语言中也有发现,如汉语吴方言、西班牙语、荷兰语、波兰语等。不同于湘乡方言,在上海和苏州等吴方言中,浊音通常表现为除阻后较小的正值 VOT,使得浊阻塞音的 VOT 与同一发音部位的不送气清音分布重叠[4, 30],而湘乡方言存在除阻前声带振动和除阻后较小的正值 VOT 两种情况。然而,汉语方言间也存在一定的相似性,如浊阻塞音在非句首位置往往呈完全浊(真浊),清擦音与对应的浊音相比具有更长、能量更强的摩擦段等(详见[20])。和汉语不同,除阻前的浊音这一特征在西班牙语、荷兰语和波兰语中更加稳定。西班牙语和波兰语并不存在清浊辅音 VOT 值的重合:浊爆发音的 VOT 为负,而清爆发音则有短暂的正值[5, 16, 18]。在荷兰语中,75% 的浊爆发音在除阻前都出现浊音段[17],这比湘乡方言中出现该情况的比例高很多(59%)。

2. 元音

本节通过三幅元音图展示了湘乡方言元音在国际音标元音图中的位置。同时,基于 20 位发音人的数据(十男十女,湘乡方言母语者,年龄在 45 至 55 岁之间),本节还提供了单元音(图 7、9—11)与双元音(图 12—14)的声学元音图。

2.1 单元音

开音节口元音在国际音标元音图中的位置。

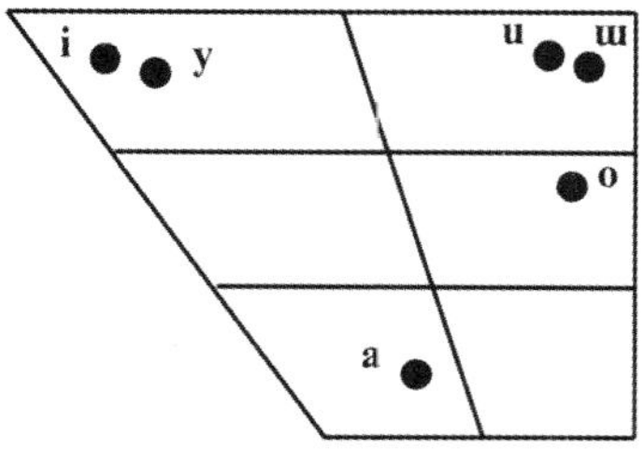

i	i^{44}	衣	tin^{44}	钉
y	y^{44}	淤		
a	ka^{44}	街	tan^{44}	针
ɯ	ɯ^{44}	乌	taŋ^{44}	当
u	u^{44}	蜗		

续表

o	o^{44}	挖		
ẽ	ẽ^{44}	烟		
õ	kõ^{44}	aa		
ã	tjã^{44}	灯	wã^{44}	弯

湘乡方言共有六个口元音(/i y ɯ u a o/),三个鼻元音(/ẽ õ ã/)和三个双元音(/eɪ aɪ aʊ/)。/y ɯ u o/只出现在开音节中,/i/和/a/可出现在开音节或闭音节中。

如图 7 所示,开音节中的/i/(/i^{44}/“衣”)在声学空间中处于最前、最高的位置。相较而言,/y/(/y^{44}/“淤”)的位置偏低且较为居中,而/a/(/ka^{44}/“街”)的位置最低且位于最中间。

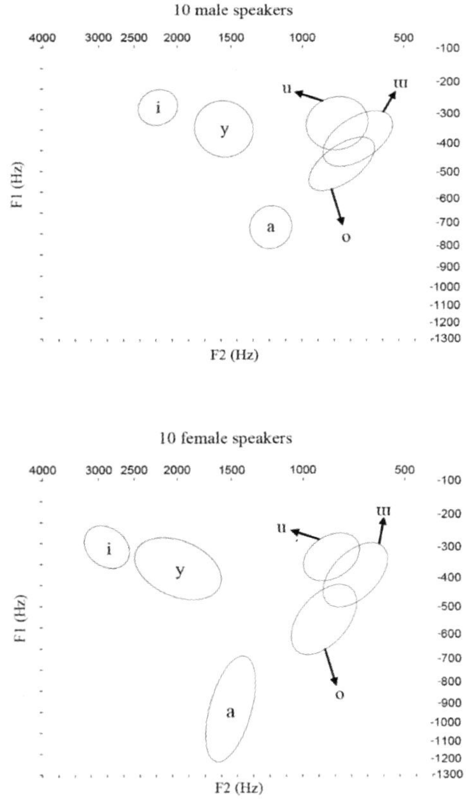

图 7　开音节口元音的声学元音图(/i^{44}/“衣”、/y^{44}/“淤”、/ɯ^{44}/“乌”、/u^{44}/“蜗”、/o^{44}/“挖”、/ka^{44}/“街”)

本节对三个后元音的转写主要基于以下两点原因。第一,正如匿名审稿人指出,后元音/ɯ u o/的唇形不同。图 8 展示了两名发音人朗读三个后元音时的唇形。如图所示,发/ɯ/(/ɯ^{44}/“乌”)时上下嘴唇相对接近,与日语中的/u/相似(严式转写为/ɯ/)[6, 7]。发/u/(/u44/“蜗”)时,嘴唇前伸。发/o/(/o^{44}/“挖”)时嘴唇也会前伸,但前伸程度比/u/小很多。第二,/u/和/ɯ/均为后高元音,/a/为后半高(back mid-close)元音。

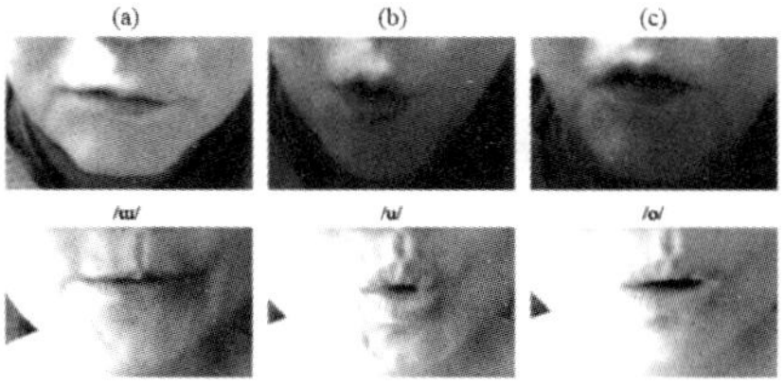

图 8　(a)/ ɯ /、(b)/u/、(c)/o/的唇形

鼻元音(下左图)与闭音节口元音(下右图)在国际音标元音图中的位置。

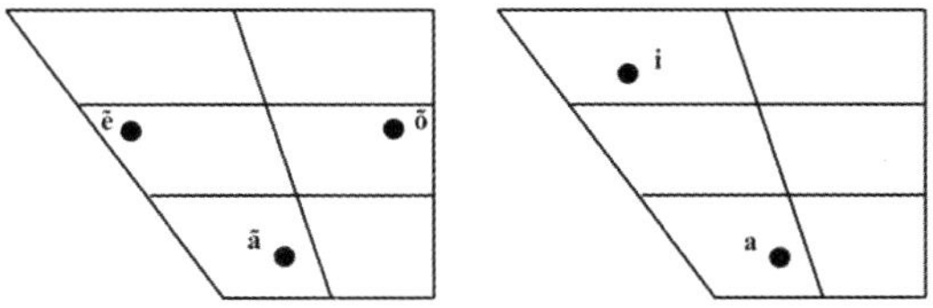

上右图展示了能出现在闭音节中的元音/i/和/a/。/i/只出现在/n/之前(/tin^{44}/“钉”),而/a/能出现在/n/或/ŋ/之前(/tan^{44}/“针”和/taŋ^{44}/“当”)。如图 9 所示,/i/在闭音节中实现为[ɪ],与开音节中的/i/相比,具有更高的 F1 和更低的 F2。而开音节与闭音节中的/a/声学空间重叠程度很高。

如上左图所示,湘乡方言中存在三个鼻元音:/ẽ/(/ẽ^{44}/“烟”)、/õ/(/kõ^{44}/“aa”)、/ã/(/tjã^{44}/“灯”和/wã^{44}/“弯”)。它们出现在开音节中,且/ã/必须前接滑音/j/或/w/。

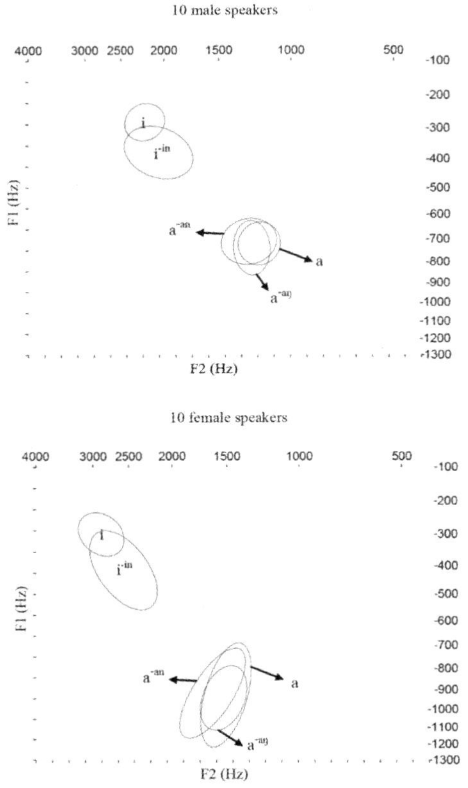

图9　闭音节口元音/i/(/tin^{44}/[tɪn^{44}]“钉”)和/a/(/taŋ^{44}/“当”)的声学元音图(图中同时呈现开音节中的/i/和/a/,以便确定闭音节口元音音值)

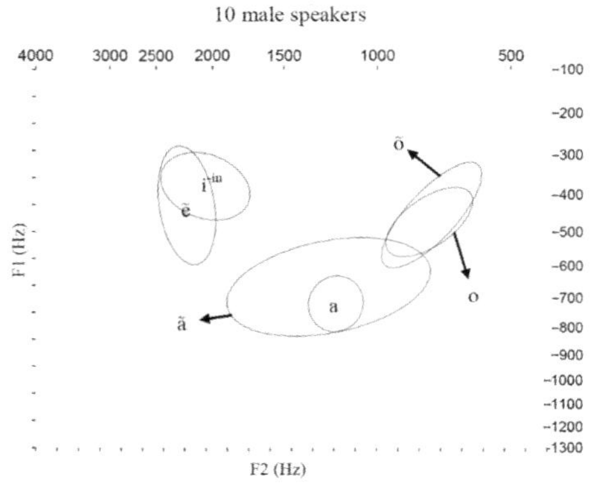

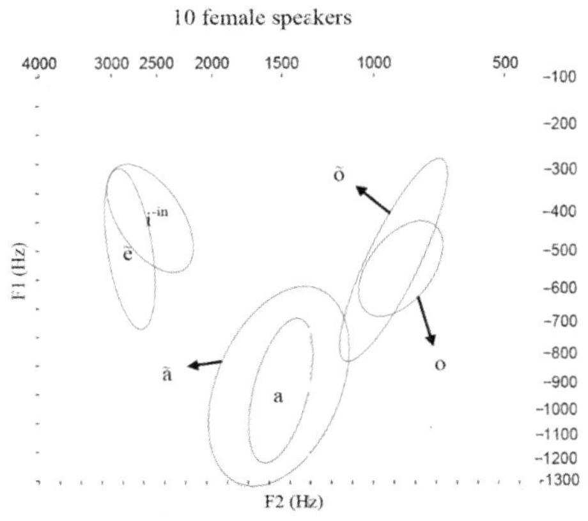

图10　鼻元音/ẽ/(/ẽ^{44}/“烟”)、/õ/(/kõ^{44}/“羹”)、/ã/(/tjã^{44}/“灯”和/wã^{44}/“弯”)的声学元音图(图中同时呈现/i/[ɪ]、/a/、/o/,以便确定鼻元音音值)

如图10所示,/ẽ/的位置比/tin^{44}/([tɪn^{44}]“钉”)中的[ɪ]更低。/o/和/õ/的声学空间重叠度较高,但/õ/的F1变化更大,尤其是在女性发音人中。男女两组发音人的数据均显示,/ã/的声学空间完全包含/a/,且/ã/的F1、F2变化更大,可能受到了前接滑音协同发音的影响。图11根据其前接滑音将/ã/进一步分为两组:与开音节中的/a/(/ka^{44}/“街”)相比,前接/j/的/ã/(/tjã^{44}/“灯”)位置更靠前,而前接/w/的/ã/(/wã^{44}/“弯”)更靠后。

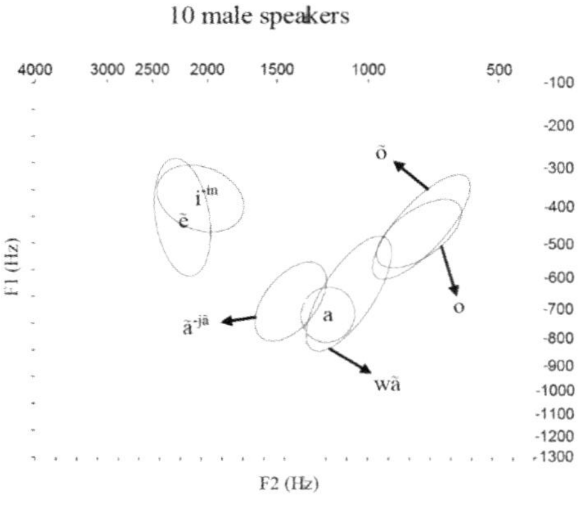

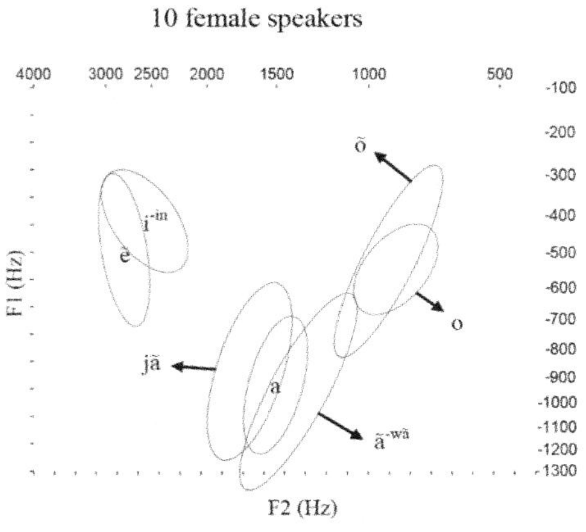

图11　鼻元音的声学元音图,其中/ã/根据前接滑音(/tjã^{44}/"灯"和/wã^{44}/"弯")分为两组(图中同时呈现/i/[ɪ]、/a/、/o/,以便确定鼻元音音值)

2.2　双元音

以下为双元音在国际音标元音图中的位置。

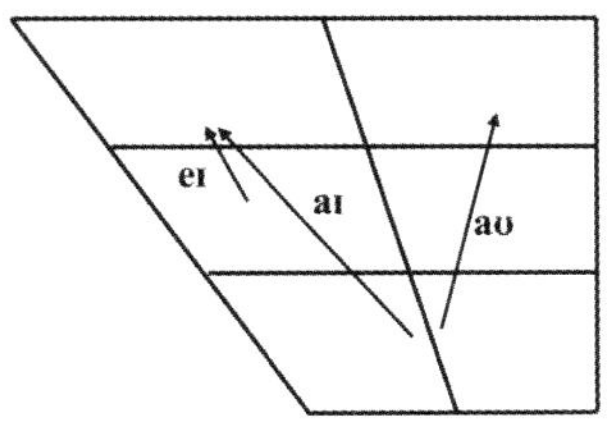

eɪ	jeɪ^{44}	优
aʊ	taʊ^{44}	刀
aɪ	taɪ^{44}	呆

湘乡方言共有三个双元音:/eɪ/(/jeɪ^{44}/"优")、/aɪ/(/taɪ^{44}/"呆")、/aʊ/(/taʊ^{44}/"刀"),都只出现在开音节中,且/eɪ/必须前接/j/。

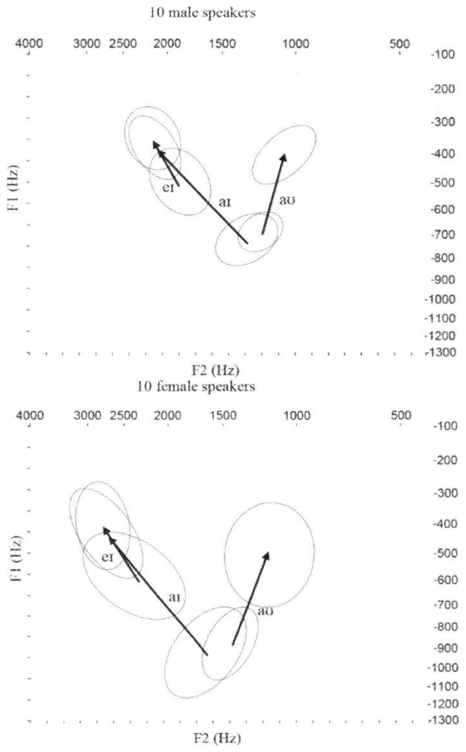

图12　双元音/eɪ/(/jeɪ^{44}/"优")、/aɪ/(/taɪ^{44}/"呆")、/aʊ/(/taʊ^{44}/"刀")的声学元音图

图12只呈现了双元音首尾成分的数值(onset and offset values)。为了更精准地描述双元音,图13同时呈现了单元音[ɪ](/tin^{44}/[tɪn^{44}]"钉")、/u/和/a/①。本文并不旨在讨论双元音是单独的元音还是由两个单元音组成的序列,以及通常作为元音音位典型形式的单元音是否同时充当了相应双元音的语音目标。对这两个问题更深入的讨论可参看[14]。

① 这种方法参考了前人的研究,例如Ladefoged和Johnson[6]通过与单元音比较来描写双元音:"一些美式英语发音人能产出首成分与head中的[ɛ]相似的双元音"。

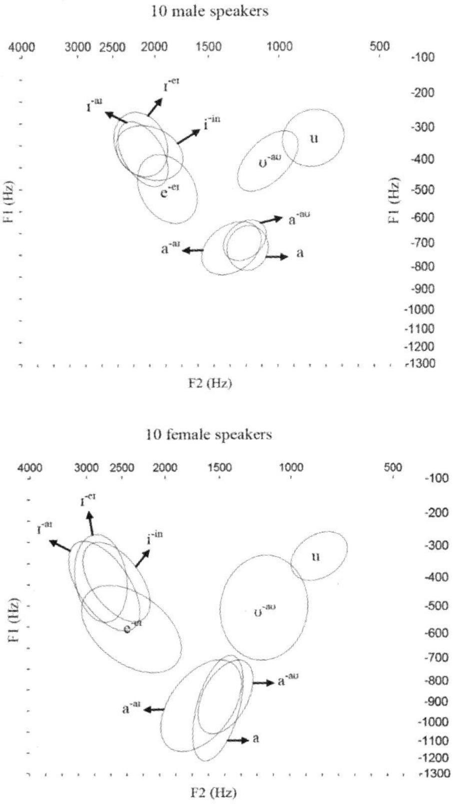

图13 双元音与三个单元音(/i/[ɪ]、/u/、/a/)的声学元音图

如图13所示,/aɪ/和/aʊ/的起始位置接近单元音/a/,随后分别移向与单元音/i/和/u/对应的松元音。/eɪ/的起始位置接近/e/,随后向[ɪ](/tin^{44}/ [tɪn^{44}]"钉")与/aɪ/的尾成分移动。

值得注意的是,前人的研究(如[27,37])多将滑音—元音组合(如/ja/、/wa/、/ɥa/)视作双元音(如/ia/、/ua/、/ya/),因此认为湘乡方言有更多双元音。然而,本研究基于以下发现将高元音与其后接元音的组合视作滑音—元音。具体而言,/ja^{34}/"热"(图14a)中滑音部分时长很短,且其元音音质变化远没有/taɪ^{44}/"呆"(图14b)中平缓。这与Ladefoged和Maddieson[7]对滑音的定义相符,即存在从高元音向下一个元音的快速移动。其他汉语方言语音系统的研究中也有类似的处理,如上海方言[4]和天津方言[11]。

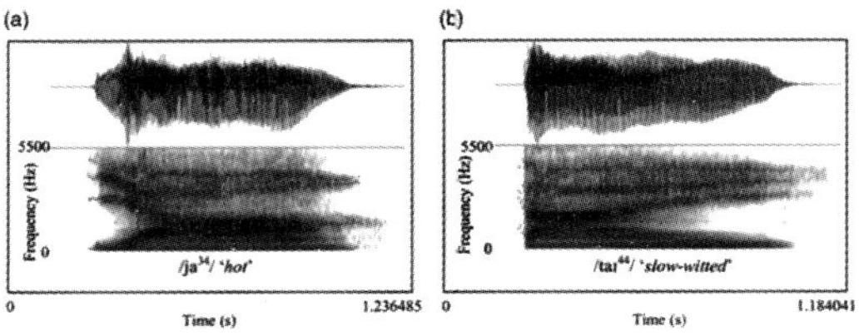

图14 (a)/ja^{34}/"热"和(b)/taɪ^{44}/"呆"的波形和频谱图

3. 音节结构

湘乡方言的音节结构为(辅音)(滑音)元音(辅音),简写为(C)(G)V(C)。音节首尾位置具有明显的不对称性:所有辅音均能出现在音节首,但仅有鼻音/n/和/ŋ/能出现在音节尾。

表1 辅音与高元音/i y u/和滑音/j ɥ w/的共现限制

		龈音				
元音/滑音	唇音	非咝音	咝音	龈后音	龈腭音	软腭音
i	是	是	否	否	是	是
y	否	是	否	否	是	否
u	是	是	是	否	否	是
j	是	是	否	否	是	是
ɥ	否	否	否	否	是	否
w	否	是	是	否	否	是

滑音(G)包括/j/、/w/和/ɥ/,均出现于音节首或辅音后,其分布存在下列限制条件。第一,如表1所示,三个滑音不能出现在龈后音/tʃ tʃʰ dʒ ʃ/之后,这些音只能后接相同发音部位的音节化近音/ɹ̩/;唇音不能后接/ɥ/和/w/。相较于另两个滑音,/ɥ/在CG组合中的分布最窄,只出现在龈腭音之后。第二,表1还展示了与滑音对应的高元音/i y u/的分布条件。尽管/j/与/i/的分布类似,但/ɥ/与/y/、/w/与/u/的分布情况并不相同。例如,唇音能后接

/u/,但不能后接/w/;齿龈非咝音(alveolar non-sibilants)/t tʰ d n/能后接/y/,但不能后接/ɥ/①。第三,就 GV 组合的共现条件而言,/j/的分布比/w/和/ɥ/广。开音节中,/j/不能后接前元音/i y ẽ/;/w/不能后接后元音/ɯ u o õ/和前圆唇元音/y/;/ɥ/不能后接除/i/和/ẽ/以外的任何元音。此外,只有/j/和/w/能出现在双元音前:/j/能后接/eɪ aʊ/,/w/能后接/aɪ/。

除上述条件以外,湘乡方言的音节结构还受音位配列限制(phonotactic restrictions)。第一,三组咝音间存在下列限制条件:/tʃ tʃʰ dʒ ʃ/只出现在相同发音部位的音节化近音/ɹ̩/前;/tɕ tɕʰ dʑ ɕ/只出现在前高元音或滑音(/i y j ɥ/)前;/ts tsʰ dz s/不与/tʃ tʃʰ dʒ ʃ/和/tɕ tɕʰ dʑ ɕ/出现在相同环境中。第二,部分软腭阻塞音不能出现在前高元音或滑音前。具体而言,/x/不出现在任何前高元音或滑音(/i y j ɥ/)前;/k kʰ g/不出现在圆唇前高元音或滑音(/y ɥ/)前;/ɣ/不出现在/ɥ/之前。第三,/ã/在三个鼻元音中分布范围最窄,只出现在/j/或/w/之后。第四,双元音/eɪ aɪ aʊ/只出现在开音节中。/eɪ/必须前接/j/;/aɪ/和/aʊ/与非滑音辅音声母或滑音共同出现(/aɪ/前接/w/,/aʊ/前接/j/)。第五,只有/i/和/a/能出现在 CVN 结构中:/i/只出现在/n/前;/a/能出现在/n/或/ŋ/前。

4. 声调

4.1 单字调

本节基于一位发音人的录音描写了湘乡方言的单字调和连读变调模式。基于多位发音人数据的声调描写详见 Zeng[20]。

第一声(T1)	44	/ka⁴⁴/	街
第二声(T2)	24	/ba²⁴/	牌
第三声(T3)	34	/ta³⁴/	达
第四声(T4)	21	/ta²¹/	打
第五声(T5)	45	/ta⁴⁵/	带
第六声(T6)	25	/ta²⁵/	太
第七声(T7)	22	/ba²²/	败

获得单字调和连读调的基频数据之后,将其归一成 T 值,公式如下:

$$T_i = 5 \times \frac{lgx_i - lgx_{min}}{lgx_{max} - lgx_{xin}} \quad (1)$$

其中,x_i 指待归一化的基频;x_{min} 和 x_{max} 分别对应给定发音人基频数据中的最小值和最大值。这种归一方式在前人研究中被多次用于减少基频的人际差异,以及将基频归一后转化为五度值,如石锋[31-33]、石锋和王萍[34]等。图 15 和 16 的 5 个间隔(0-1、1-2、2-3、3-4、4-5)分别对应调域中的五度(1、2、3、4、5,或最低、次低、中、次高、最高)[3]。

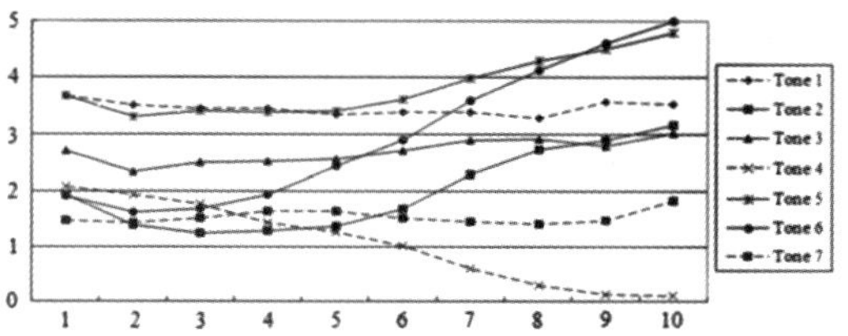

图 15 单字调的音高曲线(以五度标记法表示)

如图 15 所示,湘乡方言共有七个单字调。第一声(T1)是高平调,音高在全部时段内稳定在 4 度,因此将其调值转写为 44。第二声(T2)和第三声(T3)都是升调,分别始于 2 度和 3 度,虽然调尾在 3 度和 4 度的分界线附近,本文基于以下考量将其调值转写为 24 和 34:若将调尾视作 3 度,则 T3 将被转写为平调 33,而非升调。第五声(T5)和第六声(T6)也是升调,调首音高相差 2 度(T5 始于 4 度,T6 始于 2 度),调尾均位于 5 度,因此可分别转写为 45 和 25。虽然这四个声调的起始段略呈下降趋势,但本文将其视作升调而非凹调,原因如下:(i)下降的持续时间很短,且变化范围在一度以内;(ii)并非所有发音人都产出了下降段(详见 Zeng[20]中其他三人的数据)。反观普通话和苏州方言,降升调的起始段

① 虽然都归类于龈音,但/t tʰ d/是典型的齿—龈—龈后音(denti-alveolo-post-alveolar),/n/是典型的龈音(alveolar),/ts tsʰ dz s/是典型的齿—龈音(denti-alveolar)。

必然下降,Lau[8]以及石锋和王萍[34]提供的声学数据表明这两种方言的发音人都有意产出下降段。同样值得注意的是,T2的基频在大部分时段内低于T3,但两者调尾均为3度。T5和T6的情况与之相似,T6的基频在大部分时段内低于T5,但两者的调尾均为5度。进一步观察发现,这四个升调与不同的辅音声母共现(T2与浊阻塞音、清送气阻塞音共现,而T3与清不送气阻塞音、响音共现;T5与清不送气阻塞音、响音共现,而T6与清送气阻塞音共现)。在更抽象的层面上,T2和T3以及T5和T6在调头和调干的音高差异可部分归因于声母类型的不同。第四声(T4)是低降调21,第七声(T7)是低平调22。

如表2所示,湘乡方言中存在辅音—声调共现的制约条件。具体而言,T1、T3、T4、T5与清阻塞音或响音共现,T2与浊阻塞音、清送气阻塞音共现,T6只与清送气阻塞音共现。

表2　　声母与声调的共现关系

声调	调值	辅音声母
T1	44	清阻塞音、响音
T2	24	浊阻塞音、清送气阻塞音
T3	34	清阻塞音、响音
T4	21	清阻塞音、响音
T5	45	清阻塞音、响音
T6	25	清送气阻塞音
T7	22	浊阻塞音、响音

4.2　两字组连读变调

根据匿名审稿人的建议,本小节的目标词包括近似最小对立对(near-minimal-pair words, MP)和高频词(high-frequency words, HF),详见表3。两组目标词的连读变调模式相似:前字声调不变,而后字声调简化为三个平调,具体调值取决于其本调:如果后字的本调为45或25,则变为高平调44;如果本调为44、24或34,则变为中平调33;如果本调为21或22,则变为低平调22。上述规则只适用于两字组,多字组的变调规则有待进一步研究。

为进一步说明变调模式,图16a-n呈现了14组词的调形(tone contours)。图16a-g为七组近似最小对立对的音高曲线,每组控制后字声调不变,前字声调用从T1至T7的变量x表示,以展示前字声调调保持不变:x + T1(16a)、x + T2(16b)、x + T3(16c)、x + T4(16d)、x + T5(16e)、x + T6(16f)、x + T7(16g)。例如,图16a呈现了七个双音节词的音高曲线(T1 + T1、T2 + T1、T3 + T1、T4 + T1、T5 + T1、T6 + T1、T7 + T1)。如图所示,前字有七种不同的调形,且分别与单字调对应,说明前字声调保持不变。

图16h-n为七组高频词的音高曲线。不同于图16a-g,每组控制前字声调不变,而后字声调用从T1至T7的变量x表示,以展示后字声调变为三个平调:T1 + x(16h)、T2 + x(16i)、T3 + x(16j)、T4 + x(16k)、T5 + x(16l)、T6 + x(16m)、T7 + x(16n)。例如,图16h呈现了七个双音节词的音高曲线(T1 + T1、T1 + T2、T1 + T3、T1 + T4、T1 + T5、T1 + T6、T1 + T7),其中前字声调为44,与单字调调值一致,而后字声调变成了三个平调:T5(45)和T6(25)变为44;T1(44)、T2(24)、T3(34)变为33;T4(21)和T7(22)则变为22。

值得注意的是,图中可以观察到顺向协同发音的影响,尤其是在图16b中(T1 + T2、T2 + T2、T3 + T2、T4 + T2、T5 + T2、T6 + T2、T7 + T2)。一般情况下后字调值为33,但T5(45)和T6(25)后的声调明显高于其他五个声调。这似乎表明后字调形还受其他因素影响,如协同发音,后续研究将对这些因素进行系统分析。

表 3　　两组连读变调例词:一组为近似最小对立对(MP),另一组为高频词(HF)

前字		后字 44	24	34	21	45	25	22
44	MP	/kan^{44}ki^{44}/ 公鸡	/ty^{44}bi^{24}/ 猪皮	/ɕɪn^{44}pi^{34}/ 新笔	/kan^{44}kaɪ^{21}/ 公狗	/ɕjaŋ^{44}tẽ^{45}/ 商店	/paʊ^{44}tsʰaɪ^{25}/ 包菜	/ɕɪn^{44}bi^{22}/ 新被
	HF	/sɹ̩^{44}ki^{44}/ 司机	/pɪn^{44}daŋ^{24}/ 冰糖	/kan^{44}tsu^{34}/ 工作	/pjã^{44}taŋ^{21}/ 班长	/tʃɹ̩^{44}twaɪ^{45}/ 车队	/pẽ^{44}pʰaʊ^{25}/ 鞭炮	/kan^{44}di^{22}/ 工地
24	MP	/ran^{24}ki^{44}/ 红鸡	/dʐɥẽ^{24}bi^{24}/ 全皮	/ran^{24}pi^{34}/ 红笔	/ran^{24}kaɪ^{21}/ 红狗	/dan^{24}tẽ^{45}/ 铜店	/ran^{24}tsʰaɪ^{25}/ 红菜	/ran^{24}bi^{22}/ 红被
	HF	/dɯ^{24}ɕy^{44}/ 图书	/dzaɪ^{24}ɤ jan^{24}/ 财神	/dan^{24}ɕju^{34}/ 同学	/tɕʰja^{24}su^{21}/ 厕所	/bɯ^{24}sa^{45}/ 菩萨	/dan^{24}kʰi^{25}/ 铜器	/dan^{24}dɹ̩^{22}/ 同事
34	MP	/ɕja^{34}ki^{44}/ 黑鸡	/njeɪ^{34}bi^{24}/ 牛皮	/maʊ^{34}pi^{34}/ 毛笔	/ɕja^{34}kaɪ^{21}/ 黑狗	/ɕja^{34}tẽ^{45}/ 黑店	/ja^{34}tsʰaɪ^{25}/ 热菜	/njeɪ^{34}bi^{22}/ 绿被
	HF	/pja^{34}xaŋ^{44}/ 北方	/wi^{34}gi^{24}/ 围棋	/ɕja^{34}ɕja^{34}/ 黑色	/jan^{34}pʰɪn^{21}/ 人品	/mu^{34}tjã^{45}/ 木凳	/tɯ^{34}kʰi^{25}/ 毒气	/su^{34}dɯ^{22}/ 速度
21	MP	/mu^{21}ki^{44}/ 母鸡	/nẽ^{21}bi^{24}/ 脸皮	/xwan^{21}pi^{34}/ 粉笔	/mu^{21}kaɪ^{21}/ 母狗	/ɕjaʊ^{21}tẽ^{45}/ 小店	/njõ^{21}tsʰaɪ^{25}/ 冷菜	/xaʊ^{21}bi^{22}/ 好被
	HF	/tʰy^{21}xaŋ^{44}/ 处方	/pɪn^{21}dʐẽ^{24}/ 本钱	/tɯ^{21}pu^{34}/ 赌博	/pɯ^{21}kaʊ^{21}/ 补考	/po^{21}ɕi^{45}/ 把戏	/paʊ^{21}kʰɯ^{25}/ 宝库	/pɪn^{21}dzɹ̩^{22}/ 本事
45	MP	/tɕjaŋ^{45}ki^{44}/ 酱鸡	/ɕi^{45}bi^{24}/ 细皮	/ɕi^{45}pi^{34}/ 细笔	/tan^{45}kaɪ^{21}/ 冻狗	/ɕi^{45}tẽ^{45}/ 细店	/ka^{45}tsʰaɪ^{25}/ 芥菜	/ɕi^{45}bi^{22}/ 细被
	HF	/paʊ^{45}ɕjaʊ^{44}/ 报销	/paɪ^{45}gu^{24}/ 贝壳	/ki^{45}tɕja^{34}/ 季节	/xɯ^{45}ɕjer^{21}/ 副手	/ka^{45}ɕjẽ^{45}/ 界线	/ɕi^{45h}jaʊ^{25}/ 戏票	/paʊ^{45}dan^{22}/ 暴动
25	MP	/tsʰaɪ^{25}ki^{44}/ 菜鸡	/pʰo^{25}bi^{24}/ 白皮	/tʰjã^{25}pi^{34}/ 炭笔	/pʰo^{25}kaɪ^{21}/ 白狗	/tsʰaɪ^{25}tẽ^{45}/ 菜店	/pʰaʊ^{25}tsʰaɪ^{25}/ 泡菜	/tʰaʊ^{25}bi^{22}/ 套被
	HF	/tsʰaɪ^{25}tjã^{44}/ 菜单	/pʰa^{25}daɪ^{24}/ 派头	/pʰaɪ^{25}ku^{34}/ 配角	/kʰi^{25}tʰi^{21}/ 气体	/kʰi^{25}ɕɪn^{45}/ 气性	/tʰjeɪ^{25}kʰi^{25}/ 臭气	/tʰa^{25}dɯ^{22}/ 态度
22	MP	/da^{22}ki^{44}/ 大鸡	/mẽ^{22}bi^{24}/ 面皮	/da^{22}pi^{34}/ 大笔	/da^{22}kaɪ^{21}/ 大狗	/da^{22}tẽ^{45}/ 大店	/da^{22} tsʰaɪ^{25}/ 大菜	/da^{22}bi^{22}/ 大被
	HF	/daɪ^{22}tɕjaŋ^{44}/ 豆浆	/di^{22}dɯ^{24}/ 地图	/rwã^{22}tsu^{34}/ 饭桌	/dẽ^{22}pjaʊ^{21}/ 电表	/di^{22}tan^{45}/ 地震	/dẽ^{22}kʰi^{25}/ 电器	/daɪ^{22}dʒɹ̩^{22}/ 豆豉

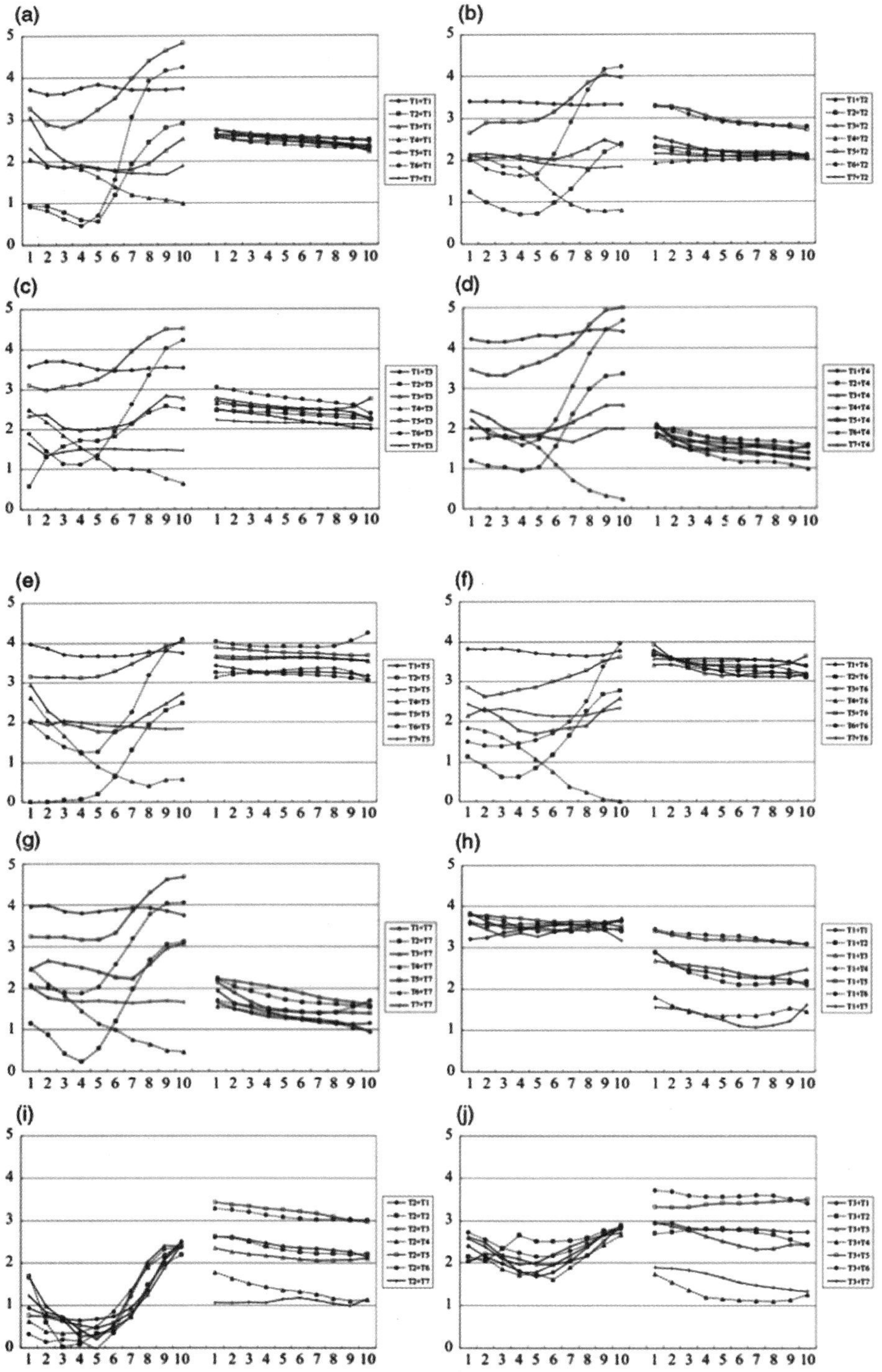
(a)
T1+T1
T2+T1
T3+T1
T4+T1
T5+T1
T6+T1
T7+T1
(b)
T1+T2
T2+T2
T3+T2
T4+T2
T5+T2
T6+T2
T7+T2
(c)
T1+T3
T2+T3
T3+T3
T4+T3
T5+T3
T6+T3
T7+T3
(d)
T1+T4
T2+T4
T3+T4
T4+T4
T5+T4
T6+T4
T7+T4
(e)
T1+T5
T2+T5
T3+T5
T4+T5
T5+T5
T6+T5
T7+T5
(f)
T1+T6
T2+T6
T3+T6
T4+T6
T5+T6
T6+T6
T7+T6
(g)
T1+T7
T2+T7
T3+T7
T4+T7
T5+T7
T6+T7
T7+T7
(h)
T1+T1
T1+T2
T1+T3
T1+T4
T1+T5
T1+T6
T1+T7
(i)
T2+T1
T2+T2
T2+T3
T2+T4
T2+T5
T2+T6
T2+T7
(j)
T3+T1
T3+T2
T3+T3
T3+T4
T3+T5
T3+T6
T3+T7

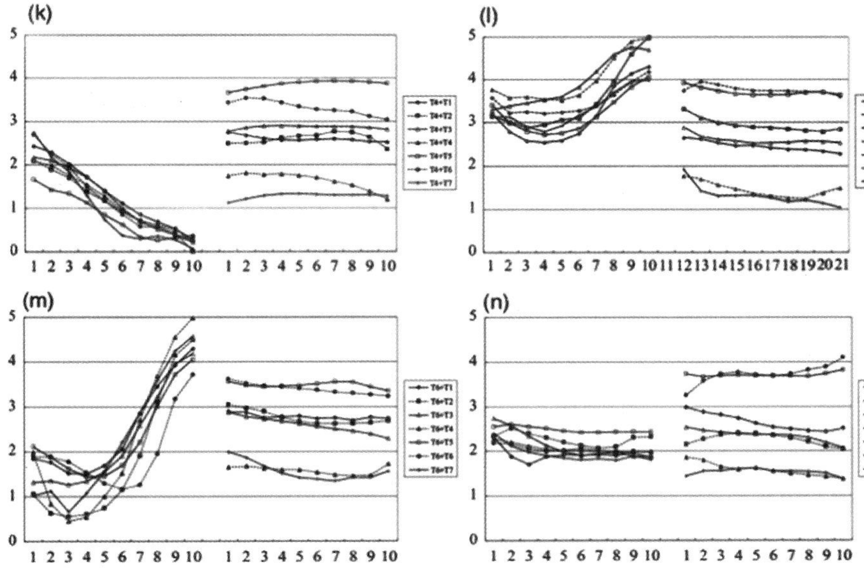

图 16 两字组连读变调模式

有学者认为这三个调域的平调是后字声调中和的结果,因为与前字相比,后字处于更弱的位置,其声学特征与林茂灿和颜景助[29]与曹剑芬[25]定义的弱化或轻声音节(weak or neutralized syllable)相似。如图 17 例词[ɕja^{34} ɕja^{33}]“黑色”(/ɕja^{34}/“黑”+/ɕja^{34}/“色”)所示,除声调弱化或中和(tonal reduction or neutralization)之外,与前字相比,后字的时长更短、振幅更小、元音音质更弱。Bao[1, 2]提出的声调表征模型将声调视作由曲拱节点(contour node)和调域节点(register node)组成的二元结构。基于此模型,上述连读变调模式可能是曲拱删除(contour deletion)的结果:曲拱删除后,高调域的两个升调(45、25)变为高平调;中调域声调(44、24、34)变为中平调;低调域声调(21、22)变为低平调。

5. 语篇录音转写

5.1 音位标音版

本小节使用湘乡方言元音表、辅音表中的符号对语篇录音进行音位转写。每个音节的右上方标有声调,变调用( )表示。[‖]表示语句(utterance)边界,[|]表示语

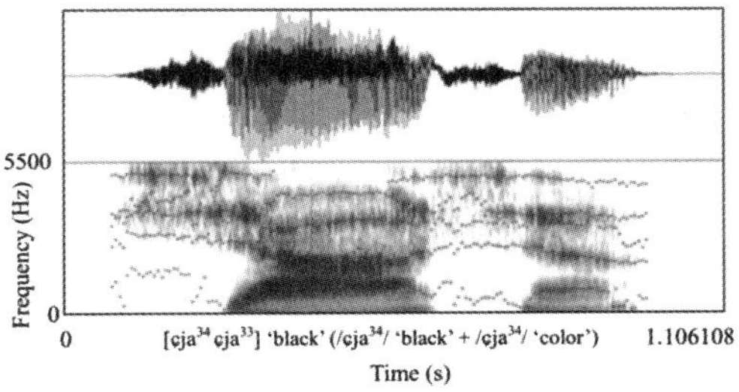

图17 [ɕja^{34} ɕja^{33}]“黑色”(/ɕja^{34}/“黑”+/ɕja^{34}/“色”)的波形和频谱图

句中的语调短语边界。

jeɪ$^{(22)}$ i$^{(33)}$ t^{h}ẽ^{44} | pja^{34} xwan$^{(33)}$ kjã$^{(33)}$ t^{h}a^{25} jaŋ$^{(33)}$ dzaɪ$^{(22)}$ nu$^{(22)}$ ni$^{(22)}$ tsõ^{44} | na^{21} ku$^{(55)}$ ti$^{(33)}$ pin^{21} dzɹ̩$^{(22)}$ da$^{(22)}$ ‖ tsõ^{44} naɪ$^{(33)}$ tsõ^{44} k^{h}i$^{(55)}$ | jeɪ^{21} ku$^{(55)}$ jan$^{(33)}$ kɯ$^{(55)}$ ɕjan^{44} | ɕjan^{44} rjaŋ^{22} t^{h}ɥẽ$^{(33)}$ ni$^{(22)}$ gẽ$^{(22)}$ raɪ^{22} ŋaʊ$^{(22)}$ tsɹ̩$^{(22)}$ ‖ t^{h}o$^{(33)}$ njã$^{(33)}$ dʑjeɪ$^{(22)}$ ɕjaŋ^{44} njaŋ$^{(33)}$ xaʊ^{21} | kaŋ^{21} | na^{21} ku$^{(55)}$ ɕjẽ^{44} jaŋ$^{(22)}$ ku$^{(22)}$ ku$^{(55)}$ kɯ$^{(55)}$ ɕjan^{44} ti$^{(33)}$ | po$^{(22)}$ t^{h}o^{44} ti$^{(33)}$ ŋaʊ^{21} tsɹ̩$^{(22)}$ t^{h}wa^{13} ro$^{(22)}$ naɪ$^{(33)}$ | dʑjeɪ$^{(22)}$ swã$^{(55)}$ na^{21} ku$^{(55)}$ ti$^{(33)}$ pin^{31} dzɹ̩$^{(22)}$ da$^{(22)}$ ‖

pja^{34} xwan$^{(33)}$ dʑjeɪ$^{(22)}$ jan$^{(22)}$ tɕɥi^{45} da$^{(22)}$ ka$^{(33)}$ kin^{45} | ro^{22} dʑin$^{(33)}$ ka$^{(33)}$ tʰy^{44} ‖ bɯ$^{(22)}$ kɯ$^{(55)}$ | tʰo$^{(33)}$ tʰy^{44} tja$^{(33)}$ ɥa$^{(33)}$ ni^{45} xaɪ$^{(55)}$ | nu$^{(22)}$ ku$^{(55)}$ jan$^{(33)}$ dʑjeɪ$^{(22)}$ po$^{(22)}$ tʰo$^{(33)}$ ti$^{(33)}$ ŋaʊ^{21} tsɹ̩$^{(22)}$ | kʰjã^{25} tja$^{(33)}$ ɥa$^{(33)}$ kin^{21} ‖ tɕɥi^{45} raɪ$^{(22)}$ | pja^{34} xwan$^{(33)}$ maʊ$^{(22)}$ tja$^{(33)}$ bjã$^{(22)}$ xwa$^{(33)}$ | tʃɹ̩$^{(33)}$ xaʊ$^{(22)}$ swã^{45} ni$^{(33)}$ ‖ kɯ^{45} ni$^{(22)}$ i$^{(33)}$ ro^{22} tɕi$^{(22)}$ | tʰa^{25} jaŋ$^{(33)}$ tʰy$^{(33)}$ naɪ$^{(33)}$ i$^{(33)}$ so^{45} | nu$^{(22)}$ ku$^{(55)}$ jan$^{(33)}$ mõ^{21} rjaŋ$^{(22)}$ dʑjeɪ$^{(22)}$ po$^{(22)}$ to$^{(33)}$ ŋaʊ^{21} tsɹ̩$^{(22)}$ tʰwa^{24} rõ$^{(22)}$ naɪ$^{(33)}$ ni$^{(22)}$ ‖ su^{21} i$^{(22)}$ | pja^{34} xwan$^{(33)}$ bɯ$^{(33)}$ tja$^{(33)}$ bɯ$^{(33)}$ dan^{24} jan$^{(22)}$ | ra$^{(33)}$ dzɹ̩$^{(22)}$ tʰa^{24} jaŋ$^{(33)}$ pi$^{(22)}$ tʰo$^{(33)}$ ti$^{(33)}$ pin^{21} dzɹ̩$^{(22)}$ da$^{(22)}$ ‖

5.2 文字转写版

有一天,北风跟太阳在那里争哪个的本事大。争来争去,有个人过身,身上穿了件厚袄子。他们就商量好,讲,哪个先让这个过身的把他的袄子脱下来,就算哪个的本事大。北风就用最大咖劲,下勤咖吹。不过,他吹得越厉害,那个人就把他的袄子箍得越紧。最后,北风冇得办法,只好算哩。过哩一下唧,太阳出来一晒,那个人马上就把只袄子脱下来哩。所以,北风不得不承认,还是太阳比他的本事大。

6. 致谢

感谢编辑 Amalia Arvaniti 和 Adrian Simpson、两位匿名审稿人、音频助理 André Radtke 以及文字编辑 Ewa Jaworska 对本文早期版本提出的建设性意见。特别感谢李倩、侯典峰在本文写作过程中给予的建议和鼓励。非常感谢 Ian Maddieson、Chris Sinha 以及 Russell Palmer 对本文的宝贵贡献。

参考文献

[1] Bao, Z. 1990. *On the Nature of Tone*. Ph. D. dissertation, MIT.

[2] Bao, Z. 1999. Tonal ontour and register harmony in Chaozhou. *Linguistic Inquiry*, 30 (3), 485 – 493.

[3] Chao, Y. R. 1980. A system of "tone-letters". *Fangyan* [Dialects], 2, 81 – 83.

[4] Chen, Y., Gussenhoven, C. 2015. Shanghai Chinese. *Journal of the International Phonetic Association*, 45(3), 321 – 337.

[5] Keating, P. A., Mikoš, M. J., Ganong III, W. F. 1981. A cross-language study of range of voice onset time in the perception of initial stop voicing. *The Journal of the Acoustical Society of America*, 70(5), 1261 – 1271.

[6] Ladefoged, P., Johnson, K. 2011. *A Course in Phonetics* (6th edition). Boston, MA: Wadsworth, Cengage Learning.

[7] Ladefoged, P., Maddieson, I. 1996. *The Sounds of the World's Languages*. Oxford: Blackwell.

[8] Lau, S. L. 2002. *Tone and tone sandhi in Suzhou*. M. Phil. thesis, City University of Hong Kong.

[9] Lee, W. S., Zee, E. 2003. Standard Chinese (Beijing). *Journal of the International Phonetic Association*, 33(1), 109 – 112.

[10] Li, F. K. 1973. Languages and dialects of China. *Journal of Chinese Linguistics*, 1 (1), 1 – 13.

[11] Li, Q., Chen, Y., Xiong, Z. 2019. Tianjin Mandarin. *Journal of the International Phonetic Association*, 48(1), 109 – 128.

[12] Li, W. 1999. *A Diachronically-Motivated Segmental Phonology of Mandarin Chinese*. New York: Peter Lang.

[13] Lin, Y. H. 2014. Segmental phonology. In Huang, C. J., Li, Y. A., Simpson, A. (eds) *The Handbook of Chinese Linguistics* (pp. 400 – 421). Oxford: Wiley-Blackwell.

[14] Miret, F. S. 1998. Some reflections on the notion of diphthong. *Papers and Studies in Contrastive Linguistics*, 34, 27 – 51.

[15] Recasens, D. 1990. The articulatory characteristics of palatal consonants. *Journal of Phonetics*, 18, 267 – 280.

[16] Rosner, B. S., López-Bascuas, L. E., García-Albea, J. E., Fahey, R. P. 2000. Voice-onset times for Castilian Spanish initial stops. *Journal of Phonetics*, 28, 217 – 224.

[17] van Alphen, P. M., Smits, R. 2004. Acoustical and perceptual analysis of the voicing distinction in Dutch initial plosives: The role of prevoicing. *Journal of Phonetics*, 32(4), 455 – 491.

[18] Williams, L. 1977. The voicing contrast in

Spanish. *Journal of Phonetics*, 5 (2), 169 –184.

[19] Zee, E., Lee, W. S., Sock, R., Fuchs, S., Laprie, Y. 2008. The articulatory characteristics of the palatals, palatalized velars and velars in Hakka Chinese. In *The 8th International Seminar on Speech Production* (pp. 113 –116).

[20] Zeng, T. 2012. *A Phonetic Study of the Sounds and Tones in Xiangxiang Chinese*. Ph. D. dissertation, City University of Hong Kong.

[21] Zeng, T. 2015. Devoicing of historically voiced obstruents in Xiangxiang Chinese. *Journal of Chinese Linguistics*, 43(2), 638 –667.

[22] 鲍厚星:《概述》,李永明主编《湖南省方言志》,湖南人民出版社2001年版,1—31页。

[23] 鲍厚星:《湘方言概要》,湖南师范大学出版社2006年版。

[24] 鲍厚星、陈晖:《湘语的分区》,《方言》2005年第3期,1—31页。

[25] 曹剑芬:《语言的韵律与语音的变化》,中国社会科学出版社2016年版。

[26] 黄伯荣、廖序东:《现代汉语》上册,高等教育出版社2011年版。

[27] 蒋军凤:《湘乡方言语音研究》,博士学位论文,湖南师范大学,2008年。

[28] 李小凡、项梦冰:《汉语方言学基础教程》,北京大学出版社2009年版。

[29] 林茂灿、颜景助:《普通话轻声与轻重音》,《语言研究》1986年第1期,77—90页。

[30] 石锋:《苏州话浊塞音的声学分析》,《语言研究》1983年第1期,49—83页。

[31] 石锋:《天津方言双字组声调分析》,《语言研究》1986年第1期,77—90页。

[32] 石锋:《天津方言双字组声调分析》,石锋主编《语音学探微》,北京大学出版社1990年版,66—83页。

[33] 石锋:《北京话的声调格局》,石锋、廖荣蓉主编《语音丛稿》,北京语言学院出版社1994年版,10—19页。

[34] 石锋、王萍:《北京话单字音声调的统计分析》,《中国语文》2006年第5期,33—40页。

[35] 王力:《中国音韵学》下册,上海书店1936年版。

[36] 袁家骅:《汉语方言概要》,语文出版社2001年版。

[37] 曾少达:《湖南省方言区划及历史背景》,李永明主编《湖南省方言志》,湖南人民出版社2001年版,211—275页。

[38] 赵元任、吴宗济:《湘乡方言》,杨时逢主编《湖南方言调查报告》,中研院历史语言研究所1974年版,584—602页。

[39] 中国语言地图集:中国社会科学院语言研究所、中国社会科学院民族学与人类学研究所、香港城市大学信息科学中心主编,商务出版社2012年版。

[40] 周振鹤、游汝杰:《湖南省方言区划及历史背景》,《方言》1985年第4期,257—272页。

曾 婷 博士,硕士研究生导师。湖南大学外国语学院副教授。专业方向为语音学、实验音系学、语音类型学。

A STUDY ON AUTOMATIC DIAGNOSIS OF MUSCLE TENSION DYSPHONIA BASED ON sEMG

FANG Qiang

Abstract Muscle tension dysphonia (MTD) is a kind of phonation disorder, in which nc obvious organic problem can be observed under laryngoscopy. In literature, researchers have investigated the acoustic, electromyographic, and breathy characteristics from a statistic point of view. In this study, we explore the possibility of diagnosing MTD based on task-related surface electromyography (sEMG) signals. In this study, the sEMG signals are collected and transformed to corresponding time and frequency domain features. Then, Flsher' s F-ratio is adopted to select task-related features for automatic diagnosis. Four traditional classification methods(K-nearest neighbor, Classification and Regression Tree, Support Vector Machine, and Logistic regression) are implemented to discriminate MTD patients from healthy people. It is found that the precision can be as high as 80% if proper task and classification method are chosen.

Keywords sEMG, F-ratio, MTD, KNN, CART, SVM, Logistic regression

基于表面肌电的肌肉紧张型发声障碍自动诊断研究

方　强

摘　要　肌肉紧张型发声障碍（MTD）是一种常见的发声障碍。这种类型的发声障碍在歌唱演员、教师及精神焦虑的人群中比较多见。这类患者的声带一般没有明显的器质性病变，但发声时喉部肌肉紧张。临床实践中，医生主要通过问诊、内窥镜检查、嗓音粗糙度评分、触诊等手段对患者的嗓音情况进行评估。可以看出，以上常规手段的诊断结果大多基于医生的主观判断，缺乏客观、定量的判断依据，严重依赖于医生的个人经验。因此，寻找客观、定量的参数，辅助 MTD 的诊断，减少 MTD 的误诊和漏诊，变得十分必要。

前人的研究比较过 MTD 患者和正常人发声过程中声学、肌电及呼吸特征的差异。本研究我们主要考察运用表面肌电信号对 MTD 进行自动诊断的可能性。因此，我们回顾了前人在 MTD 患者肌电信号方面的工作。一部分学者的研究认为 MTD 患者的肌电活动水平与正常人的肌电活动水平有显著差异［6，14］；一部分学者的研究认为 MTD 患者的肌电活动水平与正常人的肌电活动水平没有显著差异［7，17］；还有部分学者发现 MTD 患者不同肌肉肌电信号的相干性与正常人之间有显著差异。我们可以看出，前人的研究并没有取得一致的结果。造成这一现状的原因可能有如下几点：（1）大部分研究调查的人数较少（一般不多于 20 个实验被试），导致结果不稳定；（2）大部分研究只考察了肌电活动水平这一单独参数，可能 MTD 患者与正常人肌电特征存在差异，但差异并不是在肌电活动水平这一特征维度上；（3）考察的任务比较单一，MTD 患者与正常人肌电特征的差异在前人考察的任务中不明显或不稳定。

针对以上问题，在本研究中，我们收集了 47 名 MTD 患者和 22 名正常人在 14 个不同任务（8 个言语任务和 6 个非言语任务），舌骨上肌群、舌骨下肌群、环甲肌、胸锁乳突肌和斜方肌等 5 个肌群左右两侧部分的肌电信号。我们对肌电信号进行降噪和特征抽取等处理，得到 850 维的肌电特征向量。然后，我们用费舍尔 F 比值（Fisher' s F-ratio）这个指标对特征维度进行筛选，对每类任务挑选出前 10 个 F-ratio 值最大的特征维度。最后，基于挑选出来的特征，我们分别采用了 K 近邻（K－nearest neighbor）、支持向量机（SVM）、分类与回归树（Classification and Refression Tree）以及逻辑回归（Logistic

regression）四种方法对数据进行分类实验。结果表明，如果恰当地选择任务和分类方法，分类的正确率能够达到 80% 以上。
关键词 表面肌电，F 比值，肌肉紧张型发声障碍，K 近邻，分类回归树，支持向量机，逻辑回归

1. INTRODUCTION

Muscle tension dysphonia (MTD) is a kind of phonation disorder, in which no evident organic problem can be observed under laryngoscopy. It is originally coined by Morrison [11] and describes adysphonia caused by increased muscle tension of laryngeal and paralaryngeal muscles. And it has been known by other names including muscle misuse dysphonia, hyperfunctional dysphonia, and hyperkinetic dysphonia among others. It is more commonly diagnosed in women, the middle-aged, and individuals who have high levels of stress. It is also more often seen in those who use their voice often such as singers and teachers.

The symptoms for MTD vary from person to person. Hoarseness, pitch range restriction, difficulty of producing voice are typical symptoms associated with MTD. And these symptoms can be caused by a large variety of factors (such as emotional distress, drinking cold water, yelling and shouting, smoking).

MTD presumably is characterized by excessive muscular contraction, and vocal symptoms are combined with excessive glottic and/or supraglottic muscle tension. This suggests that there may exist cues in the activities of related muscles, the behavior of structures in larynx, and acoustic and aerodynamic consequences that help the differentiating of MTD patients from the healthy ones.

In clinical practice, several procedures are commonly used, such as clinical history, endoscopic assessment, harshness rating/perceptual assessment, and palpation rating. Despite the widespread use of the MTD designation, diagnosis and assessment in current clinical practice depends upon subjective interpretation of patient history and physical examination, and heavily influenced by the experience of the clinic practitioners. Hence, it is necessary to develop some objective measure for the detection of MTD.

In literature, several studies had been conducted to investigate whether muscle activity of the MTD patient were significantly different from that of the healthy control, where the sEMG was used to detect the muscle activity. Redenbaug and Reich [14] studied sEMG levels of infrahyoid muscles in normal and vocally MTD speakers. They found EMG levels were significantly larger for MTD speakers. Hocevar-Boltezar et al. [6] investigated the EMG feature in the perioral area and anterior neck before and during phonation. Their results showed a 6 – 8-fold increase of EMG activity. Stepp et al. [16] measured sEMG to explore the intermuscular coherence in the beta band as a possible indicator of MTD. They found the mean coherence in the beta band was significantly lower in MTD group than that in control group. However, there are some experiments that do not support assessing MTD with EMG features. Stepp et al. [17] investigated the sensitivity of the anterior neck sEMG to changes in MTD associated with injection laryngoplasty. They found the perceptual ratings of strain and false vocal fold (FVF) compression were both significantly reduced while sEMG was not significantly reduced. Van Houtte et al. [7] did not detect the increase of sEMG level in patients with MTD and questioned the use of sEMG as a diagnostic tool for distinguishing patients with and without MTD.

Although the above-mentioned studies did not come to an agreement, we can not conclude that sEMG is not appropriate for diagnosing MTD. It is not negligible that, most of the previous studies only explored few sEMG features (Root-Mean-Square, and coherence in beta band). None of them extensively investigated sEMG features of related muscles on vocal tasks. In addition, most of them only investigated on vocal task.

In this study, we attempt to figure out whether we can differentiate the MTD patients from the healthy people by using the activities of muscles in neck area measured by sEMG. To this end, we will collect the sEMG signals of related muscles in a few vocal/non-vocal conditions, extract extensive sEMG features, and conduct classification experiments based on the extracted sEMG features.

2. DATASET

2.1 Subject information

47 MTD patients and a group of 22 normal controls are enrolled in our experiment. The 47 patients with MTD are admitted to Beijing Tongren Hospital affiliated to Capital Medical University from June 2018 to January 2020, aged from 18 to 80 (mean = 38, std = 17.6). Among these patients, 14 of them are males and the other 33 of them are females. In the normal control group, there are 22 cases, aged from 22 to 67 (mean = 33.87, std = 11.97). Twelve of them are males, and 10 of them are females. None of the subjects has supraglottal infection, mental issue, nor muscle tension disorder caused by throat surgery or lesion. All the subjects are evaluated by subjective auditory-perceptual assessment of the voice, the Voice Handicap Index (VHI), acoustic analysis, and psychological scales assessment.

2.2 Data collection

A multi-channel physiological recorder (Australia COMPUMEDICS Grael 48 channels) is used to record the sEMG, ElectroCardioGram (ECG), nasal airflow, and breathing signals (the change of perimeter of

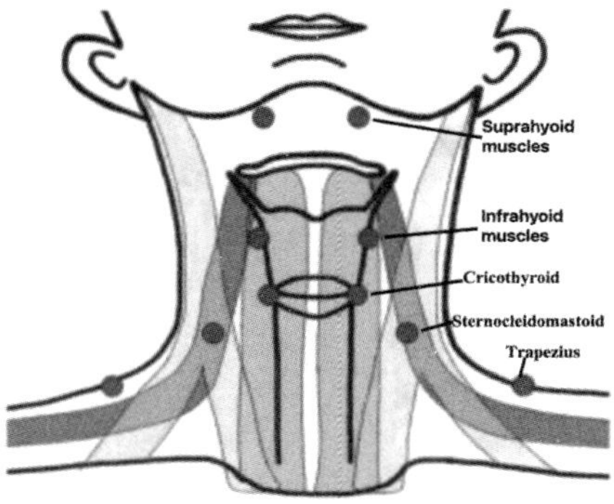

Figure 1 Locations of electrodes of surface EMG

the chest and abdomen) synchronously. The audio signal of vocal sound is recorded by a separate audio channel. In the experiment, sEMG electrodes are attached to the left and right parts of trapezius (TRA), SternoCleidomastoid muscles (SC), SupraHyoid muscles (SH), InfraHyoid muscles (IH) and CricoThyroid muscle (CT), as shown in Fig 1.

It is hypothesized that the related muscles may be activated abnormally in both vocal and non-vocal tasks for MTD patients. For this reason, the subjects are required to conduct both vocal and non-vocal tasks so as to collect task-related sEMG signals. These tasks recruited in the current study are as follows: turning head left (THL), turning head right (THR), shoulder shrugging(SS), throat cleaning (TC), swallowing (SW), deep breathing (DB), producing prolonged vowel /i/ (PI), high-pitch /i/ (HI), loud /i/ (LI), loud and high-pitch /i/(LHI), prolonged vowel /a/ (PA), high-pitch /a/ (HA), loud /a/ (LA), loud and high-pitch /i/ (LHA), short utterance (SU) (我去黑龙江,他去无锡市. "I am going to Heilongjiang, he is going to Wuxi City" in Mandarin), loud short utterance (LSU). Between two tasks, subjects are required to take a 10-second break to avoid fatigue.

In this study, the data in task SU and LSU are not used because the data in these

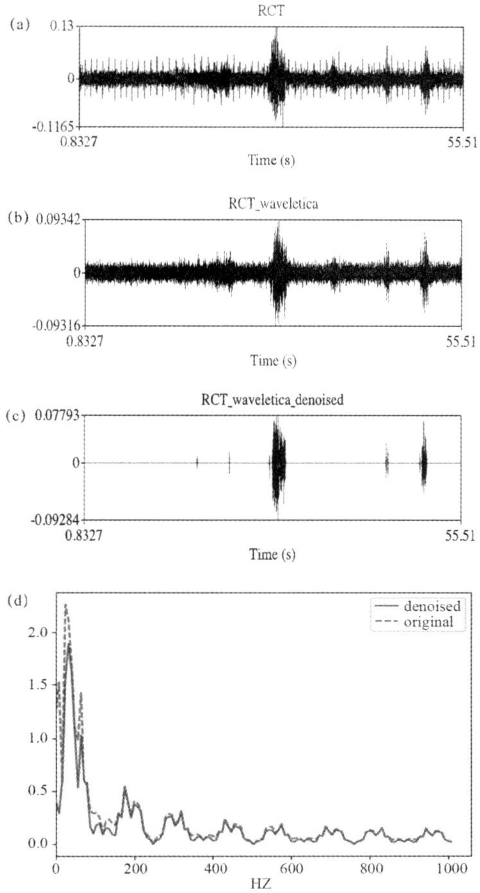

Figure 2 Examples of the original and processed EMG signal. (a) Original signal. (b) Original with ECG-like artifacts removed. (c) Original with both ECG-like artifacts and background noise removed. (d) Spectrum of original sEMG signal (dashed red) and denoised sEMG signal (solid blue).

two tasks are designed to monitor temporal variation of muscle activation and the control of respiration that are not considered in the current study.

2.3 Noise reduction

Usually, there are artifacts and background noise in the collected sEMG signal. Figure 2 (a) gives an example of recorded EMG signal, where the EMG signal sequence is contaminated by some periodic spikes, called ECG-like artifacts, and evident background noise.

The ECG-like artifacts appear when the EMG electrode is placed close to an artery. The ECG-like artifacts will change the temporal and frequency characteristics of sEMG signal. Therefore, the ECG-like artifacts should be removed before feeding sEMG signal to subsequent processing procedure.

In this study, the wavelet-ICA [1] method is implemented to suppress the ECG-like signals. To this end, firstly, a mono-channel signal sequence is transformed to a multi-channel signal sequence by wavelet analysis. Then, the multi-channel signal sequence is decomposed into several independent channels by using Independent Component Analysis (ICA) method. After that, the signals in the channel that has the same periodicity of ECG-like artifacts are removed. At last, the final signal is synthesized by reversing the aforementioned process.

As for the background noise, it is mainly introduced by the data collecting instrument and is assumed stationary. To suppress the background noise, the spectrum subtraction method [2] is applied, where the initial noise spectrum is estimated from the silence portion at the beginning of the signal sequence and updated by using the signals in silent regions dynamically.

Figure 2(b) gives an example of EMG signal of RCT (cricothyroid muscle on the right side) after removing the ECG-like artifacts. Figure 2(c) gives an example of EMG signal of RCT by removing both ECG-like artifacts and background noise. It indicates that the ECG-like artifacts and background noise in the original EMG signals can be effectively suppressed with the proposed noise reduction procedure. Figure 2(d) demonstrates an example of the spectrum of original sEMG signal (dashed red curve) and denoised sEMG signal (solid blue curve). One can see that generally the spectrum of denoised sEMG signal is close to that of the original sEMG, except that some detail frequency components are somewhat different. This indicates that the denoised sEMG signal preserves the nature of the original sEMG signal.

3. FEATURES

Traditional studies on sEMG for MTD patients are mainly based on the sEMG level [6, 7, 14]. In this study, we will extensively explore various features and evaluate their contribution to differentiate MTD patients from normal control.

Generally, features for analyzing sEMG signals can be divided into three groups: time domain, frequency domain, and time-frequency or time-scale representation. In this study, only the time and frequency domain features are considered.

Time domain features are based on sEMG time series. In this study, extensive time-domain features are adopted. They are, Duration from rest to Maximum Amplitude (D2MA), Maximum Phonation Time (MPT), Maximum AMplitude (MAM), the Duration to achieve Maximum AMplitude (DMAM), Integrated EMG, Mean Absolute Value (MAV) [19], Modified mean Absolute Value type-1 (MAV1) [12], Modified mean Absolute Value type-2 (MAV2) [12], Simple Square Integral (SSI) [4], VARiance of EMG (VAR) [13], the third, fourth, and fifth Temporal Moments (TM3, TM4, and TM5) [15], Root Mean Square (RMS) [3], the V-order (V) [18], LOG detector (LOG) feature[18], Waveform Length (WL) [12], Average Amplitude Change (AAC) [5], Difference Absolute Standard Deviation Value (DASDV) [9], Zero Crossing (ZC) [8], Myopulse Percentage Rate (MPR) [5], Wilson AMPlitude (WAMP) [19], Slope Sign Change (SSC) [8], Mean Absolute Value Slope (MAVS) [10], Multiple Hamming Windows (MHW) Histogram of EMG (HIST) [3], Auto-Regressive (AR) [3], and Cepstral Coefficient (CC) [18].

Frequency-domain features are mostly used to study fatigue of muscle and analyze motor unit recruitment. The frequency-domain features used in this study are MeaN Frequency (MNF) [4], MeDian Frequency (MDF) [12] PeaK Frequency (PKF) [3], MeaN Power (MNP) [3], and ToTal Power (TTP) [3], the 1st, 2nd, and 3rd Spectral Moments (SM1 – SM3) [4], Frequency Ratio (FR) [4], Power Spectrum Ratio (PSR) [20], Variance of Central Frequency (VCF) [4].

For the MTD patient, the asymmetry activation of muscles may occur in vocal and non-vocal tasks. This indicates that the asymmetry of corresponding features are possible indicators for diagnosing MTD. Therefore, the difference of the features between the left and right counterparts of the same muscle are calculated as additional features. Moreover, the difference of the instants when activation occurs and disappears between the left and right counterparts of each muscle is adopted to account for the temporal asymmetry. In total, there are 850 features for each vocal/non-vocal task.

4. FEATURE SELECTION

As mentioned in the previous section, there are 850 candidate features and 69 (47 +22) data samples for each task. The number of data sample is much smaller than the dimensionality of extracted feature. In order to avoid the dimension curse, it is necessary to reduce the dimensionality of features by using feature selection techniques. To this end, firstly, the original data are separated into several subsets according to their tasks (shown in section 2.1). Hence, we obtain 14 subsets in total. Then, for each subset, the Fisher's F-ratio measure is implemented to quantify the contribution of each feature dimension. Lastly, the features whose corresponding F-ratios are larger than a predefined threshold are selected. The F-ratio of the kth feature can be calculated according to Eq. 1.

$$F_{ratio}^{k} = \frac{\frac{1}{M}\sum_{i=1}^{M}(\mu_i^k - \mu^k)}{\frac{1}{\sum_{i=1}^{M} N_i}\sum_{i=1}^{M}\sum_{j=1}^{N_i}(x_i^{k,j} - \mu_i^k)^2} \quad (1)$$

where μ_i^k is the mean of the kth feature in the ith category, μ^k is the mean of the kth feature of data samples in the whole data set, $x_i^{k,j}$ is the value of the kth feature of the jth data sample in the ith category, M is the number of categories (in this study M = 2,), N_i is the number of samples in the ith category.

The denominator is a measure of within-category data dispersion, while the numerator is a measure of between-category data dispersion. Therefore, the larger the F-ratio is, the larger contribution the feature makes in discriminating MTD from healthy controls.

For each subset, the Fisher' s F-ratios of all the feature dimensions are calculated and sorted in descending orders.

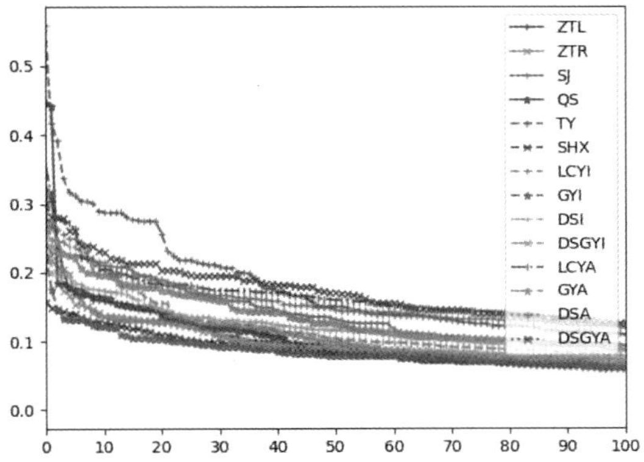

Figure 3 Sorted F-ratios for each non-vocal and vocal task

As shown in Figure 3, the Fisher' s F-ratio decreases dramatically at first, then arrives at a relative stable region. Here, we determine a predefined threshold with the elbow criterion. In this study, for each task, the feature dimensions with the first 10 highest F-ratios are selected as the inputs to classifiers. The details are shown in Table 1.

If we take a look at the details in Table 1, we can notice that the feature RMS (used to measure muscle activation level) is not one of the selected 10 features with the highest contribution to discriminating the MTD patients from the controls in most vocal and non-vocal tasks. In addition, even for similar vocal task, for example producing vowel /i/, the features that make the highest contribution to differentiating MTD patients and controls differs a lot. This may be the reason why the previous studies did not come to a consistent conclusion.

Table 1 The 10 features selected based on F-ratio for each task

Task	Muscle & feature
THL	LIH: AR_ 4 RSH: MNP, SSI, FR_ diff SC: AR_ diff_ 1, CC_ diff_ 0, CC_ diff_ 1, CC_ diff_ 2, CC_ diff_ 3, VCF_ diff
THR	SC: HIST_ diff_ 4, HIST_ diff_ 7, LSC: PKF RSC: ZC TRA: AR_ diff_ 4, CC_ diff_ 3, MDF_ diff, PKF_ diff LTRA: CC_ 3, ZC
SS	CT: MHW_ diff_ 0, MHW_ diff_ 1, MHW_ diff_ 2 IH: AAC_ diff, DASD_ diff, RMS_ diff, V_ diff, WL_ diff, SC: DASD_ diff, AR_ diff_ 2
TC	CT: MPR_ diff RCT: MPR, ZC, SC: PSR_ diff LSC: PSR LSH: DASD, MAV_ 1, RMS, V RIH: PKF

续表

Task	Muscle & feature
SW	LIH: LOG RIH: LOG LSH: LOG, MAV_ 0, MPR RSH: AAC, HIST_ 0, LOG, MPR LTRA: ZC
DB	CT: SSC_ diff, RCT: VCF TRA: AR_ diff_ 2 LTRA: CC_ 3 SC: MAV_ 2_ diff, MAVS_ diff_ 1 RSC: HIST_ 0, HIST_ 5, HIST_ 6, HIST_ 8,
PI	CT: FR_ diff SC: FR_ diff, CC_ diff_ 2 LSC: SSC RSC: DUR, AR_ 1, CC_ 0, SSC, VCF, WAMP TRA: CC_ diff_ 2
HI	CT: DUR_ diff LCT: AR_ 3 IH: MNP_ diff, SM_ 1_ diff, SSI_ diff, TTP _ diff SC: DUR_ diff TRA: AR_ diff_ 3 LTRA: AR_ 3, MAV_ 2
LI	LSH: WL, HIST_ 0, HIST_ 1, HIST_ 2, HIST_ 3, HIST_ 4, HIST_ 5, HIST_ 8 RSH: HIST_ 6 SC: PSR_ diff
HLI	IH: LOG_ diff, CC_ diff_ 2, MPR_ diff LSC: HIST_ 1, HIST_ 2, HIST_ 8 RSC: HIST_ 1, HIST_ 2, HIST_ 5, HIST_ 6
PA	LIH: DUR, SSC, WAMP RIH: DUR, SSC, WAMP LSH: HIST_ 1, HIST_ 2, HIST_ 3, HIST_ 4
HA	SC: PSR_ diff LSC: AR_ 1, AR_ 2, CC_ 0, RSC: AR_ 2, AR_ 4 TRA: AR_ diff_ 1, MDF_ diff, CC_ diff_ 0, CC_ diff_ 2, CC_ diff_ 3

续表

Task	Muscle & feature
LA	CT: MPR_ diff, LSC: DASD, HIST_ 0, INTE, AR_ 2, RMS, V, RSC: DASD, RMS, V
HLA	IH: FR_ diff RIH: SSC LSH: DASD, RMS, V RSC: DASD, INTE, RMS, V, WL

5. EXPERIMENT

5.1 Settings

Four classical classifiers are implemented to explore the possibility of discriminating MTD with EMG features. They are K-nearest neighbor (KNN), Classification and Regression Tree (CART), Support Vector Machine (SVM), and Logistic regression.

KNN is a non-parametric method for classification. It simply stores instances of the training data, and classify samples by a simple majority voting of the K-nearest neighbors. In this study, the parameter K is 7.

CART is a typical decision-tree model that can be used for both classification and regression tasks. In the training phase, the features for splitting data sample are determined by maximizing some predefined impurity measure. In this study, the 'Gini' coefficient is adopted to measure the impurity of the tree nodes. And the maximum depth of the tree is 4.

SVM is a method that seeks a best super-plane to separate negative and positive examples. The best supper-plane is obtained by maximizing the distance between a series of support vectors (SV) and the super-plane. It is formulated as Eq2:

$$\hat{y} = \sum_{i \in SV} y_i \alpha_i K(x_i, x) + b \qquad (2)$$

Where $\hat{y}$, y_i, are predicted label and the

label of the ith SV, respectively, α_i is the dual coefficient correspond to the ith SV, K is a kernel function. In practice, a number of kernel functions can be used in SVM. In this study, a 4th order polynomial kernel is adopted, and the regularization term is 1.0 in the loss function.

Logistic regression predicts the probabilities of an input by Eq3.

$$y = \frac{1}{1 + e^{-(w^T x + b)}} \tag{3}$$

Where w and b are the parameters that define the model, and can be estimated by the minimum square error criterion.

5.2 Results

Classification experiments are conducted to discriminate the MTD patients from the healthy subjects. For each task, 80% of the data is used for training, and the other 20% of the data is used for testing. Fig 4 presents the classification accuracy of different methods, namely, KNN, CART, SVM, and logistic regression, in both vocal and non-vocal tasks.

Since the purpose of this study is to explore the possibility of automatic diagnosis of MTD, we will focus on the classification accuracy of each task. As shown in Figure 4, the performance of different methods differs a lot in various tasks. If we choose 80% as the minimal acceptable accuracy of a classifier, KNN works properly in 4 tasks (THL, SW, PI, and HI), CART works properly in 4 tasks (THL, TC, HI, and LA), SVM works properly in 6 tasks (THL, TC, HI, HLI, LA, HLA), and Logistic regression works properly in 8 tasks (THL, THR, SS, TC, DB, LI, HLI, PA, HA, LA). The logistic regression method performs best on discriminating MTD patients from normal subjects in various vocal and non-vocal tasks.

For each vocal and non-vocal task, it is found at least one of the four classifiers can discriminate the MTD patients from the healthy ones with relatively high accuracies. In the non-vocal task THL, MTD patients can be recognized by all the four classifiers. In tasks TC, HI, and LA, the MTD patients can be recognized by three of the four classifiers. It indicates that MTD patients are easier to be recognized when conducting these vocal and non-vocal tasks.

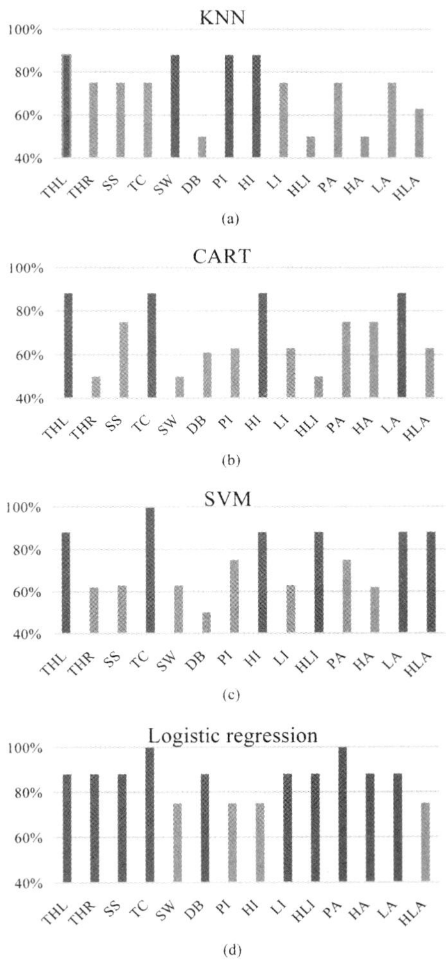

Figure 4 The precision of four classifiers for diagnosing MTD patients in various vocal and non-vocal tasks

6. DISCUSSION

In this study, we explore the possibility of automatic diagnosis of MTD based on task-related sEMG signals. To this end, the sEMG signal are collected and transformed to corresponding 850 time and frequency domain features. And Fisher' s F-ratio is adopted to select task-related features for automatic diagnosis. Four traditional classification methods (KNN, CART, SVM, and Logistic regression) are implemented to discriminate the MTD patients and normal people. It is found that the precision of discrimination can be as high as 80% if proper tasks and classification methods are chosen.

In this study, both vocal and non-vocal task show significant differences between the MTD patients and the healthy group, which is different from the results of Redenbaug and Reich' s work [14]. It is found that the MTD patients can be discriminated from normal controls with high accuracies by using Logistic regression method even for non-vocal tasks. This suggests that not only vocal tasks but also non-vocal tasks may be used in clinical practices. In the future, more data will be collected, and more advanced classifiers will be explored for tasks of discriminating MTD patients.

Acknowledgments

This work is supported by Special Program for Clinical Medicine Development of Beijing Hospitals Authority(XMLX201848).

References

[1] Abbaspour, S., Lindén, M., Gholamhosseini, H. (2015). ECG artifact removal from surface EMG signal using an automated method based on Wavelet-ICA. In Blobel B., Lindén, M., Ahmed, M. U (eds) *Studies in Health Technology and Informatics* (Volume 211), pp. 91 – 97. Amsterdam: IOS Press.

[2] Boll, S. F. (1979). Suppression of acoustic noise in speech using spectral subtraction. *IEEE Transactions on Acoustics, Speech, and Signal Processing* 27(2), 113 – 120.

[3] Boostani, R., Moradi, M. H. (2003). Evaluation of the forearm EMG signal features for the control of a prosthetic hand. *Physiological Measurement* 24(2), 309 – 319.

[4] Du, S., Vuskovic, M. (2004). Temporal vs. spectral approach to feature extraction from prehensile EMG signals. *IEEE International Conference on Information Reuse and Integration*, 344 – 350.

[5] Fougner, A. (2007). *Proportional myoelectric control of a multifunction upper limb prosthesis.* Master, Norwegian University of Science and Technology.

[6] Hocevar-Boltezar, I., Janko, M., Zargi, M. (1998). Role of surface EMG in diagnostics and treatment of muscle tension dysphonia. *Acta Oto-Laryngologica* 118(5), 739 – 743.

[7] Houtte, E. V., Claeys, S., D' haeseleer, E., Wuyts, F., Lierde, K. V. (2013). An examination of surface EMG for the assessment of muscle tension dysphonia. *Journal of Voice* 27(2), 177 – 186.

[8] Hudgins, B., Parker, P., Scott, R. (1993). A new strategy for multifunction myoelectric control. *IEEE Transactions on Biomedical Engineering* 40(1), 82 – 94.

[9] Kim, K. S., Choi, H. H., Moon, C. S., Mun, C. W. (2011). Comparison of k-nearest neighbor, quadratic discriminant and linear discriminant analysis in classification of electromyogram signals based on the wrist-motion directions. *Current Applied Physics* 11(3), 740 – 745.

[10] Miller, C. J. (2008). *Real-time feature extraction and classification of prehensile EMG signals.* Master thesis, San Diego State University.

[11] Morrison, M. D., Rammage, L. A., Belisle, G. M., C. Pullan B., Nichol H. (1983). Muscular tension dysphonia. *The Journal of Otolaryngology* 12(5), 302 – 306.

[12] Oskoei, M. A., Hu, H. (2008). Support vector machine based classification scheme for myoelectric control applied to upper limb. *IEEE Transactions on Biomedical Engineering* 55(8), 1956 – 1965.

[13] Park, S. H., Lee, S. P. (1998). EMG pattern recognition based on artificial intelligence

techniques. *IEEE Transactions on Rehabilitation Engineering* 6(4), 400 –405.

[14] Redenbaugh, M. A., Reich, A. R. (1989) Surface EMG andrelated measures in normal and vocally hyperfunctional speakers. *Journal of Speech and Hearing Disorders* 54(1), 68 –73.

[15] Saridis, G. N., Gootee, T. P. (1982). EMG pattern analysis and classification for a prosthetic arm. *IEEE Transactions on Biomedical Engineering* 29(6), 403 –412.

[16] Stepp, C. E., Hillman, R. E., Heaton, J. T. (2010). Use of neck strap muscle intermuscular coherence as an indicator of vocal hyperfunction. *IEEE Transactions on Neural Systems and Rehabilitation Engineering* 18 (3), 329 –335.

[17] Stepp, C. E., Heaton, J. T., Jetté, M. E., Burns, J. A., Hillman, R. E. (2010). Neck surface electromyography as a measure of vocal hyperfunction before and after injection laryngoplasty. *Annals of Otology, Rhinology and Laryngology* 119(9), 594 –601.

[18] Tkach, D., Huang, H., Kuiken, T. A. (2010). Study of stability of time-domain features for electromyographic pattern recognition. *Journal of Neuroengineering and Rehabilitation* 7(21).

[19] Zardoshti-Kermani, M., Wheeler, B. C., Badie, K., Hashemi, R. M. (1995). EMG feature evaluation for movement control of upper extremity prostheses. *IEEE Transactions on Rehabilitation Engineering* 3(4), 324 –333.

[20] Zhang, Q., Luo, Z. (2006). Wavelet denoising of electromyography. *IEEE International Conference on Mechatronics Automation*, 1553 –1558.

FANG Qiang Ph. D, associate professor of Institute of Linguistics, Chinese Academy of Social Sciences. His research interests include speech production and modeling.
Email: fangqiang@ cass. org. cn

AN ULTRASONIC AND ACOUSTIC INVESTIGATION OF TENSENESS IN NORTHERN YI

CHEN Shuwen

Abstract Abstract This study investigates the articulation and acoustics of tense-lax contrast in two Northern Yi dialects: Suondi and Yinuo. Suondi and Yinuo have five pairs of phonologically-defined tense and lax vowels. Previous studies have suggested that the major difference between tense and lax vowels lay in phonation types and f0, while the difference in vowel quality and lingual gesture between the two types of vowels is less known. The current study describes the articulatory and acoustic characteristics of tense and lax vowels using ultrasound imaging and spectrogram analysis. The results showed that tense vowels were articulated with more retracted tongue root and higher tongue front compared to lax vowels. Acoustically, tense vowels had higher F1 and lower F2, which was caused by the lowered and retracted tongue position. The data suggests that tense-lax distinction in Northern Yi also involves advanced tongue root/retracted tongue root ([+ATR]/[+RTR]) contrast.
Keywords Northern Yi, tenseness, ultrasound imaging, acoustics, ATR/RTR

北部彝语松紧元音的超声和声学研究

陈树雯

摘　要　北部彝语在音系上拥有 5 组松紧对立的元音：/i/（松）和/ɛ/（紧）；/ɯ/（松）和/a/（紧）；/o/（松）和/ɔ/（紧）；/ɿ/（松）和/ɿ̠/（紧）；/u/（松）和/u̠/（紧）。前人研究发现，松紧元音的主要声学区别存在于发声类型和基频，同时也在元音音质、时长、音强上存在一些差别。其中，松紧元音的音质区别存在争议。有研究指出，松紧元音的第一和第二共振峰存在差别，或仅在第一共振峰上存在差别；但也有部分研究指出，松紧元音音质不存在区别，或仅在个别松紧元音对中存在音质差别。本研究旨在通过超声成像数据和声学分析考察北部彝语松紧元音的发声生理特征和共振峰特征，探究北部彝语松紧元音的音质差别。超声数据可以直观地展示发音时的舌位差别，可为探究元音音质提供较为直接的证据。本文收集了一名北部彝语发音人的超声舌位数据及声学数据，以及另外五位发音人的声学数据。超声数据显示，紧元音发音时舌根后缩，舌前部（舌叶及前舌面）较低，整体舌位也较低；松元音发音时舌根较前，舌前部较高，整体舌位也较高。声学上，这位发音人的紧元音第一共振峰比松元音高，第二共振峰比松元音低，证明紧元音舌位较低且靠后，与超声数据呈现的特征一致。另外五名发音人的松紧元音声学特征与参加超声实验的发音人的声学数据特征一致。根据松紧元音的舌位特征和共振峰特征可知，彝语松紧元音的区别不仅仅在于发声类型，也同时具有类似非洲语言的舌根前伸/舌根后置（［+ATR］/［+RTR］）的区别，同时在第一和第二共振峰上都存在显著差异。紧元音舌根后缩（［+RTR］/［-ATR］），第一共振峰较高，第二共振峰低；松元音舌根靠前（［+ATR］/［-RTR］），第一共振峰较低，第二共振峰高。
关键词　北部彝语，松紧元音，超声成像，声学，ATR/RTR

1. INTRODUCTION

The contrast between tense and lax vowels is a main feature of many Tibeto-Burman languages spoken in Southwest China. One of the languages is Northern Yi language, a member of Lolo-Burmese subgroup of the Tibero-Burman family [4]. It is spoken in southern Sichuan Province and northern Yunnan Province in China [5]. Previous studies have showed that tense and lax vowels in Northern Yi language differ in a number of phonetic parameters: phonation type, vowel quality, duration, intensity, f0 and their effects on the initial consonants [13, 23, 25, 28]. Different from tense-lax distinction in Germanic languages, the differences between tense and lax vowels in Northern Yi (also called Nuosu langauge) lie mainly in phonation type and laryngeal constriction [5, 13, 23].

The most salient and well-investigated phonetic difference between tense and lax vowels is phonation type. Maddision & Ladegoged [23] suggested that tense vowels were produced with a greater glottal constriction because there was greater airflow in lax vowel. Acoustically, the amplitude difference between F0 and H2 (F0-H2) was larger for tense vowels [25]. F0-H2 is a measure that differentiates various phonation types [3, 9, 14, 15]. It has been shown to correlate with listeners' perception of breathiness [16]. Larger F0-H2 value in tense vowels indicates that the larynx is more restricted when producing those vowels. Anatomically, the production of tense vowels involves laryngeal sphincter, with the larynx raising and epiglottic root backing [6]. Tense vowels also have higher contact quotient when measured by electroglottograph (EGG), suggesting that tense vowels are creakier than lax vowels [13].

It has also been shown that tense vowels had slightly higher f0 [22, 23]. Studies using EEG showed that vocal folds opening was longer and the speed of vocal folds vibration was slower in lax vowels [28, 29]. In addition, aspirated or voiced consonants before tense vowels had prolonged aspiration and voicing [22, 23].

Tenseness in Yi Language is also realized with distinct patterns in duration and intensity. Tense vowels were shorter than lax vowels in falling tone in Liangshan Yi and in low falling tone in Xinping Yi (Southern Yi), but no durational difference was found in high and mid tones [23, 25]. Similar effect was found in intensity in Xinping Yi [25]. Tense vowels have lower intensity compared to lax vowels in low tone but not in other tones. The pattern in Wuding Yi is consistent with Liangshan and Xinping Yi. Wang and Kong [28] showed that tenseness in Wuding Yi was realized with different phonetic correlates for high and low tones. For syllables with a high tone, the distinction mainly lay in phonation type, while for syllables with a low tone, the major difference was in duration.

Another difference between tense and lax vowels is vowel quality. Shi and Zhou [25] reported that tense vowels consistently have larger F1 compared to their lax counterparts, suggesting that tense vowels were lower in tongue height. Similar results were reported in Yi spoken in Xinping and Jiangcheng [13]. Kuang [13] reported that tense vowels had higher F1 than the corresponding lax vowels, but no significant differences were found in F2. Edmondson et al. [6] showed that tense vowels have larger F1 and smaller F2, suggesting that the tense vowels were lower and backer. Besides the acoustic evidence, Lan and Wu [18] provided first articulatory data using ultrasound imaging. They compared two pairs of tense and lax vowels [ɿ ɿ̠ ʅ ʅ̠] spoken in Xide County. Based on their acoustic data and visual inspection of the raw ultrasound images, they suggested that lax vowels [ɿ ʅ] are higher and more fronted than the tense vowels [ɿ̠ ʅ̠]. The limitation of their study is that their ultrasound data is based on only two vowel pairs, and the ultrasound data are not subject to any statistical analysis. Some other studies, however, did not found vowel quality difference in Yi. For example, Maddision and Ladegoged [23] reported that tense and lax vowels did not differ in vowel quality in Liangshan Yi. Wang and Kong [28] demonstrated that in Wuding Yi, only /ɑ/ and /ɒ̱/ demonstrated some quality difference, and no difference was observed in other vowel pairs.

To clarify the vowel quality differences between tense and lax vowels in Northern Yi, the current study aims to investigate the vowel quality difference between all tense and lax vowel pairs in two Northern Yi dialects-Suondi and Yinuo using ultrasonic and acoustic data. Suondi and Yinuo are both dialects of Northern Yi. As a case study, only one native speaker of Suondi Yi was invited to the lab and recorded with ultrasound imaging. Acoustic data from five Yinuo speakers were recorded during a field trip to Leibo County (雷波县), Sichuan Province.

Table 1 Target stimuli used in the experiment

Ten vowels (5 tense and 5 lax) in /pV#/ and /p^{h}V#/ contexts

Vowels	Word	Gloss	Word	Gloss
i	pi^{33}	to read	p^{h}i^{33}	push aside; open
ɛ(i̱)	pɛ^{33}	to kick	p^{h}ɛ^{33}	carve
ɯ	pɯ^{33}	to exclaim	p^{h}ɯ^{33}	(no meaning)
a(ɯ̱)	pa^{33}	to exchange	p^{h}a^{33}	bladder
o	po^{33}	to rummage	p^{h}o^{33}	run away
ɔ(o̱)	pɔ^{33}	to split	p^{h}ɔ^{33}	servant
ɿ	pɿ^{33}	eagle call	p^{h}ɿ^{33}	painful
ɿ̱	pɿ̱^{33}	to poop	p^{h}ɿ̱^{33}	swing
u	pu^{33}	river deer	p^{h}u^{33}	price
u̱	pu̱^{33}	to go back	p^{h}u̱^{33}	translate; counterattack

Four apical vowels (2 tense and 2 lax) in /tsV#/, /tʂV#/, /ts^{h}V#/ and /tʂ^{h}V#/ contexts

Vowels	Word	Gloss	Word	Gloss
ɿ	tsɿ	hatch	ts^{h}ɿ	save (someone from the water)
ɿ̱	tsɿ̱	crack	ts^{h}ɿ̱	clench
ʅ	tʂʅ	urge (someone to go faster)	tʂ^{h}ʅ	becoming an orphan
ʅ̱	tʂʅ̱	pull out	tʂ^{h}ʅ̱	sprout, coming out

2. ULTRASOUNIC DATA

2.1 Participant

One male speaker of Suondi Yi participated in the ultrasound imaging. He was a native speaker of Suondi Yi, and he can also speak Mandarin and English. The speaker did not report any history of speech, hearing or mental disorder.

2.2 Stimuli

The stimuli included ten vowel phonemes which grouped as five tense-lax pairs: /i/ (lax) and /ɛ/ (tense); /ɯ/ (lax) and /a/ (tense); /o/ (lax) and /ɔ/ (tense); /ɿ/ (lax) and /ɿ̱/ (tense); /u/ (lax) and /u̱/ (tense), and two allophones of the two apical vowels ([ʅ] and [ʅ̱]) (Table 1). The 12 vowels were embedded in the /pV#/ and /p^{h}V#/ contexts. The bilabial stop /p/ was chosen to be the initial consonant because bilabial sounds did not have any coarticulatory influences on the following vowels. The lingual difference between tense and lax vowels can be better revealed without any influences from flanking consonants. The tense and lax apical vowels in /tsV#/, /ts^{h}V#/, /tʂV#/ and /tʂ^{h}V#/ contexts were also included to compare the difference between the dental/alveolar apical vowel (lax apical vowel [ɿ] and tense apical vowel [ɿ̠]) and the retroflex apical vowel (lax retroflex apical vowel [ʅ], and tense retroflex apical vowel [ʅ̠]). The 28 words were read in the carrier phrase "ŋa^{33} _ _ pi^{33}" ("I read _ _").

2.3 Procedure

Ultrasound video and the audio signal were recorded with Telemed Echo B system at the Chinese University of Hong Kong. A mid-sagittal view of the tongue was obtained by placing the ultrasonic transducer under the chin of the speaker. The participant wore a light-weight headset made by Articulate Instruments Ltd. which can stabilize the ultrasonic transducer under the chin. The ultrasound videos were recorded at the frame rate of 60 fps with Articulate Assistant Advanced (AAA) software (Articulate Instruments Ltd). The participant was asked to read through the stimuli list before the experiment to make sure that he can read the words correctly and fluently. In the recording session, the stimuli were randomized and the participants were asked to read the prompt list for five times.

2.4 Data analysis

The ultrasound video and the audio signal was automatically synchronized by AAA software. The target vowels were first labelled according to the acoustic information. In the ultrasound data, each vowel contained 9 – 16 frames of images. Among the frames corresponding to the vowel, the middle frame was chosen for further analysis, with the assumption that this frame represented the target tongue shape of the vowel. The tongue curves in the selected frames were manually tracked using AAA. The tongue splines was drawn on the lower boundary of the light line because the lighter line in the ultrasound images represents the tongue-air interface (See Figure 1 as an example). Each tongue spline was exported from AAA as 124 data points for further data analysis. Smoothing spline ANOVA (SS – ANOVA) [7], contained in the R "gss" package, was used to compare tongue curves between tense ad lax vowels. SS – ANOVA can compare the differences between two or more curves, and have been widely adopted to compare tongue splines in ultrasound studies [1, 10, 19, 20, 24]. The data points exported from AAA were first converted into polar coordinates to conduct SS – ANOVA analyses, and then converted back in Cartesian coordinates for plotting. Polar coordinates were used because it has been proposed that the tongue root position was better estimated with polar coordinates instead of Cartesian coordinates [24].

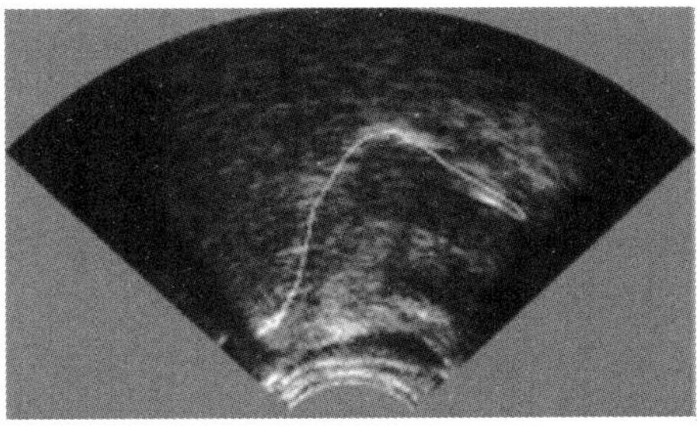

Figure 1 A raw ultrasound image of the tongue shape for vowel [ɿ] and the fitted tongue spline.

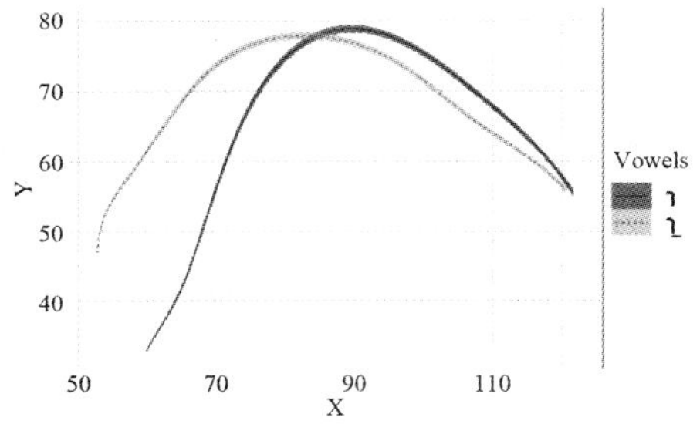

(1) Tongue shape differences between /ɿ/ and /ɿ̠/

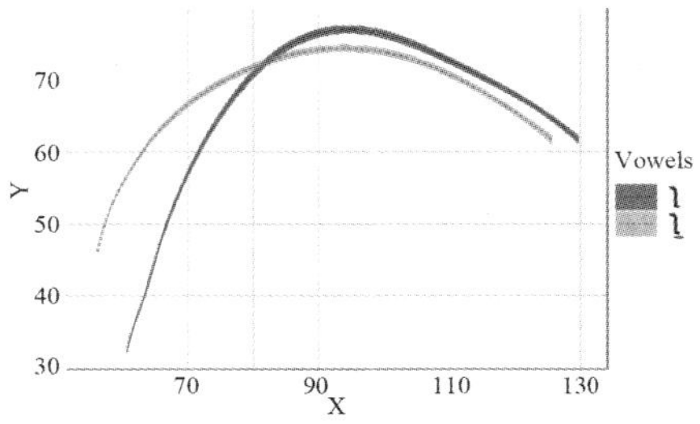

(2) Tongue shape differences between /ʅ/and /ʅ̠/

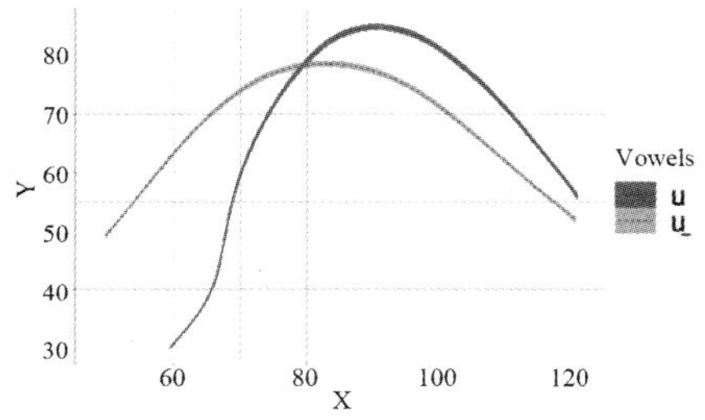

(3) Tongue shape differences between /u/ and /u̠/

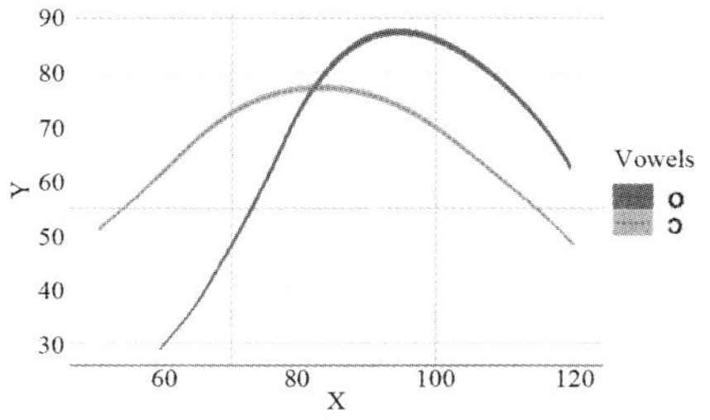

(4) Tongue shape differences between /o/ and /ɔ/.

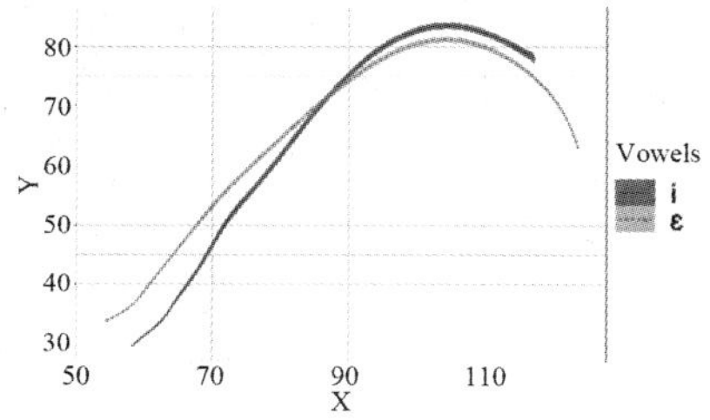

(5) Tongue shape differences between /i/ and /ɛ/.

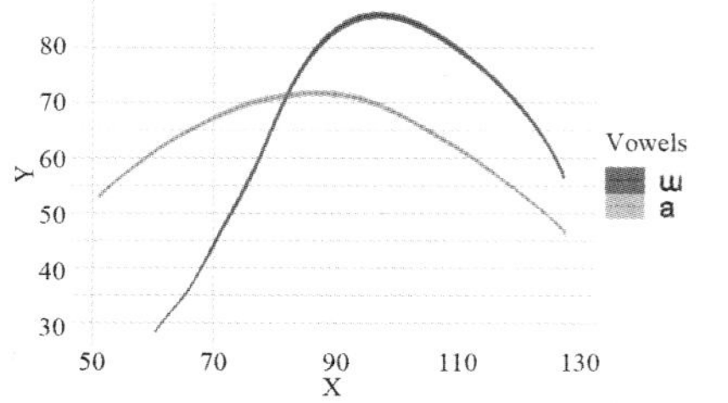

(6) Tongue shape differences between /a/ and /ɯ/.

Figure 2 The smoothing spline estimate and 95% Bayesian confidence interval for each pair of tense and lax vowels in Suondi Yi.

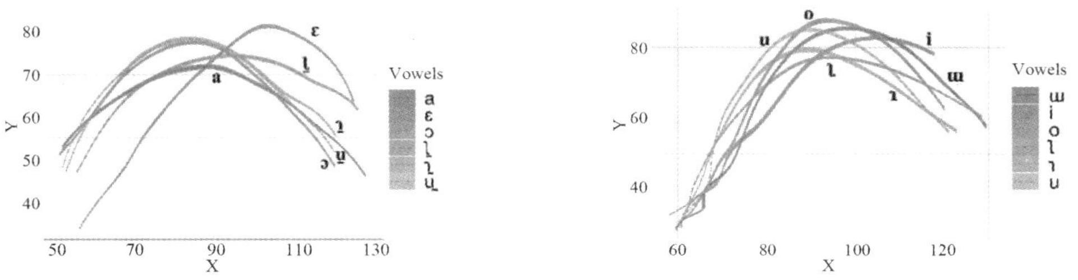

(1) Tongue shapes of tense vowels in Suondi Yi (2) Tongue shapes of lax vowels in Suondi Yi

Figure 3 The smoothing spline estimate and 95% Bayesian confidence interval for all vowels in Suondi Yi.

2.5 Results

The tongue shape differences between each pair of tense and lax vowels modelled by SS-ANOVA are shown in Figure 2, and the tongue shapes of all tense vowels and all lax vowels are demonstrated in Figure 3. In a SS-ANOVA figure, if the confidence intervals of two curves do not overlap, it means that the two curves are significantly different. As shown in Figure 2, for each pair of tense and lax vowels, the anterior part of the tongue in tense vowels is significantly lower than that in lax vowels. The tongue back is significantly higher and the tongue root is more retracted in tense vowels. This pattern is consistent for all vowel pairs. For high front vowel pairs, such as [ɿ ɿ̱], [ʅ ʅ̱], and /i ɛ/, the tongue height differences in the anterior part of the tongue are small but still statistically different. Except [ɿ ɿ̱] whose tongue height is similar, the tongue height of lax vowels is higher.

It seems that the position of the tongue root is the cause of the major differences between the tense and lax vowels, with tongue root in lax vowels being substantially more advanced than that in tense vowels, resulting in a fronted and higher tongue dorsum.

3. ACOUSTIC DATA

3.1 Participants

The acoustic data consists of two parts. The first part is from the male native speaker of Suondi who have participated in the ultrasound recording. Another part is from five native speakers of Yinuo (4 males and 1 female). Suondi and Yinuo are both dialects of Northern Yi. The native speaker of Suondi was recorded at the sound booth at the Chinese University of Hong Kong. Five native speakers of Yinuo (4 males and 1 female) were recorded with a Zoom recorder in a hotel room at Leibo County, Sichuan Province. All the speakers were in their mid-forty or mid-fifty, and they all spoke their native dialect on a daily basis. They did not report any history of speech, hearing or mental disorder.

3.2 Procedure, stimuli and data analysis

The stimuli and the carrier phrase are the same as mentioned in Section 2.1 except the word /p^{h}ɯ^{33}/. This word is omitted in acoustic recording because this word has no meaning in Northern Yi. The participants were instructed to translate the words they hear in Mandarin or Sichuan dialect into their own dialect (Yinuo or Suondi) and then say the word out loud. They were asked to practice the words until they can fluently pronounce each word. The stimuli were randomized and the participant was asked to repeat the prompt list for five times. The two sets of acoustic data (Yinuo or Suondi) are analyzed individually. As the number of speakers in the current study is rather small, pair-wise t-tests are used to compare the differences in F1 and F2 between each pair of tense and lax vowels.

3.3 Results

The first and second formant frequencies of all vowels in Yinuo and Suondi are summarized in Table 2 and Table 3. Figure 4 shows the vowel space of Suondi vowels. In the vowel chart, the five tense vowels are lower and to the right of their corresponding lax vowels. This pattern is consistent for all vowel pairs except /o/ and /ɔ/. For /o ɔ/ vowel pair, the lax vowel /o/ had a significantly higher F1 than the tense vowel /ɔ/ ($t(12) = -44.384$, $p < 0.001$), but no significant difference was found in F2. For other pairs of tense and lax vowels, the F1 of tense vowels was significantly higher than that of lax vowels ([ɿ] − [ɿ̠]: $t(38) = -16.919$, $p < 0.001$; [ʅ] − [ʅ̠]: $t(16) = -10.829$, $p < 0.001$; /u/ − /u̠/: $t(13) = -17.226$, $p < 0.001$; /i/ − /ɛ/: $t(12) = 20.882$, $p < 0.001$; /ɯ/ − /a/: $t(13) = 72.736$, $p < 0.001$). The F2 of tense vowels was significantly lower than that of lax vowels except the /o/ − /ɔ/ pair ([ɿ] − [ɿ̠]: $t(38) = 15.28$, $p < 0.001$; [ʅ] − [ʅ̠]: $t(15) = 6.722$, $p < 0.001$; /u/ − /u̠/: $t(8) = 5.143$, $p = 0.001$; /i/ − /ɛ/: $t(17) = -5.203$, $p < 0.001$; /ɯ/ − /a/: $t(11) = -24.229$, $p < 0.001$).

Figure 5 illustrates the vowel space of Yinuo vowels. Lax vowels are above and to the left of their tensed counterparts in the vowel chart for /ɯ/ − /a/, /ɛ/ − /i/, [ɿ] − [ɿ̠], and [ʅ] − [ʅ̠]. The t-tests showed that the F1 of tense vowels was significantly higher than that of the corresponding lax vowels ([ɿ] − [ɿ̠]: $t(119) = -21.216$, $p < 0.001$; [ʅ] − [ʅ̠]: $t(64) = -14.299$, $p < 0.001$; /i/ − /ɛ/: $t(54) = 19.787$, $p < 0.001$; /ɯ/ − /a/: $t(36) = 20.972$, $p < 0.001$; /u/ − /u̠/: $t(64) = -12.529$, $p < 0.001$; /o/ − /ɔ/: $t(95) = -10.448$, $p < 0.001$). The F2 of tense vowels was significantly lower than that of lax vowels in /ɯ/ − /a/, /ɛ/ − /i/, [ɿ] − [ɿ̠], and [ʅ] − [ʅ̠] ([ɿ] − [ɿ̠]: $t(156) = 7.027$, $p < 0.001$); [ʅ] − [ʅ̠]: $t(63) = 3.967$, $p < 0.001$; /i/ − /ɛ/: $t(84) = -2.168$, $p = 0.033$; /ɯ/ − /a/: $t(39) = -2.706$, $p = 0.010$). No significant difference was found in F2 between /u/ and /u̠/. Contrary to other vowel pairs, the F2 of /ɔ/ was significantly higher than /o/ ($t(94) = -5.848$, $p < 0.001$). In the vowel chart, the vowel /o/ is above but to the right of the tense vowel /ɔ/.

To summarize, the tense-lax contrast is realized similarly in Suondi and Yinuo, with tense vowels having higher F1 and lower F2. This pattern is consistent for all front vowels, but not for the high back vowel /o/ and /ɔ/. The tense vowel /ɔ/ has higher F2 compared to its lax counterpart /o/.

Table 2 First and second formant frequency of Suondi Yi in Hertz and Bark.

IPA	F1		F2	
	Hz	Bark	Hz	Bark
i	282	2.84	2031	13.1
ɛ	456	4.53	1876	12.6
ɯ	332	3.36	1700	11.9
a	837	7.49	1201	9.66
o	317	3.21	762	6.98
ɔ	498	4.9	756	6.93
u	342	3.45	865	7.67
u̠	482	4.76	786	7.15
ɿ	306	3.09	1363	10.5
ɿ̠	443	4.41	1026	8.67
ʅ	349	3.52	1582	11.4
ʅ̠	448	4.45	1401	10.6

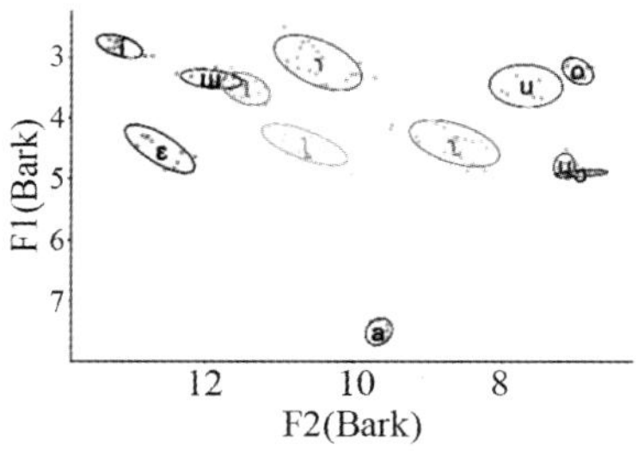

(1) The vowels of Suondi Yi.

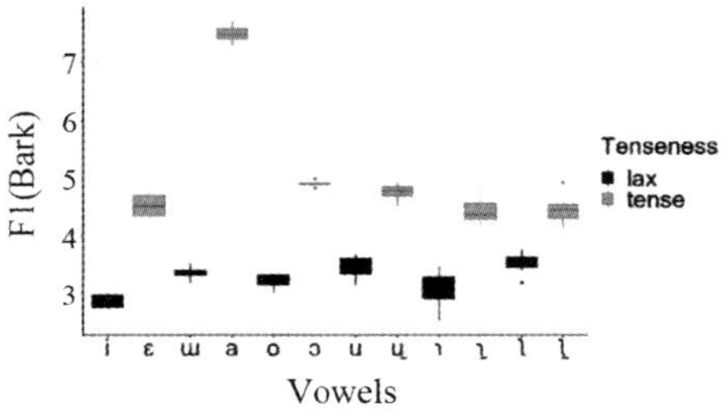

(2) The F1 of Suondi Yi vowels.

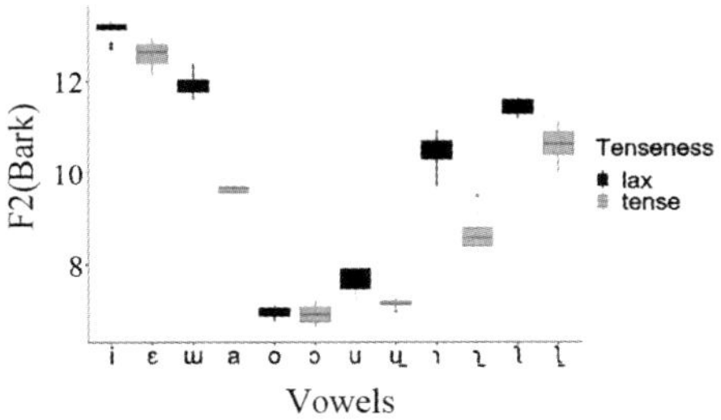

(3) The F2 of Suondi Yi vowels.

Figure4 Vowels in Suondi Yi. The upper panel demonstrates the vowel space of Suondi Yi. The middle and lower panel show the F1 and F2 of all tense and lax vowels in Suondi Yi.

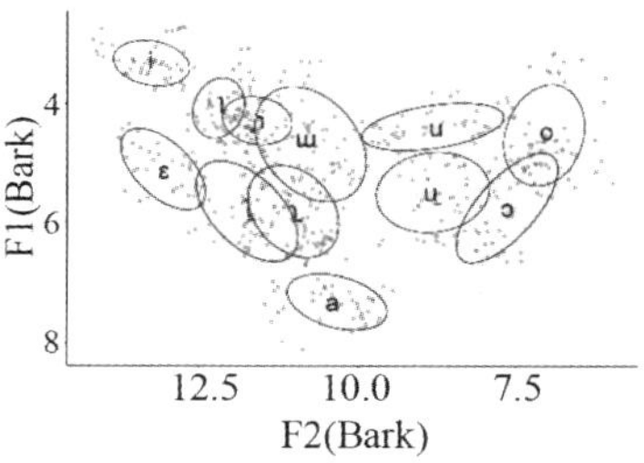

(1) The vowels of Yinuo Yi.

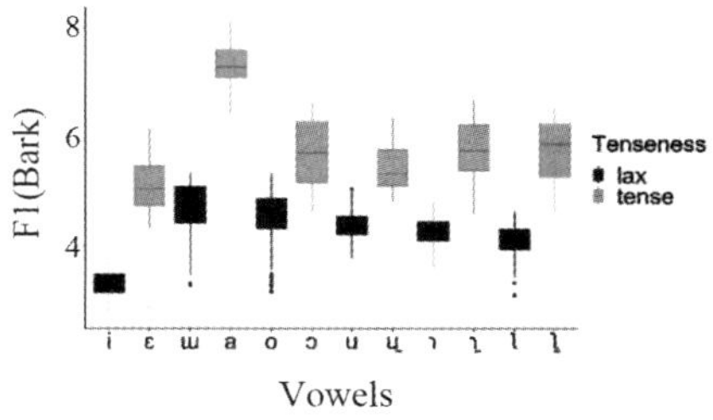

(2) The F1 of Yinuo Yi vowels.

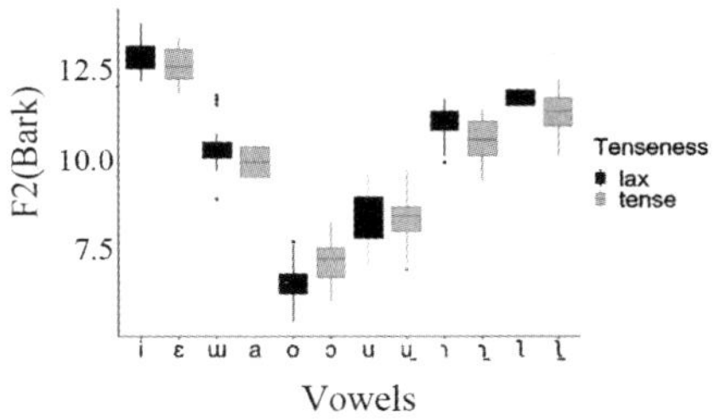

(3) The F2 of Yinuo Yi vowels.

Figure 5 Vowels in Yinuo Yi. The upper panel illustrates the vowel space of Yinuo Yi. The middle and lower panel show the F1 and F2 of all tense and lax vowels in Yinuo Yi.

Table 3 First and second formant frequency of Yinuo Yi in Hertz and Bark.

IPA	F1		F2	
	Hz	Bark	Hz	Bark
i	326	3. 29	2097	13. 3
ɛ	524	5. 11	2032	13. 1
ɯ	463	4. 57	1451	10. 8
a	811	7. 31	1355	10. 4
o	449	4. 45	768	7
ɔ	600	5. 74	859	7. 62
u	441	4. 39	1045	8. 76
u̱	567	5. 48	1058	8. 84
ɿ	427	4. 27	1612	11. 6
ɿ̱	604	5. 77	1492	11
ʅ	403	4. 03	1770	12. 2
ʅ̱	601	5. 75	1665	11. 8

4. DISCUSSION

The ultrasound data in the current study demonstrated that the tense vowels are articulated with more retracted tongue root and lower tongue front compared to the corresponding lax vowels. Acoustically, in general, tense vowels have higher F1 and lower F2 thanlax vowels. This is consistent with the results reported in previous acoustic studies [6, 25]. The ultrasound data also complements previous study by providing direct evidence on the lingual differences between tense and lax vowels.

Previous studies using laryngoscopy have shown that Yi tense vowels were articulated with raised larynx and constricted epiglottic root [21]. Our ultrasound images complemented previous data by showing that the articulation of tense vowels also involves retracted tongue root. To articulate tense vowels, the tongue is retracted, with the posterior part of the tongue raised and the anterior part lowered, while the epilaryngeal tube is constricted and the larynx is raised. When articulating the tense vowels, there is a great constriction and a tension in tongue root and throat.

Our articulatory data also showed that tenseness distinction in Northern Yi can be related with advanced tongue root(+ ATR) and retracted tongue root (+ RTR) contrast. The ART and RTR contrast is often seen in African languages [17]. It has been shown that the articulation of ART usually involves the widening of lateral pharynx walls and the lowering of larynx, whereas the production of RTR vowels involves pharyngeal constrictions and larynx raising [21, 27]. This pattern is similar to the articulation of tense and lax vowels in Yi. In Northern Yi, the tense vowels has more retracted tongue root, while the lax vowel is characterized with the advanced tongue root. According to Ladefoged and Maddieson [17], the major difference between + ATR/ + RTR contrast and tense-lax contrast is that tongue height is not correlated with tongue root position in + ATR/ + RTR contrast. For example, the difference between Akan + ATR/ + RTR vowels in tongue height is rather small compared to the changes in tongue root and pharyngeal region. In Northern Yi, the pattern is mixed. The tongue root position and the tongue height seems to be related for some vowel pairs, such as /u u̱/, /ɯ a/, and /o ɔ/. But for high front vowels and apical vowels, such as [ɿ ɿ̱], [ʅ ʅ̱] and /i ɛ/, the tongue height difference between tense and lax vowels is much smaller than the difference in tongue root, which resembles the pattern of + ATR/ + RTR contrast in African languages.

Our acoustic data confirm that tense and lax vowels have distinct vowel quality. Previous studies had controversial results regarding the acoustic correlates of tenseness. Edmondson et al. [6] and Shi and Zhou [25] suggested that there were differences in F1 and F2 between tense and lax vowels. On the contrary, Maddison and Ladefoged [23] found no difference in vowel quality, while Wang and Kong [28] found formant differences only for the /a/ and /ɒ/ vowel pair. Our acoustic result is consistent with Edmondson et al. [6] and Shi and Zhou [25]. We found vowel quality difference between tense and lax vowels in both F1 and F2. According to the Perturbation Theory [26], higher F1 represents lower tongue position, and lower F2 indicates that the tongue is backer. This prediction is consistent with our articulatory data where we found lower and backer tongue position for tense vowels.

The pattern of F2 for /o/ and /ɔ/ pair is opposite to other tense-lax vowel pairs, with higher F2 for the tense vowel /ɔ/ and lower F2 for the lax vowel /o/. According to Panel 4 of Figure 2, the tongue position of the lax vowel /o/ is more fronted, suggesting that it should have higher F2. One possible explanation for it is that the F2 of /o/ is lowered due to the lip rounding. The Perturbation Theory suggests that F2 will be lowered as the front resonating cavity is enlarged by retracting the tongue or protruding the lips[26]. It is possible that F2 of /o/ is lowered because of the extra lip protrusion in /o/. This hypothesis, however, needs to be tested in future experiment examining the lip movements of Yi vowels. Another limitation of the current study is that the number of speakers is rather small for both ultrasound imaging and acoustic analysis. Data from more speakers are needed to confirm the findings of the current study.

One unexpected pattern in the vowel chart is that /u/ vowel is to the left of /o/ in both Yinuo and Suondi, and the vowel /u/ has a higher F2 than /o/. However, in the ultrasound data, the tongue position of vowel /u/ is backer than that of /o/ (Figure 3), which means /u/ should have a smaller F2. This mismatch between articulatory and acoustic measures might be caused by the lip protrusion in the /o/ vowel as well. This possibility also needs to be confirmed in future studies with lip measures and a larger number of participants.

5. CONCLUSION

In summary, this study examined the articulatory and acoustic characteristics of tenseness in Northern Yi using ultrasound imaging. The articulatory data showed that for all five pairs of tense and lax vowel phonemes, as well as one pair of retroflex apical vowel allophones, tense vowels are articulated with more retracted tongue root and lower tongue front, while lax vowels are articulated with advanced tongue root and higher tongue front. The acoustic consequence of the tongue retraction is that F1 is increased and F2 lowered. It suggests that the phonetic correlates of tenseness in Yi lie not only in phonation types or laryngeal constriction, but also in vowel quality. The tense-lax contrast in Northern Yi also involves advanced tongue root ([+ATR]) and retracted tongue root ([+RTR]) contrast.

6. ACKNOWLEDGEMENTS

Many thanks to all the speakers who participated in the experiments. Thank Prof. Lama Ziwo from Southwest Minzu University for his help with the data collection and his insightful comments.

7. REFERENCES

[1] Ahn, S. 2018. The role of tongue position in laryngeal contrasts: An ultrasound study of English and Brazilian Portuguese. *Journal of Phonetics*, 71, 451-467

[2] Articulate Instruments Ltd. 2012. Articulate Assistant Advanced User Guide: Version 2.14. Edinburgh, UK: Articulate Instruments Ltd.

[3] Bickley, C. 1982. Acoustic analysis and perception of breathy vowels. *Speech Communication Group Working Papers*, 1, 71－81.

[4] David. B. 1979. *Proto-Loloish* (Scandinavian Institute of Asian Studies, Monograph Series No. 39). London: Curzon Press.

[5] Edmondson, J. A., Esling, J. H., Lama, Z. 2016. Nuosu Yi. *Journal of the International Phonetic Association*, 1－11.

[6] Edmondson, J. A., Lama, Z., Esling, J., Harris, J. G., Li, S. 2001. The aryepiglottic folds and voice quality in the Yi and Bai languages: Laryngoscopic case studies. *MONKHMER STUDIES*, 83－100.

[7] Gu, C. 2014. Smoothing spline ANOVA models: R packages gss. *Journal of Statistical Software*, 58 (5), 1－25.

[8] Gick, B., Wilson, I., Derrick, D. 2012. *Articulatory Phonetics.* John Wiley & Sons.

[9] Kirk, P. L., Ladefoged, P., Ladefoged, J. 1984. Using a spectrograph for measures of phonation types in natural language. *UCLA Working Papers in Phonetics*, 59, 102－113.

[10] Kochetov, A., Sreedevi, N., Kasim, M., Manjula, R. 2014. Spatial and dynamic aspects of retroflex production: An ultrasound and EMA study of Kannada geminate stops. *Journal of Phonetics*, 46, 168－184.

[11] Kong J. 1997. A study on the voice of Axi-Yi. *Collection of Essays on Chinese National Languages* (2). Kunming: Yunnan National Press. (孔江平:《阿细彝语嗓音研究》,《中国民族语言论丛(二)》,云南民族出版社1997年版。)

[12] Kong J. 1997. An acoustic study on the tense and lax vowels in Yi-Liangshan. *Studies on the Yi-Burmese Languages.* Chengdu: Sichuan People Press. (孔江平:《凉山彝语松紧元音的声学研究》,《彝缅语研究》,四川人民出版社1997年版。)

[13] Kuang J. 2011. Phonation contrast in two register contrast languages and its influence on vowel and tone. *Proceedings of the 17th International Congress of Phonetics Sciences*, 1146－1149.

[14] Ladefoged, P. 1981. The relative nature of voice quality. *The Journal of the Acoustical Society of America*, 69 (S1), S67－S67.

[15] Ladefoged, P. 1983. The linguistic use of different phonation types. In D. Bless & J. Abbs (Eds.), *Vocal Fold Physiology: Contemporary Research and Clinical Issues* (pp. 351－360). San Diego: College Hill Press.

[16] Ladefoged, P., Antoñanzas-Barroso, N. 1985. Computer measures of breathy voice quality. *UCLA Working Papers in Phonetics*, 61 (S1), 79－86.

[17] Ladefoged, P., Maddieson, I. 1995. *The Sounds of the World's Languages.* Oxford: Blackwell.

[18] Lan, Z., Wu, X. 2017. The production mechanism of Yi tense and lax vowels. *Minority Languages of China*, 4, 24－34. (兰正群、吴西愉:《彝语松紧元音对立的生成机制研究》,《民族语文》2017年第4期,24－34期。)

[19] Lee-Kim, S. 2014. Revisiting Mandarin 'apical vowels': An articulatory and acoustic study. *Journal of the International Phonetic Association*, 44 (3), 261－282.

[20] Li, Y., Zhang, J. 2021. An ultrasound and EPG investigation of coronal fricatives in Yanbian Korean. *Chinese Journal of Phonetics*, 16, 1－15.

[21] Lindau, M. 1979. The feature expanded. *Journal of Phonetics*, 7 (2), 163－176.

[22] Maddieson, I., Hess, S. 1986. "Tense" and "lax" revisited: More on phonation type and pitch in minority languages in China. *UCLA Working Papers in Phonetics*, 63, 103－109.

[23] Maddieson, I., Ladefoged, P. 1985. "Tense" and "lax" in four minority languages of China. *UCLA Working Papers in Phonetics*, 60, 59－83.

[24] Mielke J. 2015. An ultrasound study of Canadian French rhotic vowels with polar smoothing spline comparisons. *The Journal of the Acoustical Society of America*, 137 (5), 2858－2869.

[25] Shi, F., Zhou, D. 2005. Acoustic Analysis of the Tense and Lax Vowels in the Southern Yi Language. *Studies in Language and Linguistics*, 25 (1), 60－65. (石锋、周德才:《南部彝语松紧元音的声学表现》,《语言研究》2005年第25卷第1期,60—65页。)

[26] Stevens, K. N. 1998. *Acoustic Phonetics.* Cambridge, MA: MIT Press.

[27] Tiede, M. 1996. An MRI-based study of pharyngeal volume contrasts in Akan and English. *Journal of Phonetics*, 24 (4), 399－421.

[28] Wang, F., Kong, J. 2009. A study of lax/

tense voice in Wuding Yi. *Chinese Linguistics*, 2, 98 – 118. Jinan: Shandong Education Press. （汪锋、孔江平：《武定彝语松紧音研究》,《中国语言学》第2期，山东教育出版社2009年版。）

[29] Ye, Z. 2006. A study on the voice quality of Xinping Yi. *Peking University Speech Prosody Research* 2006 *research report*. （叶泽华《新平彝语松紧嗓音研究》,《北京大学语音韵律研究2006年研究报告》。）

CHEN Shuwen Ph. D, She is an assistant professor at Institute of Linguistics, Chinese Academy of Social Sciences. Her research interests include speech production, speech perception, and L2 speech acquisition.

Email: chensw@cass.org.cn